CONTROVERSIAL ISSUES
IN SOCIAL POLICY

HOWARD JACOB KARGER

University of Houston

JAMES MIDGLEY

University of California at Berkeley

C. BRENÉ BROWN

University of Houston

Editors

ALLYN AND BACON

Boston   New York   San Francisco
Mexico City   Montreal   Toronto   London   Madrid   Munich
Hong Kong   Singapore   Tokyo   Cape Town   Sydney

Series Editor: *Patricia Quinlin*
Editorial Assistant: *Annemarie Kennedy*
Marketing Manager: *Taryn Wahlquist*
Production Editor: *Paul Mihailidis*
Manufacturing Buyer: *Chris Marson*
Cover Administrator: *Kristina Mose-Libon*
Electronic Composition: *Publishers' Design and Production Services, Inc.*

For related support materials, visit our online catalog at *www.ablongman.com*

Copyright © 2003, 1994 Pearson Education, Inc.
75 Arlington Street
Boston, MA 02116

Internet: www.ablongman.com

Library of Congress Cataloging-in-Publication Data

Controversial issues in social policy / edited by Howard Jacob Karger,
James Midgley, C. Brené Brown. — 2nd ed.
   p. cm.
Includes bibliographical references.
ISBN 0-205-33745-7
   1. United States—Social Policy. 2. Public welfare—United States. 3. Welfare
state. I. Karger, Howard Jacob. II. Midgley, James. III. Brown, Brene.

HN59.2 .C66 2003
361.6'1'0973—dc21

                                 2002016389

Printed in the United States of America

10 9 8 7 6 5 4 3 2   07 06 05 04 03 02

CONTENTS

■ ■ ■ ■ ■ ▬▬▬▬▬▬▬▬▬▬▬▬▬▬▬▬▬▬▬▬▬

PREFACE

■ ■ ■ ■ ■

When Bob Pruger invited us to compile this book of debates in 1993, we had some misgivings. The task of editing a large volume of debates on controversies in social policy is a formidable one. The time and effort involved in identifying viable topics, coordinating the contributions of close to fifty authors, standardizing the material, and making the book lively presented a major challenge to two already overcommitted people. On the other hand, we were excited by the prospect that social-policy experts would have an opportunity to examine critically important issues from radically different perspectives. We had both contributed to Bob Pruger's and Eileen Gambrill's pioneering volume *Controversial Issues in Social Work*. We realized then that the debate format is an effective means for addressing controversial issues in social policy, a useful teaching device, and an important vehicle for developing knowledge in our field. Our willingness to work on the book reflected our belief that both social policy and social work are enriched by intellectual controversy and differing viewpoints on important issues.

When Allyn & Bacon asked us to do a second edition of *Controversial Issues in Social Policy*, we were again reluctant because of our time commitments. Luckily, we were able to engage the services of a third author, Dr. Brené Brown, who took the bull by the horns and helped to reconceptualize the book and find new authors for many of the debates. Some of those authors— such as Patricia Ireland, Sally C. Pipes, William Beach, and Robert Moffit—are well known to viewers of CNN, MSNBC, and other news channels. We are thankful (largely owing to Dr. Brown's efforts) to have engaged the talents of such a wide range of brilliant thinkers and authors.

Remarkably little has changed in social policy since we began the first edition of this book almost ten years ago. The country remains split between rigid hard-line conservatives and the more suffocating elements of politically correct thinking. There continues to be a dearth of independent and innovative social thinking. Moreover, the compassion in the "compassionate conservatism" of the Bush administration seems to be reserved for the needy rich instead of the needy poor. We believe that books of this kind are now more crucial than ever.

Controversy is the essence of intellectual discourse. Although it may produce sharp disagreements between persons of differing viewpoints, the role of critical disputation in furthering knowledge is universally recognized. Though scholars may strenuously promote particular positions, these positions must stand the test of analytical scrutiny before they can be accepted as valid. Critical debate facilitates the twin tasks of validation and refutation. It also heightens an understanding of the issues, permits contradictions to be resolved, and ultimately promotes correct rather than false knowledge.

Critical debate can also serve as an effective teaching device. Though rote learning has an obvious role in the educational process, the task of helping students understand the most important issues in the field requires more than just the memorization of facts. In subjects such as social work and social policy, where judgment is as important as knowledge of facts, students need to think critically, to grasp complex nuances, and to analyze issues and defend their positions. The lecture format is not always the most effective means to inculcate these kinds of intellectual skills. We hope that the debates in this book will help instructors promote passionate discussions among students and facilitate the critical thinking needed to enhance our field. Now more than ever, the profession needs innovative thinking that supports bold new ideas, not hashed-over "consensus" opinions that masquerade as truth.

Critical debate also has an important role to play in strengthening our profession. Unlike other disciplines, social work has not always encouraged critical debate. Although controversial articles do appear in some social-work journals, they rarely result in ongoing debates or rejoinders. Much to the chagrin of many social-work authors, the ideas contained in controversial articles soon disappear from the journals. This has led many authors to believe that social workers do not read their own journals, or that they simply do not care enough about the issues. Neither of these suppositions is likely correct. Many social workers fail to respond simply because there is no culture of critical debate from which to draw. This problem is especially acute in the area of social policy, which by nature is open to multiple interpretations.

Another problem is the profession's propensity to adopt a single authoritative position on complex issues. For example, one is struck by the consistency of the position statements emanating from various professional associations. Often, particular views are espoused as if they were universally accepted. It is assumed, almost *a priori*, that everyone in the profession has the same opinion on key issues. This is clearly not the case, and the diversity of viewpoints among social workers on these issues needs to be recognized. Though it is appropriate for the profession to take positions on political and social questions that affect their members, these positions are sometimes adopted with dogmatic authority. In fact, there are widely differing opinions among social workers on these important questions.

Members of the profession tend to avoid controversial discussions. For example, there are few articles in social-work journals that question whether the welfare state is in fact a failed social experiment, or whether social-welfare programs actually increase dependency. Although most social workers, including the authors, are strongly committed to the values and principles underlying the welfare state, the absence of serious discourse on these issues within the profession isolates members from much needed critical thinking about social-welfare policy. As a result, many social workers are ill informed about alternative viewpoints and ill prepared to respond to them.

This situation is unhealthy for the growth and vitality of social work as an academic subject. Social work must endorse and meet the challenges of rigorous intellectual discourse. The failure to do so will undoubtedly harm its growth as a respected field of academic endeavor.

Not only is the vitality of the discipline compromised by a lack of critical debate, but its own strength and maturity is weakened as its dearly held tenets are isolated from critique. Whatever positions social workers adopt must be strengthened by the clarification that comes from rigorous debate. Indeed, the profession's beliefs and values may calcify if it fails to exercise its intellectual muscles.

We have included debates in this book that will encourage social-work students to think critically and develop their analytical skills. For this reason, many of the debates address difficult issues. Indeed, some of the positions argued by our contributors are unpopular. However, as was argued previously, it is important that social workers understand them. We believe strongly in our readers' ability to determine for themselves which arguments are the most valid and relevant. For this reason, we do not avoid issues because of their contentiousness.

We hope that instructors will use this book in the spirit in which it was written; namely, to expose students to the varied opinions found in the rich terrain of social policy. As stated earlier, one strength of social policy is its openness to various interpretations, which makes it intellectually challenging and exciting. We hope this book will transmit the excitement and challenge of understanding and analyzing social-welfare policy.

Controversial Issues in Social Policy is divided into four parts. In the first part, we offer debates revolving around general issues in social-welfare policy. Howard Karger and James Midgley examine whether the American welfare system is compatible with the free-market system. Jon Meyer and Stephen Arch Erich debate one of the most contentious questions in social policy: Should the federal government fund faith-based social-service organizations? The privatization of social services has catalyzed heated debate for almost twenty years. Although the question remains unresolved, the nation continues to move toward privatizing social services. David Stoesz and Ira C. Colby examine whether privatization is viable and whether its promise has been realized.

Part Two examines issues involving poverty and inequality. Marion Wagner, Rebecca Van Voorhis, and John F. Longres look at whether gay-rights legislation will promote the well-being of gays and lesbians. The question of whether federal policies are addressing homelessness is tackled by Larry W. Kreuger, John Q. Hodges, Debi L. Word, and John J. Stretch. For the past twenty plus years, a debate has raged about whether welfare-to-work programs actually help the poor. This issue is skillfully addressed by poverty researchers Sandra K. Danziger and by Eileen Trzcinski and Deborah Satyanathan. The idea of providing the poor with Individual Development Accounts (IDAs) was developed by social worker Michael

Sherraden and later adopted by the former Clinton administration as well as by numerous states. Drs. Sherraden and Midgley debate whether IDAs can really help the poor in the long run. Affirmative action is also one of the most contentious social policies in contemporary society. Has it worked? If so, at what cost? What about the backlash this controversial policy has caused? Ann Rosegrant Alvarez and Sally C. Pipes examine whether affirmative-action policies have actually increased equality in the labor market. Perhaps one of the most radical policy changes under discussion is the full or partial privatization of Social Security. This discussion began in earnest during the Clinton administration and is now on the drawing boards of the Bush administration. The repercussions of privatizing Social Security are stagger-ing on many levels, including its effect on women. William W. Beach, along with Patricia Ireland of the National Organization of Women, address the implications for women of privatizing Social Security.

The access, costs, and affordability of U.S. healthcare has been an important social problem for decades. Though the Clinton healthcare bill was only one of many attempts to reform the system, all of them have failed. Since the defeat of the Clinton bill, no significant reform proposal has passed Congress. However, in light of the diminished ability of managed-care com-panies to control spiraling costs, it is likely that healthcare will again emerge as a national issue. Dawn McCarty, J. Rick Altemose, and Robert E. Moffitt debate the need for a national healthcare policy.

The Americans with Disabilities Act (ADA) was promoted as the most groundbreaking piece of legislation ever passed for the disabled. But who has really benefited? Have there been excesses and abuses? Howard Jacob Karger and John C. Bricout debate whether the ADA is meeting its intended goal or whether it is rife with abuse and unrealistic expectations. In the past few years, the War on Drugs has become a hotly contested issue. Movies such as *Traffic* question whether America's drug policy is effective or whether it is a result of self-serving and hypocritical politicians and government officials. Susan P. Robbins debates the value and effectiveness of America's drug policies in light of claims by the Office of National Drug Policy.

Part Three examines several issues in the delivery of social services. The first is outpatient mental-health commitments, which is skillfully debated by Kia J. Bentley and Melissa Floyd Taylor, along with eminent psychiatrist E. Fuller Torres and attorney Mary Zdanowicz. The term *managed care* is anathe-ma to many Americans, because it seems to stress the managed part at the expense of the care part. For many Americans, it conjures up images of cold-hearted bean counters, mountains of paperwork, and a healthcare system that is unresponsive to the needs of its clientele. Richard I. Smith, Kristin Stewart, and Heather Kannenburg debate whether managed care is really working. Interracial adoptions is another hot button. Though the National Association of Black Social Workers and other groups have taken a strong stand against interracial adoptions, others argue that there aren't enough good adoptive homes for hard-to-place children, and that these children should not become victims of America's racial tensions. This question of transracial adoptions is well argued by Elizabeth Bartholet and Leslie Doty Hollingsworth. Permitting gays and lesbians to adopt children is another contested political issue, debated here by Stephen Arch Erich and Howard Karger.

Part Four examines social-work professional and educational policy issues. Historically, one of the hottest social buttons has been abortion rights. Should the social-work profession publicly support womens' rights to secure abortions? On the surface, there appears to be a consensus in social work around a woman's right to choose. However, a less vocal element within the field questions whether the social-work profession should take a stand on this issue. Roland Meinert and John T. Pardeck debate whether abortion rights should be an accepted social-work value. The number of social-work programs has grown almost exponentially in the last twenty plus years. As a result, an increasing number of smaller schools, many of them religiously based, have been accredited by the Council on Social Work Education (CSWE), the accrediting body for social-work education. The problem is that some Christian-based schools do not accept a gay and lesbian lifestyle as viable and therefore cannot promote tolerance in that area. This difficult issue is examined by Karen E. Gerdes, Elizabeth A. Segal, and Lawrence E. Ressler.

This book could not have been written without the commitment of the contributors. Apart from delivering their debates in a timely manner, many were willing to publicly take an unpopular stand in a controversial debate, even though this action might affect their reputation. We applaud the courage of the contributors—taking an unpopular side of a debate demonstrates self-confidence and intellectual integrity. We extend our heartfelt thanks to all who contributed debates to this book. Their professionalism made the book possible and manageable.

Thanks to Judy Fifer, former social-work editor at Allyn & Bacon, and Patricia Quinlin, the current editor, for believing in this project. We would also like to express our thanks to those who reviewed our book: Mark Hanna, California State University, Fresno; Deborah Megivern, University of Michigan; Edward Scanlon, University of Washington; and Jane Walfogel, Columbia University.

Howard Jacob Karger
University of Houston
August 2001

James Midgley
University of California-Berkeley
August 2001

C. Brené Brown
Houston, TX
August 2001

PART I

SOCIAL POLICY AND THE AMERICAN WELFARE STATE

IS THE AMERICAN WELFARE STATE COMPATIBLE WITH THE MARKET ECONOMY?

Editor's Note:
Although the term *welfare state* can conjure up many meanings, it is widely used to connote a variety of government social programs designed to meet social needs and solve social problems. Most of these programs emerged at the time of the New Deal in the 1930s. Despite the popularity of these programs, critics argue that government involvement in social affairs is harmful to the economy, contrary to the American values of hard work and individual responsibility, and detrimental to freedom of choice. Supporters of the welfare state have attempted to refute these arguments, but others believe that the welfare state needs an overhaul. They argue that the basic principles of the welfare state are not compatible with a modern market economy in which virtually everyone is expected to participate in the labor force. In effect, the New Deal's outmoded collection of social programs is no longer relevant in a modern free-market society.

James Midgley, Ph.D., is Harry and Riva Specht Professor of Public Social Services and Dean of the School of Social Welfare at the University of California at Berkeley. He has published widely on issues of social policy, social work, and international social welfare. His most recent books include *Social Welfare in Global Context* (Sage Publications, 1997), *Alternatives to Social Security* (with Michael Sherraden, Greenwood Press, 1997) and *The Handbook of Social Policy* (Sage Publications, 2000).

Howard Jacob Karger, Ph.D., is Professor at the University of Houston. Along with David Stoesz, he is the coauthor of *American Social Welfare Policy* (4th ed.). He has published widely in the field of social-welfare policy, including in areas such as income-maintenance policy, poverty policy, and social development.

YES

James Midgley

The question of whether government social policies and programs are compatible with a market economy has been widely debated by social-policy experts in the past. Although strong opinions have been expressed, the topic is a complicated one. Unfortunately, the issues have been oversimplified, and conclusions seem to be based on sentiment rather than careful reasoning. This debate will show that it is possible to reach a reasoned conclusion only by addressing the complexities of the issue and by introducing caveats and qualifications. Taking these caveats and qualifications into account, it will be argued that welfare statism is compatible with the market economy—provided that the government regulates the market, links it in a planned way to social welfare, and ensures that it functions to serve people's interests.

An attempt to decide whether the welfare state is compatible with the market economy requires that the terms *market economy* and *welfare state* be defined. Both terms are used in an imprecise way not only in the academic literature but in the media and in ordinary discourse. However, they need to be understood if the relationship between the market economy and the welfare state is to be analyzed.

THE DYNAMICS OF THE MARKET ECONOMY

The term *market economy* refers to an economic system in which producers and consumers voluntarily engage in economic activities on the basis of prices determined by supply and demand (Pearce, 1992). Producers are motivated to respond to consumer demand because they wish to maximize profits, and consumers respond because they want to obtain goods and services at an optimal price. Prices are not determined by custom, personal considerations, or the government, but by supply and demand. Producers compete with each other to sell their goods and services, and this not only ensures affordability but promotes efficiency. Price efficiency is also governed by the fact that consumers can choose among the goods and services offered by different producers and distributors. Therefore, supply and demand are vital forces for determining the volume of goods and services produced, the way prices are determined, and the way the interests of producers and consumers are harmonized. Economists believe that the market economy has its own internal, self-regulatory dynamic. When supply and demand are out of balance, the market corrects itself and returns to a state of equilibrium in which the interests of both producers and consumers are satisfied. Supporters of the market economy argue that it works best when it is allowed to operate free of government control. When the market functions autonomously, competition, supply and demand, and the interests of producers and consumers ensure its smooth operation (Friedman, 1962; Friedman & Friedman, 1980).

The market economy may be contrasted with other economic systems in which supply and demand do not play such critical roles. In traditional societies, goods and services may be produced and exchanged because of cultural obligations or personal relationships. Producers provide goods and services to consumers not because they are seeking to make a profit but because they are members of the same family or clan, or because the culture prescribes particular economic exchanges. Similarly, in the former communist countries, economic exchanges were controlled and directed by the government. All citizens were expected to contribute collectively to production. Moreover, government leaders claimed that citizens did so because of a shared commitment to the common good and not because of self-interest. Government economic planners and political leaders decided what should be produced and how much goods and services should cost. The role of the market in these countries was severely curtailed.

People have strong opinions on whether the free market or the centrally planned economy is the best way of meeting demand for goods and services. Supporters of the market economy cite what they see as its obvious efficiency. A centrally planned system, they argue, creates shortages, requires rationing, and will ultimately collapse, as occurred in the Soviet Union and other communist nations. On the other hand, critics maintain that the market economy is based on greed, profits, and exploitation. They believe that claims about its effectiveness are exaggerated. It is not, they contend, a benign system of exchange based on the mutual satisfaction of the interests of producers and consumer. Rather, it thrives on the exploitation of labor, the manipulation of consumers through advertising, and the promotion of crass consumerism (Kuttner, 1997). Price gouging, environmental degradation, and other deplorable practices are integral to the way the market economy functions. Thus critics argue that the market economy, particularly in the context of economic globalization, is morally debased (Gray, 1998; Hertz, 2001; Lutwak, 1999).

Despite their opposition of the market economy, many of its detractors have recognized its positive aspects. For example, Karl Marx and Friedrich Engels—perhaps the most famous critics of the market economy—also recognized its dynamic character. They conceded that it had raised economic production to unimagined levels, and that it had obliterated oppressive feudal structures (Heilbroner, 1992). On the other hand, supporters of the market economy have recognized its limitations. The renowned economist Joseph Schumpeter praised the market's creative power but also emphasized its destructive impact. He noted that entrepreneurs, in their relentless pursuit of profits, are constantly producing new products and technologies. Although this fosters innovation, it also results in obsolescence, waste, and the decimation of producers who are unable to compete.

Of course, there is a middle way between supporters and opponents of the market economy. Many on the political left, who decry the market economy, believe that its dynamism can be harnessed for good. They want government to manage the economy not through centralized planning but through less intrusive economic-policy instruments such as interest-rate manipulation, monopoly limitation, labor and work regulations, the maintenance of fair prices, production incentives, and environmental protection. Many on the political right who lament government intervention also recognize that regulations and incentives have a role to play. For example, many are in favor of measures to limit monopolies and of efforts to stimulate economic growth and control inflation through manipulation of interest rates.

THE ROLE OF THE WELFARE STATE

It is in the context of regulating and harnessing the dynamic power of the market economy that the role of the welfare state should be discussed. Many of those who believe in the positive potential of the market economy also believe that governments must link the market economy to social policies and programs in a purposeful way. But before examining this argument in more depth, let's consider the definition of the welfare state.

The term *welfare state* is loosely used to connote an economically developed country where the government provides extensive social services to its citizens. The term was popularized in Great Britain in the years after the Second World War, when the recommendations of a committee appointed by the government to plan for postwar reconstruction were adopted (Glennerster, 1995). Chaired by William Beveridge, the committee urged the government to introduce comprehensive health, housing, education, Social Security, and welfare services. Acceptance of these recommendations resulted in a massive expansion of government social services. The British national health services was created in 1948 to provide free medical care to all citizens. Housing and educational programs were expanded; a comprehensive Social Security system was introduced in 1946; and social services for families, the disabled, and other vulnerable groups were strengthened (Hills, Ditch, & Glennerster, 1994). Other European countries also expanded their social provisions after the war. By the 1960s, most European nations were described as welfare states by social-policy writers.

Before the Second World War, it was widely believed that people should be responsible for their own welfare. However, the Great Depression of the 1930s showed that even hardworking, responsible citizens could fall into poverty and deprivation. Many workers lost their jobs, and many business people lost their livelihoods. The horrors of the Depression convinced many political leaders and ordinary citizens that government had a vital role to play in promoting the welfare of the people. As government social programs expanded, the prevailing individualist ideology that opposed government intervention gradually gave way to a collectivist ideology that stressed the importance of government provision.

It is important to note that the expansion of social services in the European countries after World War II took place within the context of wider economic policies. In an effort to promote full employment and rapid economic growth, most European governments implemented policies based on the writings of the British economist John Maynard Keynes. Therefore, welfare statism was closely linked to economic management. The social services were not intended to function in isolation from economic policy, but to complement and sustain economic development.

The term *welfare state* was also applied to other economically developed countries, such as Australia, Canada, New Zealand, and the United States. However, there has been disagreement about whether the United States is, in fact, a welfare state. Unlike the European countries, the United States has not introduced a comprehensive government-funded health service, and commercial healthcare providers continue to dominate the system. Public housing and social-welfare services are also believed to be less extensive in the United States than in Europe. For this reason, some American scholars have described the United States as a "residual" or "reluctant" welfare state (Wilensky & Lebeaux, 1965; Jannsen, 1993).

On the other hand, social-policy writers such as Theda Skocpol (1995) point out that the United States has invested more extensively in education than many European countries have and that its Social Security system is very well developed. The United States has also adopted a different approach to welfare than that favored by Europeans. Instead of maintaining a large, centralized welfare bureaucracy, the American government has promoted decentralization. It also contracts out public services to nonprofit and commercial providers. It is not that the government has failed to promote the welfare of its people, but that it has done so in a different way.

In the United States, the term *welfare state* is historically associated with the first major expansion of government social programs, which took place during the Roosevelt administration of the 1930s (Berkowitz, 1991). However, in the 1950s, when Republican President Eisenhower served two terms, social programs were also expanded. Further expansion took place under the Great Society programs of President Johnson in the 1960s, and during the Nixon and Carter administrations (Berkowitz, 1991). Despite differences between American and European approaches, the term *welfare state* was widely used to describe American social policy during these periods.

On the other hand, the term took on derogatory connotations during the Reagan administration. Several social-policy scholars associated with the political right began to attack welfare statism. For example, Charles Murray (1984) popularized the idea that government social programs caused more harm than good. By providing generous social services and benefits, Murray

wrote, the welfare state had undermined the work ethic, fostered the disin-
tegration of traditional family obligations, engendered a culture of indolence,
and promoted irresponsibility. Because of the welfare state, the United States
had not made steady social progress but had, in fact, lost ground. Many other
writers supported Murray's position, and by the mid-1990s, Republican
leader Newt Gingrich (1995) had succeeded in demonizing the term. The
goal of the Republican party, he promised, was to replace the welfare state
with the "opportunity society."

Perhaps the most serious criticism of state welfare programs came from
neoliberal or free-market economists. Some claimed that government social
programs had reduced people's propensity to save, creating a shortage of capital for investment and impeding economic growth (Feldstein, 1974). Others
argued that social programs have required high levels of taxation. As more
elderly and other needy people received social benefits, a heavy and unfair
burden was imposed on those who remained economically active (Bacon &
Eltis, 1976; Freeman, 1981). Social programs also drew criticism for supposedly harming work incentives and undermining self-reliance. Because people
were no longer required to meet their own social needs, they were becoming
dependent and irresponsible (Mead, 1992; Murray, 1984; Payne, 1998).

During the 1970s, as taxation levels increased and the United States and
many other industrial countries experienced recession and other economic
difficulties, these arguments gained support. As a result, citizens elected governments that had little sympathy for the welfare state. The most important
of these were Prime Minister Margaret Thatcher's Conservative government
in Britain, President Ronald Reagan's Republican administration, and the
military regime of General Augusto Pinochet in Chile (Glennerster & Midgley, 1991). In addition, since the 1980s, the market economy has been elevated
to a new level of importance, having promoted the maximization of profits,
tax reductions, deregulation, and the retrenchment of social programs (Kuttner, 1997). In this situation, the question of whether the welfare state and the
market economy are compatible assumes a new and urgent significance.

THE MARKET ECONOMY AND THE WELFARE STATE

The most widely accepted position today is that the welfare state and the
market economy are not compatible. Ironically, this opinion is shared by
many of those on the political right with those on the political left. Free-
marketeers, libertarians, and traditionalists agree with Marxists and radical
populists that capitalism and welfare statism are contradictory ideals.

Marxists have traditionally claimed that the welfare state is subservient
to the market and that capitalists use it to promote the interests of the wealthy
and powerful. For this reason, they argue, the welfare state cannot create a
just and equal society in which people's social needs are met (Ginsberg, 1979;

Gough, 1979). Radical populists, such as those who have recently protested at international meetings of the World Bank and World Trade Organization, agree that the global market economy is harming people's welfare.

Libertarians, traditionalists, and neoliberal proponents of the free market have a strong dislike of government, believing that people should be free of its constraints and regulations. The libertarian position is summed up in the aphorism that the best government is the government that governs least. Of course, the arguments supporting this idea are more complex than this simple maxim implies (Nozick, 1974).

Traditionalists agree! They believe that Americans have historically met their own social needs and that traditional institutions such as the family, church, and local community have effectively provided support to those who could not help themselves. Traditionalists want the government to curtail its welfare programs and to encourage churches and charities to play a greater role in meeting social needs (Olasky, 1992; 1996).

Neoliberal economists focus largely on the way in which welfare programs allegedly harm the economy. As noted earlier, they contend that social programs require high levels of public spending and impose exacting taxes on working people. High taxes in turn undermine the incentives of business firms and hardworking people. This problem worsens when people realize that their taxes are being used to support a large underclass of people who are dependent on welfare. Unless government welfare programs are scaled back, free-marketeers maintain, the economy will steadily decline. Slumping production, high unemployment, falling standards of living, and a higher incidence of poverty will result.

One variation of the free-market position concerns the privatization of social programs. Many neoliberal economists have urged government to transfer social-welfare programs to commercial providers. However, many believe that government funds should be used for this purpose. The extensive contracting out of services to commercial providers that characterizes American social policy today suggests that marketeers do not oppose government spending if commercial providers benefit from this spending. The campaign to privatize Social Security in the United States is supposedly about ensuring the program's long-term viability. In reality, however, it is about transferring huge resources to commercial insurance firms (Baker & Weisbrot, 1999; Kingson & Williamson, 1998).

The free-market position enjoys widespread popularity and support at the highest political levels today. Those who believe that the market economy and welfare state are compatible are in a small minority. Nevertheless, the latter continue to argue that the market economy can be harnessed to promote full employment, higher standards of living, and the well-being of the population as a whole. A managed market economy that is harmonized with a social-service system can, they believe, function effectively to enhance people's welfare.

Those who believe that the market economy can be harnessed for social purposes draw on the historical experience of European countries and the United States to show that attempts to regulate and manage the market economy and to link it with social policies and programs can be successful. They particularly emphasize social investments that enhance people's abilities to participate effectively in the productive economy. They show that New Deal programs in the United States provided jobs for hundreds of thousands of unemployed people and that the educational and job-training programs of the time enhanced many people's skills. Numerous communities in the United States today continue to reap the benefits of New Deal public-works programs.

Those who believe in the compatibility of the market economy and the welfare state also point out that European Social Democratic parties have raised standards of living to unprecedented levels during the last fifty years. Unlike Marxists, who favored revolution and dictatorial government, European Social Democrats achieved economic and social transformation without bloodshed, secret police terror, or concentration camps. Similarly, unlike the free-marketeers who favored unrestricted profit maximization, Social Democratic governments in Europe achieved economic development without the widespread poverty, inequalities, and social deprivation that characterize unregulated, capitalist economic development.

However, those who claim that the market economy and the welfare state are compatible are not so naive as to believe that the Social Democratic formula of the postwar years remains viable today. They recognize that fundamental economic, demographic, cultural, and social changes have taken place since the mid-twentieth century. Nevertheless, they argue, the basic principles that governed the Social Democratic approach can be reconceptualized and modernized to meet the challenges of our time. A variety of innovations that propose a reconceptualization of this kind have already been formulated, and some are being adopted by Social Democratic and other progressive governments in Europe and elsewhere. Anthony Giddens' Third Way (1998; 2001), Amartya Sen's (1999) concept of "human capabilities," James Midgley's (1995; 1999) developmentalist or "social investment" theory, the "new egalitarianism" of Samuel Bowles and Herbert Gintis (1998), and similar proposals offer strategic opportunities to once again harness the market economy for social purposes. Whether these approaches will be adopted in the United States remains to be seen.

NO

Howard Jacob Karger

For many years, the American welfare state was clearly compatible with the free market. At least as reflected in the Social Security Act of 1935, the U.S. welfare state was designed to complement rather than replace the free-market economy. In this article, I argue that the American economy has changed dramatically since the 1930s, making anachronistic the premises on which the welfare state was built.

THE AMERICAN WELFARE STATE
IN HISTORICAL PERSPECTIVE

To understand why the welfare state is incompatible with the modern U.S. economy, we must examine the ways in which the welfare state has changed in relation to the national economy. When Franklin Delano Roosevelt (FDR) assumed the presidency in 1933, he faced a country divided between right- and left-wing political factions, an industrial empire on the verge of collapse, violent labor strikes, a class society at its breaking point, and a banking system that was all but bankrupt (Cohen, 1958). FDR's response to the Depression involved a massive social experiment with the objectives of relief, recovery, and reform. FDR was not a socialist, nor was the philosophy of the New Deal welfare state Marxian. Far from being radical, FDR's New Deal programs (the foundation of the American welfare state) were designed to salvage capitalism.

Nevertheless, FDR's policies created the foundation for the modern welfare state in important ways. First, federal policy was used to ameliorate some of the more egregious inequities in the labor market. This occurred through minimum-wage laws and the establishment of workers' right to strike and collectively bargain. The New Deal welfare state set important precedents in others areas as well. First, it established the *right* of eligible people to receive public assistance. The New Deal welfare state took public assistance from the realm of "we will provide what we have" to an entitlement in which resources *must* be provided to those in need. Second, it removed the provision of public assistance from the states and planted it firmly in the federal sphere. As such, certain public-assistance rules and eligibility (but not cash benefits) were standardized and applied more evenly. FDR's New Deal programs contained an implicit policy directive that established the responsibility of the federal and state governments to provide for the needs of those citizens who were deemed worthy of receiving aid (Karger & Stoesz, 1998). Third, the New Deal welfare state firmly set the precedent of using social programs to quell and manage social unrest (Piven & Cloward, 1971). This policy would be used well into the 1960s and again in the Los Angeles riots of 1992. Fourth, it used welfare-state programs to subsidize a segment of the population for whom there were no jobs or who could not compete in the labor force. Welfare-state programs, such as unemployment insurance, also subsidized displaced workers until the economy could relocate them. To be fair, this haven provided little more than a subsistence existence for recipients. In effect, FDR's programs created a social compact that lasted for more than fifty years.

From the 1950s to the 1970s, the American welfare state grew despite sustained attacks by conservatives. Apart from some ups and downs, the

U.S. economy enjoyed an overall upward trajectory. American innovation introduced a wide range of products and services, and the productivity of U.S. industry and workers was unsurpassed in the world. The American industrial empire was clearly in the driver's seat. Thus the United States could well afford to idle a small percentage of the workforce without having a noticeable impact on the economy. In effect, the growth and productivity of the U.S. economy more than compensated for the small number of people who were subsidized.

The strategy of using welfare programs as a palliative for social unrest grew during the 1960s. Driven by massive urban riots in African American communities during the middle and late 1960s, former president Lyndon Johnson's War on Poverty programs (later referred to as the Great Society) included a variety of programs designed to ameliorate social unrest and raise people and communities out of poverty. These welfare programs bought off social discontent. Moreover, by the end of the Great Society, the number of people living below the poverty line was cut almost in half—from about 25 percent in the early 1960s to around 12 percent by 1969 (Karger & Stoesz, 1998). However, much of this reduction was offset by growth in Aid to Families with Dependent Children (AFDC) rolls.

Although former president Richard Nixon promptly dismantled the Great Society, the welfare state expanded more under his administration than it had under preceding presidents. Between 1965 and 1975, America's national fiscal priorities were reversed: In 1965, defense expenditures accounted for 42 percent of the federal budget, while social-welfare expenditures accounted for only 25 percent. By 1975, defense expenditures accounted for just 25 percent of the federal budget, while social-welfare outlays accounted for 43 percent. Even in Ronald Reagan's conservative budget of 1986 (characterized by large increases in defense spending), only 29 percent was defense related, compared to 41 percent for social welfare (DiNitto & Dye, 1987). From 1935 to the middle 1970s, the American welfare state was clearly growing.

THE GLOBAL ECONOMY AND THE WELFARE STATE

Economic health drives the welfare state. By the mid-1970s, America's economic position in the world had become uncertain. Throughout the 1970s, inflation coupled with recession (stagflation) began to erode the economic advances to which Americans had become accustomed. Late in the decade, inflation had reached double digits, and the unemployment rate was rising precipitously. The productivity advances of European and Asian nations were nipping at the heels of American industry and quality of life (Reich, 1983). The term *global economy* was finding its way into the American vernacular as legislators and policy analysts realized that the economic playing field had changed (Barnet, 1994). No longer were independent national economies the rule; instead, Americans were living in an economically inter-dependent world. This new international competition made Americans less smug about their economic dominance of the world. By the mid-1980s, all but the most daft were aware that Americans had to change their understanding of the economy.

Simultaneously, Americans also had to change their understanding of welfare. Not surprisingly, promoted welfare-to-work programs vigorously during former president Jimmy Carter's administration. Welfare reform was an important issue for the Reagan administration as well. This followed on the heels of a growing consensus among conservatives and many liberals that America would fall behind if it did not adjust to the global economy. People wondered: How should America make that adjustment? For their part, economists looked at how human resources were being deployed in Asian nations. Most of these nations did not subsidize a significant percent-age of their population, especially those who could work in some form of employment.

Americans viewed idling a percentage of the workforce through wel-fare and public-assistance programs as a perk that America could no longer afford. They could enjoy the luxury of subsidization only when the United States was the undisputed economic leader of the world, and when the huge productivity gap between America and the rest of the world could compen-sate for that indulgence. Instead, a more rational method for deploying human resources became necessary in the new global economic order. It was not coincidental that welfare reform was passed during the administration of Bill Clinton, a president firmly committed to free trade and keenly aware of the new economic realities.

With the redeployment of human resources in the global economy came the need to cut or at least stabilize taxes (Karger, 1992). When econo-mists looked at Asian economic competitors, they saw that those nations' tax burdens—on both industry and individuals—were considerably lower than in the United States. By redeploying human resources through compelling the able-bodied to work, Asian governments were able to stabilize or even lower welfare spending, which in turn helped stabilize or reduce tax rates. Thus it is no surprise that while the 1990s witnessed a period of robust eco-nomic growth, the U.S. Congress passed no new welfare-program initiatives that required significant funding. The few welfare-related programs that did pass, such as AmeriCorps, were funded by a paltry amount compared to other social programs (Karger & Stoesz, 1998).

Another adaptation to the global economy was to rely on economic inse-curity to boost productivity. This adaptation rested on the belief that job secu-rity lowers motivation and hence damages productivity. As such, workers who are threatened by the specter of dismissal will labor harder. Concepts such as employment for life thus became anachronisms. Now, middle man-agers and workers are let go as profits dip or operations are moved overseas. Even academics' jobs have been threatened as state legislatures have passed several bills weakening or eliminating tenure. In the welfare sector, economic insecurity was introduced by the Personal Responsibility and Work Opportunity Reconciliation Act of 1996 (PRWORA), which puts a five-year, lifetime cap on the receipt of public assistance (Karger & Stoesz, 1998). Welfare recipients are now subject to the same economic insecurity experienced by most of the American workforce. There are no guarantees in the new economic order.

THE EVOLUTION OF AMERICAN WELFARE POLICY

Over the past twenty years, welfare policy has undergone a radical transformation in response to changing economic conditions. For instance, New Deal public-assistance programs have shifted from maintaining people outside of the labor force to programs and policies designed to force the poor into the labor market (Karger & Stoesz, 1998). Labor-force participation is increasingly becoming the only vehicle for subsistence for the majority of the poor. In effect, the welfare state has been transformed into the work state (Kaus, 1992). Traditional social-welfare programs that had provided benefits to those unable to participate in the labor force have been replaced by labor and tax policies designed to compel the poor to work and to subsidize low-wage employment. This trend is illustrated by two recent and important welfare-related developments: the growth in the Earned Income Tax Credits (EITC) program and the passage of the PRWORA.

The Earned Income Tax Credit (EITC) was enacted in 1975 after a negative income tax advanced by the Nixon administration failed. A refundable tax credit, the EITC instructs the IRS to send a check to low-wage workers, especially those with children, who have earned income below a certain level. In 1997, a worker with two children could receive a maximum refund of $3,656. Since the creation of the EITC, other work-related tax credits have been introduced. For example, a child-care tax credit lets low-wage workers deduct the costs of day care. Moreover, several states have introduced tax credits for low-income workers, some of which are refundable (Karger & Stoesz, 1998). Again, it is not coincidental that the only public-assistance program that is growing is EITC, which is tied to labor-force participation.

On August 22, 1996, President Bill Clinton signed the PRWORA, a 900-page document that became the most important welfare legislation since the Social Security Act of 1935. The complexity of the act masked three important features. First, the responsibility for providing public assistance devolved from the federal government to the states. Second, the act disentitled the poor from receiving public assistance. In contrast to the former AFDC program, which operated under the principle of entitlement (anyone eligible for assistance had to receive it), under the PRWORA the poor are not entitled to receive public assistance. In the event that funds run out, states can turn away the eligible poor. Third, the PRWORA introduced a five-year lifetime cap on the receipt of public assistance. States had an option to reduce that cap, and most opted for two years or less (Karger & Stoesz, 1998).

The PRWORA was called welfare reform, but in fact it was labor policy. The intent of the bill was to remove the safety net of the New Deal welfare state, thereby compelling the poor to enter the labor market. By devolving public assistance to the states, removing the protection of entitlement, and instituting a lifetime cap, the government turned the welfare state into the work state. Hence, the welfare state was no longer the economic haven that the New Deal architects had envisioned. The rules of the new marketplace became the rules of welfare receipt. In the same way that no one was entitled to hold a job, no one was entitled to receive public assistance.

The conversion of public assistance into labor and tax policy is shored up by the expansion of EITC benefits—the largest public-assistance program in the nation and the only one that has been purposely enlarged in the last twenty years (Karger & Stoesz, 1998). Expanding EITC benefits while also eliminating AFDC shifted the focus from the nonworking poor to the working poor—and the circle was complete. The PRWORA forced poor people into the labor market, and the EITC subsidized their low wages. This scheme was part of the new deployment of human and economic resources that would characterize America's accommodation to the global economy. It would also become one mainstay in the U.S. strategy of remaining globally competitive. However, labor and tax policy are not welfare policy. Nor is the work state equivalent to the welfare state.

The transformation of the welfare state into the work state represents the deconstruction of the public-assistance portion of the New Deal welfare state and the final victory of market over humanitarian concerns. In no small measure, this victory is an important step in the total marketization of American society. Without a safe harbor of public assistance, almost all Americans are now more vulnerable to the vicissitudes of the marketplace.

CONCLUSION

Several years ago, U.S. carmaker giant General Motors ran an ad promoting its new line of cars that said, "This is not your father's Oldsmobile." Well, this isn't your father's economy. The global marketplace has transformed the American economy in important ways that make it incompatible with the welfare state. Like the old Pac-Man video game, the new economy devours everything in its path. The economy has converted the welfare state into the work state and replaced welfare policy with labor and tax policy. In addition, the programs it cannot deconstruct are turned into profitable ventures. This is done through the privatization and subcontracting of social services. U.S. state, local, and federal governments spend roughly half a trillion dollars a year paying public workers to deliver goods and services (Donahue, 1989). If only 50 percent of these services are good candidates for privatization, corporations could realize a half a trillion in revenues. By 1994, thirteen top human-service corporations (Columbia/HCA, CIGNA Corp., United Health Care, FHP International, PacifiCare Health, Humana, U.S. Healthcare, Tenet Healthcare, Wellpoint Health, Beverly Enterprises, Wackenhut, Community Psychiatric Centers, and Kinder Care) alone had revenues in excess of $72 billion and employed more than 471,000 people (Standard and Poors, 1995). What American corporations can't beat they join.

Though this debate has focused on the public-assistance part of the welfare state, the Social Security system—arguably the bastion of the American welfare state—is also profoundly affected by the global marketplace. The intent of the Social Security Act of 1935 was to protect workers from poverty after they retired. The act accomplished this by compelling workers to invest a portion of their earnings in the Social Security system. The money collected by the Social Security system has been invested conservatively in U.S. Treasury bills. Although a worker's contribution to Social Security does not provide a rate of return commensurate with private investment, it is safe and guarantees retired workers a stable income. However, for an increasingly voracious economic system, the protected Social Security trust fund is analogous to the hungry fox who can't squeeze through the fence to get into the chicken coop. At its present $900 billion surplus (Social Security Administration, 2000), the Social Security trust fund is an irresistible temptation for corporations and stock-market investors. Not surprisingly, several reform plans have emerged that allow the federal government or workers covered under Social Security to invest at least a portion of their trust funds in the private market. Under these plans, if the economy does well, the Social Security trust fund will be fiscally healthier than before. However, if the economy does not do well, then recipients or the federal government (which still has to cover monthly recipient payments) will suffer. Interestingly, plans to privatize Social Security did not emerge until *after* the trust fund had accumulated a large surplus. Uncertainty again replaces security as workers tie their economic security to marketplace vicissitudes.

Despite the attendant risks, some form of Social Security privatization is likely, given the large amount of capital that could be freed up for investment. Moreover, the privatization of Social Security would be the most important element in the deconstruction of the American welfare state. It would represent the triumph of the belief that the marketplace, rather than the government, is the main arbiter for meeting human needs.

Though this article has focused on the American welfare state, the ideas in it have international implications. Most industrial countries have been forced to compete in the global economy, and most have made concessions to this necessity. Welfare-state programs in virtually all industrial countries have either been stagnant or pared back (Midgley & Glennester, 1991). The entrenchment of the global economy has made the growth of the welfare state in the United States and abroad a thing of the past.

The humanitarian drives behind the original welfare state have also changed. The social unrest that led to the emergence of the New Deal in the 1930s and the growth of the welfare state in the 1960s has been replaced by relative social quiet—which in turn has led to legislative apathy. The outrage of Americans toward poverty and social injustice has given way to an acceptance of the status quo. Not only has the American economy adapted to the global economy, but citizens' sensibilities have also been transformed. The welfare state thrives during periods of compassion, concern, and outrage. Conversely, it withers when apathy and self-interest rule the day.

Is the American welfare state compatible with the free market? The resounding answer is no—at least as the U.S. economy is presently structured.

REFERENCES

Bacon, R., & Eltis, W. (1976). *Britain's economic problems: Too few producers*. London: Macmillan.

Baker, D., & Weisbrot, M. (1999). *Social Security: The phony crisis*. Chicago: University of Chicago Press.

Berkowitz, E. (1991). *America's welfare state from Roosevelt to Reagan*. Baltimore: The John Hopkins University Press.

Bowles, S., & Gintis, H. (1998). *Recasting egalitarianism*. New York: Verso.

Feldstein, M. (1974). Social security, induced retirement and aggregate capital accumulation, *Journal of Political Economy, 83*(4), 447–475.

Freeman, R. A. (1981). *The wayward welfare state*. Stanford, CA: Hoover Institution Press.

Friedman, M. (1962). *Capitalism and freedom*. Chicago: University of Chicago Press.

Friedman, M. (with Friedman, R.) (1980). *Free to choose*. London: Secker and Warburg.

Giddens, A. (1998). *The third way: The renewal of social democracy*. Cambridge: Polity Press.

Giddens, A. (2001). *The global third way debate*. Cambridge: Polity Press.

Gingrich, N. (1995). *To renew America*. New York: Harper.

Ginsberg, N. (1979). *Class, capital and social policy*. London: Macmillan.

Glennerster, H. (1995). *British social policy since 1945*. Oxford: Blackwell.

Glennerster, H., & Midgley, J. (Eds.) (1991). *The radical right and the welfare state: An international assessment*. Hemel Hempstead: Harvester Wheatsheaf.

Gough, I. (1979). *The political economy of the welfare state*. London: Macmillan.

Gray, J. (1998). *False dawn: The delusions of global capitalism*. London: Granta Books.

Heilbroner, R. K. (1992). *The worldly philosophers: The lives, times and ideas of great economic thinkers*. New York: Simon & Schuster.

Hertz, N. (2001). *The silent takeover: Global capitalism and the death of democracy*. London: Heinemann.

Hills, J., Ditch J., & Glennerster, H. (Eds.) (1994). *Beveridge and Social Security*. Oxford: Clarendon Press.

Jannsen, B. (1993). *The reluctant welfare state: A history of American social welfare policies*. Pacific Grove, CA: Brooks/Cole.

Kingson, E. R., & Williamson, J. B. (1998). Understanding the debate over the privatization of social security. *Journal of Sociology and Social Welfare, 25*(3), 47–62.

Kuttner, R. (1997). *Everything for sale: The virtues and limits of markets*. New York: Alfred A. Knopf.

Lutwak, E. (1999). *Turbo capitalism: Winners and losers in the global economy*. New York: HarperCollins.

Mead, L. M. (1992). *The new politics of poverty: The nonworking poor in America*. New York: Basic Books.

Midgley, J. (1995). *Social development: The developmental perspective in social welfare*. Thousand Oaks, CA: Sage Publications.

Midgley, J. (1999). Growth, redistribution and welfare: Towards social investment, *Social Service Review, 77*(1): 3–21.

Murray, C. (1984). *Losing ground: American social policy, 1950–1980*. New York: Basic Books.

Nozick, R. (1974). *Anarchy, state and utopia*. New York: Basic Books.

Olasky, M. (1992). *The tragedy of American compassion*. Washington, DC: Regnery.

Olasky, M. (1996). *Renewing American compassion*. Washington, DC: Regnery.

Payne, J. L. (1998). *Overcoming welfare: Expecting more from the poor and from ourselves*. New York: Basic Books.

Pearce, D. W. (1992). *The MIT dictionary of economics*. Cambridge, MA: MIT Press.

Sen, A. (1999). *Development as freedom*. New York: Knopf.

Skocpol, T. (1995). *Social policy in the United States: Future possibilities in the United States*. Princeton, NJ: Princeton University Press.

Wilensky, H., & Lebeaux, C. (1965). *Industrial society and social welfare*. New York: Free Press.

Cohen, N. (1958). *Social work in the American tradition*. New York: Holt, Rinehart and Winston.

DiNitto, D., & Dye, T. (1987). *Social welfare: Politics and public policy*. Englewood Cliffs, NJ: Prentice-Hall.

Donahue, J. (1989). *The privatization decision*. New York: Basic Books.

Karger, H. (1992). Welfare, the global economy and the state: The American experience. *Social Development Issues, 1*(14), (Fall), 83–95.

Karger, H. J. & Stoesz, D. (1998). *American social welfare policy: A pluralist approach*. (3rd ed.). New York: Longman.

Kaus, M. (1992). *The end of equality*. New York: Basic Books.

Midgley, J., & Glennester, H. (Eds.) (1991) *The radical right and the welfare state*. London: Wheatsheaf Books.

Piven, F. F., & Cloward, R. (1971). *Regulating the poor*. New York: Vintage Books.

Reich, R. (1983). *The next American frontier*. New York: Times Books.

Social Security Administration, Social Security and Medicare Board of Trustees. (2000). A summary of the 2000 annual reports, April. Retrieved June 11, 2001. Online: *http://www.ssa.gov/OACT/TRSUM/trsummary.html*.

Standard and Poors (1995). *Standard and Poors directory*. New York.

Barnet, R. (1994). Lords of the global economy. *The Nation* (December 19), 754–757.

SHOULD THE FEDERAL GOVERNMENT SUPPORT OR FUND SECTARIAN SOCIAL-SERVICE AGENCIES?

Editor's Note:
Jon Meyer and Stephen Arch Erich debate one of the most contentious questions in social policy: Should the federal government fund faith-based social-service organizations? This issue surfaced in the Personal Responsibility and Work Opportunity Reconciliation Act of 1996, which permitted the federal government to fund faith-based social-service organizations. Though this policy change delighted Christian conservatives, it troubled liberals who feared that it could further legitimize the religious right's social agenda and factions.

Jon Meyer, L.M.S.W., is a doctoral student at the Graduate School of Social Work, University of Houston. He is also the executive director for the Community-Based Services Department of the Baptist Children's Home Ministries. Mr. Meyer is a Licensed Child-Care Administrator. For the past 21 years, he has provided social services to families and children through direct practice and social-service administration.

Stephen Erich, Ph.D., L.M.S.W.-ACP, is the B.S.W. Program Director at the University of Houston-Clear Lake. He received his Ph.D. and M.S.W. from the University of Houston Graduate School of Social Work. Dr. Erich's research interests are primarily concerned with the practice of adoption and the support of families and children with special needs.

YES

Jon Meyer

The Personal Responsibility Work Opportunity Reconciliation Act (PRWORA) of 1996 posed a tremendous challenge in transferring primary responsibility for public welfare from the federal government to state and local governments. Section 104 of the PRWORA (Public Law 104–193), referred to as "Charitable Choice," opens the door for faith-based organizations to partner with government in a way that has never happened before. Numerous pundits representing an array of organizations decry this change owing to understandable concerns. However, their arguments have become distal, because the debate often lacks proper contexualization. Any time legislation has the prospect of challenging the Constitution, as is the case with "Charitable Choice," debate should and does ensue. The proper context for this debate, and thus the pro-argument, must include the legal precedents for the "Charitable Choice" legislation, the historical context for the concept of church and state separation, and the role of the church in American society. Of course, the limitation of space in this article allows for only the most pertinent points to be made. When placed in proper perspective, this article will clearly show that not only is federal funding to faith-based organizations a good idea, but it is necessary in order for genuine welfare reform to take place.

LEGAL PRECEDENTS FOR "CHARITABLE CHOICE"

The authors of "Charitable Choice," most notably Senator John Ashcroft, developed this legislation with careful thought to related decisions made by the U.S. Supreme Court. This point alone reveals that there can be no real argument against "Charitable Choice" as unconstitutional.

The following is a summary of some of the lead cases pertinent to the "Charitable Choice" legislation. Esbeck (1996) summarizes the U.S. Supreme Court decisions of *Mueller v. Allen, Witters v. Washington Department of Services for the Blind, and Zobrest v. Catalina Foothills School District.* According to Esbeck, with these cases the Supreme Court upheld an important interpretation of the First Amendment. The Court stated that "so long as individuals may freely choose or not choose religion, merely enabling private decisions logically cannot be a governmental establishing of religion." Therefore, "Charitable Choice" mandates that a choice be available in terms of secular and religious providers of social services.

Through the *Bradfield v. Roberts* and *Bowen v. Kendrick* decisions, the Court supported federal funding to directly support social services provided by a faith-based organization. Kramnick and Moore (1997) explain how *Lemon v. Kurtzman* ended in the Court's developing a baseline for the constitutionality of future legislation that may result in funding to religious organizations. From *Lemon v. Kurtzman,* the Court developed the following criteria, known as the "... *Lemon* test" (Esbeck, 1996), to protect the establishment clause as it relates to new legislation:

- Funded agencies cannot limit their services to people affiliated with any particular religious denomination.

- Services provided under an act cannot be religious in character.
- There can be no substantial risk that aid to a religious institution results in religious indoctrination.
- Religious institutions must not be the sole or primary beneficiaries of legislation.
- Any arguable effect of advancing religion must be "incidental and remote" (Kramnick and Moore, 1997).

In his presentation "A Constitutional Case for Governmental Coopera-tion with Faith-Based Social Service Providers," Esbeck (1996) states that the Supreme Court, through repeated decisions, has held that the "Establishment Clause is not violated when government refrains from imposing a burden on religion, even though that same burden is imposed on the nonreligious who are otherwise similarly situated." This discretion in burden imposition is nec-essary to maintain proper distance between church and state.

Corporation of Presiding Bishop v. Amos is another lead case important for illustrating the legal support for "Charitable Choice" (Esbeck, 1996). This case upheld an exemption for faith-based organizations in federal civil-rights legislation (Esbeck, 1996). That is why "Charitable Choice" can ease the con-cern of faith-based organizations with regard to whom they hire to work in their organizations. Churches, for example, do not have to hire staff whose belief is antithetical to that of the church.

The Court has several rationales for decisions such as the above. First, government cannot act in establishing a religion (Esbeck, 1996). In addition, Esbeck (1996) states that ". . . unlike benefit programs, religious exemptions reduce civic/religious tensions and minimize church/state interactions, both matters that enhance the nonentanglement so desired by the Establishment Clause" (p. 8). Given the legal precedents, there is no doubt that implemen-tation of "Charitable Choice" is in accordance with the Constitution.

HISTORICAL APPLICATION OF THE CHURCH/STATE "WALL"

The strongest arguments by those opposing "Charitable Choice" is based on the idea that "Charitable Choice" is a breach in the wall of separation between church and state (a phrase not explicitly found in the Constitution). Thus it makes sense to consider elements of the first American debate on church/state relations. Amazingly, strong similarities exist between the debates surrounding church and state relations in antebellum Virginia and the current debate. In addition, the modern U.S. Supreme Court has refer-enced the Virginia law regarding church and state relations (Buckley, 1995).

According to Buckley (1995), the key legislation at the time of antebel-lum Virginia was Virginia's Statute for Religious Freedom, written by Thomas Jefferson. Interestingly, this statute did not separate civil government from religious concerns—witness the many laws directly influenced by the church. The primary debate in antebellum Virginia hovered around whether religious organizations should be allowed to incorporate. The churches, and their related organizations, wanted to incorporate so they could legally receive grants, bequests, and titles. However, the Virginia Assembly argued repeatedly that to incorporate would create an establishment of religion. Eventually the Assembly realized the unequal treatment toward religious institutions, compared to other organizations desiring incorporation, was unfair. In addition, allowing the incorporation of faith-based organizations proved necessary for the good of society in general.

Just as in antebellum Virginia, "Charitable Choice" today strives to put faith-based organizations on the same footing as secular social-service providers. As stated earlier, this is not only an entitlement of faith-based organizations; it benefits all society because it can meet important needs of those in poverty.

THE ROLE OF THE CHURCH IN AMERICAN SOCIETY

Strict separation between the church and the state is a misnomer. As we've just seen, early American history and key decisions by judicial bodies have shown trying to create a "wall" between government and religion is a wasted effort. These two institutions are inextricably intertwined. Therefore, a better society will come if we can clarify the important roles of each and understand how and when they intersect in society. One crucial role of the church, without which government cannot exist, is that of a moral/value catalyst. That is not to say that moral and value development cannot occur in society without the church. However, Sievers (1995) makes an important distinction based on the idea that societal values can be "substantive" or "instrumental." In other words, when societal values are simply a means to an end ("instrumental"), the benefit to society overall and to individuals is minimized. Sievers (1995) also explains that values used instrumentally ". . . are predominately procedural—advancing choice, pluralism, and fairness—rather than substantive, and they operate as unexamined givens rather than as subjects for deliberation and action" (p. 6). One example of instrumental values would be efforts to improve the educational system without changing students' attitudes about the value of education. A second example would be attempting to improve voter registration without addressing attitudes about the value of citizenship (Sievers, 1995). In an article on John Locke, McCabe (1997) points out that in a liberal democracy, citizens must be internally motivated to act morally. McCabe cites voluntary sacrifice of personal interest for the common good as an example. Because government is constrained through its bureaucracy, it cannot address social problems at the level of substantive values and morals.

Besides the family, the only social institution able to address commitment to social values, ethics, and morals is the church. As the hidden underclass increases in size (Murray, 2001), as schools become more violent, as the economy declines, and as the physical sciences raise new moral questions, the need for strategic guidance from the church will continue to intensify. Thus it only makes sense for faith-based organizations to partner with other major social institutions, such as the federal government, to ensure social welfare.

CONCLUSION

The church and the government need each other as they perform their important roles. The government must use its legislative power to facilitate important national changes. At the same time, the church can address the moral, ethical, and spiritual well-being of citizens owing to its proximity to those in need as well as through its unencumbered legal status. Indeed, it is this partnership that has sustained this complex nation. Those who think this partnership does not exist and thus work to build separation only threaten the foundation on which this nation was built. Federal funding to faith-based organizations should occur because it is constitutional and based on legal precedents. Our forefathers recognized the important interactive relationship between church and state. And in the end, faith-based organizations are the only institutions capable of addressing issues of substantive values and morals while meeting social needs.

NO

Stephen Erich

As stated, the debate is "Should the federal government support or fund sectarian social-service agencies?" I would suggest a few changes in the wording of the question. For instance, the question could be stated as follows: "Should our federal government fund, sponsor, support, enforce, and govern the work of organized religion?" The manner in which the original question is worded suggests a narrow focus on the issue of fairness in funding. It follows then, that the federal government, through President Bush's faith-based initiative, should fund and govern sectarian social-service agencies in a manner similar to the way it funds and governs nonsectarian social-service agencies.

Bush's faith-based initiative is part of a broader effort to expand "Charitable Choice" funding. This concept changed existing law to permit public funding of "pervasively sectarian" groups in which religion permeates virtually every aspect of the organization (Conn & Boston, 2001). Charitable Choice removes all remaining safeguards that prohibit church-state co-mingling, thus allowing groups to evangelize and proselytize while providing publicly financed social services (Conn & Boston, 2001). As such, this is much more than a debate about fairness in funding.

The religious right, for whom George W. Bush is a figurehead, would also like this issue to be framed simply as a question of economic fairness. The religious right is primarily a white, middle-class movement that is well financed; well organized; and socially, politically, and theologically conservative. Generally, members believe that the Bible is inerrant and that politics should be carried out according to their interpretation of biblical law (Hardisty, 1999). This primarily Christian group comprises evangelical, fundamentalist, Pentecostal, charismatic, Reconstructionist, Protestant, and conservative Catholic members. Many different organizations are associated with this movement. The most noteworthy is the Christian Coalition (Hardisty, 1999), whose influence on Bush's policies regarding church/state separation should not be underestimated.

This debate must be discussed within a broader historical context as well as the current cultural and political trends associated with the reemergence of religious paleoconservatives in politics. Furthermore, the debate must include a discussion about the influence of power and the infusion of personal values into professional helping relationships—and the impact of these relationships on voluntary consent and self-determination.

History is an invaluable teacher. The origin of the concept of separation of church and state should be a warning about how to manage church/state relationships in the present and future. Shortly after the founding of the colony of Virginia, the Anglican church was established as Virginia's state church. A series of religiously inspired laws were quickly enacted including the banishment of Quakers and Catholics. In addition, all Virginia residents as well as many other southern colonies were forced to support Anglicanism through taxation, whether they believed in the tenets of the church or not. By the mid-1700s, Anglicanism had become a minority religion in the southern colonies, yet all residents still had to pay taxes to support Anglican ministers (Boston, 1993). Interestingly, state-sponsored religion did little to encourage piety in colonial America. In fact, estimates put the number of "religious adherents" in 1776 at around 17 percent of the population (Boston, 1993). Notably, church membership did not begin to take off in America until after the adoption of the First Amendment, which gave the country true religious freedom through the separation of church and state (Boston, 1993).

Our founders were generally spiritual but not specifically religious or even Christian (Noll, Hatch, & Marsden, 1983). Many of these great leaders had a profound belief in a higher power, yet only a few believed in the orthodox teachings of traditional Christianity—despite the erroneous claims of the religious right. The first Constitutional Convention began with no concern or provisions for official, public prayers as part of its proceedings. Furthermore, neither the preamble nor the body of the Constitution produced at the Convention makes any appeal to religious motives or authority. The only substantive mention of religion within the text of the Constitution occurs in Article VI, Clause 3, prohibits the use of any religious tests for holding political office (Boston, 1993).

The words "separation of church and state" are not found in the Constitution, although the document's creators clearly had this concept in mind. In his now famous reply to the Danbury Baptists, President Thomas Jefferson described the First Amendment as building a "wall of separation between church and state" (Whitten, 1999). The Federalist Papers, written by Alexander Hamilton, James Madison, and John Jay to "sell" the new Constitution to the American people, made no appeal to religious authorities, rationales, or purposes to legitimize the document (Whitten, 1999). Furthermore, the Supreme Court, in numerous decisions over an extended period of time, ruled that the First Amendment should be interpreted in terms of church/ state separation. Indeed, our founders recognized that "concert or union or dependency" between church and state is dangerous both to the freedom and integrity of religion and the government (Whitten, 1999).

The debate in the First Congress on the wording of the First Amendment and subsequent appeals to the First Amendment address two primary concepts: the establishment clause and the free-exercise clause. The establishment clause has generally come to mean that government cannot authorize a church, pass laws that aid or favor one religion over another, pass laws that favor religious belief, or force a person to profess a belief (Conn & Boston, 2001). The free-exercise clause has generally come to mean that one may believe anything, but that religious actions and rituals can be limited by laws that are passed for compelling government reasons. Laws aimed at a particular religion or religions in general have been considered unconstitutional by the U.S. Supreme Court (Conn & Boston, 2001). Today's religious accommodationists, who assert that the First Amendment somehow grants government the right to give nonpreferential aid to religion, do not have support for their claims. The legislative history of the religion clauses proves exactly the opposite (Conn & Boston, 2001).

President Bush's proposed faith-based initiative will clearly violate the constitutional assumption of church/state separation. His initiative will expand the federal government by creating a new government agency expressly designed to assist with the development of sectarian social-service agencies that are managed by religious institutions (Conn & Boston, 2001). In effect, this will inextricably intertwine the federal government with organized religion. Religious institutions will depend on the federal government for funding and be governed by its standards.

In spite of historical problems, the intent of the First Amendment, and the amendment's legislative history, the religious right support the comingling of political and religious agendas as a legitimate means of providing social services. The group's political outlook is tied to a number of far-right positions on a variety of social issues, including extreme hostility to the concept of separation of church and state. Its other agendas include forcing all children to pray in school; reversing *Roe v. Wade*; eradicating Equal Rights Amendment initiatives; controlling reproductive rights; legalizing discrimination against gay/lesbian, bisexual, and transgendered persons; and limiting Americans' freedom to express themselves through speech, books, and art (Hardisty, 1999).

The religious right also accuses secular humanism of undermining Christianity and turning the United States into a Godless and immoral country (Hardisty, 1999; Whitten, 1999). This claim is simply not true. In recent years, Gallup and Roper polls, along with research conducted by the Princeton Religion Research Center and other organizations, have shown the United States to be the most religious of the Western nations. A summary of some of the polls' findings reveals some interesting results: Ninety percent of Americans polled say they do not doubt the existence of God. Fifty-eight percent say religion is very important to them. Forty-two percent say they have attended a religious service within the last seven days. Fifty-nine percent maintain that religion can answer all or most of today's problems. Only 2 percent of those polled say they are atheists; another 2 percent say they are agnostics. Seventy-seven percent consider prayer an important part of their daily lives (Boston, 1993). The real problem, as far as the religious right see it, is that many Americans think they can be religious without believing in the specific theologies espoused by various camps in the fundamentalist world. In fact, many Americans are very spiritual or religious, but are unaffiliated with any denomination.

Christianity is the dominant Western religion (Frawley, 2001). According to many fundamentalist Christian sects, being a good Christian requires proselytizing and converting others to the beliefs of one's own theological mission (Bankston, 1998). Although the religious right is primarily a Protestant phenomenon, this highly prescriptive theology is common among many factions of fundamentalist Christianity.

These Christian groups have a long history of conversion through charity (Frawley, 2001). Their conversion agenda includes targeting poor, disorganized, and powerless groups (Frawley, 2001). This philosophy has far-reaching effects. For instance, in the Northeast region of India, 85 percent of the population are now Christian. About thirty-five years ago, only 20 percent of its population were Christian. The other 80 percent believed in one of many forms of religious expression native to Indian culture. During the past thirty-five years, thousands of Christian missionaries, providing a variety of needed social and medical services, launched in a comprehensive and well-coordinated effort to convert the natives of this region (Reddy, 2001). Hundreds of thousands of Indians have been manipulated into following a Christian belief system.

Another example of the ever-creeping tendrils of fundamentalist Christianity concerns the provision of medical services at a hospital in Florida.

The Bayfront Medical Center has operated and managed a publicly supported medical facility for several years. In 1997, medical services changed dramatically after Bayfront allied itself with several other facilities, including religiously managed hospitals. The facility now operates under the "Ethical and Religious Directives" of the National Conference of Catholic Bishops. Medical decisions at Bayfront were once based on patients' needs and physicians' expertise. Now religious standards determine the options available to patients and physicians. In addition, hospital employees must sign a statement saying that they will adhere to the Catholic Bishops' guidelines. This public facility no longer provides a variety of legal medical procedures, including abortions, sterilization, artificial inseminations, and emergency contraception. Religious guidelines even mandate that the hospital restrict the decisions of seriously ill patients who have presented their wishes in living wills (Conn & Boston, 2001). Since 1995, a number of mergers between Catholic and non-Catholic hospitals have occurred across the country. Many have resulted in fewer healthcare options for patients (Conn & Boston, 2001).

These examples reveal the power of fundamentalist Christian helpers to infringe on individuals' right to self-determination and ability to consent to professional help. Bush's faith-based initiative will let this kind of professional relationship flourish by funding sectarian organizations in which religious beliefs and practices pervade the entire organization. As such, the government sponsors these organizations to evangelize and proselytize while providing professional social services.

The concept of self-determination has a long history in our country. Though it is not specifically mentioned in the Constitution, the Supreme Court, in a series of due-process, equal-protection, and privacy cases, developed the position that self-determination is a fundamental right protected by the Ninth and Fourteenth Amendments (Loewenberg, Dolgoff, & Harrington, 2000). Furthermore, the National Association of Social Workers (NASW) Code of Ethics states that "social workers [should] respect and promote the right of clients to self-determination and assist clients in their efforts to identify and clarify their goals" (NASW Code, 1996, 1.02). In fact, clients' level of self-determination and consent varies with their dependency on the benefits they receive from the professional worker. The more essential and valuable the goods or services received, the greater clients' feelings of dependency on the worker and the less likely they will be to choose an option of which they believe the worker will disapprove. Stigma, loss of self-esteem, psychological and economic hardship, a lack of options, the illegitimate use of power by professional helpers, and the infusion of alien values into the helping relationship all undermine clients' ability to be self-determining (Goodban, 1985).

The concepts of self-determination and consent to treatment are interdependent. Consent to professional help is meaningful only when given freely. The intrusion of personal values into the helping relationship and the power differences between the professional helper and the client severely and inappropriately diminish the voluntary consent of clients (Corey, Corey, & Callanan, 1998). For example, how voluntary will the consent of a client be if he or she believes consent is important to gain the worker's good will? A destitute parent may agree with almost everything a worker suggests because he or she desperately needs to qualify for assistance. An uninsured, severely injured worker will sign almost any form while sitting in the emergency room. A native of Northeast India will not likely refuse the conversion attempts of Christian missionaries who provide the peoples of that area with food and medical treatment. A poor family without transportation will not be able to travel across town to a nonsectarian agency even if they feel terribly uncomfortable with the manner in which religion is co-mingled with the provision of government-sponsored social services. To be sure, these people are not forced to come to a social-service agency or to agree with the professional helper. However, their consent is certainly less than fully voluntary, and their right to self-determination has been severely diminished.

George W. Bush's plan will strip away a client's freedom of choice in other ways as well: It will fund sectarian agencies that display their religious values prominently in the form of symbols, icons, and artifacts, and it will allow the intrusion of religious values by helping professionals. This is unfortunate, because self-determination helps clients to become healthy and to guide and evaluate the course of the helping relationship (Jensen & Bergin, 1988). Researchers have also found that clients tend to change in ways that are consistent with the values of their professional helpers. This tendency leaves clients vulnerable to both overt and subtle manipulations of professionals employed in sectarian social-service agencies (Corey, Corey, & Callanan, 1998). The NASW Code of Ethics (1996) expressly discourages social workers from imposing their values on clients. Tjeltveit (1986) suggests that referrals to other agencies are appropriate when moral, religious, or political values are centrally involved in a client's problems and when the professional helper is concerned about imposing his or her values onto clients. As evidence has shown, religious entities and their followers view their values as more important than clients' right to self-determination and voluntary consent (Frawley, 2001).

In conclusion, federal funding of sectarian social-service agencies is a clear violation of the intent of the First Amendment. Bush's faith-based initiative grossly violates the principles inherent within the amendment—harming both the government and religion in the process. The United States is a spiritual country, but not in the way the religious right would have it be. Their intent is to return the nation to a mythical, Fundamentalist Christian America. Under Bush's faith-based initiative, clients' right to self-determination will include only those values and actions that are in accordance with the religious right's agenda. Furthermore, those who are most needy and vulnerable will also suffer the worst harm. Bush's plan to fund faith-based organizations will result in decreased funding for nonsectarian agencies, reducing the available choices for those who prefer not to have religious ideals forced into their lives. Social-work professionals should always be mindful of the role of spirituality and religion when working with clients. After all, these have central importance in human well-being. However, the imposition of personal values into the helping relationship serves only to grossly limit clients' right to self-determination and their voluntary consent.

REFERENCES

Bankston, C. (1998). Book review: On the padres' trail by C. Vecsey (1996). University of Notre Dame Press. Retrieved April 17, 2001, from http://www.netstoreusa .com/rkbooks/026/0268037027.shtml.

Boston, R. (1993). *Why the religious right is wrong about separation of church and state.* Amherst, NY: Prometheus Books.

Buckley, S. J. (1995, August). After disestablishment: Thomas Jefferson's wall of separation in antebellum Virginia. *The Journal of Southern History, 61*(3), 445–480. http://www.jstor.org/.

Conn, J., & Boston, R. (2001). President Bush and "faith based" initiatives. Washington, DC: Americans United for Separation of Church and State. Retrieved February 4, 2001, from http://www.au.org.

Corey, G., Corey, M., & Callanan, P. (1998). *Issues and ethics in the helping profession* (5th ed.). Pacific Grove, CA: Brooks/Cole Publishing Co.

Esbeck, C. H. (1996, August). A constitutional case for governmental cooperation with faith-based social service providers. Paper presented at the workshop on the Constitutionality of Governmental Cooperation with Religious Social Ministries, Washington, DC. Retrieved April 15, 2001, from http://www.law.emory.edu/ ELJ/volumes/win97/esbeck.html.

Frawley, D. (2001). The ethics of conversion: The religious conversions controversy. Retrieved April 6, 2001, from http://www.Pragna.org/Conver09.html.

Goodban, L. (1985). The psychological impact of being on welfare. *Social Service Review, 59*, 403–422.

Hardisty, J. (1999). *Mobilizing resentment.* Boston: Beacon Press.

Jensen, J., & Bergin, A. (1988). Mental health values of professional therapists. *Professional Psychology: Research and Practice, 19*(3), 290–297.

Kramnick, I., & Moore, R. L. (1997, November-December). Can the churches save the cities? Faith-based services and the constitution. *The American Prospect, 35*, 47–53. Retrieved July 18, 2001, from http://www.prospect.org/printfriendly/print/ V8/35/kramnick-i.html.

Loewenberg, F., Dolgoff, R., & Harrington, D. (2000). *Ethical decisions for social work practice.* (6th ed.). Itasca, IL: F. E. Peacock Publishers, Inc.

McCabe, D. (1997, Spring). John Locke and the argument against strict separation. *The Review of Politics, 59*, 233–258.

Murray, C. The underclass revisited. Retrieved July 20, 2001, from http://www.aei.org/ ps/psmurray.htm.

National Association of Social Workers. (1996). *Code of ethics.* Washington, DC: NASW.

Noll, M., Hatch, N., & Marsden, G. (1983). *The search for Christian America*. Westchester, IL: Crossways Books.

Personal Responsibility Work Opportunity Reconciliation Act of 1996, 42 U. S. C. A. § 104 (1996).

Reddy, D. (2001). Personal conversation on February 13, 2001.

Sievers, B. (1995). Can philanthropy solve the problems of civil society? *Essays on Philanthropy, 16,* Indiana University Center on Philanthropy.

Tjeltveit, A. (1986). The ethics of value conversion in psychotherapy. *Clinical Psychology Review, 6*(6), 515–537.

Whitten, M. (1999). *The myth of Christian America*. Macon, GA: Smyth.

SHOULD SOCIAL SERVICES
BE PRIVATIZED?

Editor's Note:
With the ascendance of conservative ideology, the idea that governments should provide social services for the population has come under vigorous attack. Critics of governmental involvement in social welfare claim that public social services are bureaucratic and wasteful. Unlike commercial enterprises, which must compete to survive, governmental organizations have no incentive to be efficient. For this reason, citizens everywhere complain bitterly about the quality of public services. Conservatives widely tout privatization is as an effective alternative. Proponents of privatization claim that commercial social-service enterprises are more efficient and offer better value for money compared with government efforts. By contrast, supporters of government social services contend that the profit motive does not provide a suitable basis for meeting human needs. Social programs, they say, should be regarded as collective goods to be provided for all citizens in need, irrespective of their ability to pay. Moreover, the government, rather than the business community, is the best agency for providing these services.

David Stoesz, Ph.D., is a professor at the Virginia Commonwealth University, Northern Virginia Branch. He is the coauthor (with Howard Jacob Karger) of *American Social Welfare Policy*. He is also the coauthor (with Howard Jacob Karger) of *The Politics of Child Abuse and Neglect in America* (Oxford University Press, 1995). Dr. Stoesz has published widely in the areas of international social development, social-welfare policy, and social-work education.

Ira C. Colby, D.S.W., is dean and professor of social work at the University of Houston. He serves on a number of national committees, as co-chair of ANSWER (Advocacy Network for Social Work Education and Research), a member of the Council on Social Work Education Board of Directors, chair of the CSWE Commission on Legislation and Administrative Policy, and chair of the Congressional Fellowship Selection Committee. Dean Colby's research interests are in the areas of community-based practice, homeless teenagers, social-work education, and social-welfare history. In addition, Dean Colby has presented more than fifty invitational and refereed presentations around the world.

YES

David Stoesz

In the United States, privatization has become a volatile issue in social welfare—a paradoxical development given that the private sector played an integral role in service provision even before the welfare state emerged. While it has been fashionable for leftists to view the private sector as symptomatic of a malevolent capitalism, this perspective is duplicitous. Social workers who celebrate the public sector wouldn't deign to call the local welfare department in search of financial services from the income-maintenance division, let alone look to social services for help on a personal problem. Though many critics vilify the private sector, most of what Americans receive in the form of goods and services are provided by the market. While the market economy is not a panacea, in the view of many Americans it has almost always been preferable to government provision. How many human-service professionals would elect housing from a public-housing authority, opt to drive a government-issue auto, or look forward to seeing the most recent movie from a government-information agency? Maybe a few romantic Bolsheviks, but not many more. Indeed, government provision is often reserved for the poor. This arrangement is disingenuous, at best. It not only consigns the needy to inferior service, it also segregates them from the mainstream in the process.

Given the private sector's dominant role in U.S. culture, it is only prudent to incorporate it in discussions of social policy. After all, a substantial amount of social welfare in the United States is provided under nongovernmental auspices. To that extent, American social welfare has *already* been privatized. For decades, the United Way has generated substantial revenues through hundreds of affiliates in virtually every American city for thousands of member agencies. Private philanthropy has provided billions of dollars in assistance to a range of social-welfare activities. Indeed, the training of radicals who strive to advance social justice is conducted by private organizations, such as the Industrial Areas Foundation and the Highlander Center. Finally, many health- and human-service professionals work in the private sector, having found this preferable to government service. As these facts suggest, denying the historical role of the private sector in social welfare is simply myopic.

In fact, the private sector has become the preferred basis for addressing social problems for several reasons:

- *Virtually all social change originates in the private sector.* Social movements that have benefited workers, women, and minorities are oriented around such organizations as the AFL-CIO, The National Organization for Women (NOW), the National Association for the Advancement of Colored People (NAACP), and La Raza–all private organizations.

- *The private sector provides the freedom essential for innovation.* Almost all management strategies to enhance organizational performance are derived from business.
- *The cultivation of civic culture is a function of the private sector.* Ask any resident of the former Soviet bloc about the value of government; invariably, they prefer private initiatives.
- *The dynamism of the information age is a product of the private sector.* By now it is a cliché that the best thing government can do to facilitate the postindustrial economy is to get out of the way.

So why all the brouhaha about privatization? Much of the fuss stems from the rearguard polemic parroted by liberals who have resented the success of conservatism as public philosophy, signaled by the election of Ronald Reagan in 1980. Since then, the left has chafed at the limits imposed on expansion of the government welfare state, not only in the United States, but in Europe as well. Initially, this frustration was aggravated by the far right's attempt to decimate public social programs while invoking the virtues of the private sector. More recently, a consensus has emerged that validates the private sector's contributions to social welfare, and that portrays that sector as a complement of government. Republicans, in particular, have reinforced the value of nonprofits. Witness the Points of Light Foundation established by the elder President Bush, then reinforced by the Faith-Based Social Services initiative introduced by the younger President Bush—the funding for which was proposed at $24 billion over ten years. Leftist fears that privatization would be used to *replace* government appear exaggerated.

Concomitantly, scholars began to explore the conditions under which the private sector might be desirable for service provision. In 1989, John Donahue (1989) noted that "governments in the United States spend roughly half a trillion dollars per year paying public workers to deliver goods and services directly. If only one-quarter of this total turned out to be suitable for privatization, at an average savings of, say 25 percent—and neither figure is recklessly optimistic—the public would save over $30 billion" (p. 216). Not long thereafter, David Osborne and Ted Gaebler (1992) proposed in *Reinventing Government* that the public and private sectors had different functions: Optimally, government should establish the objectives of public policy but assign the execution to the private sector. Subsequently, Osborne served as an advisor to the federal performance-review initiative.

The rhetorical virtues proclaimed by it proponents notwithstanding, privatization introduces difficult issues into the social-policy debate. Any discussion of the problems presented by privatization necessitates an appreciation of the primary sectors of American social welfare. As they have evolved historically, the *voluntary sector* consists of the private, nonprofit organizations that populate localities by the thousands; the *government sector* comprises federal, state, and local departments, which provide services directly or subcontract service provision through the private sector; and the *for-profit sector* is made up of private, commercial firms which have proliferated rapidly during the past three decades. Details of each of these can be found in *American Social Welfare Policy* by Howard Jacob Karger and David Stoesz (2001).

Because each sector has different objectives, their interaction is not always synchronous. This situation generates problems that are often associated with privatization. For example, government programs may be mandated by legislation, but the executive branch has the option of subcontracting service provision. If government provides the service directly, it will meet its mandated responsibility. However, there is no guarantee as to the program's quality, accessibility, or efficiency. For that reason, government can seek to enhance those values by contracting with private vendors. To the extent that government funnels billions of dollars to purchase services, major industries evolve—as has been the case in healthcare. These industries become powerful lobbies for the social programs on which they depend. Back in 1980, Arnold Relman (1980), editor of the prestigious *New England Journal of Medicine*, warned of the power of "the medical-industrial complex" in health policy. This concern intensified during the 2000 presidential election, when Ralph Nader claimed that "corporate welfare" endowed American business with resources that it then used to manipulate the political process.

For their part, voluntary agencies emerge when of a group of citizens agree that a community problem should be addressed and persuade the Internal Revenue Service to grant them tax-exempt status. Thousands of voluntary sector programs exist in the United States. However, they crop up irregularly throughout the society. For example, AIDS-prevention services tend not to appear in smaller, rural communities, and child day care may be in short supply in the inner city. Two features have come to typify nonprofit agencies. First, because they seek to address local problems, they are strongly community based. Second, because funding is often difficult to get, they resort to a variety of strategies to attract resources, including recruiting volunteers, holding bake sales, applying to private foundations, negotiating government contracts, and charging fees for services.

For-profit firms must perform efficiently in order to generate the profits on which investors insist. Beyond that, they enjoy a wide degree of latitude, providing they are managed responsibly. They also enjoy several advantages over their competitors in the governmental and nonprofit sectors. For instance, commercial firms have free rein to exploit new markets, and they have immediate access to capital in order to expand their operations. These advantages, coupled with business-expansion strategies such as advertising, buying competitors, and acquiring sophisticated technology, often ensure growth. The conversion of *public utilities* into *social markets* is perhaps the most controversial aspect of privatization, because it appears to come at the expense of the governmental and voluntary sectors. Though opponents of privatization decry "profiteering from human misfortune," a fundamental question remains: How humane is it to maintain an archaic prison that violates inmates' rights or a foster-care system that routinely ignores the abuses inflicted on children—when a private provider can meet cost and quality standards for comparable care?

In practice, the varying motives and prerogatives of the voluntary, governmental, and for-profit sectors have raised seminal issues in social policy, many of which converge around privatization. As tax-exempt entities, voluntary-sector organizations should be more competitive than commercial firms because they do not have to pay taxes on income, nor do they have to generate profits to satisfy investors. Yet nonprofit organizations have proven poor competitors, often losing out to for-profit firms. The focus on community service, the absence of accountability, and chronic resource problems have all made nonprofits less competitive than commercial firms. As a result, when for-profit firms enter a market that has been traditionally served by the voluntary sector, they often take a substantial portion of that market. They hold that position until nonprofits adopt many of the same management practices and boost their efficiency.

At a time when government must judiciously fund mandated activities, contracting out services becomes a desirable option. Yet which privatization strategy might be optimal? Discussions of health reform provide apt illustrations of this challenge: Should government reserve the role of single payer, as it has with Medicare, or reimburse a network of competing managed-care firms, as proposed under the Clinton Health Security Act? Should government favor nonprofit applicants because they claim to serve a broad spectrum of citizens, or for-profit firms because they boast the latest in technology? In making such decisions, should government officials be influenced by powerful lobbying agents who represent commercial providers, or elected officials who respond to the appeals of community-based nonprofits?

Conscious of their public image, commercial firms often redouble their efforts to enhance the community's welfare. They encourage employees to contribute to the United Way, and they mount community-service programs. When Blue Cross-Blue Shield went from nonprofit to for-profit status, it established health foundations to support research and demonstration projects. When for-profit providers suspect that they can generate a profit by providing superior service to a clientele, they seek subcontracts from government, as has been the case with managed-care firms seeking to enroll recipients of Medicaid and Medicare.

Unfortunately, human-service professionals have largely negated the opportunities associated with privatization. In some respects, this has been an artifact of social work, the discipline traditionally associated with social welfare. Owing to its latent socialism and reflexive preference of government social programs, social work has dismissed nonprofit agencies and has been outwardly hostile to for-profit firms. The professional education of social workers virtually ignores the knowledge and skills essential to business strategies in service provision, and lacks substantial content in finance, marketing, information systems, and contracting. For decades, social workers have managed programs to serve the public. However, rhetoric about client care notwithstanding, they have failed to generate any longitudinal data on clients' perceptions of and experiences with the services they receive.

Having failed to generate data on cost per unit of service, it is not surprising that social workers are hardly competitive in the new human-services market. Commercial firms that make superior presentations to lawmakers and government officials who want to optimize increasingly scarce tax revenues have proven far more successful. Rather than redouble their efforts to generate such information, social workers have denigrated commercial firms' motives. In this respect, social-work education is so retrograde that an altruist seeking a career in public service may be better served by a good ethics course and a program of study in the business school than a typical social-work program.

Perhaps the most salient development relating to privatization has been the expansion of information technology. Combined with economic deregulation, this development has spawned a new generation of hybrid organizations that are flat, dispersed, and nimble. Such organizations have not only demonstrated their superiority in managing a range of services domestically, they have also begun to exploit markets internationally. For social workers who were so wedded to government programs that they failed to take advantage of even industrial-era innovations, such as Employee Stock Ownership Plans, these hybrid entities are simply incomprehensible. Yet they embody the future of human-service provision. As such, the best way to access the opportunities implicit in their development is to appreciate the virtues of the private sector—in a word, to take privatization seriously.

NO

Ira C. Colby

To state that privatization is a controversial, polarizing, and emotional topic is at best an understatement. Proponents of privatization offer well-thought-out and sometimes seemingly convincing arguments. Certainly the proposition that there is a better and more efficient way to provide social services is true; the belief that such improvement is possible is not the sole domain of the public sector. But the notion that privatization of basic public social services is the answer to helping the poor move out of the grasp of poverty is an insidious and grossly erroneous assumption.

Before moving any further into this discussion, let me first define *privatization*. Doing so at the outset of a debate provides the required reference point for the ensuing discussion. Not defining essential concepts is a common debate strategy when one's position is weak. Mixing or interchanging words and concepts, without establishing a baseline definition, subtly lures the listener, or in this case the reader, into a murky, often emotion-filled, controversy. But let us ignore the debater's trickery and be reasonable and logical in our discussion.

Privatization takes many forms. It is most recognized as the subcontracting of services through the provision of public dollars to nongovernmental groups to provide direct services to clients in need. For our purposes, we'll refer to the straightforward definition set forth in Nightingale and Pindus (1997): ". . . privatization refers to the provision of publicly funded services and activities by non-governmental entities" (p. 6).

Privatizing of some social services is not a new phenomenon. Rather, it's a well-established practice that in the United States dates back to the middle of the twentieth-century, when many private, nonprofit agencies contracted with the government to provide programs and services. Typical contracting to private nonprofit agencies include United Way—funded agencies (for example, the YMCA) and member agencies of the Family Association of America (for instance, Jewish Family Services and Catholic Social Services).

History reveals that social services have long been firmly rooted in the private church community with later growth in private, nonsectarian-related organizations (Trattner, 1999; Axinn & Stern, 2000). Voluntary societies, such as the seventeenth-century Scots Charitable Society, and programs similar in design to the mid nineteenth-century Children Aids Society typify the array of social services in the private arena (Axinn & Stern, 2000). Additionally, the birth of the social-work profession can be clearly traced to the mid-to-late nineteenth-century private sectarian and nonsectarian social-aid organizations.

So why all the fuss about the privatization of social services? The recent proposals and movement to greater privatization seem to be nothing more than an effort to expand and enhance a model that is centuries old. Or is it?

On the surface, privatization appears a workable strategy, particularly if one subscribes to a politically conservative or libertarian philosophy of government. Privatization implies that the government is no longer in the welfare business. Government's new role is twofold: funding and oversight. Based on a business model, the contracting agency or organization must meet the funder's requirements, or the contract is cancelled. Provision of services becomes the province of the private sector and removes the government from a guardian and caregiver role. Competition, a source of pride in the private sector, presumably eliminates waste and incompetence—leaving only strong, efficient service providers in place.

Privatization sounds like a win-win situation for the body politic and the public. Private social service promises to reduce the size of federal and state government bureaucracies, such as the Federal Department of Health and Human Services. Private social services also promise to introduce a local flavor that reflects local needs and issues better than a national standard set by some obscure Washington, D.C., bureaucrats can. The business model also implies that social agencies will be smaller and will generate less "red tape," two characteristics that yield effective and purposeful services. And, of course, business-model proponents suggest that any private social service that can't generate its intended outcomes will lose contracts—saving the American public tax dollars in the long run.

With the new privatization efforts, a nontraditional welfare partner has emerged: *the for-profit corporation.* The Marriott Corporation and Lockheed Martin are among many new welfare providers joining the ranks of traditional, private nonprofit social agencies.

Why would private for-profit corporations ostensibly created to generate enormous profits for owners, board members, and stockholders now take on social services? Are corporations expressing a new humanitarian philosophy? Or, are these mega-corporations looking for new avenues to increase and maximize their profit margins? Certainly mega-corporations' bottom-line has always been the profit margin. The adage "If you paint a zebra colors to conceal its stripes, you still have a zebra" raises a cautionary flag. Are we to believe that the mega-corporation social-service zebra no longer has it stripes? Or, is the new corporate for-profit social-service zebra still a zebra?

We need only look back a few years to reacquaint ourselves with for-profit corporations' purported efficient and cost-saving programs. This sector's track record with federal contracts reflects, at best, the same mismanagement of funds and projects for which conservative citizens and commentators alike condemn the government. Social pundit Jim Hightower (2001) begins one of his many commentaries warning of private for-profit waste with the haunting phrase, "It's back." According to Hightower, the Pentagon's extravagant expenditures of the 1980s are commonplace once again. (Remember the $640 toilet seat?) Examples of such wastefulness include $1,887 for a machine bolt that normally costs $40 and a self-locking nut that listed for $2.69 for which the government paid $2,185. Need more? AlliedSignal overcharged the government 618 percent for spare parts, and Boeing charged $403 for a metal cylinder regularly priced $25. The government paid $714 for a bell normally priced at $47, and $76 for a screw that cost $.57. (St. Clair, 2000).

So now we want to turn public social services over to the same sector that claims efficiency as its guardian philosophy? A system that will "save" the American public millions of dollars by eliminating waste and fraud and reducing the size of government? If that's true, there's a bridge for sale in Brooklyn, some great swampland in Florida, and large estates in the desert of Arizona.

All this is interesting, but we still haven't addressed the central question: Why are we entertaining a "new" notion that mega-corporations, with their supposed newfound spirit, should provide social services to the most vulnerable and at-risk in our communities?

The ongoing privatization arguments are nothing more than an extension of the centuries-old debate concerning the role of government in welfare. As early as the Elizabethan Poor Laws of 1601, many considered welfare the sole province of the private community. The debate gained legal precedent with President Franklin Pierce's 1854 veto message of legislation that would have provided federal land to the states "for the benefit of indigent persons" (Axinn & Stern, 2000). As Pierce wrote:

> I can not find any authority in the Constitution for making the Federal Government the great almoner of public charity throughout the United States. To do so [would] . . . be contrary to the letter and spirit of the Constitution and subversive of the whole theory upon which the Union of these States is founded.

Following the Pierce veto, some publicly funded welfare programs existed, but these were more the exception than the rule. The historic public "hands-off" approach radically changed during the Great Depression with the advent of President Franklin D. Roosevelt's activist government. Public programs proliferated and became the framework for the modern-day 'welfare state.' Yet even Roosevelt seemed ill at ease with the government's emerging welfare role. In his 1935 State of the Union Address to Congress, he declared that "the Federal Government must and shall quit the business of relief" (Axinn & Stern, 2000).

Today's common catchphrases of "compassionate conservatism" and "faith-based social services" are nothing more than retreaded ideas from another era that witnessed fewer public services with a greater reliance on the private sector. It's as if President Pierce is alive and well again in the White House.

Have some governmental programs proved less than stellar? Yes, but the private sector has failed just as much in its delivery of services. How many automobile recalls have there been for defective construction? Why are product defects, such as those in the recent Firestone and Ford controversy, kept hidden from the public? How many airlines have 100 percent, or even 90 percent, on-time arrivals? How many utility "blackouts" or "brownouts" must the public suffer because of inadequate safeguards?

Mario Cuomo put it best when he wrote,

> "With unemployment insurance, worker's compensation, Social Security, fair labor standards, Aid to Families with Dependent Children (AFDC), Medicare, and Medicaid, we improved our standards and working conditions, provided services that benefit and strengthen us, and protected and nurtured our most vulnerable members. In doing so, we amplified our potential for greatness" (Cuomo, 1995, p. 17).

Government does play a central a role in providing services. It is entrusted with a basic responsibility: to ensure that all people, no matter their station in life, get the services and support they need to maximize their capacity to change, contribute to, and participate in society.

Basic social services are the business of the government. Contracting services to nonprofit social agencies is appropriate when *service*, not profit, is the ultimate end. The significant redirection of social-service programs by huge, for-profit corporations marks a dangerous return to a compassionless period. Are we foolish enough to believe that for-profit corporations are the twenty-first century's new social altruists? Do we really believe that the government has failed us over time in its public social agenda? If so, then we must explain why government should remove itself from providing health-care for seniors, preschool for poor children, protection of civil rights, safety and security through police and fire departments, funding for public education, and housing regulations.

If privatization is the answer to our collective good, then let's extend the privatization principle to other traditional governmental services. Let's privatize the U.S. military, including the army, navy, air force, Marines, and Coast Guard. By realizing significant savings from otherwise long-term expenditures that the government now pays, we could dramatically lower government costs. Under privatization, the private military contractors, not the government, would provide healthcare and other military benefits that the federal government now provides through the Veteran's Administration (VA). Closing down the Veteran's Administration alone could save U.S. taxpayers billions of dollars annually. In 1998, for example, the VA spent $43,150,218,825 on services (Veterans Administration, 2001).

Nor do we need locally funded public fire departments. Let individual citizens contract with private, for-profit fire department. Why should the average person be forced to pay taxes for a service that he or she probably will never use? Get the government out of fire protection, and let individuals elect to contract (or not) with a private fire department. Moveover, we don't need public parks; let private-sector recreation experts, such as Disney or MGM, manage our parks and compete for the contracts. Can you see a great roller-coaster ride going up and down the walls of the Grand Canyon? And while we're at it, let's privatize all libraries. If a library in one neighborhood doesn't meet its expected outcome, close it down and ship the books to one that performs better. Give people vouchers to check books out, and the strongest libraries will survive.

Privatization of public services certainly sounds ridiculous when we extend the idea to other governmental domains. Most people would agree that it is inappropriate to privatize the local fire department or military. So why do some of these same individuals seriously entertain the idea of privatizing basic social services? The poor often become the focus and flash point for public-policy discussions. For any number of reasons, many blame them directly for program failures, though they rarely praise the poor for program successes. In those instances, elected officials or policy makers claim the credit. Blaming the poor is very American; U.S. House of Representative and Republican party leader Dick Armey stated, "Poverty is a moral problem."

And former Republican Speaker of the House Newt Gingrich noted that the poor ". . . have to learn new habits" (Hudson, 1996). It is so easy to categorically blame the poor and devise reactionary policies and strategies, including contracting social services to private, for-profit corporations.

After decades of federal efforts, we know it is difficult to marshal and sustain a national collective resolve to end poverty. Throwing money into a program is not the sole answer. Shaming people for their life situations, a centuries-old intervention model, does little. Privatization is nothing more than washing our public hands of the poor under the guise of compassionate conservatism. We move human suffering and inequity into spreadsheets and bottom-line operations and make the profit motive the driving factor for the twenty-first century, for-profit corporate social agency.

Can we do better? Yes. Should we do better? Yes. Should we pass off our public responsibility to larger for-profit corporations? A resounding *no*.

REFERENCES

Axinn, J., & Stern, M. (2000). *Social welfare: A history of the American response to need* (5th ed.). Needham, MA: Allyn and Bacon.

Cuomo, M. (1995). *Reason to believe.* New York, NY: Simon & Schuster.

Donahue, J. (1989). *The privatization decision.* New York, NY: Basic Books.

Hightower, J. (February 14, 2001). Jim Hightower, Hightower's common sense commentary. National Public Radio.

Hudson, W. (1996). Economic security for all: How to end poverty in the U.S. *Economic Security Project.*

Karger, H. J., & Stoesz, D. (2001). *American social welfare policy* (4th ed.). Boston, MA: Allyn and Bacon.

Nightingale, D. S., & Pindus, N. (October 15, 1997). *Privatization of public social services: A background paper.* Washington, DC: The Urban Institute.

Osborne, D., & Gaebler, T. (1992). *Reinventing government.* New York, NY: Addison-Wesley.

Relman, A. (1980). The new medical-industrial complex. *New England Journal of Medicine (303)*(17), 80.

St. Clair, J. (July 11, 2000). *Rego and defense costs.* Retrieved July 9, 2001, from www.unrisd.org/engindex/publ/list/op/op7/op-07-01.htm.

Trattner, W. (1999). *From poor law to welfare state: A history of social welfare in America* (5th ed.). New York, NY: Free Press.

Veterans Administration (2001). Retrieved July 8, 2001, from www.bva.gov/about_va/history/expend.htm.

PART II

POVERTY, INEQUALITY, AND SOCIAL POLICY

IS LEGISLATION FOR LESBIAN AND GAY RIGHTS NECESSARY?

Editor's Note:
After centuries of oppression, gays and lesbians in the United States have campaigned effectively to counteract the prejudice and intolerance that characterize many Americans' attitudes toward homosexuality. They have educated people about sexual orientation; formed lobbying and support groups; and persuaded legislative bodies, primarily at the municipal level, to enact ordinances protecting their rights. These statutes prohibit discrimination against gays and lesbians in fields such as employment, housing, and education. However, the idea that special legislation is needed to protect gays and lesbians is not universally supported. Indeed, many opponents of gay and lesbian rights would like to use criminal law to suppress homosexuality. In addition, opponents of gay-rights legislation argue that although discriminatory legislation should be removed from the books, no special legislation for gays and lesbians should be enacted. Once gays have the same protection under the Constitution as other citizens, opponents argue, no further legal safeguards will be needed.

Marion Wagner, Ph.D., is associate professor and MSW program director at Indiana University School of Social Work. She has written in the areas of child welfare and lesbian and gay issues. Her teaching and scholarship also include women's issues, social policy, and macro social-work practice. She is a member of the CSWE Commission on Women and the NOW National Board. *Rebecca Van Voorhis, Ph.D.*, is an associate professor in the Indiana University School of Social Work. Her teaching and scholarship have focused on issues of diversity, with particular attention to women. Her publications include articles on feminist theories, cultural sensitivity, and gay and lesbian issues. Her current research examines the delivery of services for adults with serious mental illness or chemical addictions and children with serious emotional disorders.

John F. Longres, Ph.D., was professor of social work at the University of Washington. He has researched the use of social services by ethnic and racial minorities as well as adolescence and delinquency issues. He has authored

Human Behavior and the Social Environment (Peacock, 1990), and has published extensively on social-work issues in major scholarly journals.

YES
Marion Wagner and Rebecca Van Voorhis

> *You can't legislate integration, but you certainly can legislate desegregation. You can't legislate morality, but you can regulate behavior. You can't make a man love me, but the law can restrain him from lynching me.*
> Dr. Martin Luther King, Jr., 1964

Lesbian and gay people have been excluded from most federal and state legislation guaranteeing equal rights in the areas of civil rights, family rights, and protective legislation. This exclusion has deprived lesbian and gay people access to many aspects of American society. Following in the footsteps of other excluded populations in the past and supported by many heterosexual allies, lesbians and gays are currently advocating for inclusionary legislation in a variety of arenas.

OUR POSITION

We oppose laws that permit discrimination against lesbian and gay people, limit the political participation of lesbians and gay men, or make homosexual behavior criminal. We also favor laws and policies that protect the civil rights of gay and lesbian people and that prevent employment and housing discrimination, hate crimes, and discrimination against gay men and lesbians who want to marry, adopt children, provide foster care, or have custody of their children. We seek laws and policies that protect the civil rights of all gay and lesbian people—including the right to be safe, work where one chooses, marry and raise children, inherit one's partner's assets, and receive the same healthcare and retirement benefits afforded to heterosexual spouses.

Adopting new laws and eradicating existing bias in laws is necessary because existing laws and policies privilege heterosexuality and define marriage and family to exclude gay and lesbian people. The Defense of Marriage Act represents the most recent legislation asserting the privileges of heterosexuality. And the sodomy laws that remain in effect in more than twenty states are used by employers to terminate or refuse to hire gay persons and by family courts to deny custody and adoption for lesbians and gay men (Human Rights Campaign).

Opponents of inclusionary legislation for lesbian and gay people frequently deride such legislation as "special rights." Although occasionally an effective sound bite, the term "special rights" is incorrect in referring to legislation that would provide the same access and protection to lesbian and gay people as other persons have. Such legislation is necessary in the areas of civil rights, family rights, and protection against violence. This opposition is often based on religious or quasi-religious beliefs, which have no place in public policy. Bigots also used such beliefs to argue against civil rights for African American people. They quoted biblical passages and cited divine support for legal segregation. They warned of dire consequences if legal barriers to integration were dismantled. Some have used similar arguments against women's-rights legislation, including the Nineteenth Amendment to the Constitution of the United States, which provided for women's right to vote. Most arguments against racial and sexual equality have now resurfaced as arguments against equality based on sexual orientation. They are no more rational than earlier discriminatory arguments.

CIVIL RIGHTS

Civil-rights legislation became part of the American political landscape in the 1960s, when laws were passed at the federal and state level providing protection for people of color from discrimination in the areas of housing, education, employment, voting, and public accommodations. As more and more lesbian and gay people are open about their sexual orientation, the need for lesbian and gay civil-rights protection in housing, employment, and public accommodations has become apparent. One unintended consequence of discrimination based on sexual orientation seems to be discouragement of permanent relationships between lesbian, gay, or bisexual couples. Housing and public accommodations discrimination is one example. Single gay, lesbian, or bisexual people are less likely to find housing unavailable or hotels without vacancies. However, when gay or lesbian couples approach apartment managers or motel front desks, the situation may change. This is particularly true in long-term housing situations. Inclusion of sexual orientation in civil-rights legislation would allow equal access to such facilities.

The U.S. Congress has yet to pass legislation providing for nondiscrimination in employment for lesbian and gay people, even though the proposed Employment Nondiscrimination Act (ENDA) provides for multiple exceptions to the law. Employment discrimination is particularly problematic in arenas such as education, social services for children and youth, healthcare, law enforcement, and the military.

Supporters of discrimination based on sexual orientation seem to rely on stereotypes about lesbian and gay people, and to disregard research that debunks such stereotypes. Lesbians and gay men who work with vulnerable populations such as children, people with disabilities, and older adults may be subject to discrimination based on a stereotype that gay men are sexual predators. However, for over twenty years, research has shown that *heterosexual* men are more likely to sexually abuse children than gay men are, and that lesbians rarely perpetrate sexual abuse (Mallon, 2001). In fact, research also indicates that children of lesbian mothers are not only as well balanced as children of heterosexual parents, they also seem to be more accepting of difference (Laird, 1995).

Of course, lesbian and gay people have always worked as teachers, coaches, pediatricians, and social-service professionals, but often remained deeply in the closet. In the twenty-first century, fewer lesbian and gay people are willing to hide their identities from their employers, families, and colleagues. Some employers legally practice discrimination based on sexual orientation. Usually, such discrimination results from an outcry from some bigoted heterosexual employees, not from any inappropriate behavior on the part of the lesbian or gay employee. Legislation providing for nondiscrimination would ensure hiring and retention of capable employees regardless of sexual orientation. As both sides of this debate well know, sexual harassment or sexual abuse would remain just cause for termination of employment for both straight and gay employees. As an additional bonus in fields such as education and youth services, students and clients would see appropriate role models of various orientations. This is particularly important for youth who may be gay, lesbian, or bisexual themselves. Currently, such youth experience inappropriate attitudes in the child welfare system (Folaron & Wagner, 1998).

Discrimination based on sexual orientation also has pervaded law-enforcement agencies. Some federal agencies have discriminated against lesbian and gay people based on a rationale that they are more vulnerable to blackmail. Of course, this is a tautology. People can be blackmailed only if they need to keep their sexual orientation a secret, and the only reason to keep it a secret is agency policy. State and local law-enforcement agencies are gradually opening their ranks to lesbian and gay people, although a majority of agencies still seem to discriminate. As with other oppressed populations, such as people of color and women, inclusion in law-enforcement entities can decrease police officers' inappropriate behavior against such populations.

Perhaps the most blatant example of discrimination based on sexual orientation is the United States military, where the "Don't ask, don't tell" policy has brought to light numbers of service personnel discharged solely for their sexual orientation. Gay members of the military have also endured acts of violence, including murder, in a number of well-publicized cases. As in other types of employment, discrimination in the military is based on stereotypes. In particular, some people assume that gay, lesbian, and bisexual service members will sexually harass heterosexuals. Interestingly, a strong gender gap on this issue has appeared. A survey conducted by Lou Harris for the Feminist Majority found that men were 20 percent more likely than women to support military discrimination based on sexual orientation. The United States has gradually become one of the few Western nations to keep this form of discrimination. In an era when recruitment of capable persons into the military is difficult, the perpetuation of this policy seems irrational.

While the Congress and president continue to resist the inclusion of sexual orientation in employment-discrimination legislation, many state and local entities have proven more progressive. Yet corporate policies are also needed to provide full rights to gay and lesbian people. A number of companies are finding it good business to protect their lesbian, gay, and bisexual workers from discrimination. These businesses include Walt Disney Co., Adolph Coors Co., IBM, Microsoft, and many others. (Van Wormer, Wells, & Boes, 2000). With the recent action of the Purdue University Board of Trustees, in which board members adopted a policy prohibiting discrimination based on sexual orientation, such policy is now in effect at all of the Big Ten universities.

Examples of corporate policies granting domestic-partner benefits to lesbian and gay people continue to grow. For example, eighteen months after United and American Airlines led the way by offering domestic-partner health benefits to their gay and lesbian employees, now all but one of the top ten American carriers grant such benefits. Similarly, California companies such as Levi-Strauss and Apple that first adopted domestic-partner policies have been followed by many other companies, including some in the American heartland such as Cummins Engine Co., based in Columbus, Indiana.

LEGISLATION CRIMINALIZING GAY AND LESBIAN BEHAVIOR

Laws against certain types of sexual behavior remain on several states' books. Generally incorporated in laws against sodomy and other forms of sexual behavior, such laws are often applied only to gay or lesbian people, and are used as a rationale for other forms of discrimination. For example, those who oppose adoption of children by lesbian and gay people argue that "if their behavior is illegal, they shouldn't be allowed to adopt." Laws governing nonviolent consensual behavior between adults are gradually being eliminated across the country. They should be totally eliminated, as they are rarely applied. When they are applied, they are usually applied to lesbians and gays.

HATE CRIMES

Two college athletes were walking back to their dorm in Middletown, USA, after enjoying a party with friends. They turned down an alley, and a group of men emerged out of the darkness and blocked their path. Even though they were outnumbered, the athletes were not afraid. They felt confident that their strength and size could counter any attacker. The group yelled, "Faggots, you're gonna die!" Pulling out car chains, they launched their assault. Severely beaten, the athletes were taken to Middletown's hospital. There, police were called to investigate the horrible crime. When the police learned that the athletes were gay, they advised them that it would probably be impossible to find and identify the men who had assaulted them.

Declaring a crime a hate crime recognizes that the crime was meant as a signal to an entire group of people. A hate crime, such as the assault on the two gay college athletes, is a crime committed against a person or persons because she or he is a member of a particular population. Thus, in committing an act of violence or vandalism against a person or object representing a larger group, the perpetrator harms both the immediate victim and the entire represented population. The murder of Matthew Shephard sent a message to gay men everywhere that their lives are in danger because they are gay. Similarly, the lynching of African Americans throughout U.S. history warned all black people to stay in their proscribed place. Nazi symbols on a Jewish temple are intended to intimidate all Jews. Opponents of hate-crime legislation often resort to "special rights" rhetoric. One life, they say, should be as valuable in the criminal-justice system as another. This argument discounts the intention and outcome of hate crimes. In judging a crime a hate crime, the perpetrator faces more severe penalties than he or she would through the act alone.

In some areas, supporters of hate-crime legislation based on race, ethnicity, age, or religion balk at the notion of including sexual orientation. These people want to split vulnerable populations into two categories—those they approve of and those they don't. Most organizations that promote civil rights for people of color see through these arguments and have refused to support such divisive legislation. Opponents of inclusion of sexual orientation in hate-crimes legislation may base such opposition on religious beliefs. However, many religious leaders are appalled at such use of scripture and have voiced their strong support for the civil rights of gay and lesbian people, including the right to be safe from attack. Religious arguments have been a traditional tactic of human-rights opponents in the United States. The current opposition to including sexual orientation in hate-crimes legislation shows these opponents' fear that American society is becoming more inclusive.

FAMILY ISSUES

Lesbian, gay, and bisexual people have always lived together as couples and families, although sociological definitions of family did not include such partnerships until recent years. Comprehensive legislation for lesbian and gay people in the areas of domestic partnership, civil unions, adoption, foster care, and child custody is needed to ensure equal opportunity and participation for families of lesbians and gay men. Thus, we support laws such as the Vermont statute, which enable gay and lesbian couples to enter into a civil union and receive the legal rights of an officially recognized partnership. We also favor legislation such as the Wisconsin law enacted under Governor Tommy Thompson, which permits hospital visitation rights to gay and lesbian partners.

Vermont's passage of laws supporting civil unions for same-sex couples has brought discussion of such partnerships to national attention. Similar federal and state legislation allowing for domestic partnerships or marriage for such couples is necessary for the entire country. Popular culture tends to represent heterosexual love and marriage as focusing on romance and emotional commitments. Yet legal partnerships also provide many less-recognized protections. How many heterosexual couples think of their marriage as giving them the right to make medical decisions for the other partner, to share in retirement benefits, or to legally pool their economic resources in areas of credit and finance? Marriage affords these and many other rights, and divorce law protects the property and custody rights of both spouses when a marriage ends. Because families provide social stability, we believe that lesbian and gay couples merit the same rights and protections afforded by law to heterosexual couples. Legal domestic partnerships or civil unions can give partners access to all economic benefits of marriage, including Social Security, healthcare, and inheritance. In a society based on democratic principles, either all adult couples who choose to make a legal commitment should be legally allowed to do so—or none should be. Adoption and foster care are additional areas requiring equal access for lesbian, gay, and bisexual people.

LEGISLATION, NOT CONVERSION

Some people who oppose laws and policies that would protect the rights of gay and lesbian people argue instead for an "integrative" approach through which individual gays and lesbians gradually win acceptance from non-gay co-workers, neighbors, family, and friends. We agree that many heterosexual individuals have come to accept homosexuality after getting personally acquainted with a gay man or a lesbian. However, depending on such an individualized approach is unrealistic, because heterosexual people outnumber homosexual people nine to one. Thus, depending on an "integrative" approach leaves many gay and lesbian people hiding in the closet their whole lives. Generations of black Americans used the "integrative" approach and made little progress in gaining the rights and privileges enjoyed by white Americans. Only when they took to the courts and legislatures did they win rights in education, voting, employment, and housing for all African Americans. Furthermore, we oppose depending on this approach because it is another egregious example of victim-blaming. The "integrative" approach makes the gay and lesbian community responsible for changing the oppressor. Instead, it should hold the heterosexual community responsible.

BENEFITS OF GAY-RIGHTS LEGISLATION

The benefits of establishing laws and policies that extend identical rights and privileges to both heterosexual and homosexual people include the following:

- Gay and lesbian people can be open about their sexual orientation without fearing job loss, eviction, physical attack, loss of their children, denial of opportunity to adopt, refusal of admission to visit a partner in the intensive care unit, or the inability to automatically inherit a partner's estate or file a joint tax return.
- Homosexual people will experience greater emotional well-being because they won't have to expend energy hiding or passing for heterosexual in order to enjoy rights and privileges.
- Addiction and suicide among gays and lesbians will decrease owing to greater self-acceptance.
- Lesbian and gay people will be better able to contribute to the common good if they don't have to waste energy combating discriminatory practices and policies.
- Benefits from adopting protective legislation in the areas of employment, housing, and family law will be comparable to the benefits for women and people of color derived from the 1964 Civil Rights Act. Though women and people of color have not yet attained full equality, they have made huge gains in access to housing, education, and employment.

When gays and lesbians live better, more fulfilling lives, our entire society benefits.

NO

John F. Longres

Special legislation or protective regulation may be a good idea for other groups, but it is not a good idea when applied to lesbians and gays. In taking this view, I would like to make the important distinction between the need to decriminalize and the need to institute protective legislation and policies. Although they are two sides of the same coin, each side has different implications.

DEFINING THE CONTEXT: DECRIMINALIZATION
VERSUS PROTECTIVE LEGISLATION

As used here, *decriminalization* means the repeal of all existing laws, policies, and regulations that permit discrimination against homosexuals or against homosexual conduct. Conversely, it also means the rejection of any new anti-homosexual policies and laws that may be promoted. It is absolutely necessary to decriminalize homosexual behavior; the law should not intrude on sexual relations among consenting adults in the privacy of their homes as it does now in some twenty-four states. Furthermore, laws and policies should not directly or indirectly limit the participation of lesbians and gays in American society. I include here military regulations that forbid openly homosexual men and women from serving in the defense of their country and religious policies that repress homosexual behavior and forbid homosexuals from serving as religious leaders. I also include any regulations that prevent homosexuals from marrying; adopting and raising children; or working as educators, counselors, and helpers of children. Gays and lesbians ought to put all their political and moral efforts into the eradication of discriminatory laws, policies, and regulations. They must also challenge the use of homosexuality as a defense in those cases where rights are being threatened, such as the right to rent or own property, to inherit property, and to care for sick and infirm partners. In the end, gays and lesbians will need this major victory if they are to receive equal treatment under the law—a basic right of citizenship in any democracy.

Protective legislation refers to those laws, policies, or regulations that specifically identify homosexuals as a category of people whose rights must be ensured. Examples include hiring policies aimed at ensuring a homosexual presence in the workplace or policies specifying that homosexuals cannot be fired merely on the basis of their sexuality. Housing and educational policies that single out homosexuals as a category for special attention also constitute protective legislation, as do "hate-crime" laws that make physically or emotionally harming someone because of their sexuality a special kind of crime. I do not believe that gays and lesbians need such legislation to protect them from prejudice and discrimination. Why? Once discriminatory legislation is eliminated, that protection is already granted to them in the Constitution. In short, homosexuals should take aim at repealing discriminatory laws but not at promoting special protective laws.

THE LIMITS OF PROTECTIVE LEGISLATION:
WHY IT WON'T WORK

I defend this position on a number of grounds. The first is purely strategic. Homosexuals, at least those who are proudly "out," make up much less than

10 percent of all Americans. If they are to gain their equal rights, they will need allies among those more than 90 percent who consider themselves heterosexual or who are not fully willing to declare themselves homosexual. Though some of these people will support homosexuals through thick and thin, others—those on the extreme religious right–are organized to block their every move. The all-important support will have to come from that significant percent of heterosexuals that are neither particularly for nor against gays. How are these heterosexuals to be wooed? Legislation aimed at decriminalization clearly gives the message that gays and lesbians expect their due, no more or less than any other law-abiding, hardworking citizen does. Protective legislation gives a different message: It says that gays and lesbians want special treatment and special advantages. Even though this is not the case, the fact that people who are organized against homosexuals will interpret it as such will create enough doubt that the majority of heterosexuals will not go out of their way to support protective legislation.

The second reason is economic. The quest for protective legislation puts an extra financial drain on the lesbian and gay community. All too often, when protective legislation is enacted, it meets with organized efforts to either repeal or water down the law. People in the state of Oregon went through two referenda on protective legislation. In Wisconsin, the law was challenged in the courts by religious groups, by a program for delinquent boys, and by a newspaper that has refused to accept gay and lesbian advertisements. As a result, lesbians and gays, or the state on their behalf, were forced to spend hundreds of thousands of dollars defending the legislation—with no assurance of winning. In a tight economy, these dollars could be better spent on efforts to decriminalize homosexuality, reinforce the right of equal treatment, or, given present needs, strengthen research and services for fighting AIDS.

Third, sometimes the noblest of intentions go wrong. In our zeal for protection, we conjure up the image that once a policy is enacted, everyone rallies around it, and the world automatically changes for the better. Reality is often quite different. For instance, the Civil Rights Act of 1964—surely one of the most far reaching pieces of protective legislation enacted in this century—fed resentment and spawned an enormous backlash, the results of which are more apparent than ever. Many otherwise liberal Americans drifted to the right in part because of what they rightly or wrongly saw as "reverse discrimination." Conservative values became the political rallying point. Reactionary elements now can blame America's economic, political, and urban woes on readily available minority scapegoats. As for the protected groups, affirmative action and other reforms have had limited success in improving the lot of African, Latino, and Native Americans. Certainly they have not led to these groups' social and physical integration into American society.

Protective legislation for gays and lesbians may have its own unintended consequences. Allan Berube, in describing the evolution of the anti-homosexual military policy, shows that it was motivated partly by well-intentioned psychiatric efforts to exclude people who could not be expected to survive the ordeal of combat. Before 1944, the military prohibited homosexual behavior but did not prohibit homosexuals from serving their country. It was only after Harry Stack Sullivan, a major figure in psychiatry and a homosexual himself, began to work on ways of protecting emotionally vulnerable men and women that the idea of categorizing homosexuals as "psychopathic" and excluding them from military service began to surface. Although some psychiatrists and counselors fought the exclusion and strove to protect homosexuals, many others eagerly set about trapping and dishonorably discharging them.

Unintended consequences may reach down to individual homosexuals and constrain the way they think about themselves. For instance, it forces gays and lesbians to live a completely open life and to make their identification the central feature. Though coming out is an important personal and political process, the level of coming out that is necessary to take advantage of protective legislation may pigeonhole people into categories they might not have chosen. For example, protective legislation encourages people to define themselves as either gay or straight. Yet research from Kinsey to the work of Storms has shown that sexual behavior and fantasy exist on a continuum. Protective legislation divides the world into two opposite camps of sexuality. It also forces people to make their homosexuality more important than other dimensions of their identity, such as gender, race and ethnicity, religion, education, and occupation. These other dimensions tend to become secondary or even incidental.

Protective legislation may also corrode the psychological well-being of individual homosexuals. The process of bringing a suit or otherwise calling attention to a personal injustice can leave a scar on one's psyche. It is not easy to become embroiled with the police or with attorneys and the court system as a lesbian or gay person. For every hand that is offered in support, many others will be withdrawn or raised in hostility. And merely calling attention to an injustice does not mean that justice will be served. The police are likely to demonstrate indifference to what they often perceive as just one more crime against a homosexual. They might follow the letter, but not the spirit, of the law. Priorities within police departments, as well as individual officers' attitudes about homosexuals, may create a situation in which calling attention to the problem may be worse than just living with it. Working with (or against) attorneys in civil as well as criminal suits may also prove distressing. Attorneys are driven by evidence and by the professional requirement of advocating on behalf of their client. Putting together a case and defending it before a judge or arbitrator will require the ability to withstand a lot of hostile questioning. If the criminal isn't caught, if the civil or criminal case is lost, or if vindication isn't as total as the plaintiff might wish, the effects can be personally devastating.

I do not mean to suggest in any way that gays and lesbians should refrain from calling attention to injustice or from bringing suits through the court. Certainly if decriminalization is to take place, these steps will have to be taken. And homosexuals will have to endure the personal consequences associated with this process. My argument is directed only at the issue of special legislation. If a case can be brought on other grounds—grounds not rooted in homosexuality but in more universal principles—victims might get just as much redress and contribute just as much to the advancement of homosexual rights, but with less dire personal consequences. For instance, the special crime of "gay bashing" might just as well be handled as the ordinary crime of "assault." Beating up on innocent and defenseless people is a crime that must be prosecuted regardless of the victim's or perpetrator's sexual orientation. Or, being fired unjustly may be better handled on work-competence grounds, seniority rights, or procedural grounds than on the grounds of homosexual rights. There is no need to invent a special crime or a special right when others already exist to cover the situation. Fighting injustice as an individual citizen—no different from any other—brings pride and dignity to the group. Fighting injustice because homosexuals should receive special protection suggests that homosexuals are inferior to other citizens and cannot make it on their own.

REFERENCES

Carlson, B. E., & Maciol, K. (1997). Domestic violence: Gay men and lesbians. In R. L. Edwards (Ed.), *Encyclopedia of Social Work, 19th Edition 1997 Supplement* (pp. 101–111). Washington, DC: NASW Press.

Folaron, G., & Wagner, M. (1998). Children in the child welfare system: An ecological approach. In R. R. Greene & M. Watkins (Eds.), *Serving diverse constituencies: Applying the ecological perspective* (pp. 113–133). New York, NY: Aldine de Gruyter.

Human Rights Campaign. Retrieved April 15, 2001, from www.hrc.org.

Laird, J. (1995). Lesbians: Parenting. In R. L. Edwards (Ed.), *Encyclopedia of social work* (19th Ed.) (pp. 1604–1616). Washington, DC: NASW Press.

Mallon, G. P. (2001). Gay men and lesbians as adoptive parents. *Journal of Gay & Lesbian Social Services, 11*, 1–22.

Van Wormer, K. Wells, J., & Boes, M. (2000). *Social work with lesbians, gays, and bisexuals: A strength perspective.* Needham Heights, MA: Allyn and Bacon.

ARE GOVERNMENTAL POLICIES SOLVING THE PROBLEM OF HOMELESSNESS?

Editor's Note:
The problem of homelessness has worsened in recent years. Cutbacks in government support for low-income housing, deinstitutionalization, TANF time-limits, reductions in social-service expenditures, and other factors have all contributed to homelessness. In the absence of effective housing policies, many new shelters operated by voluntary social agencies have been established. Supporters argue that these shelters do a good job of caring for the homeless; providing medical and other services; and offering protection against inclement weather, violence, and crime. Opponents claim that shelters are an inefficient and haphazard response to a housing problem that should be addressed at the national level through adequate government intervention. These critics argue that although shelters do meet the immediate necessities of homeless people, they detract from the urgent need for more comprehensive, radical solutions.

Larry W. Kreuger, Ph.D., has more than thirty years of experience teaching a variety of undergraduate and graduate courses in social policy, research methods, and clinical and program evaluation. He has conducted numerous research studies, including coping strategies of widowed women, an evaluation of foster-grandparent programs, an evaluation of job-readiness training for families on welfare, a HUD-funded five-year-long study of former shelter residents, and a field screening of more than 3,600 children and adolescents exposed to a natural disaster, which was funded by Catholic Charities, USA, among others. *John Q. Hodges, Ph.D.*, is an assistant professor in the School of Social Work, University of Missouri, Columbia. He was the recipient of a National Institute of Mental Health Pre-Doctoral Traineeship at the University of California, Berkeley, while completing his Ph.D. He has served as a research associate at the Center for Self-Help Research in Berkeley. Dr. Hodges' research interests include consumer issues in mental health, homelessness among the severely mentally ill, and case-management models. *Debi L. Word*, MSW, LCSW, is a clinical instructor at the University of Missouri-Columbia, School of Social Work. She has been researching homelessness in Missouri (A Survey of Providers of Shelter Services for Homeless Persons Concerning the Impact of Welfare Reform in Missouri, October 2000).

John J. Stretch, Ph.D., is professor of social work in the School of Social Service at Saint Louis University in St. Louis, Missouri. He is a charter member of the Academy of Certified Social Workers and a Licensed Clinical Social Worker in the state of Missouri. Dr. Stretch is a nationally recognized social activist in the field of homelessness and housing. He has published extensively in major professional journals and books.

YES

Larry W. Kreuger, John Q. Hodges, and Debi L. Word

Literature abounds on the problems of providing services to hard-to-reach homeless individuals and families (Lindsey, 1998; Cummins, First, & Toomey, 1998). However, evidence suggests that the complex vulnerabilities of poverty, uprootedness, lack of affordable housing, and numerous other factors that may lead to homelessness have eased in the United States in the last several years. We think this change has stemmed from improvements in the economy overall, welfare reform (Ryan, 1999; Aber, 2000), and successful human-services programs in particular.

On August 22, 1996, President Clinton ended traditional welfare by signing the Personal Responsibility and Work Opportunity Reconciliation Act (Eaton, 1998). With this act, the existing welfare system known as Aid to Families with Dependent Children (AFDC) was repealed, as well as the Job Opportunities and Basic Skill Training Program (JOBS) and Emergency Assistance. The new federal-block grant program known as the Temporary Assistance to Needy Families (TANF) replaced these programs.

In Missouri, as noted in Table 1 below, the number of AFDC-TANF recipients rose steadily from 1960 through the early 1970s, remained fairly constant throughout the 1970s and 1980s, and then rose again in the early 1990s. But the number of welfare recipients has been considerably smaller since the passage of reform legislation in the mid-1990s, dropping over 40 percent from 1996 to 1999 (Klein, Mumford, & Thornburg,1997). Also, data recently collected by the Missouri Association of Social Welfare indicate that shelters serving homeless people have fewer residents than before.

We can't assume that the decrease in the number of welfare recipients (Dunton & Mosley, 2000) is a consequence of welfare reform alone, as noted in a multiple regression analysis of Missouri's welfare rolls analyzed by Eaton (1998). Based on data reported by the Center for Economic Information, University of Missouri, Kansas City, the reduction in the number of

TABLE 1   Number of TANF Recipients in Missouri, 1960–1998

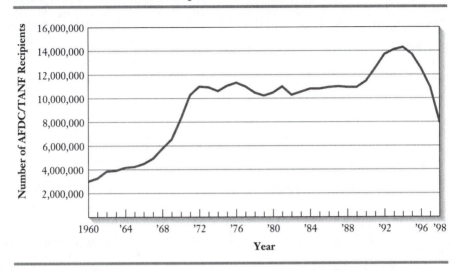

Source: Office of Social and Economic Data Analysis.

welfare recipients from 1993 to 1998 in Missouri derived from of improvements in the economy overall, especially for counties that were not near large metropolitan areas (Eaton, 1998; Rural Policy Research Institute, 1999). Numerous job opportunities provided by a strong economy decreased welfare rolls in Missouri, according to Eaton's analysis.

The key question here is: How have changes in TANF affected those who serve homeless persons in overnight and extended-stay shelters in Missouri? The Missouri Association of Social Welfare and the School of Social Work, University of Missouri-Columbia, surveyed a random sample of shelters in Missouri to find out. Out of 102 requests-to-participate letters and accompanying collection instruments that were mailed, a total of 44 were returned, yielding an overall response rate of 43.1 percent. Though the project leaders would have hoped for a higher return rate, it is not unusual for mailed surveys to produce responses in the 30–40 percent range (Ray & Still, 1987).

HOMELESSNESS AND TANF

A key question in the survey concerned the overall situation of homeless persons in the last year in Missouri. Approximately 48 percent (n=21) of the respondents reported that the number of homeless persons had increased in their part of the state in the last year. However, another 41 percent (n=18) reported that the number of homeless persons had remained constant, and 11

TABLE 2   From your knowledge have changes in TANF (welfare) caused the number of persons who are homeless in your part of Missouri to Increase, Stay About Constant, or Decrease?

TANF AND HOMELESSNESS	COUNT*	PERCENT
Decrease	3	7.7%
Stay About Constant	21	53.8%
Increase	15	38.5%
Totals	39	100.0%

*Five respondents did not answer; thus the total count is less than 44.

percent (n=5) thought that the number of homeless persons in their part of the state had declined. Thus, over half of the respondents reported either no change or a drop.

The second key question centered on whether TANF has impacted sheltered persons in the last year. Approximately 38 percent (n=15) reported that from their experience TANF had caused an increase in the number of homeless persons in the last year. But 54 percent (n=21) thought that homelessness had remained constant. About 8 percent (n=3) thought that the number of homeless persons in the last year had declined as a consequence of TANF. (See Table 2.)

The data from this study also suggested that although homelessness is still a problem, the lives of homeless persons have been improved through changes in TANF, according to shelter operators. Respondents ranked eleven issues, with housing affordability cited as the most critical concern regarding the homeless in Missouri. Table 3 presents a summary ranking of the eleven items rated.

TABLE 3   Rank Order of Overall Priority Areas

PRIORITY AREA	MEAN RANKING
Housing Affordability	4.31
Child Care	4.17
Job Training	4.13
Substance Abuse	4.12
Health/Mental Health	4.09
Transportation	3.81
Domestic Violence	3.71
Emergency Food	3.55
HIV-AIDS	2.94
Veterans Concerns	2.45
Immigration Issues	2.31

According to Dunton and Mosley (2000), most Missourians who have left welfare are currently working. These authors report that 90 percent of the respondents in their sample had worked at some point. We believe these changes are true of persons who used to be homeless. We are not arguing that welfare-reform policies have solved all of these difficult problems (Hobbs, Klein, Mumford, & Thornburg, 1999). Rather, we contend that welfare-reform initiatives and a strengthened economy have begun to show positive outcomes.

NO

John J. Stretch

Since the time of organized social services under the Elizabethan Poor Laws, there have always been shelters and shelter-type services. They have not worked as substantive solutions to serious and intransigent societal problems. The English Poor Laws of the early eighteenth century were more straightforward than modern poor laws in the United States. The poor house and the almshouse were meant to get homeless people out of sight. They were also designed to provide the least amount of support for the greatest number of people. Even then, efficiency was king in serving the homeless.

Today we engage in endless policy debates on how many and what kind of worthy and unworthy homeless people inhabit our cities and rural areas, but the problem has not gotten any better (Christian Century, 1997). The debate between the softhearted and hardheaded serves no humane objective. The Census Bureau, certainly a major hardhead, cites supposedly scientific evidence that there are very few true homeless individuals and families in the United States. Moreover, the Bureau claims, most of them are to be found in urban shelters.

It is comforting to conservative policy makers to terminologically diminish or do away with large segments of the unhoused and ill housed. Policy makers narrow and twist definitions to exclude hundreds of thousands of homeless individuals, families, and children. By their policy parameters, persons who are homeless simply do not exist. Thus out of sight, definitionally, poor people are soon out of mind programmatically.

Added to the deliberate definitional confusion is the lack of clarity of policy objectives. The new glories of privatization and welfare reform have taken their toll (Primus, 2000). The federal government has found it all too convenient to view homelessness as primarily a state issue. The states, in turn, obligingly see homelessness as a local issue. To ease the social conscience of the body politic, a new chimerical beast has been invented: so-called welfare reform, public-private partnerships, and "faith-based" initiatives. Public-private partnerships are a facile neologism for dumping responsibility on churches, the United Way, and other charity-related enterprises.

Too many shelters are unstandardized, unlicensed, unregulated, unsafe, and unsanitary. Many are firetraps. Many lump the mentally ill, the substance abuser, the chronic folks, bag ladies, abused women, and intact families with young children and infants into warehousing accommodations. Some shelters have developed specializations in serving the range of homeless populations. Some have even developed elaborate medical, dental, psychiatric, and social services to meet basic needs. Other shelters have provided a full range of rehabilitation services that include community placement, follow-up, and subsidized housing and other care. At first glance, the shelter movement—at least for some—appears to be doing the job. The fact is, there is tremendous backlash against expanding these types of expensive approaches. Furthermore, the total number of enlightened shelters that deliver solid outcomes is unknown. Little empirical support exists for the effectiveness of even the best shelters. The most damning aspect of shelter provisions is that homeless persons who seek them out have absolutely no entitlements to their services and no redress if they are turned away.

With no clarity of social purpose and no criteria for assessing their impact, shelters limp along with crumbs from uncertain and inadequate federal and state appropriations. Shelters are underrepresented as a professional group when it comes to addressing the burgeoning increases in all segments of the homeless population or devising a reliable system for dealing with the complexity of homelessness in a modern society. Shelters at best are muddling through. Sadly, as a society we feel good about that. HBO specials and network tear-jerkers make us entertainingly aware that something is wrong. We salve our collective social conscience by donating a few more dollars to our local charities. In turn, they reassure us that they are taking care of the real problems of the worthy homeless.

Given all of the above, shelters and shelter services are performing a disservice to the fundamental needs of the homeless. This situation cries out for redress. Shelters obscure the fact that we must commit the resources and the professionalism to forcibly eradicate homelessness and its grinding up of human potential. It boggles the mind that we have an epidemic of homelessness in the United States—and that the public accepts it because the homeless are hidden from public view in shelters through something called welfare reform (American Public Human Services Association, 1999). I therefore blame the policy-naive, local, and fragmented shelter nonsystem for fooling the public that something substantive is being done about homelessness. The shelters give unwarranted social comfort to the rich. They also perpetuate the myth that by using a shelter, most of the homeless—through good, old American bootstrapping—can return as better people to their communities . . . as long as they don't move next door.

Even if we accept the role of shelters as ameliorative mechanisms in a fundamentally flawed system, recent evidence suggests that they are ineffective even at this most basic of tasks. A survey of homeless providers in twenty-five large urban areas indicates that the demand for shelter increased by 15 percent in the past year, and that nearly a quarter of these requests went unmet. Similarly, there was a 17 percent increase in requests for emergency food assistance for the year 2000, of which 13 percent went unmet (United States Conference of Mayors, 2000). Despite the recent economic boom, the poorest of the poor continue to suffer, and indeed, are suffering in even greater numbers.

Lack of affordable housing and the impact of low-wage jobs were the two most-frequently cited causes of homelessness in this same study (USCM, 2000). Again, structural factors account for the increasing numbers of the homeless. No amount of temporary shelter can address a problem that has far deeper roots at the societal level. Hiding the homeless in unsafe shelters cannot disguise the utter lack of housing and jobs that would enable them to live independently.

Further, many respondents in the Missouri Association of Social Welfare survey in Missouri indicated that we have not seen the full impact of TANF, because recipients have not yet reached the sixty-month or five-year limit. People who have been on and off public assistance may not fully understand these limits, especially those who are or have been homeless. What does the future hold for these families when they reach their sixty-month limit and welfare is no longer an option? Far too much attention has been paid to the decreasing number of welfare cases without a real understanding of how recipients are faring. Findings in the MASW study also indicate that many jobs were low paying. Missourians who left welfare as a result of changes due to welfare (TANF) reform were mostly the working poor: They worked in low-paying jobs that did not allow them to rise above the poverty level. A recent study conducted by the Midwest Research Institute found that 58 percent of the 873 families interviewed still lived in poverty. The median earning of those in the study was $12,948 annually, which falls below the poverty line for a family of three (Dunton & Mosley, 2000).

As long as we tolerate a basically inequitable and inefficient economic system that perpetuates the causes of homelessness, we will continue to justify wasteful and ineffective responses such as private and "faith-based" shelters. Further, when we permit our social values to deteriorate to the point where individuals feel no responsibility for their lives, and when we do not teach citizens how to cope with the stresses of modern society, we will seek false solutions through endless social engineering and intrusive social fixings.

Welfare-reform initiatives have not worked. In the meantime, we need continued monitoring of programs intended to help homeless and poorly housed persons (Barrett & Camrud, 1999). We also need updated assessments of the impact of such efforts, perhaps obtained through statewide and national database systems. These database systems should guide effective, humane social policy to eradicate a national disgrace for the richest country in the world: homelessness in the midst of plenty.

REFERENCES

Aber, J. (2000). Welfare reform at three—Is a new consensus emerging? *News and Issues*. National Center for Children in Poverty, Volume 10, No. 1, Winter.

Barrett, L., & Camrud, K. (1999). Executive summary: Still vouchered up and nowhere to go II, Housing Comes First, November 9.

Cummins, L. First, & R., Toomey, ?? (1998, Winter). Comparisons of rural and urban homeless women. *Affilia—Journal of Women and Social Work,13*(4), 435–453.

Dunton, N., & Mosley, J. (2000). Economic well-being of former Missouri AFDC recipients. *The Midwest Research Institute, 425*. Kansas City, MO.

Eaton, P. (1998). Welfare reform in Missouri: MSCDC Economic Report Series No. 9803. Center for Economic Information, University of Missouri-Kansas City.

Hobbs, D., Klein, T., Mumford, J., & Thornburg, K. (1999, April). Poverty rates decline: Inequality persists. *Step by Step Newsletter, 108*(2).

Increased homelessness tied to welfare reform (1997). *The Christian Century, 114*(36), 1183–1184.

Klein, T., Martin, P., Mumford, J., & Thornburg, K. (1997, April). Welfare reform and child care. *Step by Step Newsletter, 8*(2).

Lindsey, E. (1998, March-April). Service providers' perception of factors that help or hinder homeless families. *Families in Society, 79*(2), 160–172.

Primus, W. (2000) Success of welfare reform unclear. *News and Issues*. National Center for Children in Poverty, Volume 10, No. 1.

Ray, J. J., & Still, L. V. (1987). Maximizing the response rate in surveys may be a mistake. *Personality & Individual Differences, 8*(4), 571–573.

A recent history of welfare reform (1999). American Public Human Services Association Retrieved April 20, 2001, from http://.aphsa.org/reform/timeline.htm.

Rural America and welfare reform: An overview assessment. Rural Policy Research Institute Rural Welfare Reform Panel (1999, February 10).

Ryan, S. et al. (1999). HHS Leaver Project. The Missouri Department of Social Services and the University of Missouri, Department of Economics.

United States Conference of Mayors. A status report on hunger and homelessness in American cities 2000: A 25-city survey, December 2000. Retrieved March 18, 2001, from http://www.usmayors.org/uscm/news/press_releases/documents/hunger_release.htm.

CAN WELFARE-TO-WORK PROGRAMS SIGNIFICANTLY REDUCE POVERTY LEVELS?

Editor's Note:
In one form or another, welfare-to-work programs have existed in the United States since the 1970s. Workfare programs are designed to encourage public-assistance recipients to find regular employment and become financially self-sufficient. The better-run programs provide job training, education, job placement, and day care, all of which help poor people secure employment. The workfare alternative to public assistance was mandated in the Personal Responsibility and Work Opportunity Act of 1996 (PRWORA), which set a maximum five-year life-time cap on income maintenance. Some have widely promoted workfare programs as the only real alternative to government assistance and as a dynamic solution to the poverty problem. Indeed, since the introduction of workfare in the PRWORA, income-maintenance caseloads have dropped 50 percent nationally. Skeptics are not convinced. They argue that workfare programs do not deliver the services needed to help the poor remain above the poverty level.

Sandra K. Danziger, Ph.D., is associate professor of social work and director, Michigan Program on Poverty and Social Welfare Policy at the University of Michigan. Her primary research interests are the impact of public programs on the well-being of families, poverty and social-welfare policies, demographic trends in child and family well-being, program implementation, and qualitative research methods. Professor Danziger's current projects address the implementation of welfare-reform policies and their impact on low-income families and children. She is a principal investigator on the Women's Employment Survey study in Michigan.

Eileen Trzcinski, Ph.D., is an associate professor in the School of Social Work, Wayne State University. She is also a coordinate faculty member in the College of Urban, Labor, and Metropolitan Affairs, and a faculty fellow at the

Fraser Center for Workplace Issues at Wayne State University. She has also been a visiting research scholar at the German Institute for Economic Research and at the Fachhochschule fuer Wirtschaft, Berlin. Her areas of research center on family policy and labor policy, on both the national and international level. Dr. Trzcinski is currently principal investigator on three research projects that focus on welfare reform. *Deborah Satyanathan* received her M.S.W. from the School of Social Work at Wayne State University, where she specialized in children, family, and youth programs and policy. She is co-editor of the Michigan Family Impact Seminars Report, titled *Moving Families Out of Poverty*. She has published on barriers to employment facing women on welfare and on domestic violence and poverty.

YES

Sandra K. Danziger

Before passage of the Personal Responsibility and Work Opportunity Reconciliation Act of 1996 (PRWORA), many states were experimenting with a work-oriented welfare system by seeking waivers from federal regulations in the Aid to Families with Dependent Children (AFDC) program. Though many types of welfare-to-work programs emerged over this period, the 1996 Act has led to a narrowing of the types of programs implemented in the states. Most states have developed variations of a "Work First" model (Nathan & Gais, 1999). In Work First programs, welfare recipients are typically required either to obtain employment on their own or to participate in short-term activities designed to move them quickly into the labor force.

However, requiring work effort and participation in employment-search programs may be supplemented or supplanted by other types of training and services and other inducements to work. These range from penalties for not working to financial incentives that increase the rewards of work. This paper summarizes research on (a) the relative effectiveness of varying approaches for moving welfare recipients into employment and (b) the possibilities for participation in these programs to change income and poverty. Because programs that incorporate the most comprehensive strategies have demonstrated promise for increased economic well-being, I argue that welfare-to-work programs *can* reduce poverty—particularly when other conditions also prevail. These include a low unemployment rate and tight labor market; other policies outside the welfare system that support poor families, including those that provide financial help with child care; access to affordable health insurance, education, and training services; tax credits such as the Earned Income Tax Credit (EITC); and minimum-wage increases. In addition, persons with physical and mental health problems or personal characteristics that reduce their chances of labor-market success must have access to services and adequate income supports.

In practice, most welfare-to-work programs now implemented in the states do not meet all these conditions. Thus they aren't likely to significantly reduce poverty. In this paper, I describe different types of welfare-to-work programs. I compare the narrower Work First approach with some experimental approaches to services that aim both to promote work and reduce poverty. I then provide evidence on the impact of these different types of programs on economic well-being. I summarize the evidence, discuss caveats, and offer policy directions that could help states improve their welfare-to-work programs.

POLICY EVOLUTION OF WORK FIRST

The phrase Work First refers to programs in which participants receive assistance in searching for work as well as to a philosophical belief about the best way to promote the economic well-being of welfare recipients. The philosophy assumes that finding a job (typically unsubsidized) as quickly as possible and developing work skills through direct experience—rather than participating in education and training—is the best way for recipients to beome self-sufficient. The assumption is that leaving welfare and taking any job will lead recipients to better jobs and eventually increase their earnings to the point where they escape poverty.

The Work First philosophy gained acceptance during the mid-1990s. During those years, many policy makers became dissatisfied with the services provided in the Job Opportunity and Basic Skills (JOBS) program, the welfare-to-work program instituted by the Family Support Act of 1988. Although many welfare recipients did not participate in JOBS, the majority who did were in education-related activities, as opposed to employment, job readiness, and job search. Policymakers and practitioners came to believe that the skills these education or training programs provided had little or no connection to those needed in the job market (U.S. General Accounting Office, 1995; Holcomb, Pavetti, Ratcliffe, & Riedinger, 1998). Additionally, according to MDRC, evaluations of the various welfare-to-work program approaches documented not only the weakness of education and training but also the strength of a Work First approach in moving recipients off assistance. For example, the Riverside, California, Work First program garnered attention for its "success" in placing recipients into jobs (Bloom, 1997).[1]

"Work first" as a concept responds to the conservative critique that shaped much of the welfare-reform debate leading to the passage of PRWORA. Conservatives argued that welfare dependency itself contributed to the problems of the poor (rather than offering a solution) and created

[1]Although the Manpower Demonstration Research Corporation (MDRC), the evaluator of Riverside and other JOBS programs, stressed some of the unique features of Riverside—including a strong management focus on job placement (Riccio, Friedlander, & Freedman, 1994)—a number of states began to implement the narrower components of Work First programs (Holcomb, Pavetti, Ratcliffe, & Riedinger, 1998; U.S. General Accounting Office, 1998).

support for the Clinton call to "end welfare as we know it." The 1996 Act aims to end dependency, in part by mandating work participation. States can most readily comply by requiring welfare recipients to engage in up-front job searches and job-readiness activities and to find work within some short period after coming onto the rolls.

A few states are incorporating broader approaches in their welfare-to-work programs. For example, Maine and Wyoming have programs that let some clients participate in post-secondary education. Washington uses community work-experience placements on a large scale. Oregon, Utah, and Tennessee have implemented assessment and service referrals for welfare clients with mental-health problems.

Even the narrow work-first focus is generally reported as a success, because almost all states experienced caseload reductions and employment increases among single mothers from the mid- to late-1990s. However, results for poverty and income changes are more mixed, as will be discussed further below. The biggest income increases and poverty reductions have resulted in a few experimental programs that provide a broader set of policies that both require work and supplement low incomes.

COMPREHENSIVE WELFARE TO WORK

Several innovative welfare-to-work strategies have not been as widely implemented as have Work First programs. A notable example is the Minnesota Family Investment Program (MFIP). Begun in 1994, MFIP operated in seven counties and required initial job searching for almost all participants (Bloom & Michalopoulos, 2001). MFIP in its fullest form (before 1998) required mandatory employment, but it also provided earnings supplements to participants who met the work requirements.

MFIP was designed to make working recipients better off financially and to increase employment (Miller, Knox, Auspos, Hunter-Manns, Orenstein, 1997). Its financial incentives included generous earned-income disregards, coupled with relatively high welfare-benefit levels. For example, in 1994, a single parent of two children who worked twenty hours a week at $6 an hour would receive in a month $599 in food stamps and cash benefits and $662 in net earnings (wages plus tax credits minus taxes)—for a total monthly income of $1261. If he or she worked forty hours per week, the earnings would rise to $1180, and the assistance would decrease to $276, for a total of $1456 (Miller, Knox, Auspos, Hunter-Manns, & Orenstein, 1997). If this same recipient stayed on welfare and had no earnings, his or her monthly income from cash assistance and Food Stamps would come to just $769. The overall income goes up because the individual's earnings gain exceeds benefits loss. MFIP proved most effective for recipients who had received assistance for at least two of the previous three years. It also provided (within the mandated employment services) job-search assistance, vocational training, and basic or post-secondary education.

HAS WELFARE REFORM HELPED?

Studies that have followed single mothers who left the public-assistance rolls between 1996 and 1999 in ten states estimate that about three-fifths of leavers were working at one point in time (Isaacs & Lyon, 2000). Annual earnings of these former recipients were quite low; many individuals continued to need Food Stamps, Medicaid, and child-care assistance. For example, in one state, 89 percent of former TANF recipients had incomes below 185 percent of the poverty line (Isaacs & Lyon, 2000). (Note: Not all sources of income are examined consistently across these studies.)

Another study analyzes the March Current Population Surveys (CPS) through 1999 (Schoeni & Blank, 2000). This research finds reduced participation in the welfare system and evidence of a small decline in poverty among single-mother families since welfare reform. However, these gains may not have accrued to women who are high-school dropouts with the very lowest incomes. Moreover, increases in other sources of family income were more important than increases in women's earnings for this poverty reduction (Schoeni & Blank, 2000). These researchers find that the 1996 policy reforms contributed significantly to these changes, but that the economic expansion over this period was primarily responsible for the increases in employment among single mothers (Schoeni & Blank, 2000). In addition, they note that no study to date has clarified which program mechanisms (whether mandated job search, sanctions for noncompliance, earned-income disregards, or some combination) are responsible for the welfare reductions, work increases, and income gains.

IS WORK FIRST SUFFICIENT?

A recent report synthesizes findings from several experimental studies and compares education-first programs with job-search-first programs and programs that offer both types of activities to clients (Bloom & Michalopoulos, 2001). These researchers find that the largest earnings gains compared to control groups can be found in programs that offer a mixed set of initial activities. They suggest that a "one-size-fits-all" approach is less likely to boost earnings than a program that tailors services to meet individual needs (Bloom & Michalopoulos, 2001).

Several studies are following the income and employment outcomes of current and former welfare recipients who are exposed to Work First reforms. They document a high prevalence of such factors as low education and work skills, physical and mental health problems, child health problems, and domestic violence—all of which may affect especially women's chances of getting and keeping jobs and leaving poverty. The Michigan Women's Employment Study (WES) provides information on the impact of these problems on employment and welfare receipt.

Multivariate analyses of 1997 data showed that lack of a high-school degree, work experience, and job skills; perceptions of discrimination; transportation problems; depression; and personal or child illness significantly reduced the likelihood that a respondent was employed at least part-time (Danziger, Corcoran, Danziger, Heflin, Kalil, Levine, Rosen, Seefeldt, Siefert, & Tolman, 2000). More recent data from this panel study indicate that respondents with two or fewer barriers to employment in 1999 (53 percent of the sample) worked on average in about 80 percent of the months between fall 1998 and fall 1999. Those with five or more barriers worked on average in about half of those months (18 percent of the sample).

Multiple barriers are also associated with longer stays on TANF. Approximately one-fifth of women who received TANF in ten or less of the forty-one months for which administrative data are available (February 1997–June 2000) had four or more barriers to employment. However, women on TANF for greater proportions of time were much more likely to have four or more barriers. Just over a third of women who received TANF in 21–30 of the 41 months, and more than half of women receiving TANF in nearly all the months, had four or more potential barriers to employment.

However, Work First programs usually do not focus on recipients with the greatest barriers to employment. For example, most states do not systematically assess a recipient's personal problems or refer him or her to treatment or other services. Certainly a few states have developed programs that screen for a wide range of problems and provide referrals for mental health, substance abuse, and other counseling or treatment services. Yet the complex needs of recipients with multiple barriers are not being met in most states. In fact, a program might sanction a recipient who seems uncooperative or who appears to have a "bad attitude," when he or she might actually be clinically depressed.

THE NEED FOR EARNINGS SUPPLEMENTS IN WELFARE TO WORK

The most significant poverty declines have been attributed to programs that provide generous earnings supplements (Berlin, 2000; Bloom & Michalopoulos, 2001). For example, according to the MDRC evaluation of the MFIP (Miller, Knox, Gennetian, Dodoo, Hunter, & Redcross, 2000), the percentage of single-parent long-term program participants who worked in an average quarter (in the first nine quarters after the program began) was about 50 percent, compared to 37 percent of the control group. The poverty rate was about

75 percent for the treatment group, but 85 percent for the controls. Over the full three-year period of the experiment, the MFIP model that combined the earnings supplement with mandated employment services had the largest effect on average annual earnings and the largest reductions in the number of people with incomes below poverty (Bloom & Michalopoulos, 2001). Thus, welfare reforms that increase both work requirements and work incentives are better able to improve welfare recipients' situation and reduce poverty.

CAVEATS

In all of these studies, it is impossible to disaggregate the effects of the "message" of Work First programs from the effects of recipient participation in various types of employment-related training, earnings incentives, or penalties for noncompliance. Poverty declines and well-being improvements are also driven by other policy expansions that have increased the value of returns to work, such as access to child health insurance beyond welfare receipt, child-care subsidies, the earned-income tax credit, and minimum-wage increases. In addition, while the economy was robust and jobs were plentiful, even entry-level wage rates tended to increase, thus improving the employment prospects of people leaving welfare.

CONCLUSIONS

Broad strategies to promote welfare to work and to support work once a recipient is employed, and that include services and supports for those who may have difficulties in the labor market, require that policymakers abandon the presumption that a complex social problem can be solved by a single strategy aimed at all welfare recipients. There are no simple solutions in any other social-policy arenas, such as child welfare, disability, early childhood, or education. As a society, we have often failed to provide sufficient resources and to allow sufficient time for implementation of new, comprehensive initiatives. However, the research reviewed here suggests that the design of welfare-to-work programs can reduce poverty.

Mandating job search and work, in the context of the economic boom of the late 1990s, moved numerous recipients into the workforce. However, many obtained low-skill, low-paying jobs. If successful, the reforms to the Work First approach suggested here would promote broader policy goals and reduce poverty further.

The MFIP results, along with post-PRWORA program outcomes, indicate that, in a booming economy, most welfare recipients can find some work. More of them escape poverty through employment, at least in the short run, than do recipients who lack access to these work-incentive programs.

The economic incentives in programs like MFIP are consistent with the goals of welfare reform.

People who succeed in Work First programs in the context of welfare reform are better off than those who are unable to respond to the new mandates. On average, women who left welfare for work and those who combine work and welfare are financially better off than nonworking female welfare recipients. More attention should be paid to developing programs that address the factors that *prevent* current recipients from going to work and improving their economic status.

Women especially who have poor physical or mental health or who lack job skills are at high risk of losing cash-assistance benefits in the next few years owing to sanctions or impending time limits. Additional policies are needed to (a) make work pay enough so that a greater percentage of working mothers can escape poverty and (b) enable greater proportions of welfare-reliant mothers to take advantage of work opportunities. Further expansion of "make-work-pay" provisions; wider access to assessment, services, and income support for those who cannot compete in the labor market; and continued improvements in mandated employment-search and job-retention training available both within and outside the welfare system should all be included in the next round of welfare-policy reforms. Comprehensive welfare-to-work strategies *can* reduce poverty.

NO
Eileen Trzcinski and Deborah Satyanathan

In this article, we address the question of whether U.S. welfare-to-work programs can significantly reduce poverty levels. To do so, we first focus on the following series of subquestions: "To what extent has welfare reform—with its emphasis on welfare to work—reduced welfare caseloads? To what extent have declining caseloads been accompanied by increased labor-market participation? Has market work significantly reduced poverty for current and former TANF (Temporary Aid to Needy Families) recipients? What conditions must be met for welfare to work to significantly reduce poverty for current and former TANF recipients? Are these conditions now being met, or will they be met in the near future?" After presenting the evidence, we conclude that welfare-to-work programs have *not* substantially eased poverty, and that they are unlikely to do so in the near future given the political climate in which we now live.

To what extent has welfare reform with its emphasis on welfare to work caused the decline in welfare caseloads?   To make the argument that welfare to work can substantially reduce poverty, we must first establish that welfare to work has both decreased welfare caseloads and increased work effort (or that it will do so). Since the passage of the Personal Responsibility and Work Opportunity Reconciliation Act in 1996, welfare caseloads have declined by almost 50 percent nationally. Many who supported welfare reform point to this fact as evidence of PRWORA's success. Few supporters of welfare reform question whether welfare-to-work programs have indeed been responsible for the dramatic decline in caseloads.

The fact that welfare caseloads significantly declined in the 1990s clearly suggests that welfare reform has met its goal of reducing welfare dependency. However, this conclusion is not strongly supported by the evidence. A number of economists and other academic researchers have attempted to disentangle the joint effects of the macroeconomy and policy changes on reducing welfare caseloads. These studies provide inconclusive evidence on whether welfare reform is responsible for the reduction in welfare rolls.

Bell (2001) reviewed published reports of the President's Council of Economic Advisors (1997, 1999) and a set of academic papers written by prominent economists. The reviewed studies included Blank (1997), Moffitt (1999), Schoeni and Blank (2000), Wallace and Blank (1999), and Ziliak et al. (2000). The results of the analyses were highly dependent on how the authors specified their statistical models; results across the studies were contradictory and not robust. Based on the evidence, Bell concluded that if caseloads are allowed to adjust sluggishly to new conditions—the natural dynamic when a stock of welfare families adjusts incrementally to the flow of entries and exits—policy effects go away. According to Bell, caseload declines have not been traced convincingly to individual reform measures such as time limits or work sanctions (2001).

In a separate review of the evidence, Blank (2001) concluded that a strong macroeconomy matters more than anything else in encouraging work and reducing poverty. She pointed out that the 1996 welfare reform corresponded with an economic expansion that set a record as the longest in U.S. history, lasting more than 106 months. During this time period, investment growth was strong, the federal government eliminated its annual deficits, productivity growth was above trend, and inflation remained low. All of these trends benefited workers. Blank argued that the strong economy of the 1990s helped fuel the decline in caseloads, growth in labor-force participation, and decreases in poverty rates. Based on her own analyses and a review of other studies, she found that between one-third and two-thirds of the caseload change in the early 1990s appeared to stem from economic factors (Blank, 2001; Figlio & Ziliak, 1999; Wallace & Blank, 1999).

Blank did not dismiss the effects of policy change on reducing welfare caseloads, but she emphasized that the precise effects are extremely difficult to measure. She concluded that "it seems more likely that economic forces have reinforced the direction of policy, and both policy and economics have worked together to change behavior more strongly than either could have accomplished alone" (2001).

To what extent have declining caseloads been accompanied by increased labor market participation?   From 1979 to 1999, U.S. Current Population

Surveys indicate that the rate of labor-market participation or preparation (work or school) increased dramatically for never-married mothers (34 percent) and widowed, divorced, or separated mothers (20 percent). Married mothers had only a steady increase in labor participation/preparation, and women without children showed no increase (Blank, 2001). However, these trends do not specifically separate out women who were TANF recipients from other women. We can better examine the specific experiences of adults who have received TANF benefits with data from the Urban Institute's National Surveys of American Families.

In 1997 and 1999, the Urban Institute conducted the National Surveys of America's Families (NSAF). These surveys were conducted on a nationally representative sample of 44,000 non-elderly families with oversamples of the low-income population. Each survey contained questions about family well-being and about the family's experience with welfare. The NSAF results provide a comprehensive look at the well-being of adults and children and reveal sometimes striking differences among the thirteen states studied in depth. They provide quantitative measures of the quality of life in America, with particular attention to low-income families.

Based on analyses of the NSAF, Zedlewski and Loprest (2001) looked at work status among current and former TANF recipients and their families in 1997 and 1999. Among current TANF recipients, the data indicated that 33 percent of adults receiving TANF benefits had no work activity in 1999, compared with 43 percent in 1997. The percentage looking for work remained unchanged—25 percent—from 1997 to 1999. Barriers to employment strongly affected the likelihood that current or former TANF recipients were engaged in market work. When current TANF recipients were separated into those with and without barriers to work, the data showed the following: More than half of the adults without barriers to work were working for pay in both 1997 and 1999. The percent of adults with multiple barriers to employment who were in paid jobs increased from 5 percent in 1997 to 20 percent in 1999. About half of the adults in the multiple barrier group were engaged in no work activity—not even job search.

Results from the NSAF indicated that most former TANF recipients were engaged in market work. Specifically, the data indicated that adults who were currently working or who had worked sometime during the year of their interview (1999) totaled 69 percent of former TANF recipients.

Individuals living with a spouse or partner who was working made up about 13 percent. Only 1 percent of adults were receiving federal disability benefits. The final 17 percent of former TANF recipients (one in six of those who left TANF in the past two years) had no known source of income. Given their precarious economic situation, these former TANF recipients were defined as "at-risk" leavers (Zedlewski & Alderson, 2001; Zedlewski & Loprest, 2001).

Zedlewski and Loprest (2001) concluded that states have clearly made progress in moving individuals, including those with significant disadvantages (multiple barriers to employment), into paid work. Despite this progress, many adults receiving TANF in 1999 were not yet engaged in work. Furthermore, a substantial percentage of TANF leavers (17 percent) were neither engaged in market work nor living with a spouse or partner who was working.

Evidence also suggests that ability to maintain employment depends on how many barriers to employment current and former TANF recipients face. Hence the long-term success of welfare-to-work programs depends on the states' willingness to address the needs of TANF recipients who face barriers to employment, particularly those who face multiple barriers. As noted in the previous section, long-term success also depends on a strong macroeconomy to create the jobs necessary for welfare-to-work programs to function.

Has market work resulted in significant declines in poverty for current or former TANF recipients?   For welfare-to-work programs to reduce poverty levels significantly, the work obtained must pay sufficient wages to move families out of poverty, or earned income must be supplemented by other sources of income. For many families, these conditions are not yet being met. Key facts regarding the working poor and children in poverty include the following: In 1999, the wage required to lift a family of four above the poverty line with full-time, full-year employment was $8.51 an hour. In 1999, the hourly wage for low-wage workers (20th percentile) was $7.35 in the United States as a whole (Mishel, Bernstein, & Schmitt, 2000). Among low-income children in the United States, 51.5 percent have parents who are employed full- or part-time (National Center for Children in Poverty, 2000). Even when parents work full-time, year-round, some children remain poor. In the United States, 7.7 percent of young children with at least one parent working full-time remain in poverty (National Center for Children in Poverty, 2000).

For children in female-headed households, poverty rates are high even in households with at least one employed person. In 1999, the poverty rate was 46.4 percent for female-headed households with children under six years of age in households with one worker. For female-headed households with children under eighteen years of age, the poverty rate was 33.9 percent in households with one worker (U.S. Bureau of the Census, 2000).

Between 1993 and 1998, TANF caseloads in the states declined by 47.2 percent; child poverty rates declined by 17.1 percent (National Center for Children in Poverty, 2000). Declines in the child poverty rate from 1993–1998 were not adequate to offset the increases that occurred between 1979 and 1993. Overall, the child poverty rate was 15.1 percent higher in 1998 than in 1979 (National Center for Children in Poverty, 2000).

Based on data from the NSAF, Loprest (2001) found that 52 percent of former TANF recipients had incomes beneath the poverty line. The median monthly earnings of former TANF recipients were $1,093; the median hourly wage was $7.15; 68 percent were working thirty-five hours or more per week. Loprest also examined indicators of economic struggles for former TANF recipients in 1999. Respondents reported that 32.7 percent had to cut the size of meals or skip meals because there wasn't enough food; 60.1 percent worried that food would run out before they got money to buy more (often or sometimes true); for 55.5 percent, food didn't last and they didn't have money for more (often or sometimes true); and 46.1 percent experienced a time in the past year when they were not able to pay the mortgage, rent, or utility bills. For many families, the evidence suggests that welfare-to-work programs have not yet prompted significant declines in poverty levels or in economic hardship.

WHAT CONDITIONS MUST BE MET FOR WELFARE-TO-WORK TO PRODUCE SIGNIFICANT DECLINES IN POVERTY FOR CURRENT OR FORMER TANF RECIPIENTS?

For welfare-to-work programs to reduce poverty significantly, states must first recognize that many TANF recipients face multiple obstacles to finding and maintaining market work. Second, states must recognize that, for many families, market work is not enough to reduce poverty and eliminate economic hardship.

Strategies to Address Barriers to Employment

Researchers have conducted many studies on potential barriers to employment for welfare recipients. The major barriers identified by Sweeney et al. (2000) at the Center on Budget and Policy Priorities include:

- little or no employment skills or education
- little or no prior work experience
- substandard housing conditions or lack of affordable housing
- having a child with special needs.

As time limits begin to run out for many families receiving TANF funds, the number of individuals without work or welfare will increase unless states pay significant attention to these barriers. Table 1 describes four policy proposals to decrease or eliminate possible barriers to work.

STRATEGIES TO SUPPORT WORK AND REDUCE POVERTY

Federal, state, and local policy makers will need to develop and implement a wide array of innovative strategies and practical programs and policies to help low-income working families with children. Many of these strategies are

TABLE 1   **Potential Strategies to Remove Barriers to Employment**

STRATEGY	RATIONALE AND DESCRIPTION
Access to Education and Training	Under the federal law, states can use TANF funds for education and training activities. Expenditures may include tuition and other educational costs, supportive services such as child care and transportation, and cash assistance for living expenses.
Transitional Jobs	By creating publicly funded transitional jobs, states can enable welfare recipients to earn wages and gain valuable work experience while also alleviating job shortages. These jobs can provide a "stepping-stone" for individuals with little or no work experience.
Housing Assistance	A housing program targeted toward current and former welfare recipients whose housing problems are a barrier to work can be an effective component of welfare-reform efforts. Housing assistance also offers a measure of security that enables parents to focus on employment goals and challenges.
Child Care for Children with Special Needs	States have access to a variety of funding sources, including TANF, the Social Services Block Grant (SSBG), or the Child Care Development Fund (CCDF) to provide care for children with special needs.

Source: Sweeney et al. (2000), Center on Budget and Policy Priorities.

already in place in some states. In *Windows of Opportunity: Strategies to Support Families Receiving Welfare and Other Low-Income Families in the Next Stage of Welfare Reform*, Sweeney et al. (2000) described an array of innovative strategies and practical ideas for helping low-income families with children. Many of these proposals are based on current state and local programs and policies that support the efforts of low-income working families. Table 2 lists of some of these proposals.

Tax strategies can also increase the earnings of low-income families and thus reduce poverty and economic hardship. Many low-income working families face a heavy state and local tax burden. States can use three basic features of a standard income-tax structure to reduce or eliminate the income-tax burden on low-income families.

Increasing personal and dependent exemptions.   Many states that do not tax poor families of three or four members allow relatively large deductions from income for all taxpayers through personal and dependent exemptions and dependent exemptions. The cost of increasing a personal exemption or credit can be mitigated in a number of ways. States can use a personal credit rather than an exemption to target relief to low-income households and

TABLE 2   **Potential Strategies to Support Work and Reduce Poverty**

STRATEGY	RATIONALE AND DESCRIPTION
Worker Stipend	In most states, parents lose eligibility for cash aid before their earnings can meet their families' basic needs. States can provide wage supplements to parents who work but earn too little to meet such needs.
Transportation Assistance	Many low-income families do not live near the areas of greatest job growth. Often public transportation is not available or is not structured to accommodate reverse commutes, nonstandard hours, or the multiple stops facing many low-income families. States can provide transportation to low-income families, and need not limit this aid to families receiving welfare.
Child Care	States can use various state and federal funding sources to create a seamless system of care for all low-income families. Effective state programs should provide affordable co-payments and access to care during nonstandard hours.
Job Retention and Advancement Services	Although many former welfare recipients are working, they are typically in short-lived, low-wage jobs that lack health insurance or other benefits and have little room for advancement or wage growth. State policies can be designed to help recipients get better jobs initially; provide extended case-management services to employed families; and ensure that low-income working families have access to all benefits to which they qualify.
Short-Term Aid	Many low-income families experience temporary crises, such as a car breakdown or the illness of a child, that can jeopardize family stability or a parent's employment. State alternatives for short-term aid include emergency-assistance programs that provide aid to prevent homelessness or utility cut-offs and cash-diversion programs that cover low-income families not eligible for welfare.
Expansion of Health Coverage for Low-Income Working Parents	While numerous states provide health-insurance coverage to many children in low-income working families, the parents in these same families frequently must go without health insurance. Studies conducted by the states consistently show that more than a third, and often more than half, of parents in families that recently left welfare do not have health coverage, either through the workplace or through public programs. States can now expand coverage for low-income working parents to whatever income level they determine is appropriate, with the help of Medicaid funds.

Source: Sweeney et al. (2000) and Lazere, Fremstad, & Goldberg (2000), Center on Budget and Policy Priorities.

reduce costs (Johnson, Zahradnik, & McNichol, 2000; Zahradnik, Johnson, & Mazerov, 2001).

Increasing the standard deduction.   By increasing the standard deduction, a state can increase the tax threshold at which families begin to pay taxes. This strategy also reduces the amount of taxes owed by families with incomes about the threshold level (Johnson, Zahradnik, & McNichol, 2000; Zahradnik, Johnson, & Mazerov, 2001).

Providing low-income credits.   A tax credit is subtracted directly from an individual's tax liability. Credits available only to low-income taxpayers can reduce the tax liability for low-income families. Credits that are refundable— that is, credits for which the taxpayer receives the entire value even if the credit amount exceeds the amount of taxes owed—can supplement wages for families at low income levels. Credits can also be restricted to families with earned income. The federal EITC (Earned Income Tax Credit) has lifted more children out of poverty than any other federal program. Tax credits for low-income working families, state EITCs, are based on the federal EITC (Bernstein, McNichol, Mishel, & Zahradnik, 2000; Johnson, Zahradnik & McNichol, 2000; Zahradnik, Johnson & Mazerov, 2001).

ARE THE CONDITIONS NEEDED FOR WELFARE-TO-WORK POLICIES TO SIGNIFICANTLY REDUCE POVERTY NOW BEING MET, OR WILL THEY BE MET IN THE NEAR FUTURE?

Exemplary state programs do exist that encourage work, reduce poverty, and address barriers to employment. For example, the Minnesota Family Investment Program (MFIP) substantially decreased the benefit reduction rate for public-assistance recipients, thus allowing them to keep more public-assistance income as they went to work. But MFIP also mandated participation in work and welfare programs. The evidence suggests that employment, earnings, and family income increased substantially for program participants, while poverty fell (Blank, 2001).

Yet most states have not integrated the available policies into a comprehensive framework that addresses the many divergent needs of families with low incomes. Many states are reluctant to follow Minnesota's example because the program did not save money for the government (Blank, 2001). For the tax year 1999, only eleven states had an EITC based on the federal EITC. Thus many families nationwide remain poor or face economic hardship even though at least one family member works in the market. Other families remain poor because family members face barriers to employment.

Comprehensive policy changes are needed to eliminate the poverty and economic hardship still endured by low-income working families. It is unlikely that the political climate will soon swing toward providing this support.

Effective policies and programs are expensive; major cost savings occur in the future, not today.

Evidence also suggests that much of the success of welfare-to-work programs rests at least in part on the existence of a strong macroeconomy. In early 2001, unemployment rates were on the rise. Other indicators suggested a substantial weakening of the strong macroeconomy that marked the early years of welfare reform. Hypothetically, the answer to the question, "*Can* welfare-to-work programs significantly reduce poverty levels?" is clearly *yes*. Based on the evidence and arguments presented in this chapter, the answer to the more urgent question, "*Have* welfare-to-work programs significantly reduced poverty levels, or will they do so in the near future?" is *no*.

REFERENCES

Bell, S. H. (2001). *Why are welfare caseloads falling?* Assessing the New Federalism, Discussion Papers, 01–02 March. Washington, DC: The Urban Institute.

Berlin, G. L. (2000). *Encouraging work, reducing poverty: The impact of work incentive programs.* New York, NY: Manpower Demonstration Research Corporation.

Bernstein, J., McNichol, E. C., Mishel, L., & Zahradnik, R. (2000). *Pulling apart: A state-by-state analysis of income trends.* Washington, DC: Center on Budget and Policy Priorities and Economic Policy Institute (http://www.cbpp.org & www.epinet.org).

Blank, R. M. (1997). *What causes public-assistance caseloads to grow?* National Bureau of Economic Research, Working Paper No. 6343. Cambridge, MA: NBER.

Blank, R. (2001). Fighting poverty: Lessons from recent U. S. history. In E. Trzcinski & D. Satyanathan (Eds.), *Moving families out of poverty* (pp. 19–25). Michigan Family Impact Seminar Briefing Report, 2001–2. Detroit, MI: Wayne State University.

Bloom, D. (1997). *After AFDC: Welfare-to-work choices and challenges for states.* New York, NY: Manpower Demonstration Research Corporation.

Bloom, D., & Michalopoulos, C. (2001). *How welfare and work policies affect employment and income: A synthesis of research.* New York: Manpower Demonstration Research Corporation.

Council of Economic Advisers. (1997). *Technical report: Explaining the decline in welfare receipt, 1993–1996.* A report by the Council of Economic Advisers. Washington, DC, May.

Council of Economic Advisers. (1999). *Economic expansion, welfare reform, and the decline in welfare caseloads: An update* [Technical Report]. A report by the Council of Economic Advisers, Washington, DC, August.

Danziger, S., Corcoran, M., Danziger, S., Heflin, C., Kalil, A., Levine, J., Rosen, D., Seefeldt, K., Siefert, K., & Tolman, R. (2000). Barriers to the Employment of Welfare Recipients. In R. Cherry and W. Rodgers (Eds.), *Prosperity for all? The economic boom and African Americans* (pp. 245–278). New York: Russell Sage.

Danziger, S. K., & Seefeldt, K. S. (2000). Ending welfare through Work First: Manager and client views. *Families in Society, 81*(6), 593–604.

Figlio, D. N., & Ziliak, J. P. (1999). Welfare reform, the business cycle, and the decline in AFDC caseloads. In S. Danziger (Ed.), *Economic conditions and welfare reform.* Kalamazoo, MI: W. E. Upjohn Institute. pp. 86–115.

Holcomb, P. A., Pavetti L., Ratcliffe, C., & Riedinger, S. (1998). *Building an employment focused welfare system: Work First and other work-orientated strategies in five states.* Washington DC: The Urban Institute.

Isaacs, J. B., & Lyon, M. R. (2000). *A cross-state examination of families leaving welfare findings from ASPE-funded studies.* Washington, DC: Office of the Assistant Secretary for Planning and Evaluation, U. S. Department of Health and Human Services.

Johnson, N., Zahradnik, R., & McNichol, E. C. (2000). *State income tax burdens on low-income families in 2000: Assessing the burden and opportunities for relief.* Washington, DC: Center on Budget and Policy Priorities.

Lazere, E., Fremstad, S., & Goldberg, H. (2000). *States and counties are taking steps to help low-income working families make ends meet and move up the economic ladder.* Washington, DC: Center on Budget and Policy Priorities.

Loprest, P. (2001). *How are families that left welfare doing? A comparison of early and recent welfare leavers.* New Federalism, National Survey of America's Families, Series B, No. B-36 April. Washington, DC: The Urban Institute.

Miller, C., Knox, V., Auspos, P., Hunter-Manns, J., & Orenstein, A. (1997). *Making welfare work and work pay: Implementation and 18-month impacts of the Minnesota Family Investment Program.* New York: Manpower Demonstration Research Corporation.

Miller, C., Knox, V., Gennetian, L., Dodoo, M., Hunter, J., & Redcross, C. (2000). *Reforming welfare and rewarding work: Final report on the Minnesota Family Investment Program. Volume 1: Effects on adults.* New York: Manpower Demonstration Research Corporation.

Mishel, L., Bernstein, J., & Schmitt, J. (2000). *The state of working America 2000–2001.* DataZone: States at a Glance Fact Sheet. Washington, DC: Economic Policy Institute.

Moffitt, R. (1999). The effect of pre-PRWORA waivers on AFDC caseloads and female earnings, income, and labor force behavior. In S. Danziger (Ed.), *Economic conditions and welfare reform* (pp. 91–118). Kalamazoo, MI: W. E. Upjohn Institute for Employment Research.

Nathan, R. P., & Gais, T. L. (1999). Implementing welfare reform. In Rockefeller Reports, October 30, 1998, 5–7.

National Center for Children in Poverty (2000). *Child poverty state fact sheets.* New York, NY: Columbia University.

Riccio, J., Friedlander, D., & Freedman, S. (1994). *GAIN: Benefits, costs and three year impacts of a welfare-to-work program.* New York: Manpower Demonstration Research Corporation.

Schoeni, R. F. & Blank, R. M. (2000). *What has welfare reform accomplished? Impacts on welfare participation, employment, income, poverty and family structure.* Cambridge, MA: National Bureau of Economic Research, Working Paper 7627.

Schoeni, R. F., & Blank, R. M. (2000, February). *The effects of welfare reform and welfare waivers on welfare participation, employment, income, poverty, and family structure.* National Bureau of Economic Research, Working Paper 7627. Cambridge, MA: NBER.

Sweeney, E., Schott, L., Lazere, E., Fremstad, S., Goldberg, H., Guyer, J., Super, D., & Johnson, C. (2000). *Windows of opportunity: Strategies to support families receiving welfare and other low-income families in the next stage of welfare reform.* Washington, DC: Center on Budget and Policy Priorities.

U. S. Bureau of the Census (2000). *Poverty statistics 1999.* Ferret Data Extraction System. Washington, DC: U. S. Bureau of the Census. Last revised: September 29, 2000 (http://ferret.bls.census.gov).

U. S. General Accounting Office (1995). *Most AFDC training programs not emphasizing job placement.* GAO/HEHS-95-113. Washington, DC: U. S. GPO.

U. S. General Accounting Office (1998). *Welfare to work: States are restructuring programs to reduce welfare dependence.* GAO/HEHS-98-109. Washington, DC: U. S. GPO.

U. S. House Committee on Ways and Means (1996). *Overview of entitlement programs, 1996.* Washington, DC: U. S. GPO.

Wallace, G., & Blank, R. M. (1999). What goes up must come down? Explaining recent changes in public assistance caseloads. In S. Danziger (Ed.), *Economic conditions and welfare reform* (pp. 144–173). Kalamazoo, MI: W. E. Upjohn Institute.

Zahradnik, R, Johnson, N., & Mazerov, M. (2001). *State income tax burdens on low-income families in 2000: Assessing the burden and opportunities for relief* and *State fact sheets.* Washington, DC: Center on Budget and Policy Priorities.

Zedlewski, S., & Alderson, D. W. (2001). *Before and after reform: How have families on welfare changed?* New Federalism, National Survey of America's Families, Series B, No. B-32, April. Washington, DC: The Urban Institute.

Zedlewski, S., & Loprest, P. (2001). How well does TANF fit the needs of the most disadvantaged families? In E. Trzcinski, & D. Satyanathan (Eds.), *Moving families out of poverty* (pp. 29–34). Michigan Family Impact Seminars, No. 2001–2. Detroit, MI: Wayne State University.

Ziliak, J. P., Figlio, D. N., Davis, E. E., & Connolly, L. S. (2000). Accounting for the decline in AFDC caseloads: Welfare reform or the economy? *Journal of Human Resources, 35*(3), 570–86.

CAN AN ASSET-BASED WELFARE POLICY REALLY HELP THE POOR?

Editor's Note:
Governmental programs for the alleviation of poverty have traditionally provided resources for consumption. Obviously, it is necessary to meet the consumption needs of the poor. But proponents of asset-based social policies
believe that the poverty problem can more effectively address these needs by
helping the poor accumulate the economic and human capital that will lift
them out of their condition. Programs that match poor people's savings
deposits with government resources, thus encouraging them to save, are far
more useful than income-support programs, which merely maintain the poor
at basic consumption levels. Critics of this approach are not so sure. Though
they agree that an asset-development program has value, they doubt that it
offers a ready solution to the problem of poverty. Poverty, they contend, is so
widespread, serious, and intractable that we need large-scale government
intervention rather than individualized programs. Solving the problem of
poverty requires economic planning, the creation of new jobs, enhanced education and training, massive social investments, and similar measures rather
than the subsidization of individual savings.

Michael Sherraden, Ph.D., is professor of social work at the George Warren
Brown School of Social Work at Washington University, St. Louis, Missouri.
He is the coauthor of *The Moral Equivalent of War: A Study of Non-Military Ser-
vice in Nine Nations* (Greenwood Press, 1990), and *Assets and the Poor: A New
American Welfare Policy* (M. E. Sharpe., 1991).

James Midgley, Ph.D., is Harry and Riva Specht Professor of Public Social Services and dean of the School of Social Welfare at the University of California
at Berkeley. He has published widely on issues of social policy, social work,
and international social welfare. His most recent books include *Social Welfare
in Global Context* (Sage Publications, 1997), *Alternatives to Social Security* (with

Michael Sherraden, Greenwood Press, 1997), and *The Handbook of Social Policy* (Sage Publications, 2000).

YES

Michael Sherraden

My great-grandparents were immigrants who homesteaded in Kansas in the 1870s. They received 160 acres of land from the federal government. They worked hard, raised twelve children, held barn dances on Saturday nights, and left the community and the country a little better off. The Homestead Act, a massive asset give-away program, was one of the most successful domestic policies in American history. It rested on the Jeffersonian idea that people become better citizens in a democracy when they have a stake, assets, and ownership. Although the United States is no longer a nation of small farmers, the concept of stakeholding is just as relevant today as it was at the birth of the republic.

Despite the prominence of asset ownership in American values and American history, social policy in the modern welfare state—especially means-tested policy for the poor—has focused almost exclusively on the distribution of income for consumption. Indeed, means-tested policy usually prohibits savings and the accumulation of assets.

Of course, income and consumption are essential—many Americans lack enough food, basic shelter, and medical insurance of any kind. But income-based policy, by itself, does not help poor households develop economically. Income-based policy traps families in a cycle of spending that goes from check to check. Yet few families manage to spend their way out of poverty. After more than fifty years of income-maintenance policy, we have confirmed that this approach is correctly named: It provides only maintenance, not development.

ASSETS: A DIFFERENT PERSPECTIVE

We must consider a different approach. Social policy, including welfare policy, should promote asset accumulation. In addition to the income and consumption policy of the current welfare state, asset-based policy would focus on savings and investment.

The rationale for this new direction can be stated in two parts. First, for the vast majority of households, the pathway out of poverty is through savings and accumulation. Reaching important economic development goals almost always requires the prior store of assets. People need assets to move to a better neighborhood, send a child to college, purchase a home, start a small business, or achieve other economic goals. Second, when people begin to accumulate assets, their thinking and behavior change as well. In other words, while incomes feed people's stomachs, assets change their heads. Accumulation of assets leads to important psychological and social shifts that people don't achieve to the same degree by receiving and spending an equivalent amount of regular income. In contrast to mainstream economic thinking, I am suggesting that assets do more than provide a storehouse for future consumption. Moreover, I contend that the psychological and social impacts of asset accumulation are vital to household "welfare," or well-being. Why do assets matter?

- They help make households stable.
- They encourage long-term thinking and planning.
- They prompt the development of knowledge and skills (human capital).
- They provide a foundation for risk taking.
- They boost personal efficacy and self-esteem.
- They increase social status and influence.
- They inspire political involvement and community participation.

Altogether, these effects of assets can contribute substantially to the well-being and development of poor households.[1]

THE DISTRIBUTION OF ASSETS

Assets are much more unevenly distributed than income. Looking at income, the top 5 percent of the population receives about as much annual income as the bottom 40 percent. But looking at assets, the top 1 percent holds about as much in assets as the bottom 90 percent.[2]

Asset statistics also tell us a great deal about racial inequality. African Americans have virtually never had the same access to asset accumulation as have European Americans. For example, at the time the federal government was doling out land to my great-grandparents, it was reneging on its promise of "forty acres and a mule" for freed slaves (Oubre, 1978). Today, the continuing discriminatory record of banks and savings-and-loan associations in making real-estate loans to African Americans is a national disgrace. Statistics show that, even when they have the same income as whites, blacks are much less likely to be granted a loan.[3] The result? African American

[1]These suggested effects of asset accumulation are discussed in Assets and the Poor (Sherraden, 1991). They are offered as propositions that have considerable intuitive appeal and certain theoretical and empirical support, although specific tests with poverty populations will be desirable.

[2]Asset-distribution data are from the Federal Reserve's Survey of Consumer Finances for 1989. Asset distribution in the United States grew considerably more unequal during the 1980s.

[3]Evidence of discrimination by race in home purchase and mortgage lending is overwhelming and pervasive. Studies consistently report steering of clients by real-estate agents, redlining of neighborhoods, and systematic loan denials by race. The Community Reinvestment Act of 1977 requires the Federal Reserve Board to keep statistics on mortgage lending. These statistics indicate strong racial bias, particularly against African Americans.

households have only about one-eleventh the assets of white households (U.S. Bureau of the Census, 1990).

ASSETS AND DOMESTIC POLICY

The importance of asset accumulation has been virtually ignored in the anti-poverty policies of the welfare state. However, through the tax system, we do support asset accumulation for the non-poor, primarily in two categories: tax expenditures for home equity, and tax expenditures for retirement pension accounts. In these two categories: the federal government spends well over $100 billion each year, and the total is rising rapidly.[4] These two categories make up the bulk of asset accumulation in most American households, heavily subsidized by the federal government. Almost everyone would agree that these asset-accumulation policies have hugely benefited the country. Thus, we have asset-based policy for the non-poor, and we spend quite a lot of money on it. But we do not have asset-based policy for the poor.

Poor people, by and large, do not benefit from asset-accumulation tax policies. That's because they have no tax rates, or they have rates too low to receive substantial tax benefits. Perhaps worse, welfare transfer recipients, under current law, are restricted from accumulating ordinary savings and even business assets. Welfare policy, as currently structured, is anti-savings policy.

This situation does not make sense. As a nation, we should not be telling welfare recipients that they cannot save for a business, a home, or their children's education.

INDIVIDUAL DEVELOPMENT ACCOUNTS

One way to improve matters is to create a system of Individual Development Accounts (IDAs). IDAs would be a relatively simple and universal system of accounts similar to Individual Retirement Accounts (IRAs). IDAs would be optional, earnings-bearing, tax-benefited accounts in the name of each individual, initiated as early as birth, and restricted to designated purposes. Regardless of the category of social policy (housing, education, self-employment, retirement, or other), the poor could accumulate assets in these long-term, restricted accounts. The federal government would match deposits for the poor, and the potential would exist for creative financing through the private sector.

---

[4]A good source for estimates of tax expenditures is U.S. Congress, Joint Committee on Taxation (1989). Estimates of federal tax expenditures for fiscal years 1990–1994. Washington, DC: U.S. Government Printing Office.

In developing a single IDA policy structure, the government would limit complexity and better integrate various asset-based initiatives into an overall national strategy. Also, the policy would be essentially direct-to-the-beneficiary, with limited intervention by a welfare bureaucracy. The following general guidelines should be considered for IDAs:

- IDAs should complement income-based policy.
- The policy should be simple in both conceptual and administrative terms.
- The accounts should be voluntary.
- The accounts should receive favorable tax treatment.
- Federal and state governments should provide deposit matches for the poor.
- Creative participation by the corporate and nonprofit sectors should be actively encouraged.

Once the structure of Individual Development Accounts is in place, even with minimal direct funding from the federal government, opportunities would exist for a wide variety of creative funding projects from the private and nonprofit sectors. To build IDA accounts, one can imagine corporations' "adoption" of schools or neighborhoods, church fund raisers, contributions from civic organizations, bake sales, car washes, carnivals, student-run businesses, and so forth. The key is to establish a policy structure that could leverage private money with tax benefits, spark creative ideas and partnerships, attract diverse funding, and gradually expand as the policy demonstrates its worth.

At this writing, discussion of asset-based policy is increasing. An Individual Development Account Demonstration bill has been introduced in the U.S. House (HR 2258, Section B) by Tony Hall (D-OH) and Bill Emerson (R-MO); it has 135 co-sponsors from both parties. A similar bill has been introduced in the Senate (S 2086) by Bill Bradley (D-NJ). The states of Oregon and Iowa are planning statewide IDA applications. Local IDA experiments have sprung up in Tupelo, Mississippi, and Bozeman, Montana.

A NEW DIRECTION: SOCIAL POLICY AS INVESTMENT

Social policy should invest in the American people—and encourage them to invest in themselves—so that they can become stakeholders and active citizens. The key is to combine social policy with economic development through a program of asset building and stakeholding.

As a closing thought, Individual Development Accounts, or some other form of asset-based domestic policy, could become for the twenty-first century what the Homestead Act was for the nineteenth: an investment-oriented policy to develop individual capacity, strengthen families and communities, promote active citizenship, and contribute to economic growth.

NO

James Midgley

Of various alternatives to conventional policies for the alleviation of poverty, the asset approach is the most original and radical. As formulated by Sherraden (1991), this approach reorients existing anti-poverty policies by encouraging the accumulation of wealth rather than the payment of benefits for consumption. By helping the poor to save, the asset approach purports to really help them enter mainstream society.

THE ASSET-BASED APPROACH

The asset-based approach is critical of conventional anti-poverty programs. Many existing programs, such as Aid to Families with Dependent Children (AFDC), Food Stamps, and Medicaid, promote the consumption of goods and services. However, they fail to encourage savings and to engender behaviors that make the poor responsible, independent, and self-reliant. Though it is obvious that people can meet their basic needs only through consumption, critics contend that the continual provision of consumption goods to the poor simply maintains them at minimal levels of living. If the goal of social policy is the eradication of poverty, the poor must have an opportunity to escape poverty. Proponents argue that the asset approach helps poor people accumulate resources to lift themselves out of poverty, and helps them become self-reliant and self-respecting citizens.

At the core of the asset approach is the Individual Development Account (IDA), which, like the Individual Retirement Account (IRA), encourages savings. These accounts would be established for all individuals, and would be tax benefited to foster asset accumulation. Depending on the financial circumstances of the depositor, individual savings would be matched by state contributions at varying rates. For example, a person in severe financial need would have a match as high as 90 percent, while someone who is working and enjoying a relatively good income would receive no match at all. The matching system would be highly flexible and permit the government to supplement savings as individuals' economic circumstances change. The individuals themselves would manage the accounts. Thus they would become familiar with investment options and learn to use their money wisely. However, the accounts would be restricted so that individuals could make withdrawals only for approved purposes, such as the purchase of a home, education, retirement, or the establishment of a business. Accumulated IDA assets could be transferred to children at death or before death if desired.

Although the asset approach would not replace AFDC or other pro-grams that help the poor meet their basic needs, it would encourage AFDC recipients to deposit a part of their benefits into IDAs and would generously match their contributions. In this way, poor people would derive concrete financial benefits, and their predilection to be dependent on the state would be reduced.

Asset accumulation through IDAs would be a long-term process but would foster thrift and responsibility among the poor.

Consonant with the tenets of Jeffersonian liberalism, the political phi-losophy underlying the asset approach is essentially individualist in charac-ter and firmly rooted in the American experience. Indeed, this approach was first used in the United States in the form of the Homestead Act of 1862, which delivered about 200 million acres of land to settlers. Similar ap-proaches have been adopted in other countries; for example, the provident funds established in many former British colonial territories to provide an alternative to social security (Midgley, 1984). An asset approach was also introduced by General Pinochet's regime in Chile to replace the country's long-standing Social Security system (Borzutsky, 1992).

CAN ASSETS REALLY HELP THE POOR?

Most economists regard the mobilization of capital through personal savings as highly desirable. Whether operated on command, corporatist, or free-market principles, modern economies require investment to renew infras-tructure and establish productive enterprises. When ordinary citizens save, those individuals *and* the economy benefits. Through savings, people accu-mulate the resources they need to purchase goods and services. In this way, they contribute to aggregate demand, stimulating more production and employment.

Few would argue with these facts. However, the role of assets in solv-ing the problem of poverty poses some problems. Indeed, the implementa-tion of an assets approach through the creation of IDAs will not likely, *in itself*, really help the poor.

The poorest sections of the population, such as AFDC recipients, do not have the financial resources to save at appreciable levels. Even if supple-mented by the government, their meager savings can do little to help them escape poverty within a reasonable period of time. AFDC benefit levels are appallingly low. Despite propagandistic claims that recipients enjoy a com-fortable level of living at taxpayers' expense, these individuals actually endure a daily struggle to survive. The poorest sections of the population subsist on incomes that are below minimal physical survival levels, and below standards of decency that any civilized society would consider mini-mal. It is unlikely that these people would somehow find the resources to contribute to IDAs, and that their savings, even if supplemented by the state, would eventually propel them out of poverty. The prospects of saving to escape poverty are even more remote for those who have lost their homes and who survive through begging, scavenging, or scrounging on the streets.

The asset approach is designed to encourage responsibility and self-sufficiency among the poor. Indeed, it has far more potential to inculcate puritan attitudes than it does of generating the material resources people need to escape poverty. It has become fashionable to indict the moral behavior of the poor, but I doubt that poverty can be solved through the cultivation of middle-class values. Those who work with welfare mothers know that they manage their meager budgets with the hard-nosed acumen of small-town bankers. Their need for material resources, realistic employment opportunities, day care for their children, and adequate housing is far greater than their need for lessons on the virtues of thrift, sobriety, and self-reliance.

In addition to the problem of inadequate resources, the asset approach presents difficult economic, organizational, and political challenges. Subsidizing IDAs would be costly, especially if the government supplements them to a significant degree. Also, implementing the IDA program on a national level would pose formidable organizational issues. Such a program would have to be flexible enough to adjust quickly to people's changing economic circumstances. However, proponents of IDAs have no doubt that these problems, as well as political obstacles, can be overcome. Although the asset approach has secured bipartisan political support, only time will reveal whether this support will endure. To finance IDAs for the poor, proponents propose abolishing a variety of tax benefits that the non-poor currently enjoy. Given the realities of the political process, it is by no mean certain that political support for these proposals will hold steady as well-organized constituents protest reductions in the benefits they currently enjoy.

More fundamentally, the asset approach, like most other attempts to deal with poverty on an individual level, fails to address the basic causes of poverty and deprivation. Poverty has deep roots in economic and social structural factors, not in individuals' inability to save. Economic decline associated with de-industrialization and global economic changes, reduced employment opportunities in traditional blue-collar occupations, falling wages for those in regular employment, deteriorating urban areas, declining educational standards, cutbacks in human services, and entrenched inequalities all contribute much more to poverty today. If we hope to address the problem of poverty at these levels, we need comprehensive economic and social policies. Like other programs that attribute poverty to individual misfortune and that assign primary responsibility for escaping poverty to the individual, attempts to encourage the poor to save cannot eradicate poverty.

The most successful programs for the alleviation of poverty have implemented macroeconomic and social policies and mobilized the resources of the state on a large scale. Despite its many shortcomings, the Johnson administration's attempts to address the poverty problem sharply reduced the incidence of poverty (Marmor, Mashaw, & Harvey, 1990). The experiences of Western Europe and the newly industrializing East Asian nations, which have highly interventionist governments, offer further evidence of the effectiveness of collectivist solutions that combine economic and social policies through the powerful agency of the centralized, interventionist state (Esping Anderson, 1985; Midgley, 1986).

Of course, such strategies are unlikely to garner much political support in America's highly individualistic, enterprise culture. Here, the power of the central government is used to promote the accumulation of wealth among those who are already wealthy, rather than deal with pressing social ills. In this political climate, the asset approach may make a contribution. However, despite its advantages, it will not *really* help the poor.

REFERENCES

Borzutsky, S. (1992). The Chicago boys, social security and welfare in Chile. In H. Glennerster and J. Midgley (Eds.), *The radical right and the welfare state: An international assessment* (pp. 79–99). Savage, MD: Barnes and Noble.

Esping Anderson, G. (1985). *Politics against markets: The Social Democratic road to power.* Cambridge, MA: Harvard University Press.

Marmor, T. R., Mashaw, J. L., & Harvey, P. L. (1990). *America's misunderstood welfare state: Persistent myths, enduring realities.* New York: Basic Books.

Midgley, J. (1984). *Social Security, inequality and the Third World.* New York, NY: John Wiley and Sons.

Midgley, J. (1986). Welfare and industrialization: The case of the four little tigers. *Social Policy and Administration* 20, 225–238.

Oubre, C. F. (1978). *Forty acres and a mule: The Freedman's Bureau and black land ownership.* Baton Rouge, LA: Louisiana State University Press.

Sherraden, M. (1991). *Assets and the poor: A new American welfare policy.* Armonk, NY: M. E. Sharpe.

U. S. Bureau of the Census (1990). *Household wealth and asset ownership: 1988.* Washington, DC: U. S. Government Printing Office.

ARE AFFIRMATIVE-ACTION POLICIES INCREASING EQUALITY IN THE LABOR MARKET?

Editor's Note:
The United States uses two basic strategies to address racial, economic, and other injustices. The first is *nondiscrimination*, in which no preferential treatment is given to selected groups. The second is *affirmative action*, whose overall goal is to admit, hire, and promote women and minorities in direct proportion to their numbers in the population. Rigorous affirmative-action policies give preferential treatment to minority and female applicants. The ostensible purpose of this policy is to right past wrongs done to these groups. Some opponents of affirmative action argue that it leads to racial quota systems, preferential treatment, and reverse discrimination. They argue that it violates equal protection under the laws guaranteed in the Fourteenth Amendment. Still others argue that affirmative-action policies benefit those minorities who do not need help and puts whites who are innocent of any wrongdoing at a disadvantage. Affirmative action is one of the most controversial issues in American social policy and can evoke great passion among both its proponents and opponents.

Ann Rosegrant Alvarez, Ph.D., is an associate professor at the School of Social Work at Wayne State University, where she is co-chair of the Concentration on Community Practice and Social Action. She is also a member of the Council on Social Work Education's Commission on the Role and Status of Women. Her research interests include issues of race and gender, community practice, multicultural community organizing, and social-work policy and history. She has published in the areas of education and training for multicultural effectiveness, participatory research, the development of critical consciousness, and women activists.

Sally C. Pipes has served as president and chief executive officer of the Pacific Research Institute for Public Policy (PRI) since 1991. She addresses national and international audiences on healthcare, education, privatization, civil rights, and the economy, and has been interviewed on such television programs as *20/20, Politically Incorrect, Dateline,* and the *Today Show.* She has been featured in *Chief Executive* magazine, in which she writes a bimonthly column. Ms. Pipes also writes a regular column for *Investor's Business Daily's* "Brain Trust" column. Her opinion editorials have appeared in the *Los Angeles Times, San Francisco Examiner, San Francisco Chronicle, Los Angeles Daily News,* and the *Orange County Register.*

YES

Ann Rosegrant Alvarez

Americans are not noted for their interest in policy. Indeed, most U.S. Americans perceive matters of policy as boring, as well as largely irrelevant to their daily lives.[1] The exception is affirmative-action policies, which evoke a strong response from the American public. Witness the lively and frequent attention to this topic in the academic disciplines, including social work, sociology, public policy, political science, economics, and education (Bergmann, 1996; Chestang, 1996; Gibelman, 2000; Hall, 1996; Hoffman, 1997; Mor Barak, 2000; Ong, 1999; Orlans & O'Neill, 1992; Peebles-Wilkins, 1996; Reisch, 2000), as well as generous coverage by news media and on numerous Web sites devoted to the topic.[2] Everyone, it appears, has an opinion on affirmative action.

Why? In part, many Americans believe that they or their loved ones have been affected by these policies. This gives almost everyone a vested interest in the implementation and results of such policies. In addition, in a country in which issues of gender and—particularly—race are incendiary and omnipresent, it offers an arena to discuss, debate, and exert an impact on the retention, or the reform and dissolution of, racist and sexist norms and practices.

I assert that affirmative-action policies are increasing equality in the labor market. In this article, I briefly address the issues of why such policies were initially put into place. The subsequent discussion examines the three primary arguments used against affirmative-action policies: (1) They are unnecessary; (2) they are discriminatory or otherwise detrimental; and

---

[1]It is common usage to refer to residents of the United States of America as "Americans." However, many residents of Mexico and Canada perceive the appropriation of this word as imperialistic and arrogant, as well as inaccurate. Nevertheless, for purposes of consistency we will use the term *American* in this debate to refer to U.S. Americans.

[2]Given ever-changing online resources, citations of those currently available are not provided. A basic search on "Affirmative Action" will yield multiple possibilities.

(3) they are not effective. My conclusion emphasizes the social-justice perspective with regard to affirmative-action policies.

BACKGROUND: THE DEVELOPMENT
OF AFFIRMATIVE-ACTION POLICIES

Despite constitutional provisions and civil-rights laws guaranteeing equality and certain rights to all U.S. Americans, racial discrimination, inequality, and the resulting problems—including poverty—have remained prominent issues nationally and locally. During the 1960s, with civil rights at the forefront of the nation's consciousness, inequities in employment and promotion practices made access to jobs an obvious area for intervention. In 1961, President John F. Kennedy issued Executive Order 10925. The order established the Committee on Equal Employment Opportunity and for the first time required affirmative action to ensure nondiscrimination in employment. In 1965, President Lyndon B. Johnson directly addressed these issues in Executive Order 11246, later amended in 1967 to include gender discrimination. Johnson outlined the directive to "take affirmative action" in a stirring oratory in 1965, when he declared, "We seek not just freedom but opportunity—not just legal equity but human ability—not just equality as a right and a theory, but equality as a fact and as a result" (Brunner, 2001, pp. 1–2).

The concept of affirmative action has broadened during the intervening years, both in terms of the populations included and the settings and venues targeted (Orlans & O'Neill, 1992). Affirmative-action battles are raging in courts, human-resource departments, and admissions offices. A consideration of some of the important questions surrounding this issue may help to assess the value and efficacy of affirmative-action policies.

IS AFFIRMATIVE ACTION NECESSARY?

To answer the question, "Is affirmative action necessary?" let's consider similarities between unions and affirmative-action policies. Labor unions arose from members' desire to change inequitable and unjust employment practices, including hiring, promoting, and firing on grounds other than qualifications and seniority. Affirmative-action policies were similarly designed to address inequities, but with a focus on those related to gender and race or ethnicity.

Many opponents of affirmative-action policies argue that circumstances no longer warrant such intervention (if they ever did), because inequality of opportunities and participation does not exist. For example, Sally Pipes, president of the Pacific Research Institute, contends that women hold more than half of all professional positions (Pipes, 1996; Pipes & Lynch, 2001) and "nearly half of all managerial and executive positions" (Pipes & Lynch, 2001,

p. 2). However, data either do not support these claims or are highly subject to interpretation.

The U.S. Equal Employment Opportunity Commission reports that in 1999, women constituted 51 percent of those in the workforce defined as "Professionals" (U.S. EEOC, 2001b). Yet this category includes such traditionally female occupations as nurse, teacher, and librarian. These occupations typically include many women while offering low pay and low status relative to many other professional jobs in male-dominated fields (U.S. EEOC, 2001a). In addition, no corroboration exists of Pipes' and her coauthor's contention regarding "managerial and executive positions" (Pipes & Lynch, 2001, p. 2). In fact, within the semantically closest category reported on by the EEOC—"Officials & Managers"—female participation drops to only 33.2 percent (U.S. EEOC, 2001b). The unevenness revealed in statistics by race (U.S. EEOC, 2001b) is even more striking. Though all "minorities" combined account for 28.4 percent of overall employment participation, the category of "Professional" employment has only 18.2 percent minority participation. Just 13.7 percent minority participation is reported for positions classified as "Officials & Managers." The work of the Federal Glass Ceiling Commission also refutes the claims of those who attempt to minimize existing inequalities and the need to address them. This bipartisan body, created by the Civil Rights Act of 1991, released extensive findings corroborating inequities in the participation of women and minorities in leadership positions in U.S. corporations. Their findings included the following:

- Of senior-level male managers in Fortune 1000 industrial and Fortune 500 service industries, almost 97 percent were white, 0.6 percent African American, 0.3 percent Asian, and 0.4 percent Hispanic (Glass Ceiling Commission, 1995).
- Compared to the earnings of white males, African American men with professional degrees earned only 79 percent, and African American women with professional degrees earned only 60 percent (Glass Ceiling Commission, 1995).
- Based on surveys and reports, 95–97 percent of senior managers in Fortune 1500 companies are men; of these, 97 percent are white. In 1994, only two women were CEOs of Fortune 1000 companies (Glass Ceiling Commission, 1995).

This and other data demonstrate that women and people of color are not represented proportionately in the most highly ranked and highly paid jobs. Given that approximately proportional representation is a potential outcome of affirmative action, current employment statistics confirm an ongoing need for policies (and enforcement) to equalize hiring processes and patterns.

Going beyond this, Bergmann (1996) presents and evaluates data on wages, employment patterns, and occupational segregation. After extensive analysis, she concludes that "the argument that affirmative action programs have already accomplished so much that we no longer need any programs of this . . . type in the workplace cannot seriously be made by anyone who has examined the evidence of what is currently going on in the workplace" (p. 47).

Returning to the example of unions, let me point out that they are not universally beloved or respected. Clearly, many people believe that they promote abuses of the system, as well as further inequities. However, they still protect the rights of people who otherwise would be subjected to the arbitrary whims of employers. Many people believe that these safeguards are necessary, owing to human nature and the general tendency of people to want to hire, work with, and promote people with whom they are comfortable. Comfort comes from commonalities—including similarities of gender and race.

This point has important implications for affirmative-action policies. Current statistics suggest an ongoing necessity for such policies as well as a future need. This need will continue until or unless people change the way they evaluate and select applicants for jobs or schools, including committing to eliminating bias in the selection process.

ARE AFFIRMATIVE-ACTION POLICIES DISCRIMINATORY OR DETRIMENTAL?

To label "discriminatory" something that is designed to oppose and remedy the effects of discrimination smacks of circular reasoning. Behind affirmative action is the assumption—borne out by history—that a policy of "no intervention" creates discriminatory practice. But many people confuse reducing the unfair advantage traditionally enjoyed by some groups with creating an unfair advantage for others.

Peebles-Wilkins (1996) points out the inconsistency of those who contend that affirmative action unfairly advantages African Americans and who suggest that such privilege is unique to "minority" groups: "As a member of the African-American community, I have always been aware that preferential treatment and special privileges have existed for the children of the influential and wealthy, for recipients of political patronage, and for individuals with white or light-colored skin" (p. 8). Reducing such preferential treatment and privilege should not be confused with discrimination.

Nevertheless, many Americans believe that affirmative-action policies promote a "double standard" and "reverse discrimination" that unjustly penalize some people while furthering the interests of others who either do not deserve or have no special claim to or need for this "favoritism." That these beliefs persist is supported by the work of Kick and Fraser (2000), who present research findings that examine three themes underlying the beliefs that affirmative action is discriminatory. They cite Wilson (1978) and Bobo and Kluegel (1993) in defining "self-interest" as the primary perspective among whites that race-targeted programs limit their own opportunities and impose "costs such as support for non-white educational and employment opportunities" (Kick & Fraser, 2000, pp. 44–45). A second theme—"racial attitudes"—originates in "beliefs about the inherent inferiority of blacks and correspondingly prejudicial treatment of them" (p. 45). Finally, "stratification beliefs" represent a point of view that a true meritocracy exists, with unlimited opportunities for all, and with low accomplishment seen as a product of low ability, effort, or merit.

Even some African Americans, who might be presumed to have reason to favor affirmative-action policies, dispute their value. For example, many African American conservative columnists, including Armstrong Williams, Ken Hamblin, and Walter Williams, argue against such policies on various grounds, contending that they are paternalistic and debilitating to blacks. These policies, they maintain, promote a "victim" mindset that only exacerbates inequalities and performance differences along racial lines.

Noted African American social-work educator Peebles-Wilkins (1996) also expresses concerns about the potential and actual consequences of affirmative-action policies, including a stigmatizing impact on African Americans who others assume have been installed in positions for which they are unqualified. However, she ultimately asserts that although existing policies are imperfect, the United States needs some version of them. With respect to affirmative-action policies in educational settings, she concludes, "In summary, the very nature of our patriarchal, racially stratified society dictates that race and sex should be considered in faculty hiring and students admissions" (p. 9).

Finally, some scholars argue that affirmative-action policies create a diversity that benefits not only the obvious targets but society as a whole. For example, Bergmann (1996) cites the value of the "differing points of view, insights, values, and knowledge of the world that members of various groups bring to their roles" (p. 106).

ARE AFFIRMATIVE-ACTION POLICIES EFFECTIVE?

Clearly, equality in the labor market has increased over time and since the implementation of affirmative-action policies. For example, Ong (1999b) reports that the representation of women in the U.S. labor force increased from 24.7 percent in 1940 to 46.1 percent in 1995. For California, the corresponding increase was from 25.5 percent to 44.7 percent. In the broadcasting industry, women constituted 23.3 percent of full-time employees in 1971, and 41 percent by 1997. People of color increased their participation in this field as well, showing an increase from 9 percent of full-time broadcasting employees in 1971 to 20 percent in 1997 (NOW Foundation, 2001).

Wages of women compared to men, and wages of people of color compared to whites, reveal further good news. For example, the female-to-male average-earnings ratios for full-time workers in California, adjusted for education and experience, increased from 57 percent in 1959 to 70 percent in 1989 (Ong, 1999). The comparable ratio by race for men in California—that is, adjusted minority-to-white annual earnings ratios—shows the following changes between 1959 and 1989: for blacks, an increase from 68 percent to 74 percent; for Latinos, an increase from 86 percent to 88 percent; and for Asian Americans, an increase from 80 percent to 94 percent (Ong, 1999). Nationally, the median employment earning for women in 1965 (when affirmative action was being implemented) was 40 percent of that of men; by 1999, that had risen to 62 percent (U.S. Census Bureau, 2001).

What has caused these changes? This question is difficult to answer. One possible solution is to estimate the potential impact of eliminating affirmative-action efforts. Following a careful analysis of the impact of affirmative action on public-sector employment, Badgett (1999) refrained from making large generalizations about the extent of change that could result from the elimination of public-sector affirmative-action programs in California. However, she did conclude that "the direction of change—a loss of opportunities for women and people of color—is clear, even if the magnitude of the change is not" (p. 100).

This issue of the extent of the change merits a closer look. Even among those who support the concept and goals of affirmative action, some have reservations. They contend that affirmative action has had such negligible impact that it should be either revised or abandoned altogether. I believe that even if the extensive efforts to date have not produced the *intended* degree of change, reducing or eliminating these efforts would severely curtail the gains toward equality that *have* been made.

In defense of existing policies, Chestang (1996b) argues that although data may not confirm enormous gains for women and minorities as a result of affirmative-action policies, we must still consider the manner and strength of the implementation when assessing their impact. Chestang points out that rather than blaming affirmative-action policies for continuing inequalities, "it is more reasonable to assume that vigorous implementation of affirmative action policies might have resulted in greater gains for African Americans" (p. 10).

Comedian George Burns responded to a query about how he felt about growing older by stating: "Considering the alternative, it's not too bad at all" (Humorous Quotes . . . , 2001, p. 1). Given our current situation, do we have anything better to propose? Various authors and social critics have considered this question (Gibelman, 2000b; Loury, 2000; Mor Barak, 2000; Stout & Buffum, 2000). Their suggestions include focusing on certain professions, targeting all those who are economically deprived, enhancing competitive skills among those who currently benefit from affirmative action, intervening within organizational contexts, and broadening exposure to and positive experiences with affirmative action.

Within corporate settings, a number of strategies have been implemented. Some seem to be effective in changing the profile of those in executive ranks. These include mentoring programs; "succession planning," in which top executives select and develop women and minority replacement candidates for their positions; and the provision of special seminars or training opportunities, such as those provided through WOMEN Unlimited, that teach "how to succeed in a male-dominated environment" (*Business Week*, 1997, p. 5).

These approaches may have merit and, in the case of some, may have created positive change. But in the end, I think they would be most useful in conjunction with current affirmative-action policies, rather than as replacement strategies. In agreeing with this, Bergmann (1996) argues against a variety of potential alternative approaches based on improving education and training, providing assistance to all who come from economically disadvantaged backgrounds, and offering apprenticeship programs. While acknowledging the value of these different strategies in a supplementary role, she points out that they do not ultimately address the root causes of the problem: discrimination, in the form of racism and sexism.

CONCLUSION

Affirmative-action policies are not a matter purely for academic discourse, but are relevant and meaningful to the daily lives of many people. Of course, the debate around these issues can grow emotional and intense. Such issues tap into some of our most deeply felt beliefs about what is fair; who we are; and how we are perceived, judged, and valued. Affirmative-action proponents and opponents alike will use the same data and draw different conclusions—although each side may think that the preponderance of evidence supports its case.

To be sure, many thoughtful and well-intentioned people oppose affirmative-action policies for the reasons mentioned, and probably for others as well. I believe that either these opponents are not fully informed on the issues and do not fully appreciate the circumstances surrounding affirmative action, or that their motives are suspect. Both data and accompanying narratives establish that (1) there is a continuing need for affirmative action, (2) it is not discriminatory, and any negative side effects are outweighed by its benefits, and (3) it has been effective, although it has not made as much of a difference to date as its proponents originally hoped for.

Moreover, a social-justice perspective ultimately mandates the continuation of affirmative-action policies and efforts. Chestang (1996a) advocates from this perspective, exhorting that "affirmative action should be supported because it is right, it is ethical, it is fair, and it is in the best of American tradition" (p. 14). It seems specious or naive to argue against this approach, when reports document that "prejudice against minorities and white women continues to be the single most important barrier to their advancement" (p. 15). If this is true—and I believe there is overwhelmingly evidence that it is—then we cannot expect huge gains in equality from programs designed to increase individual potential through improvements in education, from diversity training in the workplace, or from a laissez-faire approach. Instead, the most effective approach is to continue with a variety of supplementary efforts, but with an aggressive and progressive implementation of existing affirmative-action policies at the center of those efforts.

NO

Sally C. Pipes

Any essay that addresses "equality" and "affirmative action" must first define both terms. The slipperiness of definitions has been a constant source of vexation in the debate over preferential treatment. "Crucial terms such as *minority, equal opportunity, discrimination, racism, sexism* and even the term *affirmative action* itself, have never been given unambiguous definitions," writes philosopher Steven Yates in his 1994 book *Civil Wrongs: What Went Wrong with Affirmative Action.* "In practice, they have come to mean whatever politicians, federal judges, compliance officers, and other bureaucrats want them to mean."

Although common, the term *equality* is not self-defining. And when thrown into the politically charged debate over affirmative action, it means many different things to many different people. When we say "equal," for example, do we mean that every individual has an equal opportunity to apply for a job and that all applications will be judged by the same standards? In other words, do we mean that there shall be no signs reading that Irish or blacks "need not apply"? Or does "equal" mean that the racial and ethnic composition of a U.S. company's workforce—or perhaps the workforce of an industry—matches the overall composition of the U.S. population?

Now let's consider *affirmative action.* At times, this term describes everything from advertising in ethnic publications to increasing the applicant pool to laying off one employee rather than another based solely on the consideration of race. The latter situation happened to Sharon Taxman, a high-school business teacher in Piscataway, New Jersey. Faced with the need to reduce its staff by one teacher, the school district failed to use an unbiased method for determining which of two equally senior teachers it would lay off. Instead, citing its affirmative-action plan, it handed the pink slip to Taxman, who was white, and kept a black teacher on the payroll. In this case, race was the only factor that mattered, and Taxman was simply a member of the wrong race.

For the purposes of this essay, I base my "no" answer to the question, "Does affirmative action increase equality in the labor market?" on specific definitions of both *affirmative action* and *equality.* I define *affirmative action* to mean programs that provide individuals of preferred groups, usually (but not always) those deemed underrepresented, a bonus when they apply for admission to universities, for jobs, and for government contracts. "Affirmative action in the labor market," write two prominent economic researchers on the effects of affirmative action, "[are] policies or actions that might encourage anything other than race- or sex-blind behavior in the labor market" (Holzer & Neumark, 1999a). I'm not maintaining that race is the only factor, but only that it is an important factor and can become the only factor that matters, as in Taxman's case. (Indeed, if it were not important, why would anyone worry if affirmative-action programs disappeared?)

I define *equality* in relation to individuals, not groups. That is, equality is achieved when similarly situated individuals are judged by the same standards—treated equally—regardless of race. An athletic analogy proves instructive here. Equality means that everyone plays by the same rules: In baseball, all batters get three strikes before they are called out and four balls before they are awarded first base. In basketball, the basket is ten feet high for everyone, the free throw line is the same distance from the basket, and everyone gets two points for a bucket, unless they're firing from outside the three-point perimeter.

My definitions are not arbitrary. In fact, they cut to the heart of the matter in our constitutional republic. The Declaration of Independence—the best statement of the moral principles on which the United States was founded—speaks of the "self-evident" truth "that all men are created equal." The authors understood this equality to be an equality of rights, not an equality of condition. The former is dictated by moral philosophy; the latter is impossible given the different tastes and talents that each of us possesses. Our forefathers certainly didn't live up to the lofty principles they laid out for themselves and their progeny. But it has been in the pursuit of these principles, which Abraham Lincoln called "a standard maxim for free society," that the United States has been at its best. And indeed, it was the ability of civil-rights leaders to extol these principles and show how far the United States had to travel to achieve them that gave them the moral energy to end legal segregation and employment discrimination. Congressional backers of the 1964 Civil Rights Act assured Americans that the Act would protect individual, not group rights. "[Show me] any language which provides that an employer will have to hire on the basis of percentage or quota related to color, race, religion, or national origin," proclaimed chief Senate sponsor Hubert H. Humphrey, "[and] I'll start eating the pages one after another, because it's not there" (Pipes, 1996, p. 83).

Yet it wasn't long after the ink on the Act had dried before ambitious civil servants set about to transform it. Soon, they interpreted the Act to mandate that employers with more than one hundred employees had to report the racial composition of their workforces to the government. Any employer with fifty or more employees that contracted with the government was forced to develop affirmative-action plans with goals and timetables to achieve racial balance in their workforce. The result? An inescapable contradiction—like an elephant in a living room—sits at the center of U.S. civil-rights law. In order not to discriminate based on race—that is, not to use race as a factor in employment decisions—employers must take race into account and use it to make decisions. In the extreme, this means that Sharon Taxman loses her job based on nothing more than her race. In less extreme formulations, it means that two individuals, who are otherwise equally qualified for a job, are not equal in terms of race. The person of the preferred race is "a little more equal" and, hence, gets the job. The inescapable conclusion is that such programs do not promote—in fact they directly violate—the achievement of equality in the labor market. But setting aside the harm affirmative action does to individual equality, what of the argument that it promotes equality in the statistical sense when applied to groups? Supporters often claim that affirmative action has promoted equality, defined as increasing the absolute number and percentage of African Americans and other minorities in the labor market. However, the evidence is mixed.

Though it's convenient to mark the economic progress of African Americans after 1964, when the Civil Rights Act passed and was signed into law, such practice is misleading. African Americans were in fact making significant gains in the labor market in the decades before the passage of the Act. As economist Thomas Sowell documents, African Americans more than doubled their level of employment in technical and managerial fields from 1954 to 1964 (Sowell, 1984). "In other kinds of occupations," writes Sowell, "the advance of blacks was even greater during the 1940s—when there was little or no civil rights policy—than during the 1950s when the civil rights revolution was in its heyday" (Stephan & Thurnstrom, 1997). Hispanics and Asians made significant pre-affirmative-action employment gains as well, which contradicts the notion that all would be lost if it weren't for federally enforced race-conscious programs. "The notion that the Civil Rights Act and 'affirmative action' have had a dramatic impact on the economic progress of minorities has become part of the folklore of the land," concludes Sowell (1984, p. 80), which was "established primarily through repetition and vehemence, rather than evidence."

What about more recent evidence? Economic studies generally show that large firms with federally mandated affirmative-action programs employ a larger proportion of African Americans than firms that do not operate government-supervised affirmative-action programs (Thomas, 2000; Holzer & Neumark, 1998, 1999). As expected, these programs increase the statistical likelihood that protected minorities will be hired and decrease the likelihood that white males will be hired. "Affirmative action is associated with increases of about 15 percent in the probabilities of hiring white women and black men," conclude economists Harry Holzer and David Neumark in an extensive study of new hire data; "The probability that a white male is hired is lower by about 20 percent" (Holzer & Neumark, 1999b). And evidence suggests that the reason these programs succeed is that they give minority applicants preferences for the jobs. They do so by looking beyond simply formal qualifications, such as academic achievement, to determine whether individuals are capable of performing tasks (Thomas, 2000). Nonpreferred applicants are not afforded the same consideration, however. The result: Minorities hired into firms practicing affirmative action have lower education attainment than whites. Although these programs cost firms money, the minorities do not perform worse than their white colleagues, according to formal evaluation measures.

So these programs may increase equality by one measure, assuming that minorities are underrepresented in such firms in the jobs into which they are hired. Yet they also violate other measures of equality. How? By definition, they treat applicants differently based on their race and gender. But even if we limit ourselves to the group definition of equality, it's still not clear that they advance it in the labor market. After all, many firms are not forced to maintain government-supervised affirmative-action programs. Thus these programs may simply shift employment from the firms that don't practice affirmative action—which are smaller—to firms that do.

Which members of the preferred groups benefit most from affirmative-action programs? A 1995 study of affirmative-action programs in 138 companies in Philadelphia found that such programs concentrated the benefits among managers but didn't extend down the ranks (Bolick, 1995). An investigation of a Houston program that gives preferences to minority-owned businesses in contracting found that the benefits were concentrated among politically well connected companies (Houston Chronicle, 2001). An audit of a federal set-aside program for small minority businesses found that owners of thirty-five companies that participated were millionaires.

There's no guarantee that affirmative-action programs will continue to primarily benefit the group for which they were designed: African Americans. Along with the shift from equality of opportunity to equality of results that occurred soon after the passage of the 1964 Civil Rights Act, the justification for affirmative action has undergone a significant transformation in recent years. Originally, affirmative action was justified on remedial grounds— America had clearly wronged African Americans. Thus it was "just" to provide blacks with a leg up. "You don't take a person who for years has been hobbled by chains and liberate him, bring him up to the starting line of a race and then say, you're free to compete with all the others, and justly believe that you've been completely fair" (Pipes, 1996, p. 71), President Lyndon Johnson said in a speech at Howard University in 1964. In that speech, Johnson expressed these sentiments: "It's not enough to open the gates of opportunity. All of our citizens need to be able to walk through those gates."

But affirmative action expanded to include other groups. Many individuals who only recently immigrated to the United States were never shackled with the chains of historic U.S. wrongs. Thus the remedial justification became tenuous. Diversity—the idea that governments must manage the composition of institutions to reflect the demographics of any given area—became the reigning justification for affirmative-action programs. "As long as the rationale runs both ways" (Pipes, 1996, p. 107), said President Bill Clinton in reference to his support of Taxman's firing to meet an affirmative-action plan. Clinton later stated he would support the firing of minority teachers to preserve the jobs of a white teacher, so long as it was necessary for diversity.

This shift is important. First, remedial affirmative action should be limited in time and scope. However, managing diversity is a never-ending process that necessitates a permanent bureaucratic establishment. The concept also no longer privileges African Americans, the group whose unique history provides the most compelling justification for preferential treatment. In fact, considering that the African American population is growing, the diversity justification promises to work against their interests if ever faithfully applied. Though underrepresented in many jobs, African Americans are overrepresented in some important sectors. In California, African Americans constituted 7.8 percent of the population but 11.6 percent of the state's civil-service jobs in 1996 (Lynch, 1996a). In that same year, Shirley Paige, an African American, found she couldn't get promoted because the correctional department for which she worked needed Hispanics in senior positions (Lynch, 1996b). Many departments actually set goals and timetables for white men, who were underrepresented throughout most of the state's workforce (Lynch, 1996b). Such action is perfectly consistent with affirmative action's pursuit of diversity. "Diversity could tip the balance in favor of a white teacher if the composition of the department would have otherwise included no white teacher" (Pipes, 1996, p. 43), wrote a high-ranking government lawyer in a brief defending the Taxman firing.

Such results aren't likely to occur in the next few years. But given the reigning diversity argument for affirmative action and the changing demographics of the United States, a few isolated experiences in California may well become a pattern in other cities and states that are rich in ethnic diversity. When this occurs, it may finally be obvious to the most ardent defenders of government-supervised affirmative action that it doesn't promote true equality in the labor market. In fact, it does the exact opposite.

REFERENCES

Badgett, M. V. (1999). The impact of affirmative action on public-sector employment in California, 1970–1990. In P. Ong (Ed.), *Impacts of affirmative action: Policies & consequences in California* (pp. 83–102). Walnut Creek, CA: AltaMira Press.

Bergmann, B. R. (1996). *In defense of affirmative action.* New York: Basic Books.

Bobo, L., & Kluegel, J. (1993). Opposition to race-targeting: Self-interest, stratification ideology, or racial attitudes? *American Sociological Review, 58*, 443–464.

Bolick, C. (1995). A glimpse at private-sector preference policies. *Wall Street Journal,* October 11, A–15.

Brunner, B. (2001). Timeline of affirmative action milestones. Retrieved May 22, 2001, from http://www.infoplease.com/spot/affirmativetimeline1.html.

Business Week. (1997). Breaking through. Retrieved May 23, 2001 from http://www .businessweek.com/1997/07/b35141.htm.

Chestang, L. (1996a). Is it time to rethink affirmative action? No! *Journal of Social Work Education, 32*(1), 12–15.

Chestang, L. W. (1996b). Response to Wilma Peebles-Wilkins. *Journal of Social Work Education, 32*(1), 9–11.

Gibelman, M. (2000). Affirmative action at the crossroads: A social justice perspective. *Journal of Sociology and Social Welfare,* 27 (1), 153–174.

Glass Ceiling Commission (1995). Executive summary. Retrieved July 3, 2001, from http://www.ilr.cornell.edu/library/e_archive/gov_reports/GlassCeiling/ documents/GlassCeilingExecSummary.pdf.

Hall, R. E. (1996). Occupational aspiration among African-Americans: A case for affir-mative action. *Journal of Sociology and Social Welfare, 23*(4), 117–128.

Heritage Foundation. (2001a). The Heritage Foundation: Who we are. Retrieved February 15, 2001, from http://www.heritage.org/whoweare/.

Heritage Foundation. (2001b). The Heritage Foundation's Board of Trustees. Retrieved February 15, 2001, from http://www.heritage.org/departments/trustees.html.

Hoffman, D. M. (1997). A collection of thoughts and findings on affirmative action. *Journal of Progressive Human Services, 8*(2), 7–28.

Holzer, H., & Neumark, D. (1998). What does affirmative action do? *NBER Working Paper 6605,* June.

Holzer, H., & Neumark, D. (1999a). Are affirmative action hires less qualified? Evi-dence from employer-employee data on new hires. *Journal of Labor Economics,* 17(3), pp 534–569.

Holzer, H., & Neumark, D. (1999b). Assessing affirmative action. *NBER Working Paper 7323,* August, pp. 4–5.

Houston Chronicle (2001, January 7). Privileged few reap concessions' benefits, critics claim, p. A6.

Humorous Quotes. (2001). Retrieved June 29, 2001, from http://www.lifeisajoke .com/quotes_html.htm.

Kick, E. L., & Fraser, J. (2000). An examination of support or non-support for affirmative action, race-targeted and income-targeted policies. *Journal of Poverty, 4*(3), 43–69.

Loury, G. C. (2000). Who cares about racial inequality? *Journal of Sociology and Social Welfare, 27*(1), 133–151.

Lynch, M. (1996a). Affirmative action in California's state civil service: Who is really underrepresented and why?" Pacific Research Institute for Public Policy, October.

Lynch, M. (1996b, October 3). Reverse discrimination works both ways. *Wall Street Journal,* October 3, p. C-8.

Mor Barak, M. E. (2000). Beyond affirmative action: Toward a model of diversity and organizational inclusion. *Administration in Social Work, 23*(3/4), 47–68.

Morrison, A. M (1992). *The new leaders: Guidelines on leadership diversity in America.* San Francisco, CA: Jossey-Bass.

NOW Foundation (2001). Affirmative action in the broadcasting industry. Retrieved May 23, 2001, from http:/www.nowfoundation.org/communications/tv/affirmative.html.

Ong, P. (Ed.). (1999a). *Impacts of affirmative action: Policies and consequences in California.* Walnut Creek, CA: AltaMira Press.

Ong, P. (1999b). Race and gender in California's labor market. In P. Ong (Ed.), *Impacts of affirmative action: Policies and consequences in California.* Walnut Creek, CA: AltaMira Press.

Orlans, H., & O'Neill, J. (1992). Affirmative action revisited. *The Annals of the American Academy of Political and Social Science* (entire issue), 523.

Peebles-Wilkins, W. (1996). Is it time to rethink affirmative action? Yes! *Journal of Social Work Education, 32*(1), 5–9.

Pipes, S. (1996). Creating a crisis in a free society. In R. J. Simon (Ed.), *From data to public policy: Affirmative action, sexual harassment, domestic violence and social welfare* (pp. 1–6). New York, NY: Women's Freedom Network & University Press of America, Inc.

Pipes, S., & Lynch, M. (2001). Women don't need affirmative action. Retrieved February 15, 2001, from http://www.heritage.org/views/op-sp1.html.

Reisch, M. (2000). Social workers and politics in the new century. *Social Work, 45*(4), 293–297.

Sowell, T. (1984). *Civil rights: Rhetoric or reality?* New York, NY: Free Press.

Stephan, R., & Thurnstrom (1997). *America in black and white: One nation, indivisible* New York, NY: Aldine.

Stout, K. D., & Buffum, W. E. (2000). The commitment of social workers to affirmative action. *Journal of Sociology and Social Welfare, 20*(2), 123–135.

Thomas, W. (2000). Mitigating barriers to black employment through affirmative action regulations: A case study. *The Review of Black Political Economy*, Winter, pp. 80–102.

Thomas, W., & Garrett, M. (1999). U. S. and California affirmative action policies, laws, and programs. In P. Ong (Ed.), *Impacts of affirmative action: Policies and consequences in California* (pp. 25–58). Walnut Creek, CA: AltaMira Press.

U. S. Census Bureau (2001). Historical income tables—People. Retrieved July 3, 2001, from http://www.census.gov/hhes/income/histinc/p53.html.

U. S. Equal Employment Opportunity Commission (2001a). Job patterns for minorities and women in private industry: A glossary. Retrieved May 23, 2001, from http://www.eeoc.gov/stats/jobpat/glossary.html.

U. S. Equal Employment Opportunity Commission. (2001b). Occupational employment in private industry by race/ethnic group/sex, United States, 1999. Retrieved May 23, 2001, from http://www.eeoc.gov/stats/jobpat/1999/national.html.

Wilson, W. J. (1978). *The declining significance of race: Blacks and changing American institutions.* Chicago, IL: The University of Chicago Press.

IS PRIVATIZING SOCIAL SECURITY GOOD FOR WOMEN?

Editor's Note:
Proposals to fully or partially privatize Social Security in the United States have come from several quarters, including former president Bill Clinton. Supporters argue that privatization enables the individuals to control the Social Security portion of their retirement plan. Moreover, successful investors who never touch their accumulations could achieve higher rates of return and higher benefits than Social Security provides. The question of privatizing Social Security played an important role in the 2000 presidential election. George W. Bush proposed making personal retirement accounts part of Social Security reform, thereby letting workers divert part of their Social Security payroll tax to private investment accounts. Bush's plan would convert the 65-year-old program from one based exclusively on guaranteed benefits into one in which private markets and investment risk would figure prominently for the first time. In contrast, Bush's rival, Al Gore proposed that the government match eligible individuals' contributions with tax credits that would vary according to income. Despite the salience of these arguments, it seems likely that at least a portion of the Social Security system will be privatized in the future.

William W. Beach is director, Center for Data Analysis, The Heritage Foundation.

Patricia Ireland is a prominent national political figure and the longest-serving president (1991–2001) of the National Organization for Women. Ireland has led that organization's 500,000 members and contributing supporters in a campaign to warn women about the dangers of privatizing the Social Security system. She appears often on television and is frequently sought out for comments on current and controversial issues. Ms. Ireland is the author of the popular political autobiography, *What Women Want* (Dutton, 1996; and Plume, 1997). Currently a consultant in Washington, DC, she graduated cum laude from the University of Miami Law School in 1975.

YES

William W. Beach

Social Security's Old-Age and Survivors Insurance (OASI) program—certainly the United States' most important old-age income program—is quickly becoming the country's most expensive public policy liability. After sixty-six years of providing relatively certain income maintenance during retirement or after the premature death of a spouse, the oncoming retirement bubble of the baby-boom generation threatens to undermine the system. If Congress and the president fail to act soon, Social Security will be unable to meet its obligations by the time the boomers' children start to retire.[1]

Social Security's financial challenges are hardly news. Indeed, nearly a decade of debate and discussion by advocates and critics of the system have made these challenges clear to anyone interested in the subject. If any aspect of the current disputes over Social Security's future is settled, it is that dark financial clouds hang over the retirement system's next fifty years. So, why have Congress and the president failed to act?

Most questions about politicians' behavior can be answered by studying voters' behavior. The truth is that the politics behind the debate over Social Security's financial future have been shaped by a false opposition: that the current system is secure and that reform would be too risky. The widespread public acceptance of this opposition has, in turn, spawned complacency among political leaders. They have failed to act in the system's best financial interests.

This inaction should be particularly worrisome to groups that historically have depended most on Social Security for their retirement income: minorities and women. Women depend more on Social Security for their retirement than men. Minority women depend on it more than women generally. Why? Women's lifetime earnings commonly are below those of men. When combined with earnings discrimination and less access to pensions, these lower earnings also lead to lower lifetime savings.[2] Sparser retirement

---

[1] The Trustee's Report for 2001 states that Social Security will have exhausted its assets (principally special-issue Treasury notes) by 2038, after which it will have to cut benefits by 23 percent or raise taxes by a proportional degree to pay scheduled benefits. See *2001 Annual Report of the Board of Trustees of the Federal Old-Age and Survivors Insurance and Disability Insurance Trust Funds*, March 19, 2001, p. 10.

[2] For a discussion of savings and pension disparities between men and women, see Lois Shaw and Catherine Hill, "The Gender Gap in Pension Coverage: What Does the Future Hold," Institute for Women's Policy Research, IWPR Publication #E507, May 15, 2001.

savings is an especially acute problem among unmarried women. Poverty rates among widows and among divorced, separated, and never-married women are 66 and 47 percent higher, respectively, than their male counterparts.[3]

Given these financial challenges, one would expect that women especially would be interested in any change to Social Security's retirement program that would improve their retirement income and lifetime savings. However, the widespread impression that Social Security offers a more secure and superior retirement program compared to most private alternatives stands squarely in the way of reform.

Just how secure and superior is OASI? After the tens of thousands of dollars in payroll taxes that a worker must pay into Social Security, will the system return retirement income at a rate that is at least as good as the poorest-paying, private retirement-savings program? Is the system supporting the development of intergenerational capital in low- and moderate-income households, or is it inadvertently discouraging savings and thereby contributing to intergenerational poverty?

SOCIAL SECURITY'S RATES OF RETURN

The Social Security system's rate of return for most Americans will prove vastly inferior to what they could expect to earn by placing their payroll taxes in even the most conservative private investments. For a thirty-year-old low-income African American woman, the news is particularly grim: She is likely to receive just a little bit more from the system than she paid in taxes (after accounting for the effects of inflation). Staying in the current system likely consigns her to an inflation-adjusted return rate of only 1.2 percent. In other words, she could probably earn about as much toward her retirement by saving in an interest-bearing checking account.

If Americans were allowed to direct their payroll taxes into safe investment accounts similar to 401(k) plans, or even supersafe U.S. Treasury bonds, they would accumulate far more money in savings for their retirement years than they are ever likely to receive from Social Security. For example:

1. **Social Security pays a very low rate of return for two-income households with children.** Social Security's inflation-adjusted rate of return is only 1.02 percent for an average household of two thirty-year-old earners with children in which each parent made just under $26,000 in 2000.[4] Such couples will pay a total of about $380,400 in Social Security taxes

---

[3]Ekaterina Shirley and Peter Spiegler, "The Benefits of Social Security Privatization for Women," The Cato Institute, *Social Security Privatization No. 12,* July 20, 1998, p. 1.

[4]This rate of return calculation assumes that both adults were born in 1967.

over their lifetime (including employer payments) and can expect to receive benefits of about $403,100 (before applicable taxes) after retiring at age sixty-seven, the retirement age when they become eligible for full Social Security Old-Age benefits.[5] Had they placed that same amount of lifetime employee and employer tax contributions into conservative tax-deferred IRA-type investments–such as a mutual fund composed of 50 percent U.S. government Treasury bonds and 50 percent equities—they could expect a real return rate of over 5 percent per year prior to the payment of taxes after retirement. In this latter case, the total amount of income accumulated by retirement would equal approximately $1,203,600 (before applicable taxes).

2. **The rate of return for some ethnic minorities is negative.** Low-income, single African American men born after 1959 face a negative real rate of return from Social Security. For every dollar he has paid into Social Security, a single black man in his mid-twenties who earned about 50 percent of the average wage, or about $14,200, in 2000 can expect to get back less than 60 cents. This negative rate of return translates into lifetime cash *losses* of $74,683 on the taxes paid by the employer and employee.

Black women typically live longer than their male counterparts, yet even they have a rate of return lower than that of the general population. A twenty-one-year-old African American single mother who in 1996 made just under $20,900 (the average for black women) can look forward to a real rate of return on her Social Security taxes of only 0.97 percent. Under conservative assumptions, if she had saved those same tax dollars in a private investment account composed of government bonds, she would have received a real return of around 3 percent per year. With a mixed portfolio of bonds and equities, she could expect a return on her investments of at least 4.8 percent. This means that even with a low risk and low yield portfolio composed entirely of Treasury bonds, this single mother could have generated at least $205,000 more in savings toward her retirement (before applicable taxes) than she would enjoy under Social Security.[6]

---

[5]Total taxes paid and benefits received are expressed in nominal dollars. Social Security taxes are defined as Old-Age and Survivors Insurance (OASI) contributions, less (where applicable) an amount that would buy a life-insurance policy equivalent to the value of the coverage provided by (preretirement) Survivors Insurance. In 2000, the tax rate for OASI was 10.7 percent of all wages and self-employment income less than $80,400, as of year end. Unless stated otherwise, a discount rate is not applied to these amounts.

[6]These calculations assume that, upon retirement, this single woman annuitizes the lump sum that she accumulated at a real interest rate of 2.7 percent over 15 years. The current federal-income tax rates (with current rate structure, exemptions, tax bands, and deductions adjusted by inflation as mandated in current legislation) are applied against this annuity income.

A married woman with a good job whose husband dies before his retirement could receive a paltry $255 death benefit from Social Security—and nothing more. The current Social Security program transforms taxes from current workers into income for current retirees. However, if a married worker dies before retirement and has no children aged eighteen or younger, he or she will likely receive no benefits other than the burial fee paid to the surviving spouse.

WHY RATES OF RETURN MATTER

Defenders of Social Security argue that return rates are irrelevant to the OASI portions of the program. Social Security, they suggest, was intended to provide a basic but decent retirement income to beneficiaries and stopgap incomes for surviving spouses. Future Social Security beneficiaries, they argue, should be saving now for additional retirement income to supplement OASI benefits. Thus, they maintain that comparing rates of return on private pension investments with those from a public retirement program intended to pay out at least 35 percent of the wages an average worker earned is akin to comparing apples with oranges.[7]

This line of reasoning contains a fundamental flaw. If Social Security taxes were low enough to enable workers to save these additional dollars for their retirement, apologists for the system might conceivably be correct in characterizing Social Security as a pension program of last resort. But Social Security taxes are not low, and they are crowding out the ability of most low- and middle-income Americans to save for retirement. Thus, the rate of return on these taxes is vital, especially for those Americans for whom Social Security is their main retirement savings.

Crowding Out Savings

As payroll taxes have risen, many more Americans have fewer dollars left over for supplemental retirement investment. Over the past twenty-five years, Congress and the president have increased Old-Age and Survivors benefits so often and so much that today the high payroll taxes needed to pay those current benefits crowd out private retirement investments.[8] In 1972, the

---

[7]See Social Security Administration, "Findings and Recommendations," *1997 Annual Report of the Board of Trustees of the Federal Old-Age and Survivors Insurance and Disability Insurance Trust Funds*, Communication from the Board of Trustees of the Federal Old-Age and Survivors Insurance and Disability Insurance Trust Funds, House Doc. 104–228 (Washington, DC: U.S. Government Printing Office, 1997), Table R1, p. 36.

[8]See Martin Feldstein, "The Missing Piece in Policy Analysis: Social Security Reform," *A.E.A. Papers and Proceedings*, May 1996, pp. 1–14.

average worker (with his or her employer) paid 8.1 percent in Old-Age and Survivors payroll taxes on the first $9,000 of wages and salary (equivalent to about $24,000 in 2000 dollars).[9] In 2000, that worker paid 10.7 percent on the first $80,400 of "earned" income (or the first $19,350 in 1972 dollars).[10] Moreover, between 2020 and 2046, the Old-Age and Survivors tax rate will have to rise to 14.4 percent from today's 10.7 percent if benefit costs are not cut.[11]

Because of rising payroll taxes for retirement, increasing numbers of poor and middle-income workers do not have the after-tax funds needed to create private supplemental pension investments.[12] In fact, Social Security taxes now consume as much of the average family's budget as do outlays for housing, and nearly three times more than annual healthcare expenses.[13]

Because of the long-term financial problems of the Social Security trust fund, calculations of the rate of return for Social Security are likely to prove optimistic. The fact is that Social Security will not be able to pay out old-age benefits to the "baby-boom" generation without additional tax increases on workers or benefit cuts. These tax increases or benefit cuts will further reduce Social Security return rates for those workers currently in their twenties, members of the so-called Generation X, and their children. As these return rates fall, the relevance of rates of return on private pensions rises. That is, members of Generation X are not simply going to ignore the decaying prospects for adequate income during their retirement years. Rather, they will insist on more opportunities to create pensions to supplement Social Security's Old-Age benefits. Thus, comparing return rates for private and public pensions will become even more important to each new generation.

In addition, the rate of return is important because the crowding-out effects of high Social Security taxes on private savings for low- and middle-income workers affect the wealth that such individuals can leave to the next

[9]Social Security Administration, *2000 Annual Report of the Board of Trustees*, Table II.B1, pp. 34–35. The percentage of wages and salaries taxed to support the Old-Age and Survivors and Disability Insurance programs (Social Security taxes) equals the 50 percent paid directly by the employee plus the 50 percent paid by the employer on the employee's behalf. The employer's half comes from wages the family would have earned had there not been a payroll tax.

[10]Taxable threshold levels for 1972 and 2000 adjusted by the index value for the Consumer Price Index—All Urban Series. See *Economic Report of the President* (Washington, DC: U.S. Government Printing Office, 2000), Table B-58, p. 373.

[11]Heritage Foundation estimates based on data from the Social Security Administration's *1997 Annual Report of the Board of Trustees*, Table II.F14, p. 112.

[12]The decreasing number of firms that provide company pensions to their workers complicates this. Rising taxes of all kinds, costly regulations, and increasing pressures on the bottom line have discouraged many firms from providing pensions for long-time employees.

[13]Data on average family-consumption expenditures from the U.S. Department of Labor, Bureau of Labor Statistics, "Consumer Expenditures in 1995," June 1997, Table A. This report estimates average family income before taxes to be $36,918. An additional $2,289 was added to reflect wages the average worker would receive if the employer's share of Social Security were converted to wages.

generation. Few aspects of Social Security are as unintended or as damaging to low- and moderate-income workers as the squeeze that high payroll taxes has put on the formation of intergenerational wealth transfers. The inability of poor workers to accumulate enough savings to leave a nest egg to their children can mean that those children will be as dependent as their parents could be on their monthly Social Security check. It means that poor communities will not have as much "home-grown" capital with which to create new jobs and sources of income. Without these new jobs and income, members of the next generation will be less able to save for their retirement as well. Thus, by taxing away one generation's opportunity to help the next generation start earning at a higher level, the Social Security system acts as a drag on future generations.

SOCIAL SECURITY'S RATES OF RETURN FOR LOW AND AVERAGE INCOME HOUSEHOLDS

My colleague, Gareth Davis, and I reported in 1998 on how Social Security's return rates vary over age and income cohorts.[14] In that report, we calculated Social Security's inflation-adjusted (or "real") rates of return for various segments of the population and compared these returns with the rates workers could receive if they were allowed to invest their Social Security taxes in safe, private retirement investments.[15] These calculations showed that families at all income levels receive dismal returns for the lifetime taxes they pay.

Defenders of Social Security often argue that Old-Age and Survivors benefits help low-income workers especially. But do they? Does Social Security give low-income Americans a decent return on all of the taxes they pay into the system over their lifetime of work?[16]

A low-income family will likely receive at best a mediocre and at worst a very poor real rate of return from Social Security—despite the fact that

---

[14]See William W. Beach and Gareth Davis, "Social Security's Rate of Return," The Heritage Foundation *Center for Data Analysis Report*, No. CDA98-01, January, 1998.

[15]Davis and I reduced all rates of return and related calculations presented in this paper by the annual inflation rates for the years between 1997 and 2040, as forecast by the Board of Trustees of the Social Security Old-Age and Survivors Insurance Trust Fund in their 1997 annual report. This adjustment to rates of return, Social Security benefits, and privately managed savings mean that the reader is always shown sums and earnings ratios in terms of a dollar's purchasing power today. Thus, the statement "Social Security will pay out an annual amount of $17,000 in the year 2040" means that the program will pay enough to allow a beneficiary to purchase then what $17,000 will purchase now. In order for a beneficiary to have that much "purchasing power" in the year 2040, as he or she has today, Social Security will actually have to send this person around $100,000 annually. The difference between the two amounts is explained by the effects of inflation on the dollar's value, or by what a dollar will buy in 2040 after years of decreasing value due to inflation.

[16]Generally speaking, a low-income earner is defined in Social Security Administration simulations as someone who earns 50 percent of the average wage. In 1996, a person defined as low income earned approximately $12,862 per year.

Social Security's formulae are designed expressly to redistribute money toward low-income workers. Single-earner low-income couples born before 1935—who have paid much lower lifetime payroll taxes—fare better than do much younger workers. However, even the best-case rate of return (5.37 percent for a single-earner couple with children in which the worker was born in 1932) lies below 7 percent—a conservative estimate of what economists believe to be the long-range real rate of return on equities.[17] Every other low-income group lies below this rate of return, or well below the rates of return available to Americans who have opportunities to invest in stocks and bonds for the long term. Double-earner low-income families, as well as single low-income men and women, fare badly under Social Security. Low-income single men are hit particularly hard because of the lower male life expectancy and absence of spousal and survivor's benefits. The expected real rate of return from Social Security for low-income men falls from a high of 3.6 percent for those born in 1932 to 1.0 percent for those born in 1976—well below what these individuals could realize from a prudent private investment portfolio.

All groups fare badly under Social Security relative to the return that they could receive from a conservative private investment portfolio. A married couple with two children and a single earner fare best, receiving 4.74 percent if the earner was born in 1932. This expected rate of return falls gradually to less than 2.6 percent for those born in 1976. As in the low-income scenario, single men fare worst of all. An average-earning single man born after 1966 can expect to receive an annualized real rate of return of less than 0.5 percent (less than one-half of 1 percent) on lifetime payroll taxes.

SOCIAL SECURITY MAY IMPEDE WEALTH TRANSFERS

It is one thing for those most dependent on Social Security's retirement program to be bound to a system that yields rates of return below those for passbook savings accounts. It is quite another thing if this system also impedes the growth of supplemental retirement savings. For middle- and upper-income workers, Social Security's low rates of return are less of a problem. These workers usually have access to pension plans and other company-sponsored retirement savings programs. They also make sufficiently high wages and salaries to be able to purchase Individual Retirement Accounts (IRAs) and participate in 401(k) and 403(b) tax-advantaged savings programs. Thus, the ability of these workers to save for retirement and pass on wealth to their children seldom is impeded by Social Security's high taxes or low rates of return.

For low- and moderate-income workers, however, employers often do not provide pension plans. These individuals' incomes are so low that they sel-

[17]*Report of the 1994–1996 Advisory Council on Social Security, Vol. I: Findings and Recommendations*, p. 35.

dom have any reason to purchase tax-advantaged savings vehicles like IRAs or U.S. savings bonds. Indeed, millions of workers who pay taxes to Social Security pay little if any income taxes. Thus, for them, the tax system is FICA, or the 10.6 percent of wages that go to pay for retirement and survivors insurance.

Economists in the Center for Data Analysis (CDA) have recently completed work that provides a measure of how Social Security affects wealth creation in low- and moderate-income households. Center analysts used data from the Current Population Surveys of the U.S. Bureau of the Census and the Survey of Income Program Participation to trace the wealth-creation patterns of households at various income levels and demographic types. The construction of this database provided the CDA with a baseline of how covered workers, or those workers who pay FICA taxes, currently accumulate assets.

Center analysts then contrasted this set of baseline outcomes with those that would have occurred had these same workers had access to a Social Security system consisting of Personal Retirement Accounts (PRAs) and the traditional pay-as-you-go program. In other words, workers had the ability (in this experimental world) to invest a portion of their 10.6 percent payroll taxes that currently pays for the OASI program in a Personal Retirement Account, or an IRA that they controlled and could access only at retirement.[18] The buildup in that account would pay for part of the worker's retirement.

[18]The PRA directs a portion of Social Security worker and survivor retirement (OAS) taxes into a personal account. Three percent of the first $10,000 of earnings per year is directed to the PRA, as well as 2 percent of any earnings thereafter up to the Social Security wage cap (which was $80,400 during the year 2001). The remaining payroll tax continues to fund the Social Security retirement and survivors program. Total benefits are based on annual earnings and number of years worked, just as under current law. The PRA proposal does not change the Disability Insurance portion of the Social Security program. PRA accounts are allocated into portfolios chosen by the worker from a limited range of options (much like the federal Thrift Savings Plan). The calculations in these graphs and tables assume a portfolio of 50 percent common stocks and 50 percent government bonds, yielding a 5.0 percent inflation-adjusted rate of return.

Upon retirement, the insured worker must purchase a "Part B" annuity with a portion of the wealth accumulated in the PRA. Social Security payments under the reform plan become a two-part system (Part A and Part B). The sum of Social Security Part A and Social Security Part B equals the total benefit received under current law. Part A is that portion of the Social Security benefit that is financed through payroll taxes. Part B is a monthly stream of payments coming from the "Part B" annuity purchased with money coming from the PRA. This reform stipulates that Social Security Part B replace as much as 25 percent of the total benefit received under current law. The benefit replacement rate varies depending on the retiree's year of full-benefits retirement. For example, a worker eligible to retire at full benefits in 2021 has a benefit-replacement rate of 14.286 percent, while a worker thus eligible in 2036 sees a benefit-replacement rate of 25 percent. Income from the PRA annuity (that is, Social Security Part B) adds back an amount to Social Security Part A so that the total at least equals current law benefits.

The annuity purchase assumes the same rates and terms as the Thrift Savings Plan (TSP) annuities currently do. Upon retirement, single individuals purchase a "life only" annuity that will pay a fixed, inflation-adjusted benefit for the remaining years of life. Retiring married couples purchase an annuity that also pays an inflation-adjusted benefit, plus a survivors benefit equal to the maximum Social Security survivors benefit, which is currently two-thirds of the combined benefit.

The remaining amount (up to the full amount the worker would have received anyway from Social Security) would be paid by Social Security from the remaining payroll taxes. Thus, the "reformed" Social Security consists of a Part A and a Part B, or traditional Social Security and the Personal Retirement Account.[19]

This work shows that even this modest substitution of the PRA for a portion of the current Social Security substantially enhances low- and moderate-income families' ability to create greater retirement income or a nest egg for their children. For example, a low-income, African American woman, age thirty-three in 2001, who earns below-average wages throughout her life will retire at age sixty-seven with a monthly Social Security benefit of $861 dollars. Her net wealth at retirement will be about $12,960, principally in cash and personal property. If Part A/Part B Social Security had existed throughout her working life, she would have accumulated funds in her PRA sufficient to create a Part B annuity of $160 dollars a month. To this she would add her Part A benefit from Social Security of $701, for a total of $861 dollars. Because there remain some funds in her PRA ($11,217), she could pay herself a higher monthly benefit ($93 dollars higher), use the remaining funds to pay for a niece's college education or start a part-time business, or just leave it in the PRA. If she chose this last option, then she could leave a bequest for that niece of $24,114. This intergenerational transfer would be greater by itself than this woman's lifetime wealth accumulation without the PRA option.

Now suppose this same woman were married to a man her age who makes exactly what she does. Further assume that they remain low income throughout their working lives. Social Security promises to pay such a couple a monthly benefit of $1,866. They will accumulate about $15,870 in net wealth by the time of their retirement. As in the case of the single female, assume that another Social Security system had existed throughout this couple's working life, and that it had permitted PRA like the one described above. Had that been the case, this couple would have enough in their PRA at retirement to create an monthly annuity payment of $453. This amount would supplement the Social Security Part A payment of $1,413 to produce a total monthly benefit of $1,866. Enough would be left in the PRA to allow a $90 higher monthly payment or a bequest at death of $27,546. Despite its relatively modest size, this bequest exceeds by more than 50 percent this couple's lifetime wealth accumulation without PRAs It would likely go far to breaking intergenerational poverty in this family.

The benefits of a PRA persist at higher incomes, though the differences narrow between wealth accumulated with and without a PRA. Take the

---

[19]See Kirk A. Johnson, David C. John, William W. Beach, Ralph A. Rector, and Alfredo Goyburu, "Personal Retirement Accounts Create Wealth in Low- and Moderate-Income Families," CDA Memorandum to the Commission to Strengthen Social Security, October 4, 2001. Available upon request.

example of the forty-one-year-old, moderate-income, white single woman. If she remains moderate income throughout her working life, Social Security will pay her a monthly benefit of $1,295. She will accumulate wealth (net of liabilities) of $48,259 by the time of her retirement at age sixty-seven. The PRA, however, would be sufficient to pay $241 of this monthly benefit and create a bequest of $16,994. If she decided to invest in a small business instead of allowing her PRA to continue to grow over her retirement, she would be able put $6,278 into this enterprise.

Let's review one more example: a white, dual-earner couple who both teach, own a home, and are thirty-three years of age in 2001. Social Security promises to pay them a monthly benefit of $3,392. Their middle-income salaries permit them to accumulate significant personal wealth, which is likely to amount to $173,295 at retirement. The PRA reform, enhances even this good outcome. The funds in this couple's PRAs would be enough for a monthly annuity of at least $824. This amount would supplement the Part A monthly benefit of $2,568—for a total monthly income of $3,392. The remaining amount in the account could add another $361 to the monthly income, allow a retirement business investment of $45,633, or create a bequest of $107,954 to this couple's children.

What comes through in each of these examples is another cost of the current system. By not allowing even as small a PRA as the one used to generate these case studies, the current system costs each of these workers the lost bequest, or the lost retirement business investment, or the lost additional retirement income. These costs come despite the fact that the PRA option permits monthly incomes at least as large as those currently promised by Social Security.

CONCLUSION

When the Social Security system began, its aim was to help ordinary Americans and those in disadvantaged positions to have adequate financial security in their retirement years. However, as this analysis and a gathering body of research shows, the current system may actually decrease the lifetime well-being of many socioeconomic groups—even under the most favorable assumptions. Among the groups who will lose out under the current system are single mothers, low-income single men, average-income married couples with children, and even affluent professionals. Indeed, many ordinary Americans already understand that the Social Security system is a bad deal. Recent surveys have shown that many workers expect to pay more, in real terms, into the system than they ever expect to receive in retirement benefits.[20]

This analysis of the Social Security system almost certainly underestimates its total economic costs. For instance, it makes no attempt to include

[20]See Michael Tanner, "Public Opinion and Social Security Privatization," Cato Project on Social Security Privatization S.S.P. No. 5, August 6, 1996.

the benefits from faster economic growth, higher wages, and increased employment generated by a retirement program in which individuals are allowed to invest their Social Security tax dollars and build the wealth necessary to sustain them in their old age.

The debate on Social Security reform at times may feature technical terms (such as the "replacement ratio" and the trust fund's "long-range actuarial balance") that mean little or nothing to ordinary American families. However, there is little doubt that the outcome of the debate will have profound importance to them.

But this debate is also a concern to the thirty-something married couple who earned a combined income of $52,000 in 2000 and who struggle to put away enough for retirement while paying over one-eighth of their income into a Social Security system that is likely to yield a real return of less than 1.7 percent on their contributions. Moreover, the outcome of the debate will influence the life of people, perhaps not yet born, who quite possibly could become employed by a business that is created by the retirement investment of the young high-income New York couple.

For almost every type of worker and family, retirement under Social Security means receiving fewer dollars in old age and passing on less wealth to the next generation than they could if they placed their current Social Security tax dollars in private retirement investments instead.

NO

Patricia Ireland

Social Security lies at the heart of our nation's social-insurance program, providing universal coverage for workers and their families though a pooling of resources that guarantees benefits to all. This program has had significant success in reducing poverty in the United States by providing not only retirement, but also disability and survivor benefits to tens of millions of people. In 1959, the poverty rate of the elderly was 35 percent; by 1996, it had dropped to 11 percent.

Social Security has improved women's lives. But after a lifetime of compensated and uncompensated work, many women still face dire economic straits during what were supposed to be their golden years. With a poverty rate of 22 percent, unmarried women (never married, widowed, or divorced) aged sixty-five and older are nearly 50 percent more likely to be poor than unmarried men in the same age group, only 15 percent of whom live in poverty. Without Social Security, a shocking 52.9 percent of elderly women would be poor.

Women must be especially wary of privatization and other proposed remedies to "fix" Social Security. Social Security replaces a higher proportion of earnings for low-income workers; includes spousal, survivor, and disability benefits; pays benefits for life; and is fully adjusted for cost-of-living increases. All of these advantages are particularly important to women, and all would be lost under privatization.

Advocates for women can use the spotlight generated by the debate over Social Security's future to illuminate not only the adverse impact of reform proposals, but also the inequities facing women under the system as it is. This debate creates an extraordinary opportunity to inform public opinion and organize political pressure in order to bring greater fairness for women into the Social Security system, while preserving its essential structure.

WOMEN DEPEND ON SOCIAL SECURITY

Women, as a group, face an array of disadvantages that often mean economic hardship in retirement. Though the proportion of women covered by employer-provided pensions has increased to become nearly even with men, women's benefits are often substantially less owing to lower earnings and breaks in workforce participation. Women of color are less likely to be covered by such pensions and suffer greater pay disparity than white women.

With pay inequity and disproportionate responsibility for family care, women also have less to invest in private pensions. (In 1999, the median annual wage for women was only 72 cents for every dollar of men's median annual wage, and that pay gap has widened since 1997.)

Women are approximately 60 percent of all Social Security recipients, and nearly three out of four (72 percent) of the recipients over eighty-five are women. Older women are twice as likely as older men to depend on Social Security as their sole support. Nearly one-third of women sixty-five and older receive 90 percent or more of their income from Social Security.

UNDER PRIVATIZATION, WOMEN WOULD
LOSE IMPORTANT ADVANTAGES

Spousal and Survivor Benefits

A woman (or man) who has been married for at least ten years is eligible for spousal and survivor benefits under Social Security, irrespective of divorce or death of a wage-earning spouse. Sixty-three percent of women on Social Security receive benefits based on their husband's earnings as wives or widows, while only 1.2 percent of men receive benefits based on their wife's earnings. Thirty-seven percent of these women have no earnings history and 26 percent have a higher benefit as a wife or widow than as an earner.

Under private plans, these spousal and survival benefits would be lost. The wage-earner would own his (or her) private account. What would happen in case of divorce is an open question. However, privatization proposals that have been brought forward would allow a husband and father to leave his account to someone other than his wife and children when he dies. And, aside from these concerns, a woman could be deprived of any monetary benefit based on her husband's earnings to the extent that he manages the private account poorly, is a victim of investor fraud, or retires or dies during a downturn in the market.

Progressive Benefit Structure

Women in the waged workforce are clustered in low-paying jobs. They are helped by the Social Security benefit structure, which, as noted above, replaces a higher proportion of low-wage workers' income when they retire. Women would also lose this progressive aspect of Social Security under privatization.

Lifelong Benefits

Having the lifelong benefits provided under Social Security is especially important to women, who after reaching sixty-five have a life expectancy of 19.2 years, compared to 15.6 for men. Lifetime annuities, if available in a private system, would be prohibitively expensive. What are older women supposed to do if they exhaust their assets under a private plan before death?

Cost-of-Living Adjustments

Adjustments in benefits for increases in the cost of living are also crucial if we hope to save older women from poverty. Without such protection, even a 3 percent inflation rate cuts the purchasing power of a $100 benefit to $74 over ten years and to $55 after twenty years. Inflation-adjusted private annuities are nonexistent in this country.

Death and Disability Benefits

Seniors aren't the only ones who benefit from Social Security. Indeed, Social Security's safety net is wide; without it, vulnerable people of all ages would suffer. One-third of Social Security benefits are paid to workers with disabilities, their children, and survivors. More than seven million children and their sole caretaker parents depend on Social Security benefits after the premature death or disability of a wage-earning parent and spouse. How would skimming 2 percent of payroll taxes from the system help these workers and their families?

PRIVATIZATION WOULD BE EXPENSIVE

Young workers also should be wary of privatization. They would have to pay for the cost of the conversion to a private system. Then they would have to pay enough into their private accounts, and earn a sufficient rate of return, to offset both the one-time conversion costs and the ongoing administrative fees. Various economists estimate the transition cost of allowing workers to invest 2 percent of their payroll taxes outside the Social Security system at a whopping $1 trillion. Even the Bush administration put the figure at $900 billion in its budget proposal.

Administrative costs of Social Security in 2000 were just six-tenths of 1 percent of total income, compared to 12–14 percent for private insurers in this country. In Chile's privatized retirement system, annual administrative costs are $89.10 per retiree, compared to $18.20 for the U.S. Social Security system. A 1999 study by the World Bank found that an astounding 43 percent of funds in individually managed retirement accounts in the United Kingdom would be eaten up by administrative costs, conversion to annuities, and other fees over a projected forty-year term.

Any diversion of Social Security payroll taxes into private accounts would hasten the shortfall of Social Security revenue. Diverting just two percentage points from payroll taxes to private accounts would mean that revenue would be less than required to pay benefits. The Social Security trust fund would have to be tapped, more than a decade earlier than currently projected, and the trust fund would be entirely spent fifteen years sooner.

PRIVATIZATION WOULD BE RISKY

As the economy fluctuates, so would the yields on privatized accounts. Hard as it may be to remember in light of the recent boom, the market lost 45 percent of its value between 1965 and 1978.

The period from 1983 to 2000 was characterized by a 13 percent return on investment. That means $1,000 invested in 1983 yielded $9,000 in 2000. However, that same $1,000 invested in 1966 would have resulted in a negative 6 percent return, for a yield of $940 in 1983.

Seniors, especially women who are less likely to have other sources of support, need a steady income they can count on—not the booms and busts of the market. Once average rates of return are adjusted for risk, Social Security is a better investment than stocks or bonds and has a much higher return than any mix of financial assets in private accounts. Savings and investment are great, but not at the expense of the guarantee of Social Security—which has never missed a payment.

IT'S NOT A CRISIS, IT'S A SCAM

In light of the disadvantages, expenses, and risks, why is there such a strong call for diverting at least some portion of payroll taxes into private accounts? With the Social Security system taking in some $1.5 billion a day, the possible fees for managing even a fraction of that amount are quite an incentive. If 2 percent is diverted from payroll taxes into private accounts, the financial community's gross income from privatization could total $100 billion over the next decade. Financial companies have poured millions into a public-relations and lobbying effort, and into the election campaigns of the president and certain members of Congress, in pursuit of this windfall.

The financial industry's push for privatization of Social Security has created an atmosphere of panic. But what we are facing is not a crisis—it's a scam contrived by those who stand to gain from privatization.

The truth is that our families are not facing an imminent collapse of Social Security. Currently, payroll taxes exceed the amount needed to cover payments to beneficiaries. The excess amounts finance the Social Security trust fund. The fund is available to help the system meet the challenges of increasing life expectancy in the United States and the retirement of baby boomers beginning in 2010. If and when the fund is drawn down to zero (now projected to be 2038), the system will again be pay-as-you-go—as it was from the 1940s through the 1970s. And the projected date that the fund will be fully expended is based on a cautious economic forecast that has repeatedly proven too pessimistic.

Growth of the Gross Domestic Product (GDP) from 1960 to 1974 averaged 4.1 percent; from 1975 to 1996, it averaged 2.7 percent. Yet in 1997, the Social Security trustees estimated an annual increase in GDP, adjusted for inflation, of only 1.6 percent from 1997 to 2029. Based on this conservative assumption, they projected that the Social Security trust fund would be spent by 2029. Each year since then, the trustees have had to extend that date in light of the economy's actual performance.

By the time of their 2001 report, the trustees predicted that the fund would not be completely spent until 2038. That report also noted that even after all of the trust fund has been paid out, Social Security would be able to pay 70 percent of current benefits out of income, without any change to the system.

If the concern is that Social Security may not have sufficient income to pay full benefits after 2038, it defies common sense to propose solving that problem by moving money out of the system and into costlier, riskier private plans.

Under cover of an exaggerated funding crisis, conservative politicians want to revise or even eliminate Social Security in ways that would essentially tear holes in this safety net. In the end, the investment firms that take over even a small part of the program would line their pockets with our tax dollars, while politicians would claim they reduced government and gave taxpayers some of their own money back. Like most shell games, though, privatization is a scam. And women will likely suffer the greatest losses if it is implemented.

FOR WOMEN, SOCIAL SECURITY NEEDS UPDATING

Social Security is based on family and work patterns that have changed significantly since the system's inception in 1935. Although the essential structure of the Social Security system is sound, it is in serious need of updating to reflect the reality of twenty-first century women's lives.

The current benefit formula favors those with thirty-five years of participation in the waged workforce. Women are less likely to reach this benchmark, because they are more likely than men to hold part-time jobs and to spend time out of the paid workforce to raise families. Moreover, the effects of sex-based pay discrimination are not fully offset by the more generous treatment that lower earners receive under Social Security's benefit formula. Differences in current benefits between one- and two-earner couples and inadequacies in benefits for surviving spouses also disadvantage women.

If a woman takes time out from the waged workforce to raise small children or care for an elderly or sick family member, and then she returns to paid employment, she gets no credit at all for her care-giving years in her Social Security work record. When those zero-pay years are included in the calculation, they reduce the woman's average wages, and therefore her Social Security benefits, even further than her generally lower salary already does. Women currently receive an average of only $697 in monthly Social Security benefits, while men receive $904.

PROPOSALS FOR WOMEN

The National Organization for Women and other major women's groups have proposed changes in the Social Security system to address inequities and further reduce poverty among women. Targeting changes primarily to benefit low- and modest-income earners, these include:

- crediting women (or men, if they are the lower-earning spouse) for care-giving with a Family Service Credit of up to $5,000 annually for a maximum of ten years;
- increasing the survivors benefit from 66⅔ to 75 percent of the couple's combined benefit, capping it at the maximum earner's benefit;
- using various changes to increase the benefit for long-time, low-income workers who earn less than $9,625 annually;
- raising the benefit for divorced spouses from 50 percent to 75 percent of the former spouse's benefit; and
- raising the benefit for survivors, including divorced survivors, with disabilities to 100 percent of the deceased worker's benefits, and easing eligibility requirements.

Other changes have been proposed to more accurately reflect new socioeconomic circumstances. These include revising the ten-year marriage requirement for divorced spouses' eligibility to seven years of marriage and three years' covered work experience. Alternatively, women would be allowed to combine total number of years from two or more marriages.

The additional costs of updating the system and making it fairer to women can be met in ways that would also address the long-range solvency challenge. One possibility is to commit a portion of the federal government's projected multibillion-dollar surplus to the Social Security trust fund. Although the recent tax cut and budget resolution passed by Congress would eliminate most of the projected surplus over the next eleven years, future lawmakers should reverse those decisions to take this prudent step.

Raising the cap on wages subject to the payroll tax is another solution. Doing so would keep step with the upward distribution of income and make the payroll tax more progressive. Taxing income above the current limit of $80,400 would relieve the disproportionately heavy tax load on women and other lower-income workers.

CRITERIA FOR REFORM

Other positive proposals, beyond the scope of this chapter, have been advanced and deserve careful study. For every reform proposal, policy makers and the public should ask whether it will continue to help those with lower lifetime earnings, who are disproportionately women; maintain full cost-of-living adjustments; protect and strengthen benefits for wives, widows, and divorced women; preserve disability and survivors benefits; ensure that benefits are guaranteed and not subject to the uncertainties of the securities market; address the care-giving and labor-force experience of women; and further reduce the number of women living in poverty. As described above, privatization of Social Security fails on all counts.

Can women afford privatization of Social Security—the moving of responsibility for administering any part of the nation's social-insurance monies from Washington to Wall Street? No, they cannot. However, they can, and must, use the current debate of privatization as an opportunity to protect and strengthen Social Security—as well as make it more equitable.

DO WE NEED A NATIONAL
HEALTHCARE POLICY?

Editor's Note:
The U.S. healthcare system is driven by ideological and fiscal concerns. Primary among these is whether access to healthcare should be a right or privilege. Conservatives generally believe that health is not a right but a privilege that citizens must earn through past or present labor-force participation. Conservative Democrats believe that healthcare should be a right that is somehow tied to labor force participation, except in instances in which people are not linked to the workforce. Drawing from a European context, liberals argue that healthcare is a right that should be bestowed on each individual at birth. Despite differing orientations, most astute commentators agree that U.S. healthcare is in crisis and that changes are necessary. What form, if any, those changes will take lies at the heart of the debate.

Dawn McCarty, M.S.W., is a former medical social worker, and is the Child Welfare Education project coordinator in the department of sociology, social work, and criminal justice at Lamar University in Beaumont, Texas. In addition, she teaches courses on social problems and social welfare policy. *J. Rick Altemose, Ph.D.* is professor and director of the graduate program in the department of sociology, social work, and criminal justice at Lamar University. He also teaches courses in public policy.

Robert E. Moffit Ph.D., is director of domestic policy studies at the Heritage Foundation.

YES

Dawn McCarty and J. Rick Altemose

When debating the United States' healthcare system, we need to state which system we are talking about. One system, for the rich and for those with excellent insurance, is of outstanding quality. As the undisputed leader in high-tech medicine and medical training, the United States is where the rich and famous throughout the world come when their health problems prove life threatening. If you have money, and lots of it, America is the place to be when you're sick.

For the rest of us, the uninsured and the underinsured, the system is broken (Delaney & Hensel, 2000; Voelker, 1998). The United States is the only industrialized nation in the world that has not established universal health coverage (Redmond, 2001). Forty-five million of us have no health insurance at all. And as employers limit or eliminate their health benefits, this number is growing by over a million people a year (National Association of Social Workers, 2000). Another 33 million have limited-coverage insurance owing to excluded medical conditions, high deductibles and co-payments, and/or low maximum benefits. They risk financial catastrophe if they suffer serious or chronic illness or injury (Bertlett, 2000). Too many elders on Medicare simply cannot pay for medicines they need. Even those of us lucky enough to have "good" insurance are facing soaring premiums. Employers are dropping insurance altogether, and physicians are forced to battle HMO clerks to get us the medical care we need.

As a nation, we spend over 14 percent of our Gross Domestic Product on healthcare—about 50 percent more per capita than any other country. But we are clearly not getting what we are paying for. A World Health Organization ranking of national healthcare ranked the United States 39th, behind not only the developed nations of the world, but also Chile, Colombia, Saudi Arabia, and Singapore (Baxandall, 2001). In terms of fairness and access for all, the same report ranked us 54th (H. Bell, 2000).

THE STORIES BEHIND THE STATISTICS

But statistics alone hide the human misery involved. Stories from patients and their survivors tell of treatment delayed, treatment denied, and treatment so costly as to lead to bankruptcy. Stories from physicians tell of the time and effort taken from healing so they can jump through the hoops required by insurance companies, of patients who did not get the drug they needed because they could not afford it, of dying breast-cancer patients who never got their mammograms because they did not have money or insurance coverage (Grumbach, 2000).

What makes these stories so upsetting is not just the unnecessary suffering, but also the unfairness. The destitute have Medicaid, the affluent have insurance, but millions of full-time working people have neither. The results are almost surreal in their injustice. For example, Dr. Debra Richter tells of George and Tina, a brother and sister born to parents without insurance. Both siblings suffered from their untreated diabetes since childhood (H. Bell, 2000). As teenagers, they worked hard at full-time jobs. However, none of their employers offered insurance, and their wages were far too low to buy insurance on their own. Without the insulin, syringes, and glucometer sticks that they needed but could not afford, George went blind at age twenty. *Then* he became eligible for Medicaid. He died at twenty-one of multiple organ failure caused by his untreated diabetes. Tina had a baby who died of complications from gestational diabetes after spending five months in a hospital. Tina herself died at age twenty-five of a heart attack caused by her untreated diabetes. Although their death certificates listed diabetes and its complications, in a real sense, they died of the lack of health insurance (H. Bell, 2000).

This story illustrates many of the flaws in the current system. Denying preventive care to George and Tina saved no money. To the contrary, the hospital expenses of their final days were many times what it would have cost to provide the care that could have saved them. The alleged medical "support net" of the working poor—hospital emergency rooms, community clinics, and Medicaid—failed them. Emergency rooms do not provide treatment for chronic diseases. Community clinics and public hospitals do not have anything approaching the financial ability to provide long-term care for 45 million uninsured citizens. Medicaid is of little help to the working poor. In most states, a parent who makes even the minimum wage makes too much to be eligible. People sicken and die simply because they are poor. In the words of Dr. Martin Luther King, Jr., "Of all the forms of inequality, injustice in healthcare is the most shocking and inhumane" (anonymous, 1998, p. 2).

DO WE NEED A NATIONAL HEALTHCARE POLICY?

In light of these widely recognized problems with our current system, the need for a national policy is a bit of a no-brainer. On a matter so vital to voters as healthcare, the national government *will* have a policy, one way or another, if only a policy of neglect and leave-it-to-the-private-sector. Social workers, in particular, are called upon to develop and advocate policies that reflect the values of their profession (NASW, 2000). Through the Delegate Assembly of the National Association of Social Workers, the profession has adopted an official position on the need for a national healthcare policy: "NASW supports a national healthcare policy that ensures the right to universal access to a continuum of health and mental healthcare. . . . NASW supports efforts to enlarge healthcare coverage to uninsured and underinsured people until universal health and mental health coverage is achieved" (NASW, 2000, p. 152).

This statement clearly states that healthcare is a right, not just another commodity. This is a key distinction. If healthcare is a mere commodity— available, like diamond necklaces and yachts, to those with the ability to pay—then universal coverage might not be mandatory. But if healthcare is a right, justice demands that we all have access to it—just as justice demands that we have an equal right to vote, a jury of our peers, and equal access to certain public services such as education (Bruder, 2001). If we believe that healthcare is a positive right, then the question is not whether there should be a national healthcare policy, but rather, what policy would be most effective in providing quality healthcare to all?

IS "SINGLE-PAYER" THE BEST NATIONAL HEALTH POLICY?

Although single-payer is not the only method of attaining universal coverage (Gorin, 1997), the NASW policy is clear: "NASW supports a universal right to healthcare *under a single payer system*" (NASW, 2000, p. 153, emphasis added). What is this "single-payer" concept? The key concept is that a single payer, the government, pays all healthcare expenses with taxes. This contrasts with the current system, in which the money comes from multiple sources—taxes, insurance companies, individual consumers, HMOs, employers, and so on. It is not "socialized medicine," in which the government owns the hospitals, and healthcare workers are government employees. It is more like a much-improved version of Medicare expanded to include everybody. Of the many ideas of how a single-payer system could be structured, perhaps the most complete is the National Health Insurance (NHI) proposal by the Physicians for a National Health Program (2001). In this plan, *everybody* would be covered for *every* medically necessary service, including doctor visits, hospital stays, prescription drugs, dental and mental-health services, nursing-home and in-home care. There would be no deductibles, no co-payments, and no out-of-pocket expenses to the consumer. The NHI would pay hospitals, nursing homes, home health agencies, group practices, and health centers a monthly lump sum. Individual physicians would be paid by the NHI on the basis of a simplified, binding fee schedule. Funds for construction, major renovation, and major equipment would be provided based on need as determined by regional health-planning boards composed of both professionals and community representatives.

The insurance/HMO industry would have no role whatsoever under this proposal. Single-payer does away with the middle person, cutting drastically the cost of healthcare. Private insurers' profits and administrative costs siphon off between 13.6 percent (Physicians for a National Health Program, 2001) and 30 percent (Dufour, 2000) of premiums paid; the comparable figure for Medicare is 2 percent. The increase in taxes would be more than offset by the savings from not paying insurance companies (Newcomb, 2000). This huge savings would cover most, if not all, of the costs of covering those who now have no insurance at all (American Medical Student Association, 1999).

Another advantage of getting the insurance companies and HMOs out of the loop is that such a move would improve the quality of healthcare. As Robert Moffit argues later in this chapter, HMOs have not proved themselves to be the answer to either containing costs or improving access to quality healthcare. In fact, problems with insurance company–dominated medicine are so well known that politicians in both parties have tripped over themselves advocating various forms of a "Patient's Bill of Rights" to prevent and redress abuses. Note that these abuses came not from a tyrannical and predatory government, but from tyrannical and predatory insurance companies!

WHERE DO WE GO FROM HERE?

A plan that provides not only universal coverage (coverage for everybody) but also more comprehensive coverage (coverage for what we need) is easy to advocate. For example, does your current insurance pay for nursing-home costs? Home healthcare? A single-payer program could do so—and save billions of dollars at the same time. And all you would have to do when you go to the doctor, hospital, or pharmacy is show your NHI card. But despite the attractiveness of single-payer, advocates face very real obstacles (Gorin, 1997). Politically powerful combinations of special interests and conservative groups have successfully blocked government-sponsored health-insurance proposals at least five times in this century (Levey, Hill, & Prybil, 2000). The chances of single-payer passing Congress anytime soon are small (Gorin, 1997).

However, encouraging signs have emerged. The medical profession is rethinking its long-standing opposition to single-payer (Landa, 2001). Roadblocks at the federal level have prompted attempts to get universal healthcare at the state level. Although a Massachusetts ballot initiative was narrowly defeated in 2000, the issue is alive in that state's legislature (A. Bell, 2000). Activists in Illinois are proposing an amendment to the state constitution to guarantee universal coverage (Gaskin, 2000). There have been important successes at the federal level in expanding coverage for specific groups of people, most notably for children under the Children's Health Insurance Program (CHIP).

We suggest that national healthcare policy be seen as a two-track effort. On the track toward single-payer, any proposal that expands health coverage to those who do not currently have it is both good in itself and a step toward single-payer. In fact, universal coverage may come first, single-payer later (Gorin, 1997). Politically, universal coverage is easier to sell. For many Americans, the idea of an expanded role for government in healthcare has been demonized by accusations of "socialized medicine" or worse (Derickson, 1997). But the American people do not accept that millions should be without healthcare. A recent survey by the American Hospital Association

asked people to name one healthcare change that they thought was necessary. The overwhelming answer was healthcare for all (Lewis, 2000).

Yet as important as universal access and its financing are, our sugges-
tion for a second track is more comprehensive. That's because health policy
needs to address issues broader than just how to provide healthcare. The
NASW policy statement on Promoting the Right to Health Care calls for "economic, social, occupational, and environmental policies that contribute to
maintaining health, recognizing the relationship between these factors and
quality and longevity of life" (NASW, 2000, p. 152). Similarly, the American
Public Health Association policy statement says, "The health of the people
requires not only a universal national healthcare policy, but also social and
economic policies that foster the health, stability, and general welfare of the
population" (American Public Health Association, 1997). Therefore, we suggest working for healthcare justice by working toward a more just society.

NO

Robert F. Moffit

The United States already has a flawed health policy, which is rooted in the
federal tax code. There is a clear need for a new policy.

THE PROBLEM

Government policy on healthcare, at both the federal and state level, is often
incoherent and inequitable. It profoundly distorts healthcare markets, frustrates or eliminates consumer choice and competition, and promotes waste
and inefficiency. Relying on outdated mechanisms of political command and
control, it has created a maze of mandates and rigid regulation. It directly
contributes to reduced access to healthcare coverage, increased costs, and the
number of individuals and families without even basic health insurance coverage. It has weakened personal control over crucial healthcare decisions;
and it has progressively undermined both the personal liberty and privacy of
patients and the professional independence and integrity of their doctors and
healthcare providers.

Government finances almost half of all direct spending on healthcare,
largely through taxation to fund the huge and financially troubled Medicare and Medicaid programs as well as various public-health programs. Private healthcare spending takes place within one of the most heavily regulated environments in the U.S. economy.

Despite these problems, many of the architects of the current system—
federal and state legislators—are prepared to build upon the worst features
of their old, flawed policies and to expand their authority over the financing
and delivery of care. Bit by bit, with the serial enactment of various regula-

tory initiatives at the federal and state levels, patients are progressively losing control over the financing and delivery of medical services. If this continues, the end result will be total government control over the financing and
delivery of healthcare. In such a system, controlling costs to remain within
preordained budgetary constraints will mean the denial of medical services
to individuals and families. This, in effect, is patients' experience in single-
payer systems such as in Canada and Great Britain.[1]

In an era when individuals are increasingly empowered by rapidly
advancing information-systems technology, and competitive firms are working to customize products to individual wants and needs, the American
healthcare system remains an Industrial Age dinosaur. It is governed by corporate and government third-party payment systems. These include managed-care networks and large government programs in which the key
decisions are made by corporate bureaucrats, not by those who are directly
affected by those decisions.

In the national debate over healthcare policy, the key issues concern
power and control: Who is going to make the key decisions in the healthcare
system? Who is going to decide what doctors, benefits, and health plans are
going to be available to individuals and families? Who is going to control
the flow of the money? Ultimately, policymakers will determine whether
those decisions will continue to be made by corporate or government executives or made primarily by individuals and families.

THE SOLUTION

America needs a new national policy that empowers individuals to make
key decisions in the healthcare system, a system in which individuals are free
to choose what kind of doctor and medical specialist they want, the type of
health plan they want, and the benefits they need. America needs a system in
which individuals—rather than companies, managed-care executives, or
government bureaucrats—directly control the flow of dollars.

The only way to establish real patient control is to give individuals and
families choice. Plans and providers, with real market competition, would
then be forced to respond to patient's needs in innovative ways. Congress
and the administration can move the market in this direction by giving every
American family a tax credit to use toward the purchase of health insurance
and to offset their healthcare costs. Likewise, Congress and the administration should give refundable tax credits or direct subsidies to low-income families and individuals to mainstream them into the private healthcare system.

---

[1]See James Frogue, "A High Price for Patients: An Update on Government Health Care in Britain
and Canada," Heritage Foundation *Backgrounder* No. 1398, September 26, 2000, available at
www.heritage.org/library/backgrounder/bg1398.html.

Such tax-code changes would enable individuals to choose the plans, benefits, and medical treatments they want at prices they wish to pay.

A GOVERNMENT-CREATED MESS

Today's health-insurance system has many problems rooted in government's tax code bias[2] and its command-and-control approach to regulating the market.

First, the current system undermines the portability of health insurance. American citizens can get unlimited tax relief—in the form of an *exclusion* of the value of their benefits from taxable income—for the purchase of health insurance only if they get insurance through their employer.

Annually, the total federal tax breaks for employer-based health insurance amount to $125.6 billion. If we add in the state-based tax breaks for employer-based health insurance, the amount rises to $140.9 billion.[3] But this huge tax break is restricted almost entirely to employment-based health insurance. A worker who loses or changes her job will lose not her life insurance, auto insurance, or homeowner's insurance, but her health insurance—the very insurance that protects her and her family against serious illness or financial devastation from catastrophic illness. The reason? Her former employer owned her policy, so she could not take it with her to a new job.

Because of the enormous power of the federal tax code, government policy has tied access to health insurance almost exclusively to the workplace. It is not surprising, then, that many persons who are leaving or changing jobs have no insurance. In an age of high mobility, when workers routinely change job or careers, this policy is absurd.

Second, government policy creates inequities in the official government treatment of American workers' health insurance. If a bread winner is employed in a large corporation with a large benefits package, the tax benefits for health coverage can be very generous. That worker will get a large chunk of tax-free income. For workers making over $100,000 per year, the average annual tax break amounts to $2,638. If she is low or middle income, or employed in a smaller company, her tax breaks are less terrific. If she makes between

---

[2]On this point, there is a large and growing bipartisan consensus among healthcare policy analysts, ranging from the American Enterprise Institute to the Progressive Policy Institute. A compendium of the work of these analysts can be found in Grace Marie Arnett (Ed.), *Empowering Health Care Consumers Through Tax Reform* (Ann Arbor, MI: The University of Michigan Press, 1999).

[3]See John Shiels, Paul Hogan, and Randall Haught, "Health Insurance and Taxes: The Impact of Proposed Changes in Current Federal Policy," prepared for the National Coalition on Health Care by the Lewin Group, October 1999, p. 6. The amounts are estimated in 2000 dollars. Hereafter cited as "The Lewin Report."

$15,000 and $20,000 per year, her average family tax break for the insurance is $331; if she makes less than $15,000 per year, it is $79.[4]

If an employer offers no health insurance, a worker's only option is to purchase an individual policy. This choice may be more expensive, because smaller plans tend to have higher administrative and marketing costs. Moreover, she must purchase the policy with *after-tax* dollars, which could prove prohibitively expensive. For most middle-income Americans, of course, purchasing insurance outside of the traditional employer-based plans can be a difficult.[5]

The underlying premise of federal tax policy seems to be that healthcare is a social good—something society ought to promote. But the tax benefits for this social good are disproportionately distributed to upper-income workers who need it least. In the process, government policy contributes to the lack of insurance coverage among millions of families.

Congress does not apply the tax policies that govern health insurance to any other type of insurance coverage or to the complex purchase of goods or services in any other market. Health insurance is alone in this treatment. Policy makers who defend this arrangement in health insurance would be quick to denounce its use for auto, homeowners, or life insurance. And they would be right.

Third, today's government policy promotes waste. This tax policy is restrictive, confining Americans to one kind of health insurance (employer-based). It is also incompatible with the very idea of insurance and the functioning of a free market. Instead of insuring against risk, Congress has established tax-subsidized, prepaid medical care almost exclusively through the workplace. The tax code discourages direct payment to doctors, and encourages indirect payment to doctors through insurance. Today's policy encourages dollars that would otherwise be used for direct payment for routine medical services, like office visits, to circulate through the bureaucratic apparatus of insurance companies, thus artificially jacking up administrative costs. The tax code discourages paying small, routine medical costs out of pocket.

Fourth, government policy hides the true costs of care and prevents the operation of a free market in health insurance. Most workers do not buy their own health-insurance coverage; their employer purchases it for them. Too many

---

[4]The Lewin Report, p. ii.

[5]Congress and the Clinton administration attempted to ameliorate the problem of the absence of portability by enacting the Health Insurance Portability and Accountability Act of 1996, sometimes referred to as the Kennedy-Kassebaum bill. The legislation sought to create an artificial substitute for portability through regulation. Of course, real portability of benefits comes only with ownership of the benefits policy. So, the bill was a classic political attempt to treat the symptoms of the condition without curing it. From the standpoint of cost, it appears that the legislation may have made the situation worse. On this point, see Marilyn Moon and Joanne Silberner, "What About Health Care for the Poor?" *The Washington Post*, June 29, 1998, p. A15.

Americans think the employer's contribution to their health-benefits package is the *employer's* money, not their own. But as every labor economist knows, workers' wages are reduced by the monetary value of their company health-benefits package, for which the company takes a tax deduction. Therefore, Americans, not their employers or insurance companies, pay 100 percent of their healthcare costs.

Under today's tax-favored, third-party payment system, it is virtually impossible to control costs in a rational way. If an employer offers a traditional fee-for-service plan, the doctor being paid on a cost-plus basis makes more money if he performs more services. The more procedures he does, the more money he gets. So, the doctor has every incentive to order as many services and tests as possible, even if they might be only marginally beneficial to the patient. Under managed-care arrangements, which today cover 92 percent of the population in employer-sponsored insurance,[6] the perverse incentives of the third-party payment system are retained and reversed: Doctors, if they are paid under a capitation arrangement in a managed-care plan, can conceivably make more money if they perform fewer services. After all, managed care is a form of private-sector rationing. This has led to an understandable frustration among both doctors and patients.

HOW GOVERNMENT IS MAKING MATTERS WORSE

Millions of Americans are struggling with higher healthcare costs and having difficulty getting access to even basic coverage. Those with health insurance are sometimes dissatisfied with the quality of coverage delivered by their employer's plan—almost invariably a managed-care plan chosen by their employer.

Managed care was supposed to be the "silver bullet" of trendy healthcare policy in the early 1990s. It became fashionable when the Clinton administration proposed overhauling the entire health-insurance system and creating mandatory managed-care networks, called regional alliances, throughout the country. At that time, Congress wisely rejected the Clinton Plan. Nevertheless, millions of employers enrolled their workers (often involuntarily) in managed-care plans in order to control their healthcare costs. And Congress has itself strongly and persistently promoted managed-care.[7] For example, in 1973 Congress enacted the Health Maintenance Organization (HMO) Act, which compels employers with more than twenty-five employ-

---

[6]*The Challenge of Managed Care Regulation: Making Markets Work?* Report produced for the Robert Wood Johnson Foundation through Changes in Health Care Financing and Organization (Washington, DC: 2001), p. 3.

[7]In the Balanced Budget Act of 1997, for example, Congress enabled states to enroll Medicaid beneficiaries in managed-care plans.

ees, and subject to the minimum-wage law, to offer an HMO option if they offered health insurance to their workers.[8]

The standard response of federal and state lawmakers to complaints about the current system is to ignore the root causes of the problems—the absence of patient choice of plans and benefits and the loss of genuine competition—and to enact more laws, rules, and regulations to compensate for the shortcomings of prior policies. From 1994 to 1999, state legislatures enacted more than one thousand laws regulating managed-care alone.[9]

But every government regulation imposes a cost, and that cost is borne in higher premiums. Higher premiums make health insurance less affordable, particularly for workers and families in small firms. Because state regulation of managed-care could not address all the problems, the 107th Congress is poised to enact a "patient's bill of rights," adding yet another level of litigation atop the high level of regulation.[10] Without judging the merits of patient suits against managed-care plans over coverage, it is hard to imagine how having more people sue each other will result in an overall improvement in the healthcare system, particularly in the crucial areas of access and cost.

The Single-Payer End Game

Current government policy fuels frustration, which is paving the way for a single-payer system where the government takeover of the healthcare system would be complete. But single-payer systems, like the British National Health Service or the Canadian Medicare system—no matter how different in political structure—have similar economic dynamics. If such a system were adopted in the United States, it would probably resemble the financially troubled Medicare program, which covers 40 million senior and disabled citizens. Medicare is a cumbersome and sluggish system. According to a Mayo Foundation estimate, it is governed by almost 111,000 pages of rules, regulations, and related paperwork.[11]

The economic dynamics of a single-payer system are inescapable. If healthcare is a legal entitlement, then for all practical purposes it is what economists call a "free good." If it's a free good, then of course the demand for

---

[8]*The Challenge of Managed Care Regulation: Making Markets Work?* p. 2.

[9]Ibid., p. 1.

[10]For a discussion of the "patients' bill of rights" legislation in Congress, see John S. Hoff, "The Patients' Bill of Rights: A Prescription for Massive Federal Regulation," Heritage Foundation Backgrounder, No. 1350, February 29, 2000.

[11]The Mayo Foundation staff completed an inventory on the wide variety of Medicare's rules, regulations and paperwork, including Medicare guidelines and administrative decisions. Dr. Robert Waller, President of the Mayo Foundation, presented this information in testimony before the National Bipartisan Commission on The Future of Medicare, August 10, 1998.

this free good is unlimited. But any unlimited demand will eventually collide with limited supply. This means that government officials—not doctors or patients—are going to have to make big decisions about who gets care, how they get care, when they get care, and under what circumstances they get care. The key decisions in such a system, in other words, are political—not medical or even conventional economic ones. Advocates of these systems often insist that they successfully "control costs" while simultanesouly claiming that any problem with them could be resolved by boosting spending.

Such systems can guarantee "coverage," but they do not guarantee "access" to healthcare services. And the quality of care is certain to decline. The British case, in particular, is instructive. Waiting lists in British hospitals in 1997 topped 1.3 million. The newly elected Labour government promised to improve conditions, and made a pledge to treat one hundred thousand more patients. But the total waiting list has risen an additional one hundred thousand since 1997. Additionally, under the strange queuing system in Britain, there are more than four hundred thousand persons "waiting" to get on these lists for medical services.[12] A socialist system of healthcare financing and delivery may be internally logical. Indeed, a universal system of government-managed healthcare has strong emotional appeal. In practice, however, it can be quite cruel.

THE NEED FOR A NEW NATIONAL HEALTH POLICY

The problems of access to coverage, lack of portability, market inefficiency, waste, and loss of patient control are inherent in the current structure of the health-insurance market. But because of its peculiar structure, reform of the system cannot be effected at the state level. It must be a national priority. The reason: The dynamics of the healthcare system are driven, guided, and shaped *primarily* by the federal tax treatment of health insurance.

We cannot overestimate the impact of the Internal Revenue Code on the healthcare sector of the U.S. economy. If Congress and the administration want to reform the American healthcare system, they must first reform the health-insurance market. But they cannot hope to reform it unless they first reform the federal tax treatment of health insurance. A new national health policy should involve two major components: a universal tax-credit system and targeted tax relief.

First, establish a universal tax-credit system for health insurance and the purchase of healthcare services. Every American family should get tax relief in the form of a tax credit, regardless of place or status of employment. That tax relief should be given to individuals to use in a way that best meets their circumstances—to help offset the costs of health insurance or out-of-pocket

---

[12]Frogue, "A High Price for Patients," *op. cit.*

medical expenses, or to deposit funds in a tax-free medical savings account (MSA). An MSA is a sort of medical IRA that rolls over from year to year, from which workers and their families can pay medical bills directly. MSAs would introduce unprecedented economic efficiency in routine transactions. They would also enhance personal freedom for patients and the professional independence of physicians, who would no longer have to wrestle with insurance bureaucrats over coverage issues or the paperwork that now suffocates the third-party payment system.

Second, target tax relief or direct subsidies to families in need. Beyond a basic tax credit available to every family, the generosity of tax relief for healthcare should be determined by family healthcare needs. More help should go to lower-paid families or families with higher healthcare bills. The amount of funding for low-income families to help offset the cost of insurance or medical expenses is a purely political question. But the principle of extending assistance should be a constant.

Advantages of Reforming the Tax Treatment of the Healthcare Sector

Such a comprehensive approach would have several tangible advantages:

1. **A tax-credit approach would establish real portability.** There will never be true portability of health-insurance benefits unless individuals and families own and control their healthcare benefits package and can take it with them when they leave work or change jobs. With a tax credit for the purchase of health insurance, regardless of where individuals work or what their employment status is, they could exercise control and enjoy portability. Access to health insurance should no longer be dictated by employers' willingness to offer health insurance. A tax-credit system would end the anxiety that families feel about the continuity of their insurance coverage.
2. **A tax-credit system will establish equity.** Today, Congress authorizes unlimited tax breaks on the value of health benefits for workers who get health insurance through their employer. Those who work in firms where the employer offers no coverage get nothing. There is no reason why Congress and the administration should maintain the current inequities in the tax treatment of health insurance. A tax credit approach would establish real equity for Americans.
3. **Tax credits will encourage real insurance.** Today, many Americans are uninsured or underinsured. (They lack sufficient protection against the financial devastation of catastrophic illness.) Many are also overinsured, enrolled in costly "Cadillac" healthcare plans with benefits they do not need and would not buy if they were spending their own money directly on coverage. Every dollar increase in healthcare benefits

amounts roughly to a dollar decrease in wages and other compensation. Persons today are using insurance to cover small, routine, or purely predictable medical services. This results in workers' huge overpayments into the health-insurance system and a proportional loss of disposable income. Routine medical services should be paid directly out of pocket and given the same tax relief that is available for insurance payments. Allowing persons to pay routine medical bills from medical savings accounts would be the best way to accomplish that end.

4. **Tax credits will establish a superior consumer-based market for insurance.** Though today's employer-based healthcare system is largely private, there is no normal collision between the market forces of supply and demand. The reason? Insurance customers (employers) and insurance consumers (workers) are entirely different personalities. This creates perverse incentives for patients as well as doctors. Consumer attempts to control costs in employment-based insurance is not economically rational, because the savings from doing so will only accrue in company coffers. With tax credits for the purchase of health insurance, consumers' incentives would be rationalized. Consumers would become price sensitive and look for the best value for their money in quality, service, and price. And they would pocket the savings from their wise decisions. Federal employees do this every year in the Federal Employees Health Benefits Program (FEHBP), a consumer-driven system of hundreds of private plans that compete for the premium dollars of members of Congress and the federal workforce.[13] Moreover, instead of comparatively small employer-based insurance pools, incentives in a tax-credit system would encourage the creation of large, national insurance pools. Such pools could be sponsored by associations, professional organizations, unions, and even church and religious institutions. With large national pools, average administrative and claims costs would go down, and competing plans would have new incentives to establish long-term contracts with consumers.

5. **Tax credits will give patients control over important and sensitive healthcare decisions.** Individuals and families have little or no say in what companies offer in their healthcare benefits packages. A tax-credit system would completely reverse those dynamics. There are two emerging areas in which this will prove most vital.

   Medical ethics. President George W. Bush made a historic decision in 2001 concerning the use of federal funds for embryonic stem-cell research. Within the next few years, the first products of applied

---

[13]On the FEHBP, see Stuart M. Butler and Robert E. Moffit, "The FEHBP as a Model for a New Medicare Program," *Health Affairs*, Vol. 14, No. 4 (Winter 1995), pp. 47–61. See also Robert E. Moffit, "Consumer Choice in Health: Learning from the Federal Employees Health Benefits Program," Heritage Foundation *Backgrounder* No. 878, November 9, 1992.

research from breakthroughs in the human genome mapping project, and other advanced medical technologies, will come to fruition. Though America is in the forefront of a biomedical revolution, challenges to patients' freedom of conscience will arise. Many patients today must pay a portion of their premiums for treatments or procedures that violate their ethical, moral, or religious convictions. (Abortion is one example.) A tax-credit system would end such coercion. It would promote freedom of conscience and let persons pick health plans that are compatible with their convictions on sensitive matters. Medical savings accounts serve a similar purpose.

Medical privacy. Americans rightly do not feel confident that their health plans or their employers will safeguard their sensitive medical records. Beneficiaries enrolled in government health programs, such as Medicare, also have cause for anxiety. With a tax-credit system, however, persons would be able to pick health plans that guarantee their medical privacy, and could sue plans for breach of contract if they violated it.

6. **Tax credits can reduce or even eliminate the large number of uninsured.** Congress can make tax credits as progressive or as generous as they wish. It can combine them with marketing and insurance-market changes; it can design legal obligations that attach to accepting or rejecting a tax credit or insurance coverage. In 1991, the Heritage Foundation designed a universal tax-credit proposal with a legal requirement for individuals to purchase basic health coverage just as they are required to purchase auto-insurance coverage. This policy would have achieved universal coverage.[14] Heritage also has an updated version of the proposal.[15] Other proposals have been far less ambitious but would

---

[14]The Heritage Foundation in Washington, DC, has proposed a plan for universal coverage that would replace existing tax breaks for health insurance with a national system of tax credits for healthcare coverage. The structure of the credits, including refundable credits or vouchers for low-income persons, would be a sliding scale of tax relief. Under this formula, the amount available to families, beyond the basic credit available to everyone, would be calculated on healthcare costs compared to that income: The higher the costs compared to family income, the greater would be the credit amount for individuals and families. The Heritage proposal was examined in 1992 and re-examined in 1999 by The Lewin Group, the prominent Virginia-based econometrics firm that models healthcare policy changes. Assuming a minimum benefits package covering 365-day inpatient hospital coverage, outpatient hospital services, hospital alternatives such as home healthcare, physician services, prenatal and well child care, diagnostic tests, prescription drugs, emergency services, with deductibles, co-payments, and coinsurance requirements, The Lewin Group estimated the costs of the proposal and assumed 209.8 million Americans would qualify for the tax credit. It found that the universal approach proposed by Heritage would result in a $21.4 billion net increase in healthcare spending and a net federal cost of $55.3 billion in 2000 dollars. See The Lewin Report, pp. 41–52.

[15]See Stuart M. Butler, "Reforming the Tax Treatment of Health Care to Achieve Universal Coverage," in Jack A. Meyer and Elliott K. Wicks (Eds.). *Covering America: Real Remedies for the Uninsured* (Washington, DC: Economic and Social Research Institute, 2001), pp. 21-42.

nonetheless result in substantial reductions in the number of the uninsured.[16]

Recent research on the individual market shows that the major tax-credit proposals being offered by the Bush administration and leading members of Congress on a bipartisan basis would make health insurance affordable for millions of Americans who do not now have access to coverage. For example, representatives Richard Armey (R–TX) and William Lipinski (D–IL) have sponsored the Fair Care for the Uninsured Act (H.R.1331), which would create a tax credit of $1,000 per individual; $2,000 per couple; and up to $3,000 for family coverage. In an evaluation of the impact of the Armey–Lipinski bill, based on a large sample of twenty-thousand individual policies in the market, analysts with e.HealthInsurance.com based in Sunnyvale, California (one of the largest brokers of insurance on the Internet) found that half of the individual and family premiums purchased in that sample were within the limits of the proposed tax credits. Moreover, fully three-quarters of the policies had premiums within 75–100 percent of the tax-credit amounts.[17]

7. **Tax credits can reach millions of uninsured Americans efficiently and effectively.** Congress can design tax credits in such a way as to ensure a high take-up rate for the credits and private insurance coverage. For example, Lynn Etheredge, a prominent health-policy analyst at George Washington University, suggests administering a tax-credit system through the existing employer-based payroll system.[18] All American firms, notes Etheredge, are already part of a comprehensive payroll system and provide standard payroll deductions for employees' Social Security, Medicare, federal and state income tax, state unemployment insurance, state workers' compensation, and disability. Moreover, many firms also provide payroll deductions for pension plans, union dues, charities, and savings plans. Under a new tax-credit system, an

[16]According to Mark Pauly and Bradley Herring of the University of Pennsylvania, a 50 percent tax credit for insurance coverage would cut the uninsured population in half. See Mark Pauly and Bradley Herring, "Expanding Coverage Via Tax Credits: Trade-Offs and Outcomes," *Health Affairs*, Vol. 20. No. 1 (January-February 2001), pp. 9–26.

[17]"Analysis of National Sales Data of Individual and Family Health Insurance: Implications for Policymakers and the Effectiveness of Health Insurance Tax Credits," June 2001, available at http://www.ehealthinsurance.com/ehealthinsurance/expertcenter/ExpertCenter.html#Reports.

[18]Lynn Etheredge, presentation at a symposium on "The Uninsured: Is Tax Policy the Answer?" cosponsored by the Heritage Foundation and El Pomar Foundation, Colorado Springs, Colorado, August 10, 2001. See also Lynn Etheredge, "Tax Credits for Uninsured Workers," Health Insurance Reform Project, George Washington University (September 1999), pp. 5–7.

employee would simply notify the employer of his choice of health plan. The employer would send the payroll deductions, above the tax-credit amount, to that plan. The plans chosen by employees would notify the U.S. Treasury; and the Treasury would transmit the tax credits to health plans electronically. Existing payroll and tax deductions are very efficient, with low administrative costs.

Beyond the efficiency already built into the employer payroll-deduction system, Etheredge notes that a tax-credit system could be made very effective through a system of automatic enrollment. Under such an arrangement, workers and their families would be automatically enrolled in a plan of their choice or a "default" health-insurance plan. The exception to coverage would be a declaration by a worker, in writing, that he or she has declined the coverage and the tax credit to offset the cost of that coverage. Automatic enrollment is already a feature of many private employee-pension plans, which are characterized by high "take-up" rates. Use of the payroll-deduction system, coupled with automatic enrollment, could make a voluntary-healthcare tax-credit system virtually universal.

8. **Tax credits will restore patient satisfaction with the healthcare system.** The professional literature shows that to the extent that employers allow workers to choose options, enabling them also to pocket the rewards of wise choices, costs are contained and employees are satisfied with their healthcare offerings. But only a bare majority, 52 percent, of persons in working families have a choice of health plan through their place of work; 43 percent have no choice. Among single persons, 56 percent have no choice of health plans.[19] Dissatisfaction arises when employers force employees into health plans, particularly managed-care plans. In such circumstances, workers have not only been deprived of a choice of health plan, but they are also often deprived of their choice of doctor or specialist.

Tax credits eliminate these coercive dynamics, giving patients the power to pick the plans they want and get the medical services or treatments they need. Moreover, empowered patients empower doctors. When the patient is the key decision maker in the system, the doctor also has a natural ally in the cure and treatment of disease. Therefore, a collateral effect of the use of tax credits to expand insurance coverage is to restore the traditional doctor-patient relationship, which the rise of corporate and government third-party payment arrangements has weakened.

---

[19]See Karen Davis and Cathy Schoen, "Managed Care, Choice and Patient Satisfaction," The Commonwealth Fund August 1997, p. 3.

CONCLUSION

America already has a national healthcare policy. It is the wrong one. It distorts the health-insurance market, fuels and hides higher costs, blocks open access to coverage, compromises quality of care, inhibits portability of benefits, ties health insurance to workplace, ensures breaks in the continuity of care, discourages innovation in healthcare delivery options, and frustrates consumer choice and genuine competition. It also weakens the relationship between doctors and patients, reduces patients' freedom and privacy, and compromises doctors' professional independence and integrity.

America needs a new policy. The root structural change must be to transform the health-insurance market—ruled by corporate benefit managers and regulated by government bureaucrats—into a consumer-driven, patient-oriented system based on personal choice. To do this, Congress must reform the federal tax treatment of health insurance from one that gives almost exclusive tax breaks for the purchase of insurance through employment into one that gives individuals and families the ability to pick and choose the plans they want at the price they wish to pay. A national system of individual tax credits would allow individuals to obtain coverage through large group plans, including those sponsored by national associations, unions, fraternal organizations, and even religious institutions. Such a policy would dramatically expand access to coverage, establish portability in benefits, promote personal choice and patient satisfaction, and restore the traditional doctor-patient relationship.

What America does not need is more counterproductive and costly regulations. Nor does America need to copy the mistake of other countries, such as Britain or Canada, by giving politicians who largely created the problem an opportunity to mismanage the entire system and to play budgetary politics with medical care.

Far too many people are uninsured, and far too many who have gaps in coverage remain vulnerable to catastrophic illness and financial devastation. And, in the absence of the discipline of a genuine market, costs are rapidly rising. But these serious issues mask a more fundamental one: The healthcare debate is not simply about care; it's about power. Who will make the key decisions? Given the dynamics of recent healthcare policy, two major alternatives are emerging: government officials, who tell Americans what they can or cannot have—or individuals and families, freely choosing the plans and benefits they want. How policy makers act will profoundly shape the character and quality of American life for the rising generation. Americans should choose freedom.

REFERENCES

American Medical Student Association (1999). The uninsured. *New York Times Upfront,* *132*(6), 24.

American Public Health Association (1997). Policy statements adopted by the governing council of the American Public Health Association, November 20, 1996. *American Journal of Public Health, 87*(3), 495–519.

Anonymous (1998). Impassioned call for a single-payer national health system rings out from Chicago. *Nation's Health, 28*(8), 1–2.

Baxandall, P. (2001). Spending #1, performance #37: How U. S. healthcare stacks up internationally. *Dollars and Sense,* (235), 38–40.

Bell, A. (2000). Massachusetts voters reject universal healthcare. *National Underwriter, 104*(48), 26.

Bell, H. (2000). Life without insurance: True stories of unnecessary sickness, death and humiliation. *New Physician, 49*(6), 21–39.

Bertlett, D. K. (2000). The growth of the uninsured and the underinsured. *Journal of Financial Service Professionals, 54*(5), 62–66.

Bruder, P. (2001). Justice and managed-care: An oxymoronic notion. *Hospital Topics, 78*(4), 31–35.

Delaney, M., & Hensel, W. A. (2000). Health care epiphany: "No one could possible want a system as complex and cumbersome as ours." *American Medical News, 42*(43), 16.

Derickson, A. (1997). The house of Falk: The paranoid style in American health politics. *American Journal of Public Health, 87*(11), 1836–1844.

Dufour, J. (2000). Advocating a single-payer system. *Physician Assistant, 24*(7), 16–17.

Gaskin, I. (2000). Making a case for a single-payer system: A conversation with Quentin Young, M.D. *Birth Gazette, 16*(1), 32–33.

Gorin, S. (1997). Universal healthcare coverage in the United State: Barriers, prospects and limitations. *Health and Social Work, 22*(3), 223–231.

Grumbach, K. (2000). Insuring the uninsured. *Journal of the American Medical Association, 284*(16), 2114–2116.

Landa, A. (2001). Physicians promote universal healthcare. *American Medical News, 44*(19), 5–6.

Levey, S., Hill, J., & Prybil, L. (2000). Health care reform and the uninsured. *Health Progress, 81*(5), 20–24.

Lewis, C. (2000). No better time. *Hospitals and Health Networks, 74*(11), 92.

National Association of Social Workers (2000). *Social Work Speaks: National Association of Social Workers Policy Statements* (5th ed.). Washington, DC: NASW Press.

Newcomb, P. (2000). Arguments for a single-payer national health insurance program. *The Nurse Practitioner, 25*(11), 8–10.

Physicians for a National Health Program (2001). Proposal of the physicians' working group for single-payer national health insurance. Retrieved July 6, 2001, from http://www.pnhp.org/.

Redmond, H. (2001). The healthcare crisis in the United States: A call to action. *Health and Social Work, 26*(1), 54–57.

Voelker, R. (1998). Activist Young says "gathering storm" will propel a single-payer movement. *Journal of the American Medical Association, 280*(17), 1467.

■ ■ ■ ■ ■

HAS THE AMERICANS WITH DISABILITIES ACT (ADA) GONE TOO FAR?

Editor's Note:

About 8–17 percent of the U.S. population between the ages of twenty and sixty-four have disabilities that limit their ability to work. About half that number are disabled to the point that they cannot work or can work only irregularly. Although the range of disabilities is great, people with disabilities share a central experience rooted in stigmatization, discrimination, and oppression. The greatest stride in addressing discrimination against the disabled was made in 1990 when former president George Bush signed the Americans with Disabilities Act (ADA) (PL 101–336) into law. This act is the most comprehensive legislation for people with disabilities ever passed in the United States. The extension of civil rights to the disabled satisfied some supporters, alienated those who believed they were hurt by the act (especially some small employers), and left some members of the disabled community wondering what had actually been accomplished—and for whom.

Howard Jacob Karger, Ph.D., is professor and Ph.D. program director at the University of Houston. Along with David Stoesz, he is the coauthor of *American Social Welfare Policy* (4th ed.). He has published widely in the field of social-welfare policy, including in areas such as income-maintenance policy, poverty policy, and social development.

John C. Bricout, Ph.D., is assistant professor, George Warren Brown School of Social Work, at Washington University. Professor Bricout's professional specialty is assessing and improving organization-worker fit for employees with a disability. His current research focuses on the impacts of work and community environments on the rehabilitation and independence of people with physical or psychiatric disabilities. He has published articles on work-environment strain, supported employment, telecommuting, and computer-mediated classroom accommodations.

YES

Howard Jacob Karger

The Americans with Disabilities Act was signed into law by former president George Bush on July 26, 1990. The goal of the ADA was to further the full participation of people with disabilities by giving them civil-rights protections similar to those provided to individuals on the basis of race, sex, national origin, and religion. The ADA guarantees equal opportunity to individuals with disabilities in employment, public accommodation, transportation, state and local government services, and telecommunications. This law applies to companies with more than fifteen employees. It forbids them to discriminate against a person with a disability in hiring or promotion if the person is otherwise qualified for the job (U.S. Department of Justice, 1995).

On some levels the ADA is working extremely well. Structural barriers are being removed, much of the new building construction is designed to accommodate the disabled, public transportation is becoming more responsive, and there is an increasing awareness of the contribution of the disabled. On other levels, especially employment and education, the ADA is not faring as well. This debate will focus on those areas.

IS THE ADA WORKING?

There are several questions that should be asked of any social policy. First, who is the target population, and are they being adequately served by the policy? According to the ADA, a person is considered disabled if he or she has difficulty performing certain life functions (seeing, hearing, talking, walking, climbing stairs, and lifting and carrying) or has difficulty with certain social roles (doing schoolwork for children, working at a job, etc.). A person unable to perform one or more of these activities, or who uses an assistive device to get around, or who needs assistance from another person to perform basic activities is considered to have a severe disability. The U.S. Census reports that one in five Americans (54 million) have some kind of disability, with one in ten having a severe disability. Under this broad definition of the ADA, more than half of all those sixty-five and older have a disability (U.S. Department of Commerce, 1997). Of the 54 million Americans with disabilities, fewer than four million are legally blind, deaf, or in wheelchairs. As such, one of the key problems in the ADA is the vague interpretation of the term *disabled*. The word allows large numbers of people with varying levels of broadly defined disabilities to seek protection under the law.

The second question is whether a particular policy is accomplishing its intended goal. A major goal of the ADA is to promote employment opportunities for people with disabilities. According to the Census Bureau, between 1994 (after the passage of the ADA) and 1999, the overall unemployment rate fell from 6.6 to 4.1 percent. But the rate of unemployment for persons with disabilities rose from 71.8 to 78 percent (U.S. Department of Commerce, 1997). Moreover, only 32 percent of disabled people of working age (eighteen to sixty-four) work full- or part-time compared to 81 percent of the nondisabled population. According to the National Organization on Disabilities (2000), more than two-thirds of those unemployed said they would prefer to be working. Of those who report that they are able to work despite their disability, only 56 percent are actually working (National Organization on Disabilities, 2000). More than ten years after the passage of the ADA, people with disabilities are almost three times as likely as the nondisabled to live in households with total yearly incomes of $15,000 or less. Twenty-one percent of those with a disability and 28 percent of those with a severe disability live in poverty, compared to 8 percent of those with no disability (Diversity, Inc., 1999). Based on these statistics, the ADA has not only failed to increase employment opportunities for people with disabilities, but it may have actually worsened them.

PROBLEMS WITH THE ADA

The ADA was obviously based on good intentions. It was an open-ended act predicated on letting the courts decide the particulars of the law. This vagueness was also an invitation to lawsuits. In 1999, the U.S. Supreme Court curtailed the scope of the law in two separate decisions. In *Sutton v. United Airlines, Inc.*, United Airlines refused to hire twin sisters who were regional airline pilots because they had uncorrected vision of 20/400. The sisters maintained that their vision was correctable to 20/20 and argued that United Airlines violated the ADA when they refused them employment. In *Murphy v. United Parcel Service, Inc.*, UPS fired a mechanic because he had high blood pressure. He claimed that his medication made him able to work and that therefore his firing was unlawful under the ADA. In both cases, the Supreme Court ruled that the ADA does not cover people whose disabilities can be sufficiently corrected with medicine, eyeglasses, or other measures. These cases could profoundly affect the rights of individuals with a range of impairments—from diabetes and hypertension to severe nearsightedness, hearing loss, prostheses, and even cancer. Those able to function in the employment arena with the help of medicine or auxiliary aids may not be able to challenge employers who refuse to hire them, fail to accommodate or promote them, or discharge them based on the belief that their disabilities make them ineligible for certain jobs.

Although the ADA has resulted in the removal of important physical barriers from employment, it has erected newer and even more potent ones. Employers and most institutions are lawsuit averse. In a litigious society, many employers view hiring the disabled as an invitation to trouble. They fear that hiring disabled employees is a lawsuit waiting to happen. Others fear that ADA provisions insulate disabled employees from being fired, lest the employers risk an expensive lawsuit. Still others argue that the vague language of the ADA makes it difficult for employers to comply with the provisions of the act, thereby inviting lawsuits.

Compliance with the ADA structures employer and applicant interactions by limiting questions about an applicant's disability. Hence, many employers are not certain what questions they may legally ask a disabled applicant. Instead of encouraging an open dialogue around work expectations and allowing disabled applicants to address their strengths, employers frequently circumvent the problem by not interviewing applicants with disabilities.

Employers' fear of ADA-related lawsuits or complaints has a basis in reality. There were almost 17,000 ADA-related complaints or lawsuits filed in 1999. Though employers prevailed 95 percent of the time in ADA lawsuits and 85 percent of the time in administrative complaints handled by the Equal Opportunity Commission, the disposition was costly. Some analysts claim that employer costs in grievances and lawsuits average $10,000 and can go as high as $75,000 (Hudgins, 1999). Regardless of whether an employer is on firm ground, it is often more cost-effective to settle out of court.

Like most forms of social-policy legislation, the ADA has been subject to abuse. Some employees want to get into a protected class to grab the bludgeon and use it against their employer. On the average, more than one-third of ADA complaints are filed because of bad backs (19.5 percent), emotional problems (11.4 percent), and alcoholism and drug abuse (3.6 percent). No more than 6 percent of complainants have impaired vision or hearing. Only 12.1 percent of complaints were filed by people with spinal-cord injuries and other neurological problems—the conditions pointed to when the ADA was being written (Matthews, 1995).

In general, the most disadvantaged are frequently the last ones to reap the benefits of being in a protected social class. The ADA is no different. A Harris poll done in the middle 1990s reported that only 40 percent of people with disabilities had any substantial knowledge of the ADA (Matthews, 1995). On the other hand, many ADA complaints involve exploring the limits of the Act, including complaints around "boutique" disabilities such as Adult Attention Deficit Disorder or personality disorders.

SCHOOLS OF SOCIAL WORK AND THE ADA

Not surprisingly, the inherent problems in the ADA are also evident in schools of social work. These disability issues primarily play out in two areas: mental health and learning disabilities.

A small but important number of applicants to social-work programs experience mental-health problems, some of which are severe. These problems can range from clinical depression to anxiety disorders and even to schizophrenia. Are schools of social work obligated to accept these applicants because they are covered under the ADA? Is it ethical or socially responsible to credential social-work graduates who have significant mental-health problems, in order to comply with the ADA? Are there higher obligations than those reflected in the ADA? Should schools of social work try to circumvent problematic parts of the ADA? According to the NASW Code of Ethics: "Social workers should not practice, condone, facilitate, or collaborate with any form of discrimination on the basis of race, ethnicity, national origin, color, sex, sexual orientation, age, marital status, political belief, religion, or mental or physical disability" (National Association of Social Workers, 1999). Though most instructors in schools of social work have encountered at least a few severely mentally ill students in their classes, it is unclear how many of them have actually done something about it.

The specter of the ADA also arises in terms of grading and class performance. Most helping professionals know that it is relatively easy to obtain a diagnosis of a learning disability. Increasingly, students are turning to the excuse of a learning disability to justify inadequate class work or test performance. Occasionally, these students will request special assignments, special test-taking procedures, the use of editors or grammatical software programs, special tutors, etc. Some even argue that writing is not a necessary prerequisite for professional competence and therefore should not factor in the class grade.

Learning disabilities are a real problem, and in legitimate cases they should be accommodated in classroom settings. However, what constitutes a legitimate disability, especially since these diagnoses are relatively easy to come by? Are students who failed to master writing skills learning disabled, or have they just not mastered these skills? Is it appropriate for students who have a conceptual learning disability to enter a profession that requires a high level of conceptual thought? One of the dangers of the ADA is that it creates loopholes through which certain individuals can exploit the intent of the law. Admittedly, only a small percentage of students exploit the ADA. However, it nevertheless creates an uneven playing field that penalizes diligent students while at the same time rewarding students who have found an angle to make their social-work education easier. The net result is the demoralization of students (and faculty) who choose to play by the rules.

The exploitation of well-intentioned social policies also applies to a small number of social-work educators. Tenure is becoming increasingly difficult to secure in most American universities, and some faculty are turning to desperate measures in response to this challenge. Not surprisingly, more diagnoses of disabilities such as Adult Attention Deficit Disorder, lower-back pain, Carpal Tunnel Syndrome, mental-health problems, and so forth are being offered as a justification for why some faculty are unable to sustain research and publish. Although these disabilities may be legitimate for some faculty, for others it is a convenient ruse to cover up incompetence or the lack of self-discipline. Moreover, it begs an important question. Namely, if one has Adult ADD, then perhaps a profession that requires a high level of self-discipline, focus, and concentration may not be the appropriate career choice. It is patently wrong to assume that a particular career or vocational choice is an entitlement. If I have a writing or conceptual disability, should I demand that a university evaluate me on criteria other than research and scholarship, even though these are the currency of the academic realm?

The tension around the ADA and social-work education exists on multiple levels. Schools of social work have the implicit gate-keeping function of credentialing trained and professionally competent social-work practitioners. There is an inherent societal expectation that any student who receives an M.S.W. or B.S.W. degree is capable of helping rather than hurting clients. On the other hand, the social-work profession is committed to promoting a society free of discrimination, including discrimination toward the disabled. In the case of a student with a long history of mental illness (but who is currently in remission), which side do we err on? This is the slippery slope of the ADA.

The gate-keeping function of social-work education is frustrated by an institutional aversion to litigation. In an increasingly litigious society, greater numbers of students and faculty are willing to retain legal counsel and sue over what they consider a breach of their rights. The implicit assumption is that most of these cases will be settled out of court because universities are averse to prolonged legal battles. Unfortunately, this assumption is too frequently correct. Universities will often settle before a court hearing (even if their case is strong) to save money and avoid bad publicity. The resolve of universities and schools of social work when faced with spurious disability grievances or lawsuits is particularly weak, because neither wants to be thought of as antagonistic toward people with disabilities. As a result, many university and school of social work administrators are reluctant to question students' disability claims, even if those claims appear bogus.

CONCLUSION

The inherent problems in the ADA manifest themselves in myriad ways. First, the vague language of the ADA allows for a definition of disabilities that often stretches the imagination. Boutique disorders such as Adult ADD, environmental stress, and so forth denigrate not only the intent of the Act but also the integrity of a disability. These disabilities create a loophole whereby those who refuse to take responsibility for their behavior can comfortably hide under the umbrella of a protected class. This development reveals a societal mindset that excuses unacceptable behavior and deflects responsibility away from the actor. The most egregious part of exploiting the ADA is that it trivializes real disabilities. Those people for whom the ADA was originally designed (the physically and mentally disabled) are lumped together with those who have more suspect disabilities. Morever, as nuisance claims and lawsuits proliferate, it is likely that new legislation or judicial actions will be implemented to curtail the intent and spirit of the ADA. The unfortunate victims in this backlash will be those people who need the protection of the ADA the most.

Second, the vague language of the ADA coupled with unclear expectations regarding appropriate accommodations for people with disabilities is having a chilling effect on the employment prospects of disabled workers. These factors, in conjunction with the growth of ADA-related lawsuits and grievances, are leading a growing number of employers to be suspicious of, if not downright hostile to, the hiring of disabled workers. In an all-too-common irony in social policy, the ADA may be having the exact opposite effect of what it intended.

Last, the creation of yet another protected class has its drawbacks. By creating and implementing the ADA, we have defined people with disabilities as another group of victims in need of social protection. While the list of victims grows in our society, so too does the backlash. Moreover, the ADA makes the assumption that all people with disabilities want to be part of a protected class. This is unfair to those who choose not to enjoy the protection (and stigma) of being part of a protected class.

American social policy is predicated on the piecemeal approach of putting vulnerable populations into an almost infinite number of little "protected-class" boxes. It then proceeds to protect each little box from the other. If the purpose of the ADA is to mainstream the disabled, then how can putting people into yet another box facilitate that goal? By segregating the disabled into a protected class, we are further isolating them rather than incorporating them into mainstream American society. Given the policy blunders in the past fifty years, one would think that American policymakers would finally realize that they cannot legislate morality, responsible behavior, good citizenship, tolerance, or compassion. The goal of social policy should not be to further balkanize American society, but to create conditions that allow all people to participate as equal citizens with equal protections under the law. Piecemeal approaches to equality and fairness (such as the ADA) do not work.

NO

John C. Bricout

Today, more than a decade since it was signed into law in 1990, the Americans with Disabilities Act (ADA) has become something of a lightning rod for debates on the adequacy and appropriateness of federal legislation for protecting the rights of individuals with disabilities. The ADA is neither the first major piece of federal legislation to address the needs of individuals with disabilities (witness the Architectural Barriers Act of 1968), nor the most recent (as evidenced by the Technology-Related Assistance for Individuals with Disabilities Act Amendments of 1994). Yet the five titles of the ADA provide the most comprehensive and far-reaching legislative guidelines for protecting the rights of disabled individuals. In an effort to remove physical and attitudinal barriers to the participation of individuals with disabilities in American society, the ADA has reshaped the practices of private and public entities in the realms of employment, transportation, construction of the built environment, and telecommunications. Given such ambitious goals and the broad scope of affected organizations—ranging from small businesses to metropolitan transportation authorities, state governments, and major software manufacturers—it is little wonder that the necessity as well as the efficacy of the ADA has come into question. For this reason, the question of whether the ADA has gone too far cannot be settled by facts alone, but must include explicit considerations of values, perspectives, and power relations.

QUESTIONS RAISED BY THE ADA

At its heart, the question of whether the ADA has gone too far is one of legitimacy, which itself hangs on at least three suppositions. The first supposition is that people with disabilities face barriers that require a legislative remedy at the federal level. The second supposition is that the costs entailed in the broad civil-rights mandate of the ADA are warranted in the current social, economic, and political context. The third supposition is that the ADA has made sufficient progress in realizing some of its goals to warrant its continuation. In examining the merit of each supposition in turn, it is necessary to articulate the value positions, perspectives, and power issues that undergird arguments for and against the legitimacy of the ADA.

THE ACT

The Americans with Disabilities Act (P.L. 101–336) has five titles covering: (I) employment, (II) public services, (III) public accommodations and services operated by private entities, and (IV) telecommunications services, followed by (V) miscellaneous provisions: including insurance issues, integration, state immunity, and relations to other laws and bodies. The ADA is enforced through designated federal agencies and covers most private and public entities, including all businesses with fifteen or more employees. Despite the claim that the ADA is too exigent of covered entities, the Act allows exceptions to accommodation requirements in the face of significant implementation difficulties. Title I and Title II allow exceptions to the requirement of providing either "reasonable" (Title I), or "public" (Title II) accommodations. In Title I, reasonable accommodations are not required if they would impose "undue hardship" on an employer, or "pose a direct threat to the health or safety" of others in the workplace. In Title II, removal of architectural or communication barriers in existing buildings must be carried out only if "readily achievable." Otherwise, "alternative methods" of making goods, services, and accommodations must be provided.

The definition of disability in the ADA is very broad, but explicitly so, in order to avoid excluding anyone with a legitimate claim. An individual must meet one or more of the following three criteria to be considered disabled: (1) substantial limitation in one or more major life activities (such as work) due to a physical or mental impairment, (2) a record of such impairment, or (3) the perception by others that he or she has such an impairment. A wide range of conditions have been included within this rubric, including substance abuse and HIV infection, as well as physical, psychiatric, mental, neurological, sensory, and learning impairments.

IS THE ADA WARRANTED?

Do the barriers to social participation that people with disabilities face require a legislative remedy at the federal level? A 2001 Supreme Court ruling (*University of Alabama v. Garrett*) found that state governments are immune from lawsuits for job-discrimination claims. This decision suggests that in the eyes of the Court, the employment protections owed individuals with disabilities are not on a par with those owed individuals identified as belonging to a racial or ethnic minority. This in turn seems to question the "minority model" of disability implicit in the ADA's civil-rights protections, which are patterned on the Civil Rights Act of 1964.

A MINORITY OR MINORITIES?

Do people with disabilities fail to meet the standards of an oppressed minority population, and thus do not merit civil-rights protections at the federal level? Some have argued that by covering the estimated 54 million Americans with disabilities of varying severity and nature (from quadriplegia and schizophrenia to learning disabilities and asymptomatic HIV), the notion of "oppressed minority" is lost, and with it, the right to special civil-rights protections (e.g., Baldwin, 1997; Elvin, 2000). This argument fails to take into account several facts that narrow the range and number of persons benefiting from a "disability" designation. First, there is a trend in the U.S. Supreme Court toward excluding as disabilities impairments or conditions that can be managed or compensated (Griffin & Brown, 2000; Hall & Hatch, 1999). Second, evidence suggests (Porter, 1998) that people claiming employment protections under the ADA tend overwhelmingly to lose their cases, whether those cases are decided by a judge (92 percent) or administratively (86 percent). Others have argued that two distinct groups of people with disabilities exist: a more severely impaired group perhaps deserving of special protections, and a less severely impaired group undeserving of such protections (e.g., Johnson, 1997).

DISCRIMINATION AND JUST DESERTS

Typically, critics raise two arguments to support this declension between "deserving" and "undeserving" individuals with disabilities. First, they argue that the framers of the ADA had in mind only the most severely disabled individuals. This argument fails to take into account the role of accommodations and assistive technologies in enhancing the functional abilities of individuals with quite severe, congenital, or chronic conditions. Surely the framers of the legislation did not believe that level of functional impairment was the only criterion for ADA protections. Indeed, the Act's focus on discrimination would suggest that the framers (accurately) foresaw continued stigmatization and prejudice against even high-functioning individuals, whether they are people with asymptomatic HIV or individuals managing their mental illness with medications. Second, they maintain that the addition of difficult-to-diagnose conditions (such as soft-tissue impairments) or mild disabilities (such as chronic back pain) encourage specious claims by individuals who are malingering or who (if actually impaired) are not in need of special protections. Again, the 1998 study of EEOC records revealed that few employees won their cases owing to the difficulties in proving "substantial limitations" to functioning (Porter, 1998). These studies cast doubt on the efficacy, if not the prevalence of, malingering and gold digging.

The available evidence suggests that, as a group, people with disabilities live disproportionately with unemployment, poor education, poor housing, poor healthcare, and low incomes (Kopeks, 1995; McNeil, 2000; NOD/ Harris, 2000). Even college-educated individuals with a disability appear to earn less money over the course of their careers than their nondisabled peers do (Hendricks, Schiro-Geist, & Broadbent, 1997). This is not to suggest that there are not important in-group differences; in particular, racial and ethnic minorities seem to find less favorable employment and encounter more discrimination than white individuals with disabilities (Blanck, 1996; Kim, 1996).

It would be disingenuous to claim that all individuals with disabilities live under equally oppressive social, political and economic conditions. Clearly, individuals with more education and resources to begin with—most commonly individuals with adventitious disabilities who are able to return to work—will enjoy better economic success than those with developmental disabilities who typically have poor work histories and less-developed inter-personal skills. However, all such persons will be vulnerable to discrimina-tion. Even if a Stephen Hawking or a Christopher Reeve continues to produce creative and lasting work in their fields, the discrimination faced by others with similar disabilities is likely to be undiminished.

From the standpoint of civil rights, to deny people with disabilities minority status on exclusionary arguments grounded in notions of "deserv-ingness" divides and conquers. But it also removes discrimination from soci-etal, institutional, and organizational contexts and places it in the context of individual bad behavior. In this framework, only the most "impaired" indi-viduals would be worthy of special consideration, presumably because of their infirmity. "Discrimination" would be limited to the truculence of unkind or ignorant people who do not respond appropriately to someone in the "sick role." The impact of disablement on individual functioning and productivity reintroduces the second supposition to be explored in determining the legiti-macy of the ADA; namely, the costs of such a broad civil-rights mandate.

WEIGHING COSTS AND BENEFITS

The question of whether the costs associated with the ADA are warranted in the current social, political and economic context must include a discussion of what "costs" are, in fact, investments, and what "benefits" may engender unforeseen costs. The ADA has been widely but unfairly criticized as an unfunded federal mandate, when in fact evidence shows that the cost of most workplace accommodations is low (Batavia, 1997; Bruyere, 2000). Estimates of the average costs of job accommodations have ranged from $100 (Morely & Hyatt, 1996) to $500 (Jonse, Watzlaf, Hobson, & Mazzoni, 1996). Another study similarly found the cost of new ADA-related construction to be quite low—a modest 4.9 percent of total costs for a significant portion of respon-dents (Jonse, et al., 1996). At the same time, even job accommodations that do not incur a direct cost, such as flexible scheduling, might nonetheless be per-ceived as having a cost because of additional supervisor or coworker respon-sibilities, and coworker resentment about accommodations as "special treatment" (Frierson, 1992; Pati & Bailey, 1995).

Fortunately, employers have found reason to provide accommodations despite such concerns. Several workplace studies have reported accommo-dation costs either to be small or a good investment, allowing workers to retain their jobs longer (Bruyere, 2000; Burkhauser, 1997). In fact, the greatest cost burden of the ADA seems to be borne by the U.S. Equal Employment Opportunity Commission, which enforces Title I. The EEOC has had to absorb the costs of burgeoning caseloads and ADA training without a corre-sponding budget increase (Bruyere, 2000). The "costs" to the federal govern-men and to public and private entities seem worthwhile in a context in which an estimated 68 percent of individuals with disabilities are unemployed, 22 percent fail to complete high school, and 29 percent live in poverty (NOD/ Harris, 2000).

Some authors have argued that the ADA has improved employer attitudes by altering basic assumptions about people with disabilities, recasting people with disabilities as productive agents rather than social-service recipients (Baldwin, 1997; Wehman, 1993). In fact, the employment picture for individuals with disabilities may have improved slightly of late. In the recent 2000 NOD/Harris survey of people with disabilities, 32 percent of respondents indicated that they were employed—a 3 percent increase over the previous survey of 1998. Moreover, 56 percent of respondents with a disability who say they are able to work reported that they were working, as compared to only 46 percent in the 1986 NOD/Harris survey.

However, there may be unforeseen "attitudinal" costs in terms of employer backlash against the ADA. Although the great preponderance of employers surveyed in recent national NOD/Harris disability surveys (1998, 2000) have expressed their approval of the ADA, the employment barriers faced by individuals with disabilities, including high unemployment rates and job stagnation, persist. This strongly implies unexpressed reservations by employers about the ADA (Schall, 1998). In her review of the Title I EEOC complaint data from 1992 to 1996, Schall (1998) found that only 9.8 percent of the complaints addressed the hiring process, compared to 51.9 percent discharge-related complaints. The disparity between hiring and discharge-related complaints suggests that some employment discrimination may escape detection (Schall, 1998). The ADA may have only made employers more cautious, rather than more conscientious, thanks to managers' fears about the costs of employing individuals with disabilities. This "resistance" actually creates an argument for perpetuating the ADA, rather than desisting, because systemic change often engenders resistance (Senge, 1990). Such resistance directs the attention of "change agents" (that is, disability activists and their allies) to the underlying power relations and supportive norms (Senge, 1990). Thus, the challenge to the ADA is to foster the development of a community and to forge allied coalitions that can actively address the power inequities arising from institutional and societal structures and practices that favor nondisabled persons. This point leads to an examination of the third question: whether the ADA has made sufficient progress toward its goals.

PROGRESS THROUGH COMMUNITY

One way of appraising the progress of the ADA is to assess the satisfaction of individuals with disabilities themselves. In the most recent NOD/Harris survey, 63 percent of all respondents with a disability indicated that life has improved for people with disabilities in the past decade, which the investigators claim may be due in part to the ADA.

However, in the previous NOD/Harris (1998) survey, 58 percent of respondents who were asked directly about the impact of the ADA said that it had not made a significant impact on their lives. Ambivalence about the difference made by the ADA is understandable, given the mixed reactions of those who provide accommodations and the persistence of negative beliefs about the capacity of people with disabilities. Negative attitudes toward people with disabilities by nondisabled people endure even in the climate of civil rights fostered by the ADA. Recent studies have found negative attitudes and attributions among employers, neighbors, student peers, teachers, and others, in addition to more positive views (e.g., Bruce, Clark, 1997; Harman, & Baker, 2000; Hernandez & Keys, 2000; Silverman & Segal, 1996).

In some sense, then, the ADA may have served as a catalyst to raise the expectations of individuals with disabilities. The Act has led them to express skepticism about the very legislation that articulated a new vision of relationships between people with disabilities and their environments: social, physical, and electronic. Is there evidence that the ADA has been a catalyst to positive community building among people with disabilities in the same way that it has raised expectations? Although this is difficult to assess, it is interesting to note that disability advocates have successfully expanded the scope of ADA protections to people with psychiatric disabilities, people with learning disabilities, and people with HIV.

The federal government, some private and public institutions, and private litigants are striving to make the World Wide Web accessible by arguing an "effective communication" rationale using the ADA (Waddell, 2000a; 2000b). The ADA can also contribute to a rights-based framework for providing online accessibility to people with disabilities (Bricout, 2001). By expanding the boundaries of the community of people with disabilities, the ADA can claim to have laid a foundation for coalition building and political action to combat inequities. However, the role of the ADA in bringing about "progress"—not only on an individual or aggregated basis, but also on the basis of fostering a community of shared interest—is unclear at present. Thus, the question of whether the ADA has made sufficient progress to warrant its continuation cannot be satisfactorily answered. Certainly, the ADA offers the promise of fostering new relations between the community of people with disabilities and the institutional and societal structures that have denied them access to opportunities for participation and development. Whether such a community will develop is an issue larger than the ADA, although one in which the ADA could play an important role. The role of the ADA in fostering positive change for people with disabilities will hinge to large degree on its evolution.

EVOLUTION OR DEVOLUTION?

Like all legislation, the ADA is evolving over time, with changes in enforcement, relevant jurisprudence, social, political, and economic circumstances. At the time of this writing, the political context has taken a decidedly conservative turn. The obvious portend of this change is the emphasis on states' rights, which has already led to the granting of state immunity from ADA-based lawsuits for job discrimination. An outcome of the state-focused approach that is more supportive of the aims of the ADA is the New Freedom Initiative for People with Disabilities. The Initiative allocates money to states for assistive technologies, education, home ownership, transportation, work, and community access. Nonetheless, the slowdown of the U.S. economy may have a pernicious effect on the ADA as employers, builders, and others become more cost-conscious and scale back their plans.

It is unclear what impact a states'-rights orientation will have on federal enforcement of the ADA. However, given the need for more proactive enforcement approaches and more funding for additional staff and resources (Reichert, 2000), the outlook may not be good. The tendency of the Supreme Court to strike down lawsuits in which the plaintiff compensates for his or her disability or can take medications or other treatments that mitigate the impact of the disability has the potential to remove many individuals from the umbrella of the ADA (Griffin & Brown, 2000). Employees with disabilities who fail to take their medications, or who can attain a high level of functioning without assistive technologies for whatever reasons, may be forsaking their rights to claim ADA protections. On the other hand, it appears that employees with disabilities have reason to be more optimistic about receiving precisely the job accommodations they need, thanks to a recent ADA-based lawsuit. Recently, a federal appeals court (*Vollmort v. Wisconsin DOT*) found that employers must provide accommodations fitted to the exact needs of the job and the employee's disability (Hatch & Hall, 2000). However, costly accommodations for individuals with more severe disabilities who are employed by small businesses may still be beyond the scope of ADA protections, if the cost of the accommodation would cause undue hardship to the employer.

On balance, there are perhaps more reasons to be concerned about the efficacy of the ADA and its sustainability than to be sanguine. However, this is not to say that the ADA ought to be abandoned. The alternative to the ADA—reliance on a score of disparate federal laws, and the devolution of ADA functions and intentions to state or local legislatures—would severely undermine any real hope of ending discrimination against people with disabilities. This judgment has already been made for other minority groups for whom federal civil-rights protections are the source of legal protections and societal sanctions, public legitimacy, and distributive justice. Rather than dismantle the ADA as a failed experiment, we should recognize that the aspirations of people with disabilities for equality require a reinvigoration of the Act's purpose, mandate, and resources.

REFERENCES

Baldwin, M. L. (1997). Can the ADA achieve its employment goals? *Annals of the American Academy, AAPS*, 37–52.

Batavia, I. A. (1997). Ideology and independent living: Will conservatism harm people with disabilities? *Annals of the American Academy*, AAPS, 53–70.

Blanck, P. D. (1996). Empirical study of the ADA (1990–1994). *Behavioral Science and the Law, 14*(1), 5–27.

Bricout, J. C. (2001). Making computer-mediated education responsive to the accommodation needs of students with disabilities. *Journal of Social Work Education, 37*(2), 15–30.

Bruce, A. J., Harman, M. J., & Baker, N. A. (2000). Anticipated social contact with persons in wheelchairs: Age and gender differences. In F. Columbus (Ed.), *Advances in psychology research, Vol. 1* (pp. 219–228). Huntington, NY: Nova Science Publishers.

Bruyere, S. M. (2000). Civil rights and employment issues of disability policy. *The Journal of Disability Policy Studies, 11*(1), 18–28.

Burkhauser, R. V. (1997). Post-ADA: Are people with disabilities expected to work? *Annals of the American Academy, AAPS, 549*, 71–83.

Clark, M. D. (1997). Teacher response to learning disability: A test of attributional principals. *Journal of Learning Disabilities, 30*(1), 69–79.

Diversity, Inc. (1999). The bureaucrats keep count. Retrieved June 3, 2001, from http://www,diversityinc.com.

Elvin, J. (2000). ADA's good intentions have unintended consequences. *Insight on the News, 16*(7), 18.

Freedom Network (2000). Good intentions and the ADA. Retrieved June 7, 2001, from http://www.free-market.net/spotlight/ada.

Frierson, J. G. (1992). An employer's dilemma: The ADA's provisions on reasonable accommodations. *Labor Law Journal, 43*(1), 309–312.

Griffin, J. W., & Brown, B. D. (2000). Chipping away at the ADA. *Trial, 36*(13), 48.

Hall, J. E., & Hatch, D. D. (1999). Supreme Court decisions require ADA revision. *Workforce, 78*(8), 60–66.

Hatch, D., & Hall, J. E. (2000). ADA requires disability-specific accommodations. *Workforce, 79*(2), 92.

Hendricks, W., Schiro-Geist, C., & Broadbent, E. (1997). Long-term disabilities and college education. *Industrial Relations, 36*(1), 46–60.

Hernandez, B., & Keys, C. (2000). Employer attitudes toward workers with disabilities and their ADA employment rights: A literature review. *Journal of Rehabilitation, 66*(4), 4–16.

Hudgins, E. L. (1999, May 24). Counterpoint on ADA and HIV. *Physician's Weekly*, 1–5.

Johnson, W. G. (1997). The future of disability policy: Benefit payments or civil rights? *Annals of the American Academy, AAPS, 549*, 160–172.

Jonse, D. L., Watzlaf, V. J., Hobson, D., & Mazzoni, J. (1996). Responses within non-federal hospitals in Pennsylvania to the Americans with Disabilities Act of 1990. *Physical Therapy, 76*(1), 49–60.

Kim, P. S. (1996). Disability policy: An analysis of the employment of people with disabilities in the American federal government. *Public Personnel Management, 25*(1), 73–88.

Kopeks, S. (1995). The Americans with Disabilities Act: A tool to combat poverty. *Journal of Social Work Education, 31*(3), 337–346.

Mathews, J. (1995, April 16). Disabilities act failing to achieve workplace goals: Landmark law rarely helps disabled people seeking jobs. *The Washington Post*, 3A.

McNeil, J. M. (2000). Employment, earnings and disability. 75th Annual Conference of the Western Economic Association International. Vancouver, BC, June 29–July 3, 2000.

Morely, G., & Hyatt, D. (1996). Do injured workers pay for reasonable accommodating? *Industrial and Labor Relations Review, 50*(1), 92–98.

National Association of Social Workers (1999). Code of ethics of the National Association of Social Workers, approved by the 1996 NASW Delegate Assembly and revised by the 1999 NASW Delegate Assembly. Silver Spring, MD.

National Organization on Disabilities (2000). Americans with disabilities trail non-disabled in key life areas, benchmark NOD/Harris survey finds. Retrieved June 3, 2001, from http://www.nod.org/hsevent.html.

NOD/Harris (1998). Survey program on participation and attitudes. Americans with disabilities still face sharp gaps in securing jobs, education, transportation and in many areas of daily life. Retrieved June 16, 2001, from http://www.nod.org/pressurvey.html.

NOD/Harris (2000). Survey program on participation and attitudes. The 2000 NOD/Harris survey of Americans with disabilities. Retrieved June 18, 2001, from http://www.nod.org/hs2000.html.

Pati, G. C., & Bailey, E. K. (1995). Empowering people with disabilities: Strategy and human resource issues in implementing the ADA. *Organizational Dynamics, 23*(3), 52–69.

Porter, R. (1998). Employees lose ADA suits, study shows. *Trial, 34*(9), 16–18.

Reichert, J. L. (2000). Poor federal enforcement weakens ADA, disability group asserts. *Trial, 36*(9), 93.

Schall, C. M. (1998). The Americans with Disabilities Act—Are we keeping our promise? An analysis of the effect of the ADA on the employment of persons with disabilities. *Journal of Vocational Rehabilitation, 10*(3), 191–203.

Scotch, R. K., & Schriner, K. (1997). Disability as human variation: Implications for policy. *Annals of the American Academy, AAPS, 549*, 148–154.

Senge, P. M. (1990). *The fifth discipline: The art and practice of the learning rganization.* New York: Doubleday.

Silverman, C. J., & Segal, S. P. (1996). When neighborhoods complain: Correlates of neighborhood opposition to sheltered care facilities. *Adult Residential Care Journal, 10*(2), 137–148.

U. S. Department of Commerce (1997). Census brief. Disabilities affect one-fifth of all Americans: Proportion could increase in coming decades. U. S. Department of Commerce, Economics and Statistics Division, CENBR/97-5, December 1997.

U. S. Department of Justice (1995), ADA/EEOC. Retrieved June 6, 2001, from http://www.usdoj.gov/crt/ada/adahom1.asp.

Waddell, C. D. (2000a). Electronic curbcuts: The ADA in cyberspace. Retrieved June 11, 2001, from http://www.abnet.org/irr/hr/winter00humanrights/waddle.htm.

Waddell, C. D. (2000b). The National Federation of the Blind sues AOL. Retrieved June 11, 2001, from http://www.abnet.org/irr/hr/winter00humanrights/waddle2.html.

Wehman, P. (1993). Employment opportunities and career development. In P. Wehman (Ed.), *The ADA mandate for social change* (pp. 45–68). Baltimore, MD: Paul H. Brookes Publishing.

HAS THE WAR ON DRUGS BEEN EFFECTIVE?

Editor's Note:
The U.S. War on Drugs has become a "moral panic," the sort of melodrama that an insecure middle class creates in order to retain its social standing. A moral panic is manifested by policies and professionals that seek to reestablish social control over a phantom threat. In the case of the War on Drugs, conservative politicians and law-enforcement officers have convinced the public that the nation suffers from a new generation of violent minority youth who must be held in check. The evidence presented for the law-and-order agenda consists largely of the arrest rates for violent and repeat offenders. Yet most of these "violent" offenses stemmed from overzealous police officers' overcharging miscreants, and most "repeat" offenders were rearrested for drug-related offenses. Not coincidentally, many black leaders, including Jesse Jackson, argue that minorities are the real target of the War on Drugs. In that sense, the "war" has become a war on minorities as much as a war on drugs.

The White House Office of National Drug Control Policy (ONDCP), a component of the Executive Office of the President, was established by the Anti-Drug Abuse Act of 1988. The principal purpose of ONDCP is to establish policies, priorities, and objectives for the nation's drug-control program. The goals of the program are to reduce illicit drug use, manufacturing, and trafficking; drug-related crime and violence; and drug-related health consequences. To achieve these goals, the director of ONDCP is charged with producing the National Drug Control Strategy. The Strategy directs the nation's anti-drug efforts and establishes a program, a budget, and guidelines for cooperation among federal, state, and local entities.

Susan P. Robbins, Ph.D., is an associate professor at the University of Houston Graduate School of Social Work. She has taught substance-abuse courses at both the graduate and undergraduate levels for over twenty years. Dr.

Robbins also trains child-protective service workers throughout Texas and New Mexico on substance-abuse-related issues. A founding member of the Drug Policy Forum of Texas, she also serves on their board of directors. Dr. Robbins has published in several areas, including human development and substance abuse.

YES[1]

ONDCP

EVOLUTION AND OVERVIEW OF THE NATIONAL DRUG CONTROL STRATEGY

National drug-control strategies were produced annually between 1989 and 1999. These strategies increasingly recognized the importance of preventing drug use by young people and a recognition that no single approach can rescue the nation from drug abuse. Consensus was reached that drug prevention, education, treatment, and research must be complemented by supply-reduction abroad, on our borders, and within the United States. Each strategy expressed a commitment to maintain and enforce anti-drug laws. All the strategies, with growing success, tied policy to a scientific body of knowledge about the nation's drug problems. The *1996 Strategy* established five goals and thirty-two supporting objectives as the basis for a coherent, long-term national effort. These goals remain the heart of the current *Strategy* and will guide federal drug-control agencies over the next five years. These goals are useful for state and local governments as well as the private sector.

Drug abuse and related crime permeate every corner of our society, afflicting inner cities, affluent suburbs, and rural communities. Drugs affect rich and poor, educated and uneducated, professionals and blue-collar workers, young and old. Seventy-seven percent of drug users in America are employed (SAHMSA, 2000). Some of the elderly suffer from addiction as do people in the prime of their lives. Drug abuse is prevalent among the young although it is not as widespread as many children and adolescents think.

The history of drug abuse in America indicates that this blight is cyclic in nature. When the nation fails to pay attention and take precautions, drug abuse spreads. The introduction of cocaine in the late nineteenth century exemplifies how attitudes affect the incidence of drug abuse. Cocaine use skyrocketed, in part because the psycho-pharmacological effects of this drug were poorly understood. The alleged benefits of cocaine were touted by health authorities whose unproven claims were the basis for commercial

---

[1]Excerpted from The Office of National Drug Control Policy (ONDCP), *The National Drug Control Strategy: 2001 Annual Report.* Washington, DC: ONDCP, 2001.

advertising. Only when the negative consequences of cocaine addiction were recognized and publicized did perceptions change. Drug abuse was condemned, and new laws were passed producing a healthier nation with a lower crime rate.

When people forgot, ignored, or denied the problem of drug abuse, it resurfaced. Cultural amnesia allowed new drugs to be introduced, some of which were more potent than their predecessors. Associated with these new drugs were subcultures with special appeal for the young and impressionable. Once again, drug abuse increased as did its deleterious consequences. Twice in this century drug use rose and then fell. Illegal drugs never disappeared entirely although the percentage of Americans who used them declined dramatically.

If we aren't careful, the number of drug abusers could rise again. Drug use among children is a particularly urgent concern. Beginning around 1990, teens and preteens adopted more permissive attitudes toward drugs. Soon thereafter, actions followed perceptions, and use of illegal drugs increased among young people. This trend continued through 1996 before stabilizing in 1997. In 1999, 6.7 percent (14.8 million) of Americans twelve and older were current users of illicit drugs. This figure is down from the 14.1 percent of the U.S. population twelve and older who were current users in 1979.

Drug abuse and its consequences can be reduced. By historical standards, present rates of drug use are relatively low. With the concerted effort outlined in the *National Drug Control Strategy* and this Annual Report, we can lower them further. Indeed, the will of the American people is such that we aim to slash rates of drug use by half over the next several years.

THE NATIONAL RESPONSE TO DRUG ABUSE: PROTECTING PUBLIC HEALTH AND SAFETY

The *National Drug Control Strategy* takes a long-term, holistic view of the drug problem and recognizes the devastating effect drug abuse has on the country's public health and safety. The *Strategy* maintains that no single solution can solve this multifaceted challenge. The *Strategy* focuses on prevention, treatment, research, law enforcement, shielding our borders, drug-supply reduction, and international cooperation. It provides general guidance while identifying specific initiatives. Through a balanced array of demand-reduction and supply-reduction actions, we strive to reduce drug use and availability by half and the consequences of drug abuse by at least 25 percent by 2007. If this goal is achieved, just 3 percent of the household population aged twelve and over will be using illegal drugs. This level would be the lowest documented drug-use rate in American history; drug-related health, economic, social, and criminal costs are expected to drop commensurately.

Preventing drug abuse in the first place is preferable to addressing the problem later through treatment and law enforcement. The *Strategy* focuses on young people, seeking to teach them about the many negative consequences associated with illegal drugs, alcohol, and tobacco. In addition to drug-prevention for children, intervention programs must help young adults as they leave home to start college or join the workforce.

There are approximately five million drug abusers who need immediate treatment and who constitute a major portion of domestic demand. Without help, many of these adults and their families will suffer from the impact of poor physical and mental health, unstable employment and family relations, and possible involvement with the criminal-justice system. Since parental substance abuse is a significant predictor of youth drug use and often contributes to child abuse and neglect, treatment for parents is key to breaking the inter-generational cycle of addiction. Accordingly, the *Strategy* focuses on treatment. Research clearly demonstrates that treatment works. We must take advantage of all opportunities—in the workplace, the health and social-services system, the criminal-justice system, and our communities—to encourage drug abusers to become drug-free.

Substance abuse by law breakers is another area of concern. A December 1998 Bureau of Justice Statistics study found that 33 percent of state and 22 percent of federal prisoners said they committed their current offense while under the influence of drugs, and about one in six of both state and federal inmates said they committed their offense to get money for drugs (Mumola, 1999). Approximately 20 percent of state prisoners and 60 percent of federal prisoners are incarcerated for a drug-related crime. A drug program that includes treatment for substance abuse disorders during and after incarceration is essential for safe reentry into the community. Prisons and detention centers are just a temporary response that address a third of the offenders under government supervision; the remaining 4.4 million offenders are in community programs.

Treatment, in lieu of incarceration, will help large numbers of non-violent, drug-related offenders. Experience proves that drug courts, drug testing, and drug treatment within the criminal-justice system can reduce drug consumption and recidivism. Over time, expanded alternatives to incarceration promise to decrease the addicted population and reduce both crime and the incarceration rate in America. The ultimate goal is to help people with drug problems renounce crime and enter the workforce as productive, self-sufficient, tax-paying members of society. Education, job training, and social skills instruction are important accompaniments to treatment.

Over the years, we have come to understand that drug abuse is a complex phenomenon that affects both public health and safety. We also realize that breaking the cycle of drugs, violence, and crime is an important first step toward securing the health of individuals and communities.

THE PUBLIC-HEALTH DIMENSION
OF SUBSTANCE ABUSE

Drug abuse, whether directly or indirectly, is now a major vector for the transmission of infectious diseases, including acquired immunodeficiency syndrome (AIDS), hepatitis B, hepatitis C, and tuberculosis. Increasing numbers of such cases are being reported among the partners of intravenous drug users. Most HIV-infected newborns have mothers who acquired this disease through their own drug use or sexual activity with a drug user. In addition, research is demonstrating that minority populations may face unique risks that must be addressed. The National Institutes of Health has developed a strategic plan, for reducing and ultimately eliminating health disparities among minority groups, which currently suffer disproportionately from HIV and AIDS. Because drug abuse causes a complex set of health problems, we must continue addressing it through a variety of educational and other prevention efforts, early intervention, treatment, and research.

To address these health disparities as well as other factors that affect the health of the nation, the Surgeon General developed "Ten Leading Health Indicators"[2] intended to elicit wide participation in improving health. These indicators are designed to act as a national health report card for the next decade so communities, counties, states, and the entire country can assess individual and collective progress in achieving a nation of healthy people.

As we continue strengthening our efforts to reduce the use of illegal drugs, underage alcohol, and tobacco, while improving overall physical and mental health, we will need to rely on scientific advances consistently. Particularly over the past decade, science has increased our understanding of addiction and better approaches for dealing with it. Research now defines substance abuse as preventable behavior and addiction as a treatable, chronic, relapsing disease of the brain. Addiction is characterized by compulsive drug-seeking that results from the brain's prolonged exposure to drugs. Animal and human studies have demonstrated that chronic drug use changes the brain in fundamental ways that persist long after drug use has stopped. By using advanced brain imaging technologies, we can see what we believe to be the biological basis of addiction.

---

[2]These indicators are: (1) physical activity, (2) overweight and obesity, (3) tobacco use, (4) substance abuse, (5) responsible sexual behavior, (6) mental health, (7) injury and violence, (8) environmental quality, (9) immunization, (10) access to healthcare. Seven of these ten indicators are directly linked to the goals and objectives of the Strategy, particularly those related to reducing the incidence of drug use, co-occurring disorders, crime, and violence.

PUBLIC-SAFETY DIMENSIONS OF SUBSTANCE ABUSE

Hundreds of thousands of people enter the criminal and juvenile-justice systems each year due to substance-use disorders. Our prisons and jails hold approximately 2,054,694 persons (Bureau of Justice Statistics, 2000), and 4.4 million offenders are in community programs. On any given day, our jails house more than 25,000 people suffering from both mental illness and substance-use disorders. Over 300,000 are affected by one or the other type of disability. Over half the inmates in state and federal prisons have a mental-health or substance abuse disorder—nearly 700,000 in all (National GAINS Center, 1997).

A million offenders under criminal justice supervision need, and are not getting, drug treatment. Each year over 550,000 people return to their communities from state and federal prisons; most are untreated, and many are dangerous, unemployable, or sick. Over 350,000 (two-thirds) will be rearrested within three years of release. With treatment during and after incarceration, this level of recidivism can be sharply reduced (U.S. Department of Justice, 1999).

Drug treatment has been shown to have an immediate impact on the level of drug use and associated crime, and retention in drug treatment is also significant for future behavior. Longitudinal studies have repeatedly shown that drug use and criminal activity decline upon entry into treatment and remain below pre-treatment levels for up to six years. Public safety is the primary beneficiary of drug treatment programs.

LAW ENFORCEMENT

Effective law enforcement is essential for reducing drug-related crime within the United States. Illegal drug trafficking inflicts violence and corruption on our communities. The criminal activity that accompanies drug trafficking has both a domestic and international component. Domestic traffickers are often linked with international organizations. Federal, state, and local law enforcement organizations, working together through programs like the Organized Crime Drug Enforcement Task Force (OCDETF) and High Intensity Drug Trafficking Area (HIDTA), must share information and resources in order to maximize their impact on criminal drug trafficking organizations.

The *Strategy* stresses the need to protect borders from drug incursion and cut the supply of drugs in communities along our borders. Sharing intelligence and making use of the latest technology can make a big difference. The Southwest border is a major gateway for the entry of illegal drugs into the United States. Resources have been allocated to close other avenues of drug entry into the United States, including the Virgin Islands, Puerto Rico, the Canadian border, and all air terminals and seaports.

INTERNATIONAL INITIATIVES

The United States seeks to curtail illegal drug trafficking in the transit zone between source countries and the U.S. multinational efforts in the Caribbean, Central America, Europe, and the Far East are being coordinated to exert maximum pressure on drug traffickers. The United States supports a number of international efforts against drug trafficking that are being coordinated with the United Nations (UN), the European Union (EU), and the Organization of American States (OAS).

Supply-reduction operations can best be mounted at the source: the Andean Ridge for cocaine and heroin; Mexico for methamphetamine, heroin, and marijuana; and Southeast Asia and South Central Asia for heroin. Where access to source regions is limited by political complications, we support international efforts to curtail the drug trade.

RESEARCH-BASED POLICY

The *National Drug Control Strategy* is based on sound research, technology, and intelligence. The *Strategy* will be adjusted according to feedback from ONDCP's Performance Measures of Effectiveness system. Conditions are fluid, so the *Strategy* will change to respond to emerging issues. We can measure—target by target—how successful we are in achieving goals and objectives. The *Strategy* receives input from a wide range of organizations, individuals, and government branches.

The overriding objective of our drug-control strategy is to keep Americans safe from the threats posed by illegal drugs. We hope to create a healthier, less violent, more stable nation unfettered by drugs and drug traffickers as well as the corruption they perpetrate.

Goals of the National Drug Control Strategy

1. *Educate and enable America's youth to reject illegal drugs as well as alcohol and tobacco.*

   Drug use is preventable. If children reach adulthood without using illegal drugs, alcohol, or tobacco, they are unlikely to develop a chemical-dependency problem later in life. To this end, the *Strategy* fosters initiatives to educate children about the dangers associated with drugs. ONDCP involves parents, coaches, mentors, teachers, clergy, and other role models in a broad prevention campaign. ONDCP encourages businesses, communities, schools, the entertainment industry, universities, and sports organizations to join these national anti-drug efforts.

2. *Increase the safety of America's citizens by substantially reducing drug-related crime and violence.*

Researchers have identified important factors that place youth at risk for drug abuse or protect them against such behavior. Risk factors are associated with greater potential for drug problems while protective factors reduce the chances of drug involvement. Risk factors include a chaotic home environment, ineffective parenting, anti-social behavior, drug-using peers, general approval of drug use, and the misperception that an overwhelming majority of peers are substance users. Protective factors include, but are not limited to, parental involvement; success in school; strong bonds with family, school, and religious organizations; knowledge of dangers posed by drug use; and the recognition by young people that substance use is unacceptable.

3. *Reduce health and social costs to the public of illegal drug use by reducing the treatment gap.*

   Drug addiction is a chronic, relapsing disorder that exacts an enormous cost on individuals, families, businesses, communities, and nations. Addicted individuals may engage in self-destructive and criminal behavior. Treatment programs have been found to reduce the consequences of addiction for the individual and society. The ultimate goal of treatment is to help people stop using drugs and maintain drug-free lifestyles while achieving productive functioning within families, at work, and in society. Providing access to treatment for America's chronic drug abusers is a worthwhile endeavor. It is both compassionate public policy and a sound investment.

4. *Shield America's air, land, and sea frontiers from the drug threat.*

   The United States is obligated to protect its citizens from threats posed by illegal drugs crossing our borders. Interdiction in the transit and arrival zones disrupts drug flow, increases risks to traffickers, drives them to less efficient routes and methods, and prevents significant quantities of drugs from reaching the United States. Interdiction operations also produce information that can be used by domestic law-enforcement agencies against trafficking organizations.

5. *Break foreign and domestic drug sources of supply.*

   The rule of law, human rights, and democratic institutions are threatened by drug trafficking and consumption. International supply-reduction programs not only reduce the volume of illegal drugs reaching our shores, they also attack international criminal organizations, strengthen democratic institutions, and honor our international drug-control commitments. The U.S. supply-reduction strategy seeks to:

   - Eliminate illegal drug cultivation and production.
   - Destroy drug-trafficking organizations.
   - Interdict drug shipments.
   - Encourage international cooperation.
   - Safeguard democracy and human rights.

The United States continues to focus international drug-control efforts on source countries. Drug-trafficking organizations and their production and trafficking infrastructures are most concentrated, detectable, and vulnerable to law enforcement in source countries. In addition, cultivation and production of coca and opium poppy into cocaine and heroin are labor-intensive activities. Consequently, cultivation and processing are relatively easier to disrupt than other aspects of the trade. The international drug-control strategy seeks to bolster source-country resources, capabilities, and political will to reduce cultivation, attack production, interdict drug shipments, and dismantle trafficking organizations, including their command and control structure along with its financial underpinnings.

DRUG CONTROL IS A CONTINUOUS CHALLENGE

The metaphor of a "war on drugs" is misleading. Although wars are expected to end, drug education—like all schooling—is a continuous process. The moment we believe ourselves victorious and drop our guard, drug abuse will resurface in the next generation. To reduce the demand for drugs, prevention must be ongoing. Addicted individuals should be held accountable for their actions and offered treatment to help change destructive behavior.

Cancer is a more appropriate metaphor for the nation's drug problem. Dealing with cancer is a long-term proposition. It requires the mobilization of support mechanisms—medical, educational, social, and financial—to check the spread of the disease and improve the patient's prognosis. Symptoms of the illness must be managed while the root cause is attacked. The key to reducing the incidence of drug abuse and cancer is prevention coupled with treatment and accompanied by research.

NO

Susan P. Robbins

It is somewhat remarkable that at the beginning of the new millennium, debates about the war on drugs continue. By all empirical measures, the War on Drugs has been one of the most costly, enduring, and ineffective social policies ever undertaken in the United States. And yet the war continues, as do the debates, fueled by empty rhetoric and promises of future success that rely on spending more money in ways that have produced failure in the past. In order to evaluate the overall impact of the War on Drugs, it is important to examine not only if its stated mission has been achieved, but also what the consequences that drug-war policies have had for this and other countries.

Although certain drugs have been under some degree of federal control since the early 1900s, the "War on Drugs" as we know it today began during

Richard Nixon's presidential campaign in 1968 (Baum, 1996). Since that time, we have enacted a myriad of policies with the stated mission of reducing illegal drug use in the nation (demand reduction) and stopping the flow of illegal drugs from entering the country (supply reduction). In order to achieve this, the federal government has spent billions of dollars, with a drug-war budget that has increased dramatically over the last twenty years—from $1 billion in 1980 to over $19.2 billion in 2001. When combined with state and local monies, annual expenditures on the War on Drugs now amount to over $40 billion a year (Bureau of Justice Statistics, 1999; Drucker, 1998; Office of National Drug Control Policy, 2000b).

Even though a vast amount of money has been spent to reduce drug use and keep illicit drugs out of this country, the War on Drugs has done neither—despite claims to the contrary. In fact, the data indicate that the availability of illicit drugs has not only increased in the last two decades, but the drugs themselves are cheaper and purer than they were twenty years ago (Department of Health and Human Services, 1999; Lindesmith Center, 2000; National Institute of Drug Abuse, 1999; Office of National Drug Control Policy, 1999). In addition, there has been an increase in drug-overdose deaths as well as an increase in emergency-room drug episodes (Substance Abuse and Mental Health Services Administration, 1996).

Another measure of the ineffectiveness of the War on Drugs can be seen in an examination of government data on illicit drug use throughout the 1990s—the period in which governmental expenditures for the War on Drugs steadily escalated. After an initial and steady rise in illicit drug use among adolescents during the last decade, drug use in this group has fluctuated slightly from year to year (see NIDA, 1998, 1999, 2000), typically with decreases in the use of some drugs accompanied by increases in the use of others. Those who support current prohibition policies have proclaimed temporary downward fluctuations as proof that the War on Drugs is working. Careful analyses of these data suggest otherwise. These data show that decreases in use of most drugs are relatively minor and are offset by increases in the use of other drugs, as well as overall increases when viewed longitudinally. For example, although youth in the eighth, tenth, and twelfth grades showed very minor decreases in the use of most drugs between 1999 and 2000, a minor increase was seen in the use of hallucinogens other than LSD and "other" narcotics for twelfth-graders, and larger increases were seen in the use of MDMA (Ecstasy). Likewise, although minor decreases were found in the use of any illicit drug between 1999 and 2000 (from −.07 to −1.5), the levels of self-reported drug use were still significantly higher in 2000 than in 1991 (+8.1 to +15.0) (National Institute of Drug Abuse, 2000). The reporting of carefully selected data such as these creates the illusion of incremental success in the War on Drugs. In reality, drug use waxes and wanes owing to a variety of social, cultural, and individual factors—although some have argued that the War on Drugs has helped to create a more plentiful and less expensive supply of dangerous drugs such as crack (Gray, 1998).

Data from the National Household Survey on Drug Abuse collected annually from 1993 to 1999 show that incidents of current illicit drug use rose from 11.7 million in 1993 to 14.8 million in 1999. That said, illicit drug use has decreased for some populations since record high use was reported in the late 1970s through early 1980s (Walker, 1998). However, is a far stretch to attribute this decrease to the War on Drugs, because use also began to steadily increase again, particularly among teenagers, during the 1990s when record amounts of money were spent on drug-use prevention and drug inter- diction. Some attribute the escalating reports of drug use in the early 1980s to the advent of crack, which created open drug markets and disproportion- ately affected poor and disenfranchised minorities. However, Inciardi (1992) points out that the crack "epidemic" reported by the media presented a dis- torted picture of drug use, because powder cocaine was more plentiful and more widely used than crack.

Not surprisingly, marijuana has consistently been the most commonly used illicit drug, accounting for at least four-fifths of all current drug use, and with the majority of marijuana users using no other illicit drugs (National Institute of Drug Abuse, 1998, 1999, 2000). Earlier data such as these prompted Baum (1996, p. 126) to observe that "were marijuana legal, the country's problem with illegal drugs would shrink to the tiny number of heroin and cocaine users, obviating a federal drug enforcement budget the size of the DEA's." Drug-war rhetoric notwithstanding, the failure to significantly and consistently reduce either casual or steady drug use despite our ever- increasing expenditures led Sweet, a federal judge and former prosecutor, to conclude that "our present prohibition policy has failed, flatly and without serious question" (Sweet, in *The National Review*, 1996 p. 11).

However, data on drug use, even when accurately reported and inter- preted, are deceptive. They place the focus on use rather than on acute and chronic drug abuse, and the War on Drugs has been instrumental in blurring this crucial distinction (Benjamin & Miller, 1993; Robbins & Mikow, 2001). As Nadelmann (1996) points out, most drug use results in no harm, and demo- nizing drug use leads to a host of other problems. On the other hand, drug abuse and chronic dependence do create significant problems for the indi- vidual user and society at large. Many believe that these problems should be a primary focus of our national drug policy. The economic costs of abuse and chronic dependence can be easily seen in the increased costs of medical care, loss of productivity, and death—much of which can be mitigated by referrals to treatment to reduce abuse.

However, current drug-policy funding ensures that those who are most in need of treatment are least likely to receive it, despite the fact that treatment upon request has been federal law since 1988 (See the Anti-Drug Abuse Act of 1988.) According to the Office of National Drug Control Policy (2000a), 57 percent of Americans who need drug treatment receive none. Although some have debated the efficacy of treatment (see Bender & Leone, 1998), an impor- tant study by the RAND Drug Policy Research Center found that each dollar invested in drug-abuse treatment saves taxpayers more than $7 in societal costs (such as drug-related emergency-room visits and crimes committed to support a drug habit). The study also found that treatment is ten times more effective at reducing cocaine use than interdiction is, that it is less expensive than law enforcement, and that treatment reduces demand (Caulkins, 1998; Rydell & Everingham, 1994). Despite these findings, the Network of Reform Groups (1999) notes that the current ten-year national drug strategy plan fails to make treatment-on-request a reality. This is not surprising, given that approximately two-thirds of the federal budget is allocated for law-enforcement and criminal-justice initiatives related to the drug war, and only one-third of it is spent on treatment and prevention (Massing, 2000). Although there have been modest increases in allocations for treatment and prevention in 2001, the largest percentage increase has been allocated to interdiction and criminal justice (Office of National Drug Control Policy, 2000b).

The abysmal failure in achieving the stated goals of reducing supply and demand is only part of the picture, however. The ever-escalating War on Drugs has had a profoundly negative impact on society as a whole in a variety of ways. The prison population grew from 200,000 in 1970 to 1.7 million in 1997, with over 60 percent of federal prisoners being jailed for nonviolent drug offenses, many of them first offenses (Bureau of Justice Statistics, 1997). According to Friedman (1998) and Walker (1998), drug prohibition is the major source of the tremendous growth in our prison population.

This has led to a disproportionate imprisonment of minorities, especially black men, with one out of three either in prison or on some form of supervised release. Current drug policy has been racist in its effect, even if that was not its stated intent. The federal sentencing guidelines that impose differential penalties for crack and powder cocaine have been cited as "the most blatant aspect of bias in the system" (Austin, Bruce, Carroll, McCall, & Richards, 2001; Walker, 1998).

The War on Drugs affects not only black men and their families, but also the inner cities. As Friedman (1998) points out, the destruction of the inner city in major metropolitan areas is a direct consequence of drug prohibition. Sellers, who are heavily concentrated in these areas, compete aggressively with one another, and the resulting violence has left many inner-city areas looking like war zones. Children who live in these areas face the greatest risk of falling victim to drug-gang violence (Benjamin & Miller, 1993). Inasmuch as one of the arguments used to justify the War on Drugs is to "save the children," the effect appears to be quite the opposite when we consider the long-term social, economic, and cultural impact of our current prohibition policies. In addition, the large amounts of money involved in the illegal drug trade provide a strong inducement to otherwise law-abiding citizens to forgo traditional careers in favor of fast money.

Many who support the current War on Drugs cite drug use as a significant causal factor in crime, replete with images of the crazed drug addict who robs or burglarizes to support his or her habit. Although some crimes are related to drug use, very few burglaries or robberies are drug related (Walker, 1998). Despite the common misperception that drug use causes a significant rise in crime, the relationship between the two is complex, and the data do not support this connection. According to Walker (1998), the National Household Survey data show that few who use illicit drugs become addicts or engage in other criminal activity. Quite to the contrary, a wealth of data demonstrates a clear causal link between *drug prohibition* and crime (Benjamin & Miller, 1993; Gray, 1998). Moreover, the rise in crime that occurred with alcohol prohibition is analogous to the rise in crime that has resulted from the War on Drugs. Not surprisingly, organized crime plays a central role in the distribution of illicit drugs, and the War on Drugs has led to a significant rise in organized crime and violence associated with drug dealing (Benjamin & Miller, 1993).

Not only does drug prohibition lead to increased crime, it also spawns corruption in law enforcement, the criminal-justice system, and interdiction efforts. McNamara (1996) points to grave instances of corruption in the police force, the Federal Bureau of Investigations, the Drug Enforcement Administration, and the Coast Guard. He points out that the violence and corruption stem from the competition for illegal profits rather than drug use itself, and notes that "the drug war is as lethal as it is corrupting" (p. 9).

Citing a National Institute of Drug Abuse study, the Network of Reform Groups (1999) notes that 60 percent of societal costs of illicit drug use are due to drug-related crime and the black market. This includes "police, legal and incarceration costs, lost productivity of incarcerated criminals, and victims of crimes, as well as the lost productivity due to drug-related crime careers" (p. 1). Significantly, less than 30 percent of the societal costs were found to be caused by the effects of ingesting the drugs themselves. The authors conclude that "our failing War on Drugs actually creates the majority of costs our communities pay when considering illegal drugs" (p. 1). There are numerous other negative effects of the War on Drugs that are unrelated to prisons, crime, or corruption—effects that are just as insidious and harmful to our citizens and communities. These deserve a more detailed discussion than is possible in this brief chapter, but they merit mention owing to their importance. Of major significance is the fact that drug prohibition compounds the harm to the individual user. Friedman (1998) notes that in addition to making drugs dangerously adulterated and more expensive than if they were legally produced, users are forced to associate with criminals to purchase drugs. They are also at constant risk of infection from unclean needles (which is responsible for the unnecessary spread of disease), and many must admit to criminally using drugs in order to qualify for treatment. For these reasons, many involved in the drug-reform movement advocate harm-reduction strategies that recognize the reality of drug use but seek to limit the harm to the user and society that results from drug prohibition. Another facet of this harm that is rarely discussed is the undertreatment of chronic pain by medical doctors who fail to prescribe adequate doses of pain medications to patients with chronic pain, owing to pressure from the Drug Enforcement Administration (Friedman, 1998). Further, the loss of constitutional rights and freedoms has been well publicized in the drug-war debate, and is a significant threat to a continued democratic society.

Finally, we must also consider the harm done to foreign countries in our quest to solve the drug problem in America. Friedman (1998) points out that the War on Drugs has led to instability, loss of wealth, and loss of sovereignty in countries such as Colombia, Peru, and Mexico. A critical examination of the failed War on Drugs cannot help but demonstrate that its effects have been far reaching and extremely damaging to our citizens, our communities, our freedoms, and other countries.

As the November Coalition (2001) notes, "In thirty years of 'The War On Drugs,' our government hasn't even managed to accomplish even a small reduction in drug dealing and abuse, yet we have spent almost a trillion dollars. ONE TRILLION DOLLARS!" To address the very real problems associated with drugs, especially those of acute and chronic drug abuse, and achieve a more effective allocation of taxpayer dollars, we must refocus our efforts and seriously examine a wider and more rational choice of policy options. Clearly, it is time to rethink drug policy.

REFERENCES

Anti-Drug Abuse Act of 1988 (1988, November 18). Public Law 100–690.

Austin, J., Bruce, M. A., Carroll, L., McCall, P. L., & Richards, S. C. (2001). The use of incarceration in the United States: National policy white paper, American Society of Criminology National Policy Committee. *The Criminologist, 26*(3), 14–16.

Baum, D. (1996). *Smoke and mirrors: The War on Drugs and the politics of failure.* New York: Little, Brown & Co.

Bender, D. L., & Leone, B. (Eds.) (1998). *The War on Drugs: Opposing viewpoints.* San Diego, CA: Greenhaven Press.

Benjamin, D. K., & Miller, R. L. (1993). *Undoing drugs: Beyond legalization.* New York: Basic Books.

Bureau of Justice Statistics (1997, August 14). Nation's probation and parole population reached almost 3. 9 million last year. (Press release.) Washington, DC: U.S. Department of Justice.

Bureau of Justice Statistics (1999). *Sourcebook of criminal justice statistics 1998.* Washington, DC, p. 462.

Bureau of Justice Statistics (2000). Prison and jail inmates at midyear 1999, April.

Caulkins, J. P. (1998). Drug abuse treatment programs are effective. (In D. L. Bender and B. Leone (Eds.) *The War on Drugs: Opposing viewpoints* (pp. 68–73). San Diego, CA: Greenhaven Press.

Department of Health and Human Services (1999). *Preliminary estimates from the Drug Abuse Warning Network.* Washington, DC: Department of Health and Human Services.

Drucker, E. (1998, Jan./Feb.). Drug prohibition and public health. *Public Health Reports.* U.S. Public Health Service. Vol. 114.

Duke, S. B., & Gross, A. C. (1993). *America's longest war: Rethinking our tragic crusade against drugs.* New York: Tarcher/Putnam.

Friedman, M. (1998, January 11). There's no justice in the war on drugs: Can our laws be moral if they have so racist an effect? *New York Times,* p. 19.

Gray, M. (1998). *Drug crazy.* New York: Random House.

Inciardi, J. A. (1992). *The War on Drugs II: The continuing epic of heroin, cocaine, crack, crime, aids, and public policy.* Mountain View, CA: Mayfield Publishing.

John Jay College of Criminal Justice (2000). Remarks of the Honorable Janet Reno, Attorney General of the United States, on the reentry court initiative. New York, February.

Johnston, L. D., O'Malley, P. M., & Bachman, J. G. (1998, December 18). Drug use by American young people begins to turn downward. (National press release). University of Michigan News and Information Services, Ann Arbor, 27 pp.

Lindesmith Center (2000). Shadow conventions 2000: The failed drug war. Retrieved May 12, 2001, from http://www.lindesmith.org/shadowconventions/factsheet.html.

Massing, M. (2000). The elephant in the room: Response to Robert Houseman's letter. *Salon.* Retrieved May 16, 2001, from http://www.salon.com/health/feature/2000/04/05/drug_debate/index.html.

McNamara, J. D. (1996, February 12). The war on drugs is lost. *National Review.* Retrieved May 11, 2001, from http://www.nationalreview.com/12feb96/drug.html.

Mumola, C. (1999). Substance abuse and treatment, state and federal prisoners, 1997 NCJ-172871. Bureau of Justice Statistics. Released January 5.

Nadelmann, E. A. (1996, February 12). The war on drugs is lost. *National Review.* Retrieved May 7, 2001, from http://www.nationalreview.com/12feb96/drug.html.

National GAINS Center (1997). The prevalence of co-occurring mental and substance abuse disorders in the criminal justice system. *Just the Facts.* Spring.

National Institute of Drug Abuse (2000). Monitoring the future survey, 2000. Washington, DC: Department of Health and Human Services.

National Institute of Drug Abuse (1999). Monitoring the future survey, 1999. Washington, DC: Department of Health and Human Services.

National Institute of Drug Abuse (1998). Monitoring the future survey, 1998. Washington, DC: Department of Health and Human Services.

Network of Reform Groups (1999). The effective drug control strategy, 1999. Retrieved May 22, 2001, from http://www.csdp.org/edcs/.

November Coalition (2001). Alarming facts in the war on drugs. Retrieved May 22, 2001, from http://www.november.org/Alarming.html.

Office of National Drug Control Policy, (April, 1999). Drug data summary. Washington, DC: Government Printing Office, p. 4.

Office of National Drug Control Policy (2000a). National Drug Control Strategy. Washington, DC: Government Printing Office.

Office of National Drug Control Policy (2000b). Executive summary: National Drug Control Strategy budget summary, February 2000. Retrieved May 22, 2001, from http://www.whitehousedrugpolicy.gov/policy/budget00/exec_summ.html.

Robbins, S. P., & Mikow, J. (2001). Designing effective drug prevention programs for minority youth. Philadelphia, PA: Center for the Study of Youth Policy, University of Pennsylvania.

Rydell, C. P., & Everingham, S. S. (1994). Controlling cocaine. (Prepared for Office of National Drug Control Policy and the United States Army.) Santa Monica, CA: Drug Policy Research Center, RAND, p. xvi.

Substance Abuse and Mental Health Services Administration (August, 1996). Historical estimates from the Drug Abuse Warning Network. Washington, DC: Department of Health and Human Services. p. 38.

Substance Abuse and Mental Health Services Administration, Office of Applied Studies (2000). Summary of findings from the 1998 national household survey on drug abuse (NHSDA), DHHS Publication No. (SMA) 00–3466. Rockville, MD: U.S. Department of Health and Human Services.

Substance Abuse and Mental Health Services Administration, Office of Applied Studies (2000). *Full Report: 1999 National Household Survey on Drug Abuse.* Retrieved May 16, 2001, from http://www.health.org/govstudy/bkd376/.

Substance Abuse and Mental Health Services Administration, Office of Applied Studies (1994, July). *National Household Survey on Drug Abuse, 1993.* Advance Report Number 7, Washington, DC: U.S. Department of Health and Human Services. Retrieved May 21, 2001, from http://www.health.org/govstudy/bkd376/.

Sweet, R. W. (1996, February 12). The war on drugs is lost. *National Review.* Retrieved May 16, 2001, from http://www.nationalreview.com/12feb96/drug.html.

U.S. Department of Justice, Office of Justice Programs (1999). Reentry courts: Managing the transition from prison to community. A call for concept papers, September.

Walker, S. (1998). *Sense and nonsense about crime and drugs: A policy guide.* Belmont, CA: West/Wadsworth Publishing Co.

PART III

ISSUES IN SOCIAL-SERVICE POLICY

IS OUTPATIENT COMMITMENT A STEP FORWARD FOR MENTAL-HEALTH CLIENTS?

Editor's Note:

The shift to deinstitutionalization that began in the United States in the 1970s was a blessing for states economically burdened with the maintenance of archaic state hospitals. As states discharged patients from institutions, they realized immediate savings. Moveover, the continuing fall in the number of hospitalized patients provided justification for state governments to abandon expensive capital-investment projects designed to renovate existing state hospitals. The substantial cost savings from "deinstitutionalizing" patients received wide support from both conservative and liberal politicians. Unfortunately, the transfer of patients from state to community-based institutions was ill planned and characterized by severe fragmentation. Little effective coordination emerged at the state or national level. Moreover, the Supreme Court determined that states could not forcibly confine mentally ill persons who were not dangerous to themselves or others, who were not being treated, and who could survive outside the hospital. This mandate had several consequences, including the discharge of severely mentally ill people into the community. Some of these individuals could not follow a treatment plan or monitor their medication use. As a result, calls arose for greater latitude in psychiatric commitments.

E. Fuller Torrey, M.D., is a research psychiatrist and executive director of the Stanley Medical Research Institute, president of the Treatment Advocacy Center, and professor of psychiatry at the Uniformed Services University of the Health Sciences. *Mary Zdanowicz, J.D.,* is an attorney and executive director of the Treatment Advocacy Center. The Center is a nonprofit legal-advocacy organization dedicated to eliminating legal and clinical barriers to timely and humane treatment for millions of Americans with serious mental illness, who are not receiving appropriate medical care. Information about the Center is available at www.psychlaws.org.

Kia J. Bentley, Ph.D., is a professor and director of the Ph.D. program in social work at Virginia Commonwealth University. She is the author of *The Social Worker and Psychotropic Medication: Toward Effective Collaboration with Mental Health Clients, Families and Providers* (2002 with Joseph Walsh, 2nd ed., Wadsworth) and the editor of *Social Work Practice in Mental Health: Contemporary Roles, Tasks and Techniques* (2002, Wadsworth). Dr. Bentley has numerous publications in the area of mental health, including the social worker's role in medication management, the right of patients to refuse medication, family psychoeducation, peer-leadership training for consumers, prescription-writing privileges for social workers, and psychosocial interventions for people with schizophrenia. *Melissa Floyd Taylor, Ph.D., LCSW*, is an assistant professor of social work at the University of North Carolina—Greensboro. Her current research interests include the operationalization of social-work values in practice with persons who have serious mental illness, as well as practice and policy implications of changing conceptualizations of mental health and mental illness.

YES

E. Fuller Torrey and Mary Zdanowicz

Outpatient commitment involves a court order mandating that a person follow a treatment plan or risk sanctions for noncompliance, such as potential involuntary hospitalization and treatment. Because of its role in enhancing compliance, some treatment advocates regard outpatient commitment as a form of assisted treatment. Therefore, they consider it one possible treatment approach for persons with severe psychiatric illnesses, such as schizophrenia and bipolar disorder, who refuse or neglect to take their medications needed to control their symptoms.

Outpatient commitment has been shown to be highly effective in improving compliance with medications. Studies in Arizona (Van Putten, Santiago, & Berren, 1988), North Carolina (Hiday & Scheid-Cook, 1987), Ohio (Munetz, Grande, & Kleist, et al., 1996), and Iowa (Rohland, 1998) showed that outpatient commitment at least doubled rates of treatment compliance. The Iowa study, for example, reported that "outpatient commitment promotes treatment compliance in about 80 percent of patients while they are on outpatient commitment."

Because outpatient commitment improves treatment compliance, it also sharply reduces the need for readmission to a psychiatric hospital by 50 to 80 percent (Munetz, Grande, & Kleist, et al., 1996; Rohland, 1998; Zanni & deVeau, 1986; Fernandez & Nygard, 1990). In a recent controlled study of outpatient commitment in North Carolina (Swartz, Swanson, & Wagner, et al., 1999), "subjects who underwent sustained periods of outpatient commitment beyond that of the initial court order had approximately 57 percent fewer readmissions and 20 fewer hospital days than control subjects." Another study also found that "the predicted probability of any violent behavior was cut in half from 48 percent to 24 percent" in subjects who underwent extended outpatient commitment and also had regular outpatient visits (Swanson, Swartz, & Borum, et al., 2000). In these studies of outpatient commitment, commitment alone was not sufficient but had to be combined with available and adequate outpatient services.

WHY IS OUTPATIENT COMMITMENT NEEDED?

We argue that outpatient commitment is needed because many individuals with severe psychiatric illnesses lack awareness of their illness. This deficit is biologically based (Young, Zakzanis, & Bailey, et al., 1998; Bare, 1998) and is not the same thing as psychological denial. Both schizophrenia and bipolar disorder affect the prefrontal cortex, which is used for insight and understanding into one's needs. When this area of the brain is damaged by disease, the affected person loses self-awareness. This loss characterizes some neurological disorders, such as Alzheimer's disease, and some individuals with cerebrovascular accidents (strokes). In the disorder's most extreme form, a post-stroke individual may lack awareness that his or her leg is paralyzed, despite obvious evidence to the contrary.

More than one hundred studies of awareness of illness and insight in schizophrenia and bipolar disorder have been conducted in recent years. The studies have shown that between 40 and 50 percent of individuals with severe psychiatric illnesses have moderately or severely impaired awareness of illness (Amador, Flaum, & Andreason, et al., 1994; David, Buchanan, & Reed, et al., 1992; personal communication, David, 1993). For some individuals, awareness may fluctuate over time. For others, it may improve with medication. For many others, however, the lack of awareness neither fluctuates nor improves with medication.

Understanding this lack of awareness of illness is crucial to understanding the need for assisted treatment. Individuals with heart disease, rheumatoid arthritis, and cancer occasionally refuse treatment, but in such cases it is assumed that their cognitive functioning and awareness of their illness are intact. One cannot make this assumption about an individual who has a severe psychiatric disorder and impaired awareness of illness.

Failure to take medication may have many unfortunate consequences for those with severe psychiatric disorders, including homelessness, incarceration, violence, and suicide. At least a third of the U.S. homeless population—150,000 persons—have severe psychiatric disorders (Torrey, 1997). In one follow-up study of patients discharged from a state psychiatric hospital, 82 percent of those who continued to live in stable housing took their medication, whereas only 33 percent of those who became homeless took their medication (Drake, Wallach, & Hoffman, 1989). A study in Boston found that only 11 percent of homeless individuals with severe psychiatric illnesses were taking medications (Bassuk, Rubin, & Lauriat, 1984). A similar study in Columbus, OH (Belcher, 1988a; Belcher, 1988b) reported that only 6 percent of such individuals were taking medication and that most "were resistant to traditional methods of psychiatric intervention that relied on voluntary compliance."

Incarceration is another apparent consequence of the failure to take needed medication. A recent Department of Justice study reported that 16 percent of inmates in local jails and state prisons—275,900 individuals—were mentally ill, and many were presumed to have been noncompliant with treatment (Ditton, 1999). One follow-up study of individuals released from state hospitals reported that 32 percent were arrested and jailed within six months; "psychotropic medication had been prescribed upon their discharges from state hospitals, but the respondents failed to take their medications" (Belcher, 1988c).

Violent behavior is another potential consequence of the failure to take medication. A Department of Justice study indicated that almost one thousand homicides each year are committed by persons with a history of mental illness (Dawson & Langan, 1994). A significant correlation between the failure to take medication and violent behavior has been reported in several studies (Kasper, Hoge, & Feucht-Haviar, et al., 1997; Smith, 1989), including one in which "71 percent of the violent patients . . . had problems with medication compliance, compared with only 17 percent of those without hostile behaviors" (Bartels, Drake, & Wallach, et al., 1991).

Suicide is still another potential consequence of inadequate medication. In one study of patients who committed suicide, 71 percent "who were depressed in their last episode were not receiving adequate antidepressant or lithium carbonate medication at the time of suicide" (Roy, 1982). In another study that compared 63 individuals with schizophrenia who committed suicide and 63 individuals with schizophrenia who did not, "there were seven times as many patients who did not comply with treatment in the suicide group as in the control group" (De Hert, McKenzie, & Peuskens, forthcoming 2001).

FOR WHOM IS OUTPATIENT COMMITMENT NEEDED?

We propose that outpatient commitment, as a form of assisted treatment, should be considered for any individual with a severe psychiatric disorder who has impaired awareness of his or her illness and is at risk of becoming homeless, incarcerated, or violent or of committing suicide.

One example is the case of Phyllis Iannotta, who supported her parents for twenty-two years before developing schizophrenia (Kates, 1985). Although she responded to medication, Iannotta had no awareness of her illness and so neglected to take the medication. She became homeless in New York City and was eventually found raped and murdered in an alley. At that time, there was no provision for outpatient commitment in New York state. Iannotta's few possessions when she was found consisted of a can of cat food and a plastic spoon.

George Wooten is another example. Wooten developed schizophrenia during high school (Kilzer, 1984). He responded to medications when hospitalized but neglected to take them when released. He abused alcohol and glue and was incarcerated in the Denver County Jail more than one hundred times before he died on the streets. No outpatient commitment was ever instituted. Here are a few other sad examples:

Russell Weston developed paranoid schizophrenia in his early twenties. His symptoms improved when he was on medication, but because he had no awareness of his illness, he rarely took the medication. Even though he assaulted a hospital worker and threatened to kill the president and others, he was never put on any form of assisted treatment. He traveled to Washington, DC, and has been charged with killing two police officers at the Capitol.

Thomas McGuire was a college graduate who had worked steadily for fifteen years. He became acutely manic. During an early episode, he was successfully treated with medication. However, he exhibited no awareness of being ill and refused to continue to take medication or to be hospitalized. Despite his family's pleas that he be placed on some form of mandated treatment, the hospital released him untreated. Six hours later, he hanged himself (Torrey, 1997).

Phyllis Iannotta, George Wooten, Russell Weston, Thomas McGuire, and other individuals like them are candidates for outpatient commitment. Overall in the United States, approximately 3.5 million people have active symptoms of schizophrenia or bipolar disorder at any given time (Report of the National Advisory Mental Health Council, 1993). As noted above, between 40 and 50 percent of them—1.4 to 1.75 million—have significantly impaired awareness of their illness or their need for treatment (Amador, Flaum, & Andreason, et al., 1994; David, Buchanan, & Reed, et al., 1992). Other studies have shown that between 36 and 50 percent of individuals with schizophrenia and bipolar disorder are not being treated at any given time (Von Korff, Nestadt, & Romanoski, et al., 1985; Regier, Narrow, & Rae, et al., 1993). For a small subset of them—probably around one hundred thousand individuals— outpatient commitment could be the most effective form of assisted treatment.

Outpatient commitment is only one possible form of assisted treatment. The number of patients who might need outpatient commitment depends partly on the relative availability of other forms of assisted treatment. All forms of what we refer to as assisted treatment include some form of explicit or implicit coercion. Other forms of assisted treatment to outpatient commitment are described below.

Advance Directives

Psychiatric advance directives are legal documents that permit mentally ill persons to authorize and specify treatment in anticipation of future periods of mental incapacity. These directives may be effective for mentally ill persons who have regained awareness of their illnesses and seek to authorize treatment when they need help in the future. Advance directives will not help those who are unable to recognize that they will need assistance in the future.

Assertive Case Management

Many studies have shown that the Program for Assertive Community Treatment (PACT) and similar programs, in which teams actively assist with treatment in the home, improve treatment compliance. However, for at least a third of patients, assertive case management is not effective, suggesting the need for additional assisted interventions (Dixon, Weiden, & Torres, et al., 1997).

Representative Payees

Appointing a representative payee for Supplemental Security Income, Social Security Disability Insurance (SSDI), and Veterans Affairs benefits is another approach. Studies have shown that this form of assisted treatment, in which a mentally ill person permits a trusted individual to help him or her use funds wisely, reduces hospitalization (Luchins, Hanrahan, & Conrad, et al., 1998) and homelessness. However, no study has shown its effectiveness in improving treatment compliance (Stoner, 1989). The U.S. Third Circuit Court of Appeals ruled that a man with epilepsy was not entitled to SSDI unless he took his prescribed antiseizure medication (*Brown v. Bowen*, 1988). Thus a legal precedent has been set for use of this mechanism to enforce compliance.

Conditional Release

In many states, patients involuntarily committed to a state psychiatric hospital can be released on the condition that they follow their treatment plan, including taking medication (Slobogin, 1994). A study in New Hampshire, a state in which conditional release is widely used, showed that this policy was very effective in increasing medication compliance and reducing episodes of violence by mentally ill persons (O'Keefe, Potenza, & Mueser, 1997).

Conservatorship or Guardianship

In conservatorship or guardianship, a court appoints an individual to make decisions for a legally incompetent individual. This legal tool is widely used for individuals with mental retardation but is used only sporadically for individuals with severe psychiatric illnesses. Studies of conservatorship showed it to be highly effective in improving treatment compliance (Geller, Grudzin-skas, & McDermeit, et al., 1998; Lamb & Weinberger, 1992).

Mental-Health Courts

A growing number of mentally ill persons face incarceration, even for "nuisance" crimes like vagrancy. Mental-health courts, although still uncommon, have emerged to offer mentally ill persons an alternative to incarceration through supervised treatment. In 2000, the U.S. Congress passed legislation establishing a series of mental-health courts to serve as models for states to follow.

Some consumers, a few mental-health professionals, and—most prominently—civil-liberties groups and the Bazelon Center for Mental Health Law have voiced objections to outpatient commitment. These objections have included the following:

- **Outpatient commitment is not necessary**. If you improve mental-illness services, severely psychiatrically ill individuals will seek them out. In response, we argue that members of the target population suffers from impaired awareness of their illness, which clouds their judgment about the need for treatment. Even if available mental-illness services are excellent, it seems that people who do not believe that they are ill will not use them.
- **It is wrong to involuntarily commit people to mental-illness services when the services are deficient**. We agree that public mental-illness services are deficient in almost every U.S. state. However, many severely psychiatrically ill persons are at risk or victimized. They live on the streets and eat out of garbage cans. They are periodically jailed. Some are a clear danger to themselves or others. We believe that the public should not have to wait for services to improve while vulnerable persons and the public are at risk.
- **The threat of outpatient commitment drives away the people who need treatment**. This objection alleges that individuals who have been treated involuntarily or threatened with involuntary treatment will thereafter avoid treatment. Studies have demonstrated that the majority of severely psychiatrically ill patients who have been coerced into taking medications in the past agree that in retrospect it was in their best interest (Greenberg, Moore-Duncan, & Herron, 1996; Lucksted & Coursey, 1995). One study (Schwartz, Vingiano, & Perez, 1988) found that 71 percent of the patients agreed with the statement: "If I become ill again and require medication, I believe it should be given to me even if I don't want it at the time."
- **Outpatient commitment siphons off resources from the mental-illness treatment system, so that fewer resources are available for patients who want to use the services voluntarily**. If one assumes that

a fixed amount of total resources is available for treatment, this statement is true. But resources can also be increased, as they were in 1999, when New York implemented outpatient commitment. In addition, because outpatient commitment appears to lower treatment costs by reducing hospital use, it should make more funds available for all patients. Implicitly, opponents of outpatient commitment are also arguing that individuals who voluntarily seek services and have awareness of their illness are more entitled to treatment than those who shun treatment and lack awareness of their illness.

- **Outpatient commitment increases the stigma of mental illness by making mentally ill people targets of coercion.** Studies in the United States (Thornton & Wahl, 1996) and Germany (Angermeyer & Matschinger, 1996) have shown that the single largest cause of stigma is episodes of violence perpetrated by severely mentally ill persons. By providing a means by which severely mentally ill persons who lack awareness of their illness can be treated, and thereby decreasing episodes of violence, outpatient commitment and other forms of assisted treatment should ultimately decrease the stigma associated with mental illness.

- **Individuals should never be coerced into taking antipsychotic medications, because these medications are dangerous.** According to Dr. Ross J. Baldessarini of the Harvard Medical School (1979), "antipsychotic agents are among the safest drugs available in medicine." Like all medications, they have side effects. However, as a group, these side effects are comparable to those of drugs used to treat heart disease or rheumatoid arthritis.

- **Outpatient commitment will be a dragnet, ensnaring many individuals who do not need it.** Because outpatient commitment is usually predicated on a need-for-treatment standard and not just overt dangerousness, critics fear that it will ensnare many individuals who do not need it. Experience suggests that there is no basis for such fears. For example, in December 1996, Wisconsin adopted a new need-for-treatment standard. In the first twenty-two months following adoption of the standard, only thirty-five requests for commitment were made (Treffert, 1999). Individuals mandated into outpatient treatment should always have legal representation, regularly scheduled reviews of the commitment, and the right to appeal a decision. Also, the legal standards governing commitment decisions should be neither vague nor ambiguous.

- **Outpatient commitment infringes on a person's civil liberties; no one should ever be involuntarily treated.** In the United States, individuals with medical illnesses such as active tuberculosis who refuse to take medication are regularly hospitalized involuntarily and treated. In New York City alone, an average of one hundred such involuntarily hospitalizations take place each year, and many more such patients agree to take medication only after being threatened with involuntary treatment (Fujiwara, Larkin, & Frieden, 1997). We do not suggest that severe mental illness is analogous to a communicable disease. However, the rationale is similar: Medically necessary treatment should be provided in the best interest of individual and society.

We argue that the real liberty question regarding individuals with severe psychiatric disorders is whether they are in fact free when they are ill. If one's thoughts and behavior are driven by delusions and hallucinations owing to a disease over which one has no control, is this condition truly liberty? This point was best expressed by Herschel Hardin, a former member of the board of directors of the British Columbia Civil Liberties Association (1993). He wrote, "The opposition to involuntary committal and treatment betrays a profound misunderstanding of the principle of civil liberties. Medication can free victims from their illness—free them from the Bastille of their psychoses—and restore their dignity, their free will, and the meaningful exercise of their liberties" (A15). One may also argue that outpatient commitment is not merely an optional action but is a duty of psychiatrists and the state to protect individuals for their own safety.

CONCLUSIONS

Outpatient commitment is one form of assisted treatment that we argue is useful for individuals with severe psychiatric illnesses who have limited awareness of their illness. It is not, nor is it claimed to be, a panacea for the problems facing the nation's mental-health systems. In the absence of assisted treatment, we have witnessed rising rates of homelessness, incarceration, violence, and suicide among persons with severe mental illness. Both common sense and compassion argue for the use of assisted treatment, including outpatient commitment, when needed.

NO

Kia J. Bentley and Melissa Floyd Taylor

At first blush, the question "Is outpatient commitment a step forward for mental-health clients"? seems lopsided. Who could possibly argue *against* a policy that, at its core, has the delivery of much-needed, state-of-the-art treatment to individuals experiencing severe symptoms of serious mental illness—one of our most troubling social problems and medical challenges? So-called "assisted outpatient treatment" seems to offer an opportunity to ensure that folks who really need psychiatric medication and won't take it *will* get it—and *will* take it, and perhaps receive other psychosocial interventions as well. Society can do this without having to pay for expensive inpatient hospital stays, without stripping away consumers' "right" to be in the community, and, in some states, without even having to legally declare these individuals a danger to themselves or others. Well-meaning people have argued that, for a subset of individuals with mental illness, assisted outpatient treatment represents a healthy compromise between an individual's right to liberty and his or her need for care and supervision (Scheid-Cook, 1991). It all seems quite attractive on the surface. And indeed, as the other side will argue, recent "assisted outpatient treatment" laws do enjoy the support of the general public—including most family members of persons with mental-illness, some mental health providers, and at least one renowned psychiatrist.

However, we are not among the supporters. Instead, we argue that "assisted outpatient treatment" is a rather transparent euphemism for outpatient *commitment*. Moreover, the term is used to hide the affront to humanistic values and civil liberties that policies like these represent. We join with the vast number of mental-health consumers, client-advocacy organizations, civil-liberties proponents, and even members of our own professional organization who maintain that these laws can perpetuate negative stereotypes about people with mental illness and divert attention (and money) away from other real problems and solutions in the mental-health system. Mulvey, Geller, & Roth (1987) summarized their analysis of the issue by noting that outpatient commitment is a failed attempt at "benevolent coercion," much like probation and parole, juvenile justice, and protective services. And, they add, it cancels out the well-established (and we believe crucial), right to refuse treatment.

THE ANTITHESIS OF HUMANISTIC VALUES

Belief in the basic dignity and worth of individuals is a core value in the social-work profession, and certainly the notion is not unique to human services. But recent discourse in the media by proponents of outpatient commitment seems to fly in the face of that value. These proponents' portrayal of persons with mental illness can be quite disturbing. For example, there has been a great deal of rhetoric in the media about "Kendra's law" in New York—the outpatient-commitment law enacted following the tragic death of a young woman who was pushed in front of a subway by a man with untreated schizophrenia. Proponents seemed to rely heavily on negative and infantilizing characterizations of people with mental illness to get the law passed. Governor Pataki of New York argues that if the mentally ill refuse to act responsibly by taking their medication, we must take action to protect all New Yorkers. In a very recent *Baltimore Sun* article, Steven Sharfstein and Mary Zdanowicz (2001) published an article touting outpatient commitment.

The article contains graphic accounts of recent sensational crimes committed by "noncompliant" men with a history of schizophrenia. Zdanowicz is executive director of the Treatment Advocacy Center (TAC), an organization founded by E. Fuller Torrey and a major proponent of increased use of involuntary treatment. TAC was originally affiliated with the National Alliance for the Mentally Ill (NAMI), until ethical opposition by some members led to its splitting off. But a general alignment between the leaders of TAC and NAMI remains. Consumer groups have understandably criticized NAMI for being two-faced on important consumer-rights issues. Members of the powerful family-focused organization portray themselves as advocates for the mentally ill. They expose the sweeping generalizations and negative stereotypes that undergird stigma but then either support or maintain silence on outpatient-commitment laws, which some members complain rely too often on myths about violence and mental illness. The organization has also been known to selectively use high-profile cases to argue for causes that benefit itself. Upon analysis, we are left with some troubling questions: Is this selective use of the media a marketing necessity, a needed trump card in the fight for people with mental illness and their families, or something else? Is NAMI inappropriately exploiting tragic cases in the news—whether it's the case in New York, the Unabomber, or the murders of the Capitol police—and actually *perpetuating* stigma and fear? As some antipsychiatry consumer groups have claimed, is NAMI creating divisiveness in the consumer community by aligning itself with drug companies and organizations (such as TAC) known to be against consumer rights?

Even more disturbing in terms of humanistic values is the recent tack taken by increasingly extremist psychiatrist/author E. Fuller Torrey. Dr. Torrey jumps to the conclusion that because severe mental illnesses are thought of as brain disorders, people who have them are incapable of fully appreciating their illness and are therefore unqualified to make meaningful decisions about their treatment (Torrey, 1997). His leap of logic stems from his inappropriate and specious equation of "brain disordered" with "brain diseased," and more recently with "brain damaged." He tries to strengthen his argument by pointing to research that demonstrates damage in the frontal lobes of some persons diagnosed with schizophrenia (see Moran, 2000; Torrey & Zdanowicz, 1999). Though we support current biological and stress-vulnerability models of mental illness, we do not use them as ammunition to disenfranchise those who suffer from them—any more than we would argue that cancer patents, patients with HIV, or persons with mental retardation or brain tumors should have reduced decision-making rights. As consumer advocate Judi Chamberlain (1998) exclaims, "Why does the supposedly medical diagnosis of 'mental illness' carry such a profound effect on the rights of those so labeled?' (p. 405). Indeed, psychiatry is virtually the only medical specialty that includes coercive treatment (Shore, 1997), and outpatient commitment is merely an expansion of this alarming reality.

The slanted portrayal of persons with severe mental illness is a key point in our argument. For example, Torrey's recent writings have stressed the poor judgment and insight of persons with severe mental illness. He says "they" cannot know or accept what is best for them. He also says that physicians cannot assume that people with severe mental illness can think clearly (see Moran, 2000). The economic and political implications of Torrey's "people as brain damaged" tact in terms of preserving medical dominance is discussed more fully elsewhere (see Taylor & Bentley, 2000). The point here regarding Torrey is that his views naturally set up a logical progression toward institutionalization of some type and/or forced treatment. A recent article in *Mental Health Weekly* reports that Torrey admitted that he himself has intentionally dispensed less psychotropic medication than medically indicated to homeless individuals who were awaiting competency hearings, in order to keep them off the streets (Murder suspect in 'Kendra's Law' case, 2000). Presumably he believes that this is the humane thing to do. Indeed, proponents of outpatient commitment passionately argue that they have the "true" best interests of the mentally ill person at heart. They insist that they are helping "the lost," caring for people caught in a "revolving door," and providing for the "least restrictive alternative" (Staghenko, 2000).

Needless to say, the reaction by individual mental-health consumers and organized consumer-advocacy groups to those arguments, to Torrey, and to "Kendra's Law" and others like them has been loud, clear, and unwavering. Web sites such as MadNation (*http://www.madnation.org*) and Support Coalition International (*http://mindfreedom.org*) are filled with hundreds of personal testimonies of self-identified consumers outraged by the outpatient-commitment laws. These laws, they contend, signal a pendulum swinging away from the human rights of mental-health consumers. Some radical consumers passionately warn of the expansion of "forced psychiatric drugging" and the "government's chemical crusade." They even offer a Sanctuary Network for nonviolent consumers who want to move out of their state to escape involuntary medication. Most of the vignettes are an impressive testament to the sound judgment, clear thinking, and articulation of people with mental illnesses. They serve as a powerful reminder that consumers' voices are critical to this discussion.

AN INFRINGEMENT ON CIVIL LIBERTIES

In our own profession of social work, self-determination is a core value. As one of our foremothers said, it's a "foundation stone" (Richmond, 1917). The notion of self-determination is simple: It means that social workers should support and assist clients in making decisions about treatment goals, choice of interventions, and the timing of termination, to name a few areas. Except in cases in which a "client's actions or potential actions pose a serious risk of *foreseeable and imminent risk to themselves or others"* (NASW, 1997, emphasis added), we honor these client freedoms. Using legal, ethical, and philosophical arguments, Bentley (1993) explains why social workers should specifically uphold a client's right to decline medication except in the most extreme situations: that of *present* violence or self-destruction, or in cases in which there is *substantial likelihood of extreme violence.* Even Murdach (1996), a social worker who advocates for beneficence or acting "for the good of the consumer," does not propose that involuntary intervention become the "norm of practice" (p. 31) and urges careful individualized assessment.

This gets at the center of consumer-rights advocates' worry about outpatient commitment: The criterion for imminent dangerousness, a longstanding safeguard to premature involuntary treatment, is noticeably lacking. In New York (and about ten other states), you can now force someone to take medication through an order for "assisted treatment" just because they are legally determined to *need* it. Someone petitions the court after predicting that a person (whose history is problematic in terms of adherence to treatment) will deteriorate if he or she doesn't get forced help. This seems quite contradictory to leaving people with mental illness alone when they want to be left alone, as long as they abide by the law and do not hurt themselves or others. We argue that outpatient-commitment laws are socially unjust because they can and do set up intrusive interventions in the absence of what has historically been seen as sufficient cause. U.S. society has heretofore been unwilling to tolerate that level of personal infringement on the "presumed innocent," even if it means the public must accept that some undesired outcomes will occur. Thus, as Solomon (1996) notes, we end up applying criminal-justice sanctions to a mental-health issue. The probationlike restrictions associated with outpatient commitment represent a sentence associated with a guilty verdict—except that it is applied to people found guilty of nothing. Moreover, outpatient commitment is a social-justice issue, because it may disproportionately impact (and some would say, target) African American males (e.g. Scheid-Cook, 1991). It thus represents yet another legally sanctioned avenue for social control of those individuals society fears most.

BLAMING THE VICTIM

The basic values of self-determination and belief in the dignity of all play a key role in our understanding of the goal of social justice. As we see it, social justice is about creating societal, governmental, and corporate structures and processes that are characterized by individual and collective fairness, that allow for equality of opportunity, and that reflect sensitivity to our similarities and differences. For people with mental illness, it means, among other things, that we should try to create systems of care that provide up-to-date medical treatment and psychosocial interventions in ways that convey respect for their humanness and their right to pursue life goals not unlike those of us without mental illness. The implications of our failure to fully deliver on this promise are crucial. For one, outpatient-commitment laws rest on blaming the victims of an underfunded system of care. Psychologist Dr. Robert Bernstein, executive director of the widely respected Bazelon Center for Mental Health Law, as acknowledged that "commitment laws are being used to compensate for the substantial holes in our public mental health system" (in Moran, 2000). In the same article, psychiatrist Paul Appelbaum refers to a "slowly starved" system in which care on a voluntary basis should be the first priority. Upon passage of Kendra's law, the president of the Mental Health Association in New York stated, "Today we saw a law signed that is well-intentioned. But what it does in actuality is punish the innocent and provide some absolution to a system that is guilty of total failure" (Pataki signs "Kendra's Law" as family looks on, 1999). According to one article in the *Mental Health Weekly*, in addition to the state's chapter of NASW, Kendra's Law was also opposed by the state's NAMI chapter, the New York Council for Community Behavioral Health, and the Coalition of Voluntary Mental Health Agencies (N.Y. lawmakers agree to toughen involuntary commitment laws, 1999). Moran (2000, p. 26) noted that some New York physicians had said that Kendra's Law "replicates all the mistakes of the past by mandating care in the community without providing the necessary supports."

It has been rightfully pointed out that Andrew Goldstein, the man who pushed Kendra Webdale in front of the subway, was not refusing treatment at all but rather seeking help he couldn't find. He had sought help and been turned away. According to a report released by New York's Commission on Quality of Care for the Mentally Disabled, he had complained about auditory hallucinations and anxiety, and had received extensive inpatient and emergency-room services in the two years before the subway incident (Murder suspect in 'Kendra's law' case, 2000). Apparently, there was grossly insufficient follow-up and continuity of care. *New York Times* writer Michael Winerip (1999) noted that supervised housing and daily case-management services would have cost 75 percent less than the fragmented care Goldstein actually received ($25,000 versus $100,000 per year) *and* they would have been more responsive to his needs. But after Kendra's death, when one might expect public outrage about the inadequacy of services and calls for massive increase in mental-health budgets to reduce waiting lists, something else happened. Opponents of outpatient commitment launched a well-orchestrated campaign that seemed to focus on further stereotyping the mentally ill as dangerous and the need for laws that could force treatment. Lost opportunity became a secondary tragedy.

The proponents of outpatient commitment argue that current laws "carefully guard civil liberties by providing strict standards and due process protections" (Sharfstein & Zdanowicz, 2001). Proponents additionally discount civil-liberties concerns as "unfounded." They reassure the mental-health community by pointing to eligibility rules that require persons under the statute to have a significant history of noncompliance as judged to be in danger of deterioration. They also criticize plans that advocate *alternatives* to outpatient commitment, such as increased use of advanced directives. All assurances aside, the National Stigma Clearinghouse notes that the subjective interpretation of the language in the law about predicting deterioration could lead to high numbers of persons' being deemed eligible for outpatient commitment. They point to the dangerousness of forced medication *itself*, and the lack of available court-appointed lawyers and medical personnel for second opinions (Seven misconceptions about Kendra's' Law, 2000).

A CUMBERSOME MISUSE OF FUNDS
AND A PRACTICAL NIGHTMARE

Other important but admittedly less philosophical concerns have been offered about outpatient commitment for several decades (Appelbaum, 1986; McCafferty & Dooley, 1990; Miller & Fiddleman, 1984; Wilk, 1988). For example, it has been pointed out that the monitoring and tracking of those committed for outpatient treatment may be unwieldy, especially without increased funding. Fiscal responsibility may be ambiguous. To illustrate, who pays for medication when it is prescribed and delivered against the patient's will? What about liability? Are providers liable for inadequate treatment, or for harm caused by medication administered against someone's will? What about the research that shows that—in general—forced treatment doesn't work very well, and is actually contradictory to the newer partnership and empowerment approaches to mental-health care? Or is such research really an example of a backlash against those approaches, which some scholars believe threaten the traditional "medical model" way of doing business? Do these laws subtly, or even not so subtly, favor psychopharmacological treatments over other kinds of treatment? And if so, what are the implications for the role of clinicians and human service agencies? Will social workers and other clinicians become mental-health parole officers or some new brand of societal regulator?

The New York Association of Psychiatric Rehabilitation Services (NYAPRS, 1999), a coalition of providers and consumers, voiced strong opposition to Kendra's Law. They disseminated a lengthy "Memorandum of Opposition," which continued attacks on the empirical foundation of the law. For example, recent research seems to suggest that extended participation in a court-ordered assisted-outpatient-treatment program may reduce violence among subjects, but an array of outpatient services as well as medication adherence over the long haul is necessary (Swanson, Swartz, Borum, Hiday, Wagner, Ryan, & Burns, 2000). Importantly, in addition to improved adherence on the part of the individual consumer, important *mechanisms for improvement* are thought to stimulate case management and the mobilization of resources (Swanson, Swartz, George, Burns, Hiday, Borum, Wagner, & Ryan, 1997). Note that both speak to *improving the responsiveness of the system.* The jury is still out about effectiveness of outpatient commitment, however. Several scholars have acknowledged that well-controlled, ethically sound studies with rigorous methodology and high-quality, relevant measurement tools are only now being conducted on assisted outpatient programs (Lidz, 1998; Draine, 1997).

NYAPRS raised dozens of other provocative questions about outpatient commitment. Specifically, it mentioned that outpatient commitment represents a new, unfunded mandate on local governments and their mental-health centers, that it has substantially expanded the responsibilities of local police (and turned treatment teams into police), and that it amounts to preventive detention based on the *prediction* of dangerousness—a task that has never really been proven reliable.

ALTERNATIVE PARADIGMS

So, if not outpatient commitment, then what? This is a fair question, especially given that people on both sides of this debate agree that the existing system is wholly inadequate. We have said that the ideal service system is one that builds on the values of self-determination and respect for dignity and uniqueness. This calls for a reconceptualization of services away from authority and toward empowerment and individual strength—services whose goal is recovery of the whole person (Bentley & Taylor, in press). Hiday, well published in the area of outpatient commitment, would agree. She writes, "Better service may even be able to ameliorate much of the apparent need for formal legal coercion" (1996, p. 36). If we start holding the mental-health system responsible, at least in part, we move toward funding such things as well-qualified case managers with small caseloads, the expansion of consumer/peer-operated services, transportation to clinics and other community resources, child care for consumers in programs, and financial assistance for expensive new-generation medications. We involve consumers and families in the planning and evaluation of services in nontrivial ways, including the development of meaningful procedures for advanced directives as well as effective discharge planning and aftercare services. We start delivering services associated with success and abandon those not associated with success. So, intensive case-management teams might be expanded, as well as family psychoeducation, skills training, supportive group interventions, and vocational training and supports. We would finally create and maintain the array of housing options and residential supports so desperately needed by mental-health consumers. In this way, we would cease to "blame the victim" of poor services and instead would keep our promise to provide a high-quality, accessible, client-focused, community-based system of mental-health care. We would place accountability for results where it belongs—with the community, its providers, and policy-makers. And at the same time, we would protect and honor the voice of consumers in directing their lives.

REFERENCES

Amador, X. F., Flaum, M., Andreason, N. C. et al. (1994). Awareness of illness in schizophrenia and schizoaffective and mood disorders. *Archives of General Psychiatry, 51,* 826–836.

Angermeyer, M. C., Matschinger, H. (1996). The effect of violent attacks by schizophrenic persons on the attitude of the public towards the mentally ill. *Social Science and Medicine, 43,* 721–1728.

Appelbaum, P. S. (1986). Outpatient commitment: The problems and the promise. *American Journal of Psychiatry, 143,* 1270–1272.

Baldessarini, R. J. (1979). The neuroleptic antipsychotic drugs. *Postgraduate Medicine, 65,* 108–128.

Bare, W. B. (1998). Neurobehavioral disorders of awareness and their relevance to schizophrenia. In X. F. Amador, & A. S. David (Eds.), *Insight and psychosis.* (pp. xx–xx). New York: Oxford University Press.

Bartels, J., Drake, R. E., Wallach, M. A., et al. (1991). Characteristic hostility in schizophrenic outpatients. *Schizophrenia Bulletin, 17,* 163–171.

Bassuk, E. L., Rubin, L., Lauriat, A. (1984). Is homelessness a mental health problem? *American Journal of Psychiatry, 141,* 1546–1550.

Belcher, J. R. (1988a). Defining the service needs of homeless mentally ill persons. *Hospital and Community Psychiatry, 39,* 1203–1205.

Belcher, J. R. (1988b). Rights versus needs of homeless mentally ill persons. *Social Work, 33,* 398–402.

Belcher, J. R. (1988c). Are jails replacing the mental health system for the homeless mentally ill? *Community Mental Health Journal, 24,* 185–195.

Bentley, K. J. (1993). The right of psychiatric patients to refuse medication: Where should social workers' stand? *Social Work, 38,* 101–106.

Bentley, K. J., & Taylor, M. F. (in press). A context and vision for excellence in mental health practice. In K. J. Bentley (Ed.), *Social work practice in mental health: Contemporary strategies, tasks and techniques.* Belmont, CA: Wadsworth.

Brown v. Bowen, 845 F 2d 1211 (3d Cir 1988).

Chamberlin, J. (1998). Citizenship rights and psychiatric disability: Speaking out. *Psychiatric Rehabilitation Journal, 21*(4), 405–408.

David, A., Buchanan, A., Reed, A., et al. (1992). The assessment of insight in psychosis. *British Journal of Psychiatry, 161,* 599–602.

Dawson, J. M., Langan, P. A. (1994). *Murder in families.* Bureau of Justice Statistics Special Report. Washington, DC: U.S. Department of Justice, Office of Justice Programs.

De Hert, M., McKenzie, K., Peuskens, J. (2001). Risk factors for suicide in young people suffering from schizophrenia; a long term follow-up study. *Schizophrenia Research*.

Ditton, P. M. (1999). *Mental health and treatment of inmates and probationers*. Bureau of Justice Statistics Special Report. Washington, DC: U.S. Department of Justice, Office of Justice Programs.

Dixon, L., Weiden, P., Torres, M., et al. (1997). Assertive community treatment and medication compliance in the homeless mentally ill. *American Journal of Psychiatry, 154*, 1302–1304.

Draine, J. (1997). Conceptualizing services research on outpatient commitment. *Journal of Mental Health Administration, 24*, 306–315.

Drake, R. E., Wallach, M. A., Hoffman, J. S. (1989). Housing instability and homelessness among aftercare patients in an urban state hospital. *Hospital and Community Psychiatry, 40*, 46–51.

Fernandez, G. A., Nygard, S. (1990). Impact of involuntary outpatient commitment on the revolving-door syndrome in North Carolina. *Hospital and Community Psychiatry, 41*, 1001–1004.

Fujiwara, P. I., Larkin, C., Frieden, T. R. (1997). Directly observed therapy in New York City: History, implementation, results, and challenges. *Clinics in Chest Medicine, 18*, 135–148.

Geller, J., Grudzinskas, A. J. Jr, McDermeit, M., et al. (1998). The efficacy of involuntary outpatient treatment in Massachusetts. *Administration and Policy in Mental Health, 25*, 271–285.

Greenberg, W. M., Moore-Duncan, L., Herron, R. (1996). Patients' attitudes toward having been forcibly medicated. *Bulletin of the American Academy of Psychiatry and the Law, 24*, 513–524.

Hardin, H (1993, July 22). Uncivil liberties. *Vancouver Sun*, p. A15.

Hiday, V. A. (1996). Outpatient commitment: Official coercion in the community. In D. L. Dennis & J. Monahan (Eds.), *Coercion and aggressive community treatment* (pp. 33–47). New York: Plenum Press.

Hiday, V. A., Scheid-Cook, T. L. (1987). The North Carolina experience with outpatient commitment: A critical appraisal. *International Journal of Law and Psychiatry, 10*, 215–232.

Kasper, J. A., Hoge, S. K., Feucht-Haviar, T., et al. (1997). Prospective study of patients' refusal of antipsychotic medication under a physician discretion review procedure. *American Journal of Psychiatry, 154*, 483–489.

Kates, B. (1985). *The murder of a shopping bag lady*. New York, NY: Harcourt Brace Jovanovich.

Kilzer, L. (1984, July 3). Jail as a "halfway house". . . . or long-term commitment? *Denver Post*, p. 1.

Lamb, H. R., Weinberger, L. E. (1992). Conservatorship for gravely disabled psychiatric patients: A four-year follow-up study. *American Journal of Psychiatry, 149*, 909–913.

Lidz, C. W. (1998). Coercion in psychiatric care: What have we learned from research? *Journal of the American Academy of Psychiatry & the Law, 26*, 631–637.

Luchins, D. J., Hanrahan, P., Conrad, K. J., et al. (1998). An agency-based representative payee program and improved community tenure of persons with mental illness. *Psychiatric Services, 49*, 1218–1222.

Lucksted, A., Coursey, R. D. (1995). Consumer perceptions of pressure and force in psychiatric treatments. *Psychiatric Services, 46*, 146–152.

McCafferty, G., & Dooley, J. (1990). Involuntary outpatient commitment: An update. *Mental & Physical Disability Law Reporter, 14*, 277–287.

Miller, R. D., & Fiddleman, P. (1984). Outpatient commitment: Treatment in the least restrictive environment? *Hospital & Community Psychiatry, 35*, 147–151.

Moran, M. (2000). Coercion or caring? *American Medical News, 43*, 26–31.

Mulvey, E. P., Geller, J. L., & Roth, L. H. (1987). The promise and peril of involuntary outpatient commitment. *American Psychologist, 46*, 571–584.

Munetz, M. R., Grande, T., Kleist, J., et al. (1996). The effectiveness of outpatient civil commitment. *Psychiatric Services, 47*, 1251–1253.

Murdach, A. D. (1996). Beneficence re-examined: Protective intervention in mental health. *Social Work, 41*, 26–31.

Murder suspect in "Kendra's Law" case off medication for trial. (2000, February 28). *Mental Health Weekly*, p 5.

National Association of Social Workers (1997). *Code of ethics*. Washington, DC: Author.

New York Association of Psychiatric Rehabilitation Services (NYAPRS). (1999, May). Memorandum of Opposition A.8477 "The assisted outpatient treatment act." Retrieved July 16, 2001, from http://www.madnation.org/new/kendra/opposition.htm.

N. Y. lawmakers agree to toughen involuntary commitment laws (1999, August 9). *Mental Health Weekly*, p. 2.

O'Keefe, C., Potenza, D. P., Mueser, K. T. (1997). Treatment outcomes for severely mentally ill patients on conditional discharge to community-based treatment. *Journal of Nervous and Mental Disease, 185*, 409–411.

Pataki signs "Kendra's Law" as family looks on. (1999, November 25). *Times Union*. p. 812.

Regier, D. A., Narrow, W. E., Rae, D. S., et al. (1993). The de facto U.S. mental and addictive disorders service system. *Archives of General Psychiatry, 50*, 85–94.

Report of the National Advisory Mental Health Council (1993). Health care reform for Americans with severe mental illnesses. *American Journal of Psychiatry, 150*, 1447–1465.

Richmond, M. E. (1917). Social diagnosis. New York, NY: Russell Sage Foundation.

Rohland, B. M. (1998, May). The role of outpatient commitment in the management of persons with schizophrenia. Iowa City, Iowa Consortium for Mental Health, Services, Training, and Research.

Roy, A. (1982). Risk factors for suicide in psychiatric patients. *Archives of General Psychiatry, 39*, 1089–1095.

Scheid-Cook, T. L. (1991). Outpatient commitment as both social control and least restrictive alternative. *The Sociological Quarterly, 32*(1), 43–60.

Schwartz, H. I., Vingiano, W., Perez, C. B. (1988). Autonomy and the right to refuse treatment: Patients' attitudes after involuntary medication. *Hospital and Community Psychiatry, 39*, 1049–1054.

Seven misconceptions about Kendra's Law (2000, August 12). *National Stigma Clearinghouse* Retrieved July 20, 2001, from *http://community.webtv.net/stigmanet*.

Sharfstein, S. S., & Zdanowicz, M. (2001, March 1). Courts must be able to order help. *Baltimore Sun*. p. A18.

Shore, M. F. (1997). Psychological factors in poverty. In L. M. Mead (Ed.), *The new paternalism: Supervisory approaches to poverty* (pp. 305–329). Washington, DC: Brookings Institution.

Slobogin, C. (1994). Involuntary community treatment of people who are violent and mentally ill: A legal analysis. *Hospital and Community Psychiatry, 45,* 685–689.

Smith, L. D. (1989). Medication refusal and the rehospitalized mentally ill inmate. *Hospital and Community Psychiatry, 40,* 491–496.

Solomon, P. (1996). Research on coercion of persons with severe mental illness. In D. L. Dennis & J. Monahan (Eds.), *Coercion and aggressive community treatment* (pp. 129–145). New York: Plenum Press.

Stashenko, J. (2000, June 1). Advocates challenge NYC's enforcement of Kendra's Law. *Associated Press.* p. 812

Stoner, M. R. (1989). Money management services for the homeless mentally ill. *Hospital and Community Psychiatry, 40,* 751–753.

Swanson, J. W, Swartz, M., Borum, R., Hiday, V. A., Wagner, H. R., & Burns, B. J. (1999). Involuntary outpatient commitment and reduction of violent behavior in persons with severe mental illness. *British Journal of Psychiatry, 176,* 324–331.

Swanson, J. W., Swartz, M., George, L. K, Burns, B. J. Hiday, V. A., Borum, R., & Wagner, H. R. (1997). Interpreting the effectiveness of involuntary outpatient commitment: A conceptual model. *Bulletin of the American Academy of Psychiatry & Law, 25,* 5–16.

Swartz, M., Swanson, J. W., Wagner, H. R., Burns, B. J., Hiday, V. A., & Borum, R. (1999). Can involuntary outpatient commitment reduce hospital recidivism: Findings from a randomized trial with severely mentally ill individuals. *American Journal of Psychiatry, 156,* 1968–1976.

Taylor, M. F., & Bentley, K. J. (2000, February). Changing conceptualizations of mental health and mental illness: Implications for social work education in the 21st century. Paper presented at the 46th Annual Program Meeting of the Council of Social Work Education, New York City.

Thornton, J. A., Wahl, O. F. (1996). Impact of a newspaper article on attitudes toward mental illness. *Journal of Community Psychology, 24,* 17–25.

Torrey, E. F. (1997). *Out of the shadows: Confronting America's mental illness crisis.* New York, NY: John Wiley & Sons.

Torrey, E. F., & Zdanowicz, M. T. (1999). Hope for cities dealing with the mental illness crisis. *Nation's Cities Weekly, 22*(16), 2–3.

Treffert, D. A. (1999). The MacArthur coercion studies: A Wisconsin perspective. *Marquette Law Review, 82,* 759–785.

Van Putten, R. A., Santiago, J. M., & Berren, M. R. (1988). Involuntary outpatient commitment in Arizona: A retrospective study. *Hospital and Community Psychiatry, 39,* 953–958.

Von Korff, M., Nestadt, G., Romanoski, A., et al. (1985). Prevalence of treated and untreated DSM-III schizophrenia: Results of a two-stage community survey. *Journal of Nervous and Mental Disease, 173,* 577–581.

Wilk, R. J. (1988). Involuntary outpatient commitment of the mentally ill. *Social Work, 20*(6), 133–137.

Winerip, M. (1999, November 4). Man who pushed woman onto tracks needed supervision, report says. *New York Times,* p. A21.

Young, D. A., Zakzanis, K. K., Bailey, C., et al. (1998). Further parameters of insight and neuropsychological deficit in schizophrenia and other chronic mental disease. *Journal of Nervous and Mental Disease, 186*, 44–50.

Zanni, G., deVeau, L. (1986). Inpatient stays before and after outpatient commitment. *Hospital and Community Psychiatry, 37*, 941–942.

■ ■ ■ ■ ■

IS MANAGED CARE CONTAINING COSTS AND IMPROVING ACCESS TO QUALITY HEALTHCARE?

Editor's Note:
"Managed care" became a household phrase during the 1990s. About 81.3 million Americans are enrolled in health-maintenance organizations (HMOs), up from 33.3 million in 1990. An estimated 89 million more are enrolled in preferred provider organizations (PPOs), which cost more but allow patients more flexibility. HMOs have been embraced by the nation's employers as a way to increase access and control health costs.

Heather Kanenberg, LMSW holds a Bachelors of Social Work from Murray State University and a Masters in Social Work from the University of Houston Graduate School of Social Work. She has worked with the State Children's Health Insurance Program and with the County Health Department. Mrs. Kanenberg is currently the Public Policy Analyst at a local children's advocacy organization in Houston Texas and an adjunct faculty member at the University of Houston-Clear Lake. Mrs. Kanenberg's primary interest areas include Children's issues, Women's issues, Poverty, and Health Care.

Richard I. Smith, J. D., at the time this chapter was written, was Vice President, Policy and Research at the American Association of Health Plans (AAHP). Mr. Smith holds a J.D. from the University of Maryland School of Law, an M.A. in Political Science from Johns Hopkins University, and a B.A. from Wesleyan University. Prior to joining AAHP, Mr. Smith served as Vice President, Health Care Policy at the Assocation of Private Pension and Welfare Plans; Director; Public Policy, Washington Business Group on Health; and Staff Director of the Maryland Governor's Commission on Health Care Policy and Financing.

Kristin Stewart, M.H.A., is Executive Director, Private Market Issues, at the American Association of Health Plans (AAHP). Ms. Stewart holds a M.H.A. from the School of Business and Public Management at The George Washington University and a B.A. from Bates College. Prior to joining AAHP, Ms. Stewart worked in the U.S. Senate and House of Representatives as a

Legislative Assistant. AAHP is the largest national trade organization representing more than one thousand health plans that provide healthcare coverage to more than 140 million Americans.

The authors want to thank Terry Sollom of AAHP for providing assistance in writing and editing the text.

YES

Richard I. Smith and Kristin Stewart

Managed-care organizations have benefited American consumers by improving the quality and affordability of the medical care they receive. For the first time, an infrastructure is in place that allows performance in the healthcare system to be measured. This creates opportunities for continuous quality improvement that have long been commonplace in other industries. The task of reforming our healthcare delivery system is enormous. Much work remains to be done by health plans, healthcare practitioners, and healthcare institutions so that all Americans can realize the promise of high-quality medical care.

SETTING THE STAGE: THE ORIGINS OF MANAGED CARE

Managed-care organizations and their precursors have been part of the American healthcare landscape for nearly a century. Prepaid group practices began to form as early as 1910, and several health plans that continue serving members today were founded in the 1930s and 1940s.[1] Though the debate over managed care typically is viewed as a recent phenomenon, it actually began with the emergence of these alternative healthcare delivery systems.

Like contemporary managed care, the early alternative systems faced strong opposition from organized medicine.[2] For instance, in 1937, the Group Health Association (GHA) was founded in Washington, DC, but not without opposition. Six years after its creation, the U.S. Supreme Court ruled that the DC Medical Society and the American Medical Association (AMA) had violated federal antitrust laws because of their actions against GHA: "Group Health doctors were systematically denied medical society membership, which limited their ability to get malpractice insurance, and were also denied privileges to admit patients to local hospitals."[3]

---

[1]For a brief overview of the origins of managed-care organizations in the United States, see P. Fox, "An Overview of Managed Care," in P. Kongstvedt (Ed.), *The Managed Care Handbook, Fourth Edition*, Aspen Publishers, Inc., 2001.

[2]Fox, 2001, op cit.; M. Millenson, *The New American Health Care System: A Report to the American Association of Health Plans*, Washington, DC, October 8, 1997.

[3]*American Medical Association v. United States*, 317 U.S. 519, January 18, 1943.

The development of new managed options and strategies continued in the post–World War II years. The first type of independent practice association (IPA) HMO was formed by a California county medical society in 1954. Moreover, the origins of utilization-review organizations can be traced to the late 1950s, when a Blue Cross plan, a county medical society, and a hospital council in Pennsylvania retrospectively analyzed hospital claims for utilization that was significantly above the average. Finally, PPOs began to form in the 1970s.[4]

Policy makers turned to managed care as one strategy in addressing the nation's serious health-system problems in the 1970s. In 1973, Congress passed the federal HMO Act to encourage growth in HMO enrollment. One year before passage of the Act, *un*managed care in government-funded health programs ended when Congress gave the Medicare program the right to disallow "any costs unnecessary to the *efficient* [emphasis added] provision of care," an authority that was automatically extended to the Medicaid program.[5] Enactment of the HMO Act was followed by the creation of the Medicare risk program in 1982, which offered beneficiaries a managed-care alternative to traditional Medicare. Nonetheless, as late as 1981, fewer than 10 million Americans were enrolled in HMOs. Although membership thereafter began to grow rapidly, not until 1986 did the number of HMO members reach about 10 percent of the nation's population.[6]

Shift in Focus: Assessing Quality in the Health System

In light of this low enrollment in managed-care plans well into the 1980s, the performance of the nation's health system in the 1970s and 1980s provides a baseline for assessing the effects of managed care as it developed into the predominant form of health coverage in the 1990s. Though policy experts often recall the healthcare cost problems that emerged during this period, they tend not to discuss the voluminous research documenting extensive and serious quality problems in the American healthcare system in the pre-managed care era.

Most prominently, quality of care came into question in a report issued in 1976 by a U.S. House of Representatives subcommittee investigating healthcare costs and quality issues. Congressional researchers estimated that some 2.4 million unnecessary operations every year were causing fifteen

[4]A. Enthoven, "The History and Principles of Managed Competition," *Health Affairs*, Supplement 1993.

[5]K. Davis (Ed.), *Health Care Cost Containment: Johns Hopkins Studies in Health Care Finance and Administration, Volume 3*, Johns Hopkins University Press, 1990.

[6]Group Health Association of America, *Patterns in HMO Enrollment, Fourth Edition*, (p. 198).Washington, DC, June 1995.

thousand deaths.[7] During this period, U.S. Surgeon General William Stewart, among other distinguished physicians and researchers, characterized the nation's healthcare system as "often of low quality, fragmented and impersonal."[8]

The HMO Act focused public and research attention on managed care, with one key question being asked at the time: "Does less costly care mean lower quality care?" In 1978, one of the first studies to examine the quality issue found that while prepaid groups reduced hospital stays by about a third, thereby reducing costs by 10–40 percent, the quality of care was comparable to that offered by indemnity plans.[9]

COST AND QUALITY IN MANAGED CARE

Some observers view managed care as a direct response to the spiraling cost increases inherent in the fee-for-service system. Others view it as a response to the well-documented quality problems that pervaded fee-for-service. The reality is that managed care has been successful. It has responded to both cost and quality concerns—reinforcing early findings that affordable healthcare coverage does not necessitate any sacrifice in quality, and in fact, goes hand in hand with improved quality of care.

Making Health Coverage Affordable: A Success Story

By some estimates, managed care has saved the U.S. economy billions of dollars annually—upward of $150 billion in 2000 alone.[10] During the 1990s, the economy benefited from stability in healthcare costs brought about largely through the use of managed-care practices. These savings helped companies avoid price hikes associated with rises in employee benefits costs. An analysis of U.S. Department of Labor data noted that healthcare costs, in particular, "stabilized and in some cases declined in the mid-1990s as more and

---

[7]U.S. House of Representatives, Subcommittee on Oversight and Investigations of the Committee on Interstate and Foreign Commerce, *Cost and Quality of Health Care: Unnecessary Surgery*, 84th Congress, U.S. Government Printing Office, 1976.

[8]M. Millenson, *Beyond the Managed Care Backlash: Medicine in the Information Age*, Progressive Policy Institute, July 1997.

[9]H. Luft, "How Do Health Maintenance Organizations Achieve Their 'Savings'? Rhetoric and Evidence," *New England Journal of Medicine*, June 15, 1978.

[10]U. Reinhardt, "Managed Care Is Still a Good Idea," *Wall Street Journal*, Nov. 17, 1999; H.E. Frech and J. Langenfeld, "Managed Health Care Effects: Medical Care Costs and Access to Health Insurance," University of California, Santa Barbara, November 2000.

more companies adopted managed-care plans, which kept a lid on overall healthcare and workers' compensation costs."[11]

Positive Impact on Out-of-Pocket Expenses. Managed care's ability to address the spiraling costs of the fee-for-service system has benefited consumers in the form of lower out-of-pocket costs. As managed care has become more prevalent, consumers' out-of-pocket spending on healthcare has grown at a much smaller rate than national health expenditures and spending by private health insurers. According to a recent economic trend analysis of healthcare spending patterns: "The share of national health spending from consumer out-of-pocket sources declined for the 11th straight year, reaching a low of 16.5 percent in 1996 [compared to 20.7 percent in 1990]. . . . This slowdown has paralleled the growth in managed care, which generally requires more limited copayments on insured services and smaller deductibles than indemnity insurance requires."[12]

Positive Impact on Prescription Drug Costs. Prescription medications are more widely available to patients owing to the generous insurance coverage under managed care. In 1980, patients paid about two-thirds of the cost of prescription drugs directly. However, by 1999, they paid only one-quarter of that cost.[13] Private health-insurance payments for prescription drugs grew an average of 19 percent per year between 1994 and 1997. During that same time, consumers' out-of-pocket payments for prescription drugs increased just 2.2 percent per year.[14] Similarly, a recent study found that between 1992 and 1997, as health-plan spending on prescription drugs was growing rapidly, consumers' out-of-pocket spending decreased from 53 percent to 37 percent of total private spending on prescription drugs.[15]

Affordability Expands Coverage. Given that every 1 percent real increase in health-insurance premiums results in an additional 300,000 to 500,000 Amer-

[11]Y. Dreazen, "Rise in Benefit Costs Takes on Urgency," *Wall Street Journal*, (p. 16). June 2, 2000.

[12]K. Levit, et al., "National Health Spending Trends in 1996," *Health Affairs*, Jan./Feb. 1998, 46.

[13]R. Samuelson, "Beware of a Regulatory Overdose," *Washington Post*, Sept. 5, 2000.

[14]Calculations based on data from the Health Care Financing Administration, Office of the Actuary, National Health Statistics Group, *www.hcfa.gov*, 1998.

[15]Barents Group LLC, *Factors Affecting the Growth of Prescription Drug Expenditures*, July 1999, prepared for the National Institute of Health Care Management.

icans losing their health-insurance coverage,[16] the importance of managed care's impact on cost cannot be overstated. By keeping health coverage affordable, managed care has enabled millions of Americans who would otherwise be uninsured to afford health coverage. In addition, given that low-income workers are disproportionately affected by an increase in healthcare spending, managed care's success at keeping health coverage affordable has been of particular benefit to low-income workers.[17]

Positive Impact on Entire Health Care System.   Numerous studies have found that the presence of managed-care plans in the healthcare marketplace helps to reduce costs throughout the healthcare system. For example, a 1997 study reported that the price competition associated with managed care slows the rate of growth in health expenditures for all payers in the market, resulting in long-run savings in future years for both healthcare plans and other types of coverage in the market area.[18] Further supporting this "spillover" effect, recent research shows that total employer insurance costs are 8–10 percent less in areas where HMO market share is above 45 percent, compared with areas where HMO enrollment is below 25 percent.[19]

Public Insurance Programs: Managed Care's Contribution

The benefits of managed care have increasingly been recognized by federal and state purchasers who have contracted with managed-care plans to cover tens of millions Americans. Since 1982, federal purchasers have selected health plans in the Medicare+Choice program, Medicaid managed care, and the managed-care option in the Federal Employees Health Benefit Program. State purchasers have selected managed-care plans for public-sector employees and Medicaid beneficiaries.

---

[16]Lewin Group LLC, Feb. 1999, calculations prepared for AAHP; AFL-CIO, *Paying More and Losing Ground: How Employer Cost-Shifting Is Eroding Health Coverage of Working Families*, 1998, study prepared by Lewin Group LLC; and the White House, *Statement of Administration Policy*, "S.1052—Bipartisan Patient Protection Act," June 21, 2001.

[17]R. Kronick and T. Gilmer, "Explaining the Decline in Health Insurance Coverage, 1979–1995," *Health Affairs*, March/April 1999.

[18]Lewin Group LLC, *Managed Care Savings for Employers and Households: 1990–2000*, May 23, 1997. In general, the studies referred to in the report indicate that each 10-percentage-point increase in managed-care enrollment is associated with a 1.0-percentage-point reduction in the rate of growth in health spending for all plans, including traditional indemnity plans.

[19]L. Baker, et al., "HMO Market Penetration and Costs of Employer-Sponsored Health Plans," *Health Affairs*, Sept./Oct. 2000.

Health Plans Serve Many Financially Vulnerable Medicare Beneficiaries.
Similar to the experience in the private sector, Medicare+Choice managed-care plans have particularly benefited financially vulnerable Medicare beneficiaries. Because the traditional Medicare fee-for-service program does not cover a large portion of beneficiaries' healthcare costs, most Medicare beneficiaries fill in the gaps in their Medicare benefits by purchasing either indemnity supplemental coverage or enrolling in a Medicare+Choice managed-care plan.

Data shows that Medicare+Choice managed-care plans serve many financially vulnerable beneficiaries and do so at premiums that are typically lower than if beneficiaries had purchased indemnity supplemental coverage.[20] In fact, lower-income beneficiaries without supplemental coverage were more likely to choose a Medicare+Choice managed-care plan than higher-income beneficiaries. For Medicare beneficiaries of limited or modest means who are not eligible for Medicaid, the availability of health plans has enabled them to afford supplemental coverage.

Medicaid Eligibility Has Expanded Under Managed Care. Likewise on the Medicaid side, the savings attributed to managed-care plans have enabled state Medicaid programs to expand their ranks. In the early 1990s, when enrollment in Medicaid HMOs was voluntary, several states obtained waivers from the federal government to establish demonstration programs that required certain groups or counties to be enrolled in managed-care plans. These states argued that savings gained through managed care could be used to enable expansions in eligibility or benefits.

This trend has been so persistent that the federal government no longer requires states to obtain waivers to require managed-care enrollment as long as certain requirements are met. Health Care Financing Administration (HCFA) detailed the benefits of these demonstration programs in 1997, reporting that a survey of seven states with programs showed Medicaid coverage was expanded to an additional one million beneficiaries who otherwise would have been ineligible for coverage.[21]

Improving Quality of Care: Much Progress and Future Promise

Medical- and health-services researchers have reported that the 1990s saw continuing improvement in major indicators for Americans' health status.

---

[20]American Association of Health Plans, "Medicare HMOs Serve Many Financially Vulnerable Beneficiaries," *Facts & Figures*, Washington, DC, May 2000.

[21]Health Care Financing Administration, *Medicaid Managed Care Enrollment, 1985–1997*, 1997.

These indicators showed improvement in life expectancy, infant mortality, and mortality rates for various diseases, among other areas.[22] Simultaneously, use of numerous types of services (such as immunization rates for preschool children), the number of surgical procedures for conditions such as heart disease, and the number of prescription drugs dispensed all increased significantly.[23]

The strong and growing presence of managed care—with its emphasis on prevention, access to care, coordination of care, and support for the dissemination of exemplary practices—facilitated these improvements. It was during this same period of continuing improvements in health-status indicators that combined HMO and PPO enrollment soared from 73 million to 172 million.[24]

Independent Studies Compare Fee-for-Service and Managed Care. Numerous studies have made direct comparisons between care delivered to enrollees in managed-care plans and care delivered to individuals with fee-for-service (FFS) insurance. The cumulative research shows a pattern of largely positive findings about the quality of care in managed-care plans. Even the American Medical Association has acknowledged that "most studies comparing the quality of care in managed-care plans and traditional indemnity plans have found the quality of care to be comparable."[25]

Most notably, favorable findings have been documented in comprehensive literature reviews published in 1994 and 1997 and have continued to hold true in studies published since early 1997.[26] The most recent review (1997) of fifteen studies on the quality of care published between late 1993 and early 1997 found that for eighteen of twenty-four indicators of quality of care, HMO care was better than or as good as care provided in other settings.

Numerous additional studies have documented that individuals in managed-care plans receive superior or comparable quality care than those with fee-for-service coverage. Much of the research examines the quality of

[22]National Center for Health Statistics, *Health, United States, 1999*, U.S. Public Health Services, 1999.

[23]Ibid.

[24]InterStudy, *Competitive Edge 10.1, HMO Industry Report*, 2000; Hoescht Marion Roussel, *HMO/PPO Digest*, 1999.

[25]Statement before the U.S. House of Representatives Judiciary Committee on HR 4277, July 29, 1998, 1069.

[26]R. Miller and H. Luft, "Managed Care Plan Performance Since 1980," *Journal of the American Medical Association*, May 1994; R. Miller and H. Luft, "Does Managed Care Lead to Better or Worse Quality of Care," *Health Affairs*, Sept./Oct. 1997.

care provided by health plans to individuals who have serious conditions, chronic illnesses, and debilitating ailments, or who need emergency treatment. These findings cover a wide variety of illnesses, a broad range of treatment settings, and an expansive spectrum of patient populations.[27]

For example, a review of seventeen studies published between 1987 and 1995 examining the quality of cardiovascular care found that the process and outcomes of care in HMOs were better than or equal to care in non-HMO settings. Of the 107 measures studied, thirty-five (33 percent) showed better performance by HMOs, sixty-seven (63 percent) showed no difference between HMO and non-HMO settings, and only five (5 percent) yielded better performance by non-HMO settings.[28]

MYTHS AND REALITIES

As the leading agent of change in the American healthcare system, managed care has made health coverage more affordable and created a new emphasis on quality, but not without attendant controversy. Oftentimes, these discussions have been fueled by statements that do not reflect how managed care actually works. As the debate over the direction of the nation's healthcare system continues, it is essential that claims about how the system is working be subjected to critical analysis so that the solutions recommended will be appropriate.[29]

---

[27]Other studies not described here that document the quality of care provided by managed-care organizations include: D. Angus, "The Effect of Managed Care on ICU Length of Stay," *Journal of the American Medical Association*, Oct. 1996; J. Holtzman, "The Effect of HMO Status on the Outcomes of Home-Care after Hospitalization in a Medicare Setting," *Journal of the American Geriatrics Society*, May/June 1998; H. Greenwald and S. Henke, "HMO Membership, Treatment and Mortality Risk among Prostatic Cancer Patients," *American Journal of Public Health*, Aug. 1992; A. Potosky, et al., "Breast Cancer Survival and Treatment in HMO and FFS Settings," *Journal of the National Cancer Institute*, Nov. 1997; P. Braveman, et al., "Insurance-Related Differences in the Risk of Ruptured Appendix," *New England Journal of Medicine*, Aug. 18, 1994; Piper and Bartels, "Medicaid Primary Care: HMOs or Fee-for-Service?" *Public Welfare*, Spring 1995; A. Potosky, et al., "Breast Cancer Survival and Treatment in HMO and FFS Settings," *Journal of the National Cancer Institute*, Nov. 1997; Braveman, et al., "Insurance-Related Differences in the Risk of Ruptured Appendix," *New England Journal of Medicine*, Aug. 18, 1994; Piper and Bartels, "Medicaid Primary Care: HMOs or Fee-for-Service?" *Public Welfare*, Spring 1995.

[28]J. Seidman, et al., "Review of Studies That Compare the Quality of Cardiovascular Care in HMO versus Non-HMO Settings," *Medical Care*, Dec. 1998.

[29]For a more thorough discussion of claims made about managed care, see R. Smith, et al., "Examining Common Assertions about Managed Care," in P. Kongstvedt (Ed.), *The Managed Care Handbook, Fourth Edition*, Aspen Publishers, Inc., 2001.

Physician-Patient Interactions: Relationships Growing Stronger

Office Visits Increasing in Length and Frequency. Critics of managed care say that physicians are forced to see too many patients and spend too little time with each patient, when, in fact, physicians are spending more time with patients. According to calculations based on AMA data, physicians spent more time on patient-care activities per visit in 1998 (29.5 minutes) than in 1985 (26.3 minutes).[30] This encompasses visits in all settings, including hospitals, clinics, and office visits. During the 1990s, when managed-care enrollment more than doubled, physician visits increased. Overall, between 1990 and 1998, visits to physicians increased, from an average of 2.9 visits per person per year to 3.1 visits.[31]

Access to Specialty Care Readily Available. A widely repeated charge against managed care is that enrollees have a difficult time accessing specialty care. However, studies published in the last five years show that health-plan members have good access to specialists. Most recently, a 1999 physician survey conducted by the journal *Medical Economics* showed that in eight of nine non–primary care specialty areas, HMO patients had as many as or more office visits per patient than non-HMO patients.[32] An Arthritis Foundation–sponsored study of HMO patients with rheumatoid arthritis found no significant difference in number of office visits with rheumatologists, number of outpatient surgeries, or number of hospital admissions when compared with indemnity patients.[33]

Hospital Lengths of Stay Match Surgeons' Recommendations. Opponents of managed care contend that health plans are not providing coverage for the medically necessary length of hospital stay. However, an analysis of length-of-stay patterns among commercially insured patients shows a gap between

---

[30]American Medical Association, *Socioeconomic Characteristics of Medical Practice 1997–1998*, 1998; AMA, *Physician Socioeconomic Statistics 1999–2000*, 1999. The time spent per patient was calculated by dividing the mean number of hours spent in patient-care activities per week by the mean number of total patient visits per week (1985: 51.3 and 117.1, respectively; 1998: 51.7 and 105.0, respectively).

[31]National Center for Health Statistics, *Health, United States, 1999*, U.S. Public Health Service, 1999; NCHS, *Health, United States, 1992*, 1993.

[32]K. Terry, *Medical Economics*, Dec. 6, 1999.

[33]E. Yelin, "Health Care Utilization and Outcomes Among Persons with Rheumatoid Arthritis in FFS and Prepaid Group Practice Settings," *Journal of the American Medical Association*, Oct. 2, 1996.

rhetoric and reality. Using data collected by the MEDSTAT Group, an independent health-information research company, the American Association of Health Plans determined that 95 percent of both HMO and indemnity hospital admissions had a length of stay that fell within the range, or exceeded the high end of the range, recommended by surgeons surveyed by the American College of Surgeons. The other 5 percent of admissions fell below the recommended range for both HMO and indemnity enrollees.[34]

CONCLUSION

Based on an evaluation of the facts, we believe that managed-care organizations have made important contributions to Americans' ability to obtain quality medical care at an affordable cost. Looking forward, managed-care organizations continue to evolve to meet consumers' preferences and to take advantage of the opportunities created by new medical approaches.

Responding to Consumers

Before the widespread adoption of managed care, consumers were limited to indemnity coverage, with its high costs and many financial and other barriers to quality care. In recent years, managed-care organizations have expanded coverage options and developed innovative new insurance products for consumers. For instance, many network-based plans let consumers obtain coverage of non-network providers for additional cost-sharing.

Many plans that previously required individuals to obtain referrals for specialty care from primary-care providers have developed "open-access" products. These products give individuals the choice of continuing to obtain a referral, or of self-referring to specialists, sometimes with a slightly higher co-payment. According to American Association of Health Plans survey data, the percentage of plans offering an open-access product increased from 7 percent in 1996 to 27 percent in 1999.[35]

Another major development in health-plan design has come with the narrowing of the scope of services subject to preauthorization. One major national plan has adopted a policy that eliminates nearly all preauthorizations in favor of a care-coordination role. This role emphasizes providing information to patients and providers about their treatment alternatives. Other health plans have determined that preauthorization has continuing

---

[34]American Association of Health Plans, *An Analysis of Inpatient Hospital Lengths of Stay for Selected Diagnosis Related Groups*, Washington, DC, Oct. 1997.

[35]American Association of Health Plans, *Portrait of a Changing Industry*, Washington, DC, November, 2001.

value but have reduced the range of services subject to preauthorization. Typically, plans focus remaining preauthorization requirements on services with high variation in use or indications of inappropriate overuse, or services for which there are treatment alternatives that merit consideration.

American Association of Health Plans survey data shows that prior authorization of specialist office visits was already low by 1996 (ranging from 9 percent to 23 percent among seven different specialties) and had declined even further by 1999 (from 3 percent to 11 percent among the seven specialties).[36] Likewise, among four categories of outpatient services (cardiac catheterization, outpatient surgery, endoscopy, and CT and MRI scans), prior authorization requirements dropped significantly from 1996 to 1999.

New Opportunities

In recent years, new opportunities have emerged to effectively treat chronic illnesses that previously had a poor prognosis. Many health plans have adopted a "disease-management" approach. These programs have several goals: Use "evidence-based" guidelines to promote appropriate treatment; systematically identify individuals with specified chronic diseases; closely monitor health status and adequacy of medication and trigger clinical interventions when needed; and educate patients through outreach programs in lifestyle changes that can improve health and prescription-drug regimes.

American Association of Health Plans survey data shows that over 70 percent of plans operate disease-management programs for diabetes, asthma, and congestive heart failure.[37] Other diseases covered by this emerging approach include coronary artery disease, high-risk pregnancy, chronic obstructive pulmonary disease, and depression. Recent research points to the promise of this approach for patients—namely, that disease management makes a significant difference in slowing the progression and reducing the cost of congestive heart failure.[38]

The Challenge Ahead

As the American healthcare system grapples with the twin challenges of improving the quality and affordability of healthcare, managed-care plans have much to contribute. The central question we as a society must face is whether we are willing to truly reform the healthcare system along principles of evidence-based medical-care and quality measurement—or whether

[36]Ibid.

[37]P. Welch, C. Bergsten, C. Cutler, R. Smith, "Disease Management Practices in Health Plans," *American Journal of Managed Care*, April 2002.

[38]C. Tilney, et al., "Improved Clinical and Financial Outcomes Associated with a Comprehensive Congestive Heart Failure Program," *Disease Management*, Vol. 1, No. 4, 1998.

we are content to return to a system that frequently ignores the best available medical evidence, allows for unjustifiable variations in medical treatment from patient to patient, and makes no meaningful effort to systematically improve quality.

Managed-care organizations have taken great strides to promote evidence-based care, and much more remains to be done. Policy makers, consumer advocates, organized medicine, and the media have much to consider as they decide whether they will promote this vision of better medical care for Americans, or whether they will be content to preserve the status quo.

NO

Heather Kanenberg

Without looking in your wallet at your insurance card (assuming you have one, which is a big assumption) are you a member of an *HMO* or a *PPO*? Do you have separate co–pays for brand name and generic prescriptions? Can you get a brand name prescription without having to pay full price? I know that you probably don't have to check in your wallet to know the answers to these questions. When we get sick we want to be able to be treated. Even more so, we want the opportunity to go to the doctor on a regular basis for 'check-ups' that will help prevent us from getting sick in the first place.

For those with health insurance, it seems there are constant battles over services, payments, coverage, and authorization issues. Those without health insurance are keenly aware of the activities in which they choose to participate, how far they can push their bodies, and what they will do in the future as aging continues. In my work with the State Children's Health Insurance Program (S-CHIP), I once met a mother of three who was a schoolteacher. She and her husband were without insurance for themselves and their children. They were afraid to let their children play outside in fear of the kids hurting themselves and having no way to receive necessary medical attention. Imagine being afraid to let your children participate in one of the most fundamental activities of childhood because you didn't have health insurance.

In our nation, healthcare has undergone incredible changes over the past decades, leaving us with the current system of care known as managed care. As Bertrand states, "Managed care is simply medical care that is provided by a corporation established under state and federal laws—a company that makes medical decisions for you in much the same way a financial adviser takes charge of your investment portfolio. Your managed-care provider tells you which physician to consult, monitors the medications and treatments they prescribe and ensure, that your costs remain as low as possible. For these services, you pay a set insurance premium each year" (n.d. 2).

IS MANAGED CARE SUCCESSFULLY CONTAINING COSTS AND IMPROVING ACCESS TO QUALITY HEALTH CARE?

Is Managed Care Containing Cost?

Despite consumers' disgust over the hassles and restrictions associated with managed care at its inception, employers loved it. They were able to pay significantly less money for a few years in order to offer health insurance benefits to their employees. In addition, consumers were fairly pleased, being able to see their HMO doctor for approximately ten dollars a visit. Some experts are currently estimating next year the nation will see the largest increase in premiums since managed care began. They are predicting a ten to thirteen percent increase in cost for larger employers and an increase of twenty percent or more for smaller employers. These prospects leave purchasers more frustrated than ever, and leave authorities on the subject questioning the future of health insurance. Medical inflation is back and it is outwitting managed care at the very game it was designed to play (Appleby, 2000).

Quoted in Appleby (2000), Kenneth Sperling of the benefits firm Hewitt Associates shares, "In the early '90s, we saw these kinds of cost increases, but we had the alternative of managed care as a low-cost option." Looking at the current state of affairs, Sperling indicates, "We are in the same mess as ten years ago, however now, we don't have managed care to 'resolve' our problems. Thanks to medical technology, costly new treatment methods and prescriptions, an aging society, and the ability of hospitals and physicians to refuse to accept managed-care reimbursement cuts, we are looking at exponential growth in spending on health care. Spending on health care is quietly growing to total fourteen percent of gross domestic product and some estimates show that by 2010, nearly one out of every five dollars could be spent on medical care, products, and services" (Appleby, 2000).

The managed-care industry is struggling. Many healthcare plans held their rates at unprofitable levels during a long industry price war in an attempt to gain market share. Now these plans want to increase their profitability. However, they have already reaped the easy savings by squeezing payment to doctors and hospitals. Other ways of saving money—further reducing hospital stays, restricting patient access to specialists and expensive medical tests, limiting patient choice of physicians—are all ones patients are coming to hate (Froomkin, 1999, p. 9).

The cost of private health insurance is continually growing in the United States. The average cost of a family health plan purchased by an employer is $6,351 per year. This leaves any employers in the predicament of both wanting to provide healthcare benefits for their employees and also needing to balance the company's budget. Many employers simply cannot afford to offer their employees an insurance plan. Similarly, pricing has increased in the private market such that purchasing health insurance coverage as an individual can potentially drain middle–income family earnings. This only makes sense when we hear that ninety-one percent of those who have private insurance receive this coverage through an employer–sponsored plan. Simply put, Americans cannot afford the coverage otherwise (Key Facts, 2001).

Americans experience anxiety over possible increases in premiums, co-payments, and cost of treatment. The emergence of new reports and nightly exposés on prescription drug cost increases has left many chronically ill or prescription dependent consumers pondering how to possibly forecast their medical expenses and simultaneously plan for the future. These increases in costs leave many with the difficult decision between spending from their monthly budget on needed medical care or alternately on basic needs such as shelter, transportation, and food.

Consumers want a simple solution to the challenge of minimizing spending on healthcare while ensuring everyone comprehensive, quality healthcare. The answer Americans thought they had found in managed care was only a smoke screen. "The fact is, we've never had the answer to this question," says Levitt. "We just stopped looking for a few years." (Appleby, 2000).

Is Managed Care Improving Access to Quality Health Care?

The Agency for Health Care Research and Quality (2000) provided the following statistics vital to understanding who experiences health insurance coverage and most importantly, they help define who is **not** receiving coverage for healthcare:

- Hispanics are three time as likely to be uninsured as non-Hispanic whites (35.3 percent uninsured vs. 11.9 percent of non-Hispanic whites, 21.1 percent of Asians and Pacific Islanders, and 22.2 percent of African Americans).
- 84 percent of Americans who lack health coverage are working or are the dependent of a worker.
- People 18 to 24 years of age are more likely than other age groups to lack coverage (30 percent of this group is uninsured). Young adults without health insurance may have "aged out" of a family policy, Medicaid, or may have foregone buying health coverage because they didn't think they would need it or couldn't afford it.
- In households with incomes of less than $25,000, a quarter are uninsured; only eight percent of those in homes with incomes of $75,000 or more lack coverage.

■ Uninsured persons are more likely to be employed in the wholesale and retail trade industry. They also tend to work in agriculture, forestry, fishing, mining, and construction.

■ Almost half of uninsured workers (48 percent) are either self-employed or work in private sector firms with less than 25 employees.

■ Single individuals and individuals in single parent families are more likely to be uninsured than married couples.

■ The number of uninsured women is increasing, but not the number of men.

It is difficult to discuss "access to care" when we know that 44 million of our nation's population is without insurance, thus leaving us with a system that inherently does not provide access to healthcare for all individuals. More specifically, we see that people of color, children, and people living in poverty are least likely to have insurance. A total of 11.1 million children lacked coverage in 1998—15.4 percent of all children (2000 Statistics, 2001).

These families, workers, and children have a greater likelihood of being hospitalized for preventable conditions, such as pneumonia and uncontrolled diabetes. Uninsured adults and children are less likely to receive preventative care. Uninsured cancer patients are more likely to be diagnosed with late-stage cancer rather than experiencing early detection. Tragically, mortality rates for uninsured women with breast cancer are appreciably higher than rates for women with insurance. Uninsured adults are more than thirty percent less likely to have had a check-up in the past year. And most astonishingly, the uninsured, when they receive the care they desperately need and deserve, are often charged more than the rest of us. Given that major insurers, including Medicare and Medicaid, contract for sizable discounts with hospitals and other medical service providers, providers often offset these reduced rates by raising the prices to uninsured individuals (Key Facts, 2001). Understanding the economic roots and the facts of uninsured individuals makes it difficult, at best, to agree that a managed-care system of health insurance is working to increase access to all individuals. We see both the vulnerable and strong experiencing barriers to accessing healthcare, left solely to rely on the fragile public health safety net.

However, for those individuals fortunate enough to be members of a managed-care plan, access issues are entirely different. American consumers expect an inherent freedom of choice in all that they do. This expectation is also maintained in the highly personal area of healthcare. Limited choice inherent in managed care, thanks to networks, is not a good thing. Many consumers find it disheartening to search for a physician in a specific network. If one has been fortunate enough to have secured a primary care physician, his/her next hurdle is the specialist care. Many encounter difficulty, frustration, and flaws in the referral process for specialty care.

In addition, there are national debates among healthcare providers and their managed-care organizations regarding the providers' right and freedom to treat their patients. In the healthcare world, where there are monetary incentives to order fewer tests and prescribe fewer medications, it is difficult to argue that patients have access to their needed care. Inherent in these debates rests the premise that there are physicians currently practicing medicine in the country being pressured to provide less for their patients despite medical necessity.

The National Center for Policy Analysis [NCPA] suggests that a number of studies and media reports point to the financial arrangements between Health Maintenance Organizations (HMOs) and doctors reward physicians and hospitals for deferring or withholding care that is considered too costly or excessive. This sets in opposition the financial interest of the doctor and the medical needs of the patient. For example:

- The brain tumor of a five-year old Florida girl was repeatedly misdiagnosed as the flu until her mother took her to a facility outside the HMO—which refused to pay for the surgery resulting from the correct diagnosis.
- Long Island Jewish Hospital in Queens replaced private doctors in its anesthesia department with lower-paid and less-experienced salaried physicians, and in one ten-week period four patients died from anesthesia-related complications after successful surgery.
- A California HMO was fined $500,000 by the state for refusing to refer a young girl to a specialist for her Wilm's tumor and instead assigning a physician who had never operated on children or on a Wilm's tumor (Problems with Managed, 2001).

A Survey conducted by the United States Department of Health and Human Services, of more than 4,000 enrollees and disenrollees from 45 Medicare HMOs across the country, found an "alarmingly high level of dissatisfaction" among chronically will and disabled patients.

- The study found that 20 percent to 25 percent of disenrollees said they failed to receive primary care, referrals to specialists, and HMO coverage of emergency care they needed.
- Of those who received care, 16 percent of enrollees and 18 percent of disenrollees reported waiting more than twelve days to see their primary care doctor.
- And, 24 percent of enrollees and 26 percent of disenrollees reported having to wait more than twelve days to see a specialist (Problems with Managed, 2001).

HMOs often reimburse doctors a fixed amount of money per covered patient, together with "withholds" and bonuses for delivering frugal care.

Thus, incentives discourage doctors from referring patients to specialists for care, authorizing high-tech procedures, or approving costly operations. There is usually a review board the doctor can appeal to if HMO management refuses to cover a treatment or procedure, but it also has the power to deny care (Problems with Managed, 2001).

So, I will ask the question that begs to be answered: Who benefits by this? Not the unassuming individuals who seek their doctor's medical attention for chronic or temporary illness. I would venture to say that it also is not the patient who is unwittingly prescribed a medication that might not be the most effective or suitable. I also firmly believe the physician does not benefit when the patient is not referred to a specialist, even when it would be the most appropriate course of treatment.

So what are we left with? We are left with a health insurance system pleading to be reformed or re-evaluated. The current managed-care system has experienced such condemnation, and the public outcry is so loud, that it has been heard in the hallowed halls of Washington. We now have a congress that thinks it knows how to help. The Patient's Bill of Rights is our national leaders' way of assisting the HMOs, once renowned as super-efficient, progressive organizations that were capable of putting the required pressure on doctor and hospital bills against the current public criticism. This criticism that frequently accuses HMOs of negligent and potentially dangerous penny-pinching at the price of patients.

Political officials responded to the public clamor against managed care with proposals establishing certain "patient's rights." Both parties are promising action on the issue, but Republicans and Democrats are submitting different prescriptions. Both parties state that they support the idea of codifying what people should get from their health insurance providers, surveys show that no other action by Congress would be as welcomed by the American people.

Currently we are left with two separate bills passed by the House and the Senate. Despite wide overlap between the measures that the House and Senate adopted during July 2001, the versions contain essential differences that are proving to lead to the most polarizing question in the patient's rights debate: "How much legal recourse should people have if their health plans deny them care?" The Senate would give consumers easier access to state courts, permit more class actions, and allow greater damage awards. Many outside policy analysts and congressional aides from both parties say that substantive differences can be resolved. As the Washington Post reported, Capitol Hill staffers predicted that there might be middle ground to be reached regarding limits on damage awards as well as the language in the differing bills regarding lawsuits against employers who buy their employees health insurance (The Patients', 2001).

Squabbles regarding lawsuits aside, isn't a bill of patient's rights what we need? Don't we, as American consumers of healthcare, want to halt "drive-through" deliveries? Don't we want to ban "gag clauses" in managed-care contracts with physicians that limit what can be discussed with patients? Don't we want our health plans to respond within 72 hours to appeals of care denials? Don't we believe that Medicare beneficiaries should receive side-by-side comparisons on costs, benefits, and other key features in managed-care options? We need to get behind this movement and begin demanding that the lumbering bureaucracies known as health plans treat us as consumers with value and rights. Most importantly, we are paying customers that deserve consistent quality services.

A snapshot of what the Patient's Bill of Rights would cover:

Senate and House Leaders agree upon:

1. Who: all Americans in health plans who have group or individual insurance coverage.
2. Access to Doctors: guarantees patients direct access to pediatricians and obstetrician-gynecologists. Requires insurers to offer a kind of plan that gives a choice of doctors, at a higher cost.
3. Emergency Room Treatment: health plans must pay for care at the nearest emergency room. This includes emergency services, care to medically stabilize the patient, and "post-stabilization" care.
4. Prescription Medication: even if a health plan has a formulary of drugs it typically pays for, the plan must allow patients other drugs at no extra charge if their doctor says they are necessary.
5. Clinical Trials: health plans must pay routine medical costs for patients participating in clinical trials approved or funded through the National Institutes of Health, the Food and Drug Administration, the Defense Department, or the Department of Veteran Affairs.

Senate and House Department disagree upon:

1. Where Lawsuits against HMO's can be filed. Senate: Patients may sue health plans over care in state court; lawsuits over contract disputes must be filed in federal courts; a compliant must first be heard by an outside appeals board unless delay would cause death or immediate harm. House: Patients may sue plans over care in state courts; patients must fist complete an outside appeals process; if patients lose during the appeals process they may sue anyway but face a much higher legal burden to prove their health plan was wrong.
2. Damage Awards. Senate: In state courts, patients can collect whatever state allows. In federal court, patients may collect unlimited noneconomic damages and punitive damages of up to 5 million dollars. House: In either state or federal court, patients can collect up to 1.5 million dollars in noneconomic damages. Patients may also collect up to 1.5 million

dollars in punitive damages in rare cases in which a health plan has refused to provide care, even after an outside appeals board orders it.
3. Employer Liability. Senate: Legislation attempts to shield employers from getting tangled in lawsuits by workers against health plans. Lets people sue companies only if the companies participate directly in the healthcare decisions. House: agreement with Senate legislation, adds a restriction of lawsuits against employers to federal courts.
4. Tax provisions. Senate: None. House: Allows permanent, unlimited access to medical savings accounts. Creates "association health plans" that allow small employers to band together to buy coverage through professional or trade groups (Dueling Legislation, 2001).

Essentially, the Patient's Bill of Rights is an attempt to reform a system of health coverage that is ailing on its own. The reality is that we deserve to be stakeholders in all decisions made regarding our care and medical treatment. We have fundamental rights to information, freedom of choice, ease of access, care without discrimination, and privacy in our treatment that cannot be overlooked or usurped. The current system is costly and does not offer all consumers quality services based on these concepts. Simply, managed care does not contain cost nor does it offer quality care or access to all.

REFERENCES

Appleby, J. What happens when the band aides run out? *USAtoday.com.* Retrieved August 15, 2001, from http://www.usatoday.com/life/health/hcare/lhhca140 .htm.
Bertrand, C. A. Managed care—solution or problem? Retrieved August 15, 2001, from www.medicineuptotheminute.com/mgdcare.htm.
Dueling legistation on patients' rights in the house and senate. (2001, August 5) *Washingtonpost.com.* Retrieved August 21, 2001, from http://www.washingtonpost .com/wp-srv/pnpolitics/transcripts/patientscompared_080501.html.
Froomkin, D. (1999, February 23) Backlash builds over managed care. *Washingtonpost.com.* Retrieved from http://www.washingtonpost.com/wp-srv/health/ policy/managedcare/overview.htm.
Key facts about the uninsured. (2001, April) Retrieved August 10, 2001, from http://www.familiesusa.org/media/pdf/uninsuredkeyfacts.pdf.
Problems with managed care. Retrieved August 27, 2001, from http://www.ncpa .org/health/pdh19.html.
2000 Statistics for U.S. health insurance coverage. (2001, July) Agency for Healthcare Research and Quality. Rockville, MD. Retrieved from http://meps.ahrq.gov/ pubdoc/h022/HIC2000Stats.htm.

SHOULD TRANSRACIAL ADOPTIONS BE ALLOWED?

Editor's Note:

Transracial adoption is an emotionally charged issue for many of America's minority members and prospective white adoptive parents. In the 1980s, the National Association of Black Social Workers (NABSW) noted that an unacceptably high percentage of black children were being placed with white families. NABSW contended that these cross-racial adoptions deprived the children of their racial identity and would eventually result in cultural genocide for the black community. However, research on cross-racial adoption was inconclusive regarding the potential negative effects of African American children growing up in white families. In 1996, President Clinton signed legislation forbidding interference in child placement for reasons based on race, though the law exempted Indian tribes.

Without basic health, education, and employment supports, minority families are likely to have difficulty adopting children. For example, the number of African American children available for adoption far outstrips the number of African American families recruited to adopt children, despite the fact that black families adopt at a rate 4.5 times greater than white or Hispanic families.

Elizabeth Bartholet is the Morris Wasserstein Public Interest Professor of Law at Harvard Law School, where she teaches civil rights and family law. She specializes in child welfare, adoption, and reproductive technology. Before joining the Harvard faculty, she was engaged in civil-rights litigation, first with the NAACP Legal Defense Fund, and later as founder and director of the Legal Action Center, a public-interest law firm in New York City that focuses on criminal-justice and substance-abuse issues. Professor Bartholet's publications include *Nobody's Children: Abuse and Neglect, Foster Drift, and the Adoption Alternative* (Beacon Press, 1999) and *Family Bonds: Adoption, Infertility, and the New World of Child Production* (Beacon Press, 1999). Professor Bartholet has won three "Friends of Adoption" awards for her writing and her related advocacy work.

Leslie Doty Hollingsworth, Ph.D., is an assistant professor at the University of Michigan. Professor Hollingsworth's research focuses on the identification and correction of disparities in the adoption and foster care of children of color, children in poverty, and children of women with severe and persistent mental illness. She teaches courses in human behavior and interpersonal practice with families.

YES

Elizabeth Bartholet

Some twenty-five years ago, a trial court in Virginia upheld the state ban on interracial marriage. The court reasoned that God had created different races and, accordingly, that it was natural to maintain racial purity and unnatural to engage in racial mixing.[1] At that time, many other state laws banned both interracial marriage and transracial adoption. In *Loving v. Virginia,*[2] the United States Supreme Court struck down the Virginia antimiscegenation law, reversing the trial court's decision and holding that it was unconstitutional for states to mandate racial separatism in the family.

Later, in *Palmore v. Sidoti,*[3] the Court ruled that it was unconstitutional to transfer custody of a white child from mother to father solely because the mother was living with a black man. Though the Court acknowledged that living in a transracial family might not be in the child's best interests, it held that the equal-protection doctrine prevented consideration of a potential parent's race in custody decisions.

In the 1960s and 1970s, the courts in this country outlawed formal state bans on transracial adoption, finding them similarly inconsistent with the equal-protection doctrine. A similar development has arisen in South Africa today, where the ban on transracial adoption has just recently been lifted as part of the move to abolish apartheid. But in the United States, a strange thing happened in 1972. The National Black Social Workers Association (NABSW) issued a statement calling for a new ban on transracial adoption. Actually, this development was not so strange. At that time, the black-power movement was at the height of its popularity, and movement supporters were calling for various forms of black separatism.

The NABSW statement had an immediate impact on the foster-care system. The child-welfare establishment—which had moved cautiously in the 1960s and early 1970s to open up transracial adoption as a means of placing black children languishing in foster care—acquiesced to the demands of the NABSW. The NABSW's position, maintained to this date, has been a key force behind the adoption policies we have today.

---

[1] *Loving v. Virginia,* 388 U.S. 1, 3 (1967) (quoting from trial judge's unpublished opinion).

[2] 388 U.S. 1 (1967).

[3] 466 U.S. 429 (1984).

Pursuant to these policies, public-adoption agencies throughout the nation make race a primary factor in child placement. The agencies routinely separate children and prospective parents into racial categories, assign children to racially matched parents, and hold children for whom there is no racial match available. Agencies have made extensive affirmative-action efforts over the past two decades to recruit black parents to adopt the overwhelming number of black children waiting for homes. The state and federal governments have provided financial subsidies to encourage these adoptions. Agencies have radically revised parental-fitness criteria for black adopters to permit more of them to qualify, and have mounted advertising campaigns to reach out to the black community. However, these efforts have not produced enough black adoptive parents for all of the waiting black children. Nonetheless, public-adoption agencies refuse to consider transracial placement except as a last resort. Some agencies refuse under any conditions to place children across racial lines.

What is the difference between the old and the new cry for racial purity in the family, the old and the new insistence on race barriers in adoption? The difference, of course, is the added voice of some members of the black community, particularly the voice of the NABSW's leadership. In my view, this is not enough of a difference. The new barriers to transracial adoption seem to me just as wrong as those that existed in our segregationist past.

Why are barriers to transracial adoption wrong? First, they hurt black children. I do not consider this issue worth much of our time because the evidence is so clear.[4] The opponents of transracial adoption have devoted most of their energy to arguing that their position serves the best interests of black children. I assume that opponents see these arguments as the only ones likely to meet general acceptance among policy makers. But in the end, these arguments must be rejected as frivolous.

The evidence demonstrates overwhelmingly that transracial adoption works well for the children involved. Studies show that transracial adoptees flourish in every respect assessed by the social scientists, including measures of self-esteem and identity. Indeed, transracial adoptees do at least as well as children raised in same-race families. Moreover, the evidence demonstrates overwhelmingly that delays in and denials of permanent placement have devastating effects on children.

Opponents of transracial adoption have no good response to this evidence that race-matching policies damage black children. Sometimes they rely on anecdotes indicating that in certain individual cases a black child has apparently suffered a loss of racial identity or encountered other problems growing up with white parents. However, anecdotes can be cited on both

---

[4]For specifics on the negative impact that transracial adoption prohibitions have on black children, including documentation of evidence, see Elizabeth Bartholet, *Where Do Black Children Belong? The Politics of Race Matching in Adoption*, 139 U. Pa. L. Rev. 1163, 1201-1226 (1991).

sides of the debate. A *60 Minutes* program[5] that aired in 1992 told the story of a black child who was taken from his white foster parents in order to prevent them from adopting him. He was killed shortly thereafter by the black adoptive parents with whom he had been placed. Though anecdotes can be cited on both sides, the entire body of social-science research evidence tells one consistent story—a story that provides not a shred of evidence supporting the claim that transracial adoption poses problems for children.

Opponents of transracial adoption also claim that not enough has been done to recruit black adopters. It is true that more could be done, but blacks are already adopting at the same rates as whites. This represents a significant accomplishment, given that black families are disproportionately at the bottom of the socioeconomic ladder.[6] The problem is not that black adults are not adopting, but that there are so many black children in need of homes. Roughly 40 percent of children in foster care are categorized as black or African American, and roughly half are categorized as children of color. Blacks would have to adopt at many times the rate of whites to provide homes for all of the waiting black children.

Opponents of transracial adoption also argue that we should not be removing so many black children from their biological families. They claim that if we did more to preserve these families, we would not need to worry about transracial adoption. But for years the child-welfare establishment has made family preservation and reunification policy priorities. In fact, many are now questioning whether we have gone too far in this direction, preserving families at the cost of subjecting children to unconscionable abuse and neglect.

Finally, opponents of transracial adoption claim that whites would not be interested in adopting the black children who most need placement. They claim that whites are interested only in healthy black babies, rather than the older children and the children with disabilities who disproportionately populate the foster-care system. But when whites are asked whether they are interested in adopting older black children with significant disabilities, they say "yes" in significant numbers.[7] Whites who express interest in such children are regularly turned away by public-adoption agencies. It seems disingenuous in the extreme for the NABSW and its allies to argue adamantly for the preservation of barriers to transracial adoption on the ground that if those barriers were removed whites would not want to adopt the children anyway. Let us remove the barriers and see what happens.

---

[5]*60 Minutes*: "Simple as Black and White" (CBS television broadcast, Oct. 25, 1992).

[6]Those who volunteer for the kind of intentional parenting that adoption represents tend to be relatively privileged in socioeconomic terms.

[7]See, e.g., James Breay, *Who Are the Waiting Children? An Overview of the Adoption Services System in the Massachusetts Department of Social Services*, 17, Table 3.3, reporting that out of 308 approved pre-adoptive white families in Massachusetts, 52 would consider adopting a minority race child, 101 would consider adopting a "special-needs" child, and 141 would consider adopting a sibling group, 1994.

In addition to their harmful impact on black children, I also think these barriers to transracial adoption are wrong because of their goal. I see race separatism in the family as the goal at the heart of these policies. If this were a valid goal, then some harm to the black children denied permanent homes would be justified. However, I do not see this goal as valid.

Most opponents of transracial adoption are reluctant today to speak the race-separatist rhetoric that characterized the famous 1972 NABSW policy statement describing transracial adoption as a form of racial genocide. Indeed, many often express outrage, at least in public forums, at the notion that their position has anything to do with race separatism. But race-matching policies only make sense when seen as part of a more general move for race separatism, a modern move reminiscent of the earlier trend that gave rise to the 1972 NABSW position. These policies make sense only in conjunction with a kind of racial fundamentalism that is newly popular. And, as demonstrated earlier, they make no sense whatsoever as a means of advancing the best interests of children, although these are the terms in which they are typically justified.

Arguments by the opponents of transracial adoption reveal the separatist nature of their position. For instance, some say that only black parents can teach black children the "coping skills" necessary to survive in a racist society. Yet studies indicate that transracial adoptees actually cope very well. What seems to lie at the heart of the "coping-skill" claim is a concern that black children develop a particular mode of interacting with whites, one that is arguably designed to advance the interests of the larger black community.

Another classic argument made by the opponents of transracial adoption is that it produces children with confused racial identities. However, the evidence shows that transracial adoptees develop a positive sense of self-esteem and are not at all confused about the fact that they are black. Quite clearly, the real concern is that they may not be sufficiently committed to the black community. They may not have what certain black leaders see as an "appropriate" black identity or an "appropriate" set of attitudes about racial relations. As one former president of the NABSW said, transracially adopted black children may end up with "white minds," which he saw as problematic for the black community because "our children are our future."[8]

These kinds of arguments could also be used to oppose integrated education and interracial marriage. If we think that black children can develop appropriate coping skills and racial identities only under the tutelage of black adults, then we should send them to schools with all-black faculties. Furthermore, according to this logic, we should also do our best to prevent marriage and procreation across racial lines so as to protect black children from the problems involved in being raised by a white parent and the confusion of

[8]*President's Message*, Nat'l Ass'n of Black Social Workers Newsletter (Nat'l Ass'n of Black Social Workers, Atlanta, Ga.), Spring 1988, at 1–2.

racial roles inherent in their own mixed-race status and their parents' interracial relationship. In fact, many of the arguments mounted against interracial marriage some decades ago sound remarkably similar to those now made against transracial adoption. Nine years ago, in reaction to claims that the children of interracial marriage would necessarily suffer identity confusion and related problems, Dr. Alvin Poussaint conducted an interview study of such children.[9] Interestingly, but not surprisingly, empirical-research evidence generally shows that the children of interracial marriage look much like the transracial adoption group on measures of self-esteem, racial identity, and basic attitudes about race relations.[10]

There are calls today for creating all-black schools for teenage boys, and there are many expressions of disgust with the failure of the integration strategy to empower the black community. And there is ongoing hostility toward interracial unions from many quarters. Last spring, a school principal in Montgomery, Alabama threatened to cancel the high school prom to prevent interracial couples from attending, calling one student who had interracial parents "a mistake."[11] Debate within the black community over the pros and cons of interracial marriage is intense, with many expressing opposition.[12]

But race separatism is not the direction our country is taking as a general matter. And it is not the direction I think we should take.

I want to end with a call for courage and a call for action. A call for courage because I think it takes courage for blacks and whites to stand up against those black leaders who have opposed transracial adoption. The reason we have the policies that we have today is that many of those who know what is happening, and who care about children, have felt silenced. Whites have been too ready to assume that the limited number of black leaders who have opposed transracial adoption speak for the entire black community. Many whites have felt they have no right to a voice on issues involving black children, and have no right to question any black leader's claim to represent the entire black community. And many have undoubtedly simply felt intimidated. The price often involved in supporting transracial adoption is to be attacked as racist, and that is a label that white liberals do not relish.

Whites should not be ashamed to assert that they care about the fate of black children, and that they see these children as belonging not simply to the

---

[9]Dr. Alvin F. Poussaint, *Study of Interracial Children Presents Positive Picture,* 15 Interracial Books for Children Bull. 9, 9–10 (No. 6 1984) (challenging the notion that biracial children suffer identity crises and suggesting that it may actually be an advantage in our country to come from an interracial background).

[10]See, e.g., William E. Cross, *Shades of Black: Diversity in African-American Identity,* 108–114 (1991) (summarizing and comparing empirical research on biracial and transracially adopted children).

[11]Ronald Smothers, "Principal Causes Furor On Mixed-Race Couples," *New York Times,* March 16, 1994, A16.

[12]See Derrick Bell, *Race, Racism and American Law,* § 2.4 (3d ed., 1992).

black community but to the larger human community. It is absurd, and arguably racist, to assume that the black community is monolithic, and that any black person who speaks on an issue should be seen as representing the entire community's view.

In fact, there is no reason to assume that the NABSW leadership position on transracial adoption represents a majority position in the black community. The NABSW has never even taken a poll of its membership on the issue. A number of NABSW's members quit the organization in 1972 to protest the new policy statement opposing transracial adoption. Those polls that have been taken of black people indicate no significant support for NABSW's position or for today's race-matching policies. The private decisions of many black adults indicate significant and increasing support for interracial family relationships. The number of interracial marriages has jumped in the last two decades from 310,000 per year to 1.1 million, and mixed-race births have multiplied at twenty-six times the rate of any other group.[13] Biracial people are sufficiently proud of their identities that they are now demanding their own census category. In addition, black birth mothers who feel that they want to exercise choice in placing their children for adoption often choose the private over the public adoption system *precisely because* they want their children to be placed as soon as possible, without regard to race.

In my call for action, I must first note the urgency of the situation. The foster-care population is exploding, with figures projected to continue to escalate dramatically in coming years. Many now talk of the need to build orphanages. They engage in this talk knowing that orphanages have failed children miserably in the past. But these people see no other way to house the overwhelming numbers of children whose birth parents cannot care for them. Yet orphanages seem necessary only to the degree that we buy into the necessity of maintaining current barriers to transracial adoption. Foster-care population numbers are overwhelming because of our refusal to place children for adoption whom we easily could place. We must do something to bring people to their senses.

There are many obvious targets for action. We need to challenge the organizations that purport to care about civil rights and children to take a stand on transracial adoption—and to take the right stand. We need to pass state laws such as the one recently enacted in Texas that prohibits child-welfare agencies from using race to delay or deny placement, and from otherwise discriminating in the foster-care and adoption processes.[14]

There is much else that can and should be done. But before taking action, we need to decide whether race separatism is an appropriate goal for

---

[13]See Jill Smolowe, "Intermarried . . . With Children," *Time*, Fall 1993, Special Issue, p. 64.

[14]Tex. Fam. Code Ann. § 16.081 (West Supp. 1994); Tex. Hum. Res. Code § 47.041 (West Supp. 1994).

this country in the new millennium. We need to decide what lessons to take from the racial hostilities that are tearing the world apart. Should we see these hostilities as reason to despair that we will ever create an integrated, multicultural society, as reason to put our hopes for oppressed peoples in racial separatism and racial-group empowerment? As South Africa lifted its ban on transracial adoption, do we want to insist that ours remains in place?

I suggest that we instead view current racial hostilities as reason to embrace the special kind of diversity represented by the transracial family, and as reason to celebrate the success that these families have experienced in crossing racial lines. I suggest that the right move for this country is to shed the particular remnant of our apartheid history represented by the barriers to transracial adoption.

NO

Leslie Doty Hollingsworth

In the United States, the controversy surrounding transracial adoption has focused primarily on the adoption of African American children by white parents. To understand the opposition to this practice, two steps are necessary. First, the reader must accept that Africa-descended people in the United States constitute a separate cultural group, distinct from their U.S. citizenship. Building on the work of other scholars, Robbins, Chatterjee, & Canda (1998) describe the emergence of a bicultural perspective when considering members of minority groups in the United States. Using this perspective, we can view the culture of a minority-group family "as one that may operate independently from the larger societal culture" (p. 128). Second, the reader must have some knowledge of the history of Africa-descended people in the United States. At least three historical facts are important.

First, Africa-descended people brought into slavery an orientation to extended family life in which the community had a primary role in the socialization of children. Second, among traditional Africans—believed to have influenced contemporary African American identity—the identity of the individual is subsumed under the group identity (Mbiti, 1969). There can be no individual self separate from the group. Third, the institution of slavery forced African American people to create an extended family life, in the form of plantation communities (James, 1992), as a mechanism of survival.

These experiences contributed to the development of a group identity among African American people and united them in a common heritage and a common set of values, beliefs, and practices. Baldwin (1981) explained this concept clearly in his theory of African self-consciousness. Race, or what Baldwin calls one's "collective biogenetic definition," defines an individual's social identity. The worldview of African American people emerges from this identity. A core personality system is part of the self of African American people and becomes expressed, according to Baldwin, in "a congruent pattern of basic traits (beliefs, attitudes, and behaviors) which affirm African American life and the authenticity of African heritage." These traits are organized into four dimensions of competency for African American people: (1) awareness and recognition of one's African identity and heritage; (2) the prioritization of ideologies and activities that seek black survival, liberation, and proactive and affirmative development; (3) prioritization of activities that specifically facilitate self-knowledge and self-affirmation (i.e., Africentric values customs, institutions, and the like); and (4) a posture of resolute resistance toward forces that threaten the survival of black people generally (Baldwin, summarized in Hollingsworth, 2000).

In the category of broader sociological theories, Baldwin's (1981) theory of African self-consciousness can be conceptualized under symbolic interactionism. According to this framework, individuals are not born with a "self" but develop the self (the I) and personal identity through interaction with others in a social group (Cooley, 1902/1956). Children learn appropriate social behavior and develop personal values through observation and empathy with others. The family is the setting in which social learning and development occur (Burgess, 1926; Waller, 1938). Thus, African American families who are themselves products of the African American group help children develop a social identity necessary for participation in the group. The cultural self and the cultural group are therefore maintained.

It was within this sociohistorical context that the practice and increase in transracial adoptions of African American children became cause for concern among members of the National Association of Black Social Workers. In 1971, 2,500 African American children had been transracially adopted, representing 35 percent of all adoptions of black children that year (McRoy, 1989). Between 1967 and 1972, ten thousand African American children were adopted by white families. This discovery led NABSW members to issue a resolution that remains relevant as an explanation of why transracial adoption should not occur. The group wrote:

- Black children belong physically and psychologically and culturally in black families where they can receive the total sense of themselves and develop a sound projection of their future. Only a black family can transmit the emotional and sensitive subtleties of perceptions and reactions essential for a black child's survival in a racist society.
- Human beings are products of their environment and develop their sense of values, attitudes, and self-concept within their own family structures.
- Black children in white homes are cut off from the healthy development of themselves as black people (Simon & Alstein, 1977, p. 50, and in McRoy, 1989, p. 150.) (Bullets inserted by the current author.)

The association based its position on "the necessity of self-determination from birth to death of all Black people, the need of [young black people] to begin at birth to identify with Black people in a Black community, and the philosophy that we need our own to build a strong nation" (Simon & Alstein, 1977, p. 52). Participants in the formation of the resolution "committed [themselves]" to go back to their communities and work to end what they referred to as "this particular form of genocide" (p. 52). They agreed to professionally pursue alternatives to transracial adoption "and to develop other alternatives and ways of implementation if necessary based on [their] experience as Black people" (p. 52).

The position taken by the National Association of Black Social Workers was consistent with the wording of the United Nations Convention on the Rights of the Child (1989). In its preamble, the Convention "[took] due account of the importance of the traditions and cultural values of each people for the protection and harmonious development of the child" (p. 2). Article 8.1 of the Convention document reads: "[Countries party to the Convention] undertake to respect the right of the child to preserve his or her identity, including nationality, name and family relations as recognized by law without unlawful interference" (p. 4). With regard to children who cannot remain with their biological families, Article 20.3 of the Convention document reads in part: ". . . When considering solutions, due regard shall be paid to the desirability of continuity in a child's upbringing and to the child's ethnic, religious, cultural and linguistic background" (p. 7).

Considering the soundness of these arguments, adoption agencies began to step up the recruitment of African American adoptive families and to prioritize same-race placements for black children. Soon, advocates of transracial adoption called for empirical verification of the assertions made by the National Association of Black Social Workers. But while researchers were beginning to pursue the requested research (reviewed in Silverman, 1993, and Hollingsworth, 1997), transracial-adoption advocates were pursuing legislative means to eliminate any interference with transracial adoption. It was at this point that the use of power became a primary element in the controversy.

THE IMPOSITION OF POWER

In his writings, postmodern philosopher Michael Foucault (cited in Robbins, Chatterjee, & Canda, 1998) linked knowledge and power. Rules of discourse allow certain people to produce fields of knowledge and to determine what is accepted as truth or falsehood, or as good or evil. Outcomes are determined by those who know the rules, and who have produced the rules. What may seem an objective reality is actually the result of power relations. The imposition of power is therefore not necessarily violent or even coercive but the result of who holds knowledge of the rules.

The approach taken by advocates of transracial adoption to eliminate any interference with the practice represents the use of social power to accomplish the desired goal. Organizational skills, language reconstruction, the media, and research were used in this process, which is described below.

First, advocacy groups formed to support and facilitate transracial adoption. The Open Door Society in Canada and the Council on Adoptable Children in the United States (Simon & Alstein, 1992) were two examples of the use of expert knowledge. Knowledge of how to establish and use advocacy groups in the direction of a desired end facilitated the effectiveness of these groups.

Second, transracial adoption was said to be necessary because of the small numbers of African American families adopting black children. In that regard, African Americans were blamed for the situation requiring transracial adoption. The implication was that if enough African Americans adopted, there would not be a need for transracial adoption. In fact, large proportions of African Americans did adopt—through informal mechanisms. In his study of African American families spanning 1969 to 1976, Dr. Robert Hill (1977) found that 90 percent of African American children born out of wedlock were kept by the extended family. The majority of these children (57 percent) were cared for by one or both grandparents.

Third, advocacy groups used the media to call attention to the large numbers of children in the foster-care system. African American children, overrepresented in these numbers, were portrayed as languishing in the foster-care system or as caught up in foster-care drift. The implication was that the crisis of African American children in the child-welfare system would be greatly reduced, if not eliminated, by transracial adoption.

Fourth, language designed for the legal protection of African Americans was directed against African Americans. Groups such as the National Association of Black Social Workers were accused of discriminating against African American children by interfering with the children's right to the permanent homes and families offered by transracial adoption. This accusation did not address the fact that alternative methods of solving and interpreting the African American situation had not been fully examined. Interestingly, this same approach has been used recently in efforts to dismantle affirmative-action programs in higher education—programs that were established to correct inequities imposed over centuries on people of African descent living in the United States. Affirmative-action programs are accused of discriminating against others by pursuing the very goals for which they were intended.

Fifth, language used in the resolution by the National Association of Black Social Workers was reconstructed. In criticizing transracial adoption as "genocide," African Americans were accused of being self-serving, of demanding that the well-being of African American children be sacrificed for the benefit of the group. However, in December 1948, the United Nations held the Convention on the Prevention and Punishment of the Crime of Genocide (United Nations Convention, 2001). According to the agreement approved at the convention, "genocide means . . . acts committed with intent to destroy, in whole or in part, a national, ethnic, racial or religious group, as such . . . forcibly transferring children of the group to another group." Use of the term *genocide* was appropriate within the context described in this paper.

Sixth, and finally, the responsibility was placed on African American people to prove that transracial adoption was detrimental to African American children, or that same-race parenting was uniquely beneficial. Empirical proof was demanded if the assertions of the National Association of Black Social Workers were to be accepted. It was undoubtedly this final step that led Goddard (1996) to write: "The position statement adopted by the National Association of Black Social Workers represented the clearest socio-cultural formulation of Black opposition to transracial adoption. Hence one could expect that for many researchers the empirical testing of a reality deemed to be understood and conclusive seemed unnecessary" (p. 275).

In 1994, the Multiethnic Placement Act became law. The legislation made it illegal to delay or deny the foster or adoptive placement of a child on the basis of race or ethnicity. The wording left a provision that a child's best interest could be considered in the decision-making. However, in 1996, the Interethnic Adoption Section of the Small Business Job Protection Act was passed. This legislation removed the "best-interests" wording and attached financial penalties to agencies and states found guilty of breaking this law. Patton (1999) points out that in the same year the Interethnic Adoption legislation was passed, the Personal Responsibility and Work Opportunity Act of 1996 was also passed, limiting to five years the amount of time unmarried women with dependent children could receive income-support benefits. She adds that this latter legislation had the potential of making it harder for unmarried women living in poverty to parent their children, at a time when the previous legislation was making it easier for more advantaged families to adopt.

Also noteworthy was the use of the word *research* by transracial-adoption advocates. A content analysis of media-reported interviews with adolescent and adult transracial adoptees between 1986 and 1996 (Hollingsworth, Unpublished manuscript) made two discoveries. First, the number of published interviews substantially increased in the years transracial-adoption legislation was being considered. Second, many media reports (and congressional committees) cited the results of a single twenty-year longitudinal study by Simon and Alstein (1992). Criticism had been directed at the study. For example, McRoy (1994) noted that in their conclusions, the researchers "reported that they did not discern any significant racial identity problems occurring for African American children . . . [in] transracial adoptive families" (p. 68). McRoy (1994) observed that this was in spite of figures from the third wave of that study indicating that 11 percent of the transracially adopted adolescents stated they would prefer to be white and that 27 percent of the transracial adoptive parents believed that their adopted children self-identified as white. Further, the study had an attrition rate of 128 families over its twenty years (from an original 204 families in 1971–1972, to 76 in the final year, 1991) (Hollingsworth, 1997).

In 1997, the Adoption and Safe Families Act was passed. Though not restricted to transracial adoption, the law makes it easier to terminate parental rights while freeing up children to be adopted at a younger age. Because African American families are more heavily represented in the child-welfare system, their likelihood of being negatively affected by this law increases.

CONCLUSIONS

Transracial adoption was not necessary in 1972 when the National Association of Black Social Workers put forth its resolution. The small number of African American families adopting black children stemmed from stringent adoption-eligibility standards that were difficult for many African American families to meet, and the preference of African Americans to adopt informally. The ability of same-race parents to socialize their children in the development of a racial self or identity has never been in question.

Transracial adoption is not necessary today. Only about 8 percent of all adoptions are believed to be transracial, including international adoptions (Stolley, 1993). This indicates that there is not a strong market for this practice. Moreover, the systematic removal of barriers to transracial adoption has not resulted in significant reductions in the number of African American children in foster care. There were 560,000 children in the public foster-care system at the end of 1998 (the most recent year data are available) (ACF Press Room, 2001). The number has consistently increased in the past fifteen years. An estimated 43 percent (n = 241,000) of the children in foster care in 1998 were African American (Evan B. Donaldson Adoption Institute, 2000), in spite of the fact that African American children make up only 15 percent of all U.S. children.

In summary, transracial adoption should not be allowed because it removes children from the protection and assistance of their cultural group (a right protected by Conventions of the United Nations) through the imposition of power by persons in a position of political, economic, and educational advantage. The revised position statement offered by the National Association of Black Social Workers in 1994 constitutes an appropriate alternative:

> Family preservation, reunification, and adoption should work in tandem toward finding permanent homes for children. Priority should be given to preserving families through the reunification or adoption of children with/by biological relatives. If that should fail, secondary priority should be given to the placement of a child within his own race. Transracial adoption of an African American child should only be considered after documented evidence of

unsuccessful same-race placements has been reviewed and supported by appropriate representatives of the African American community. Under no circumstance should successful same-race placements be impeded by obvious barriers (i.e., legal limits of states, state boundaries, fees, surrogate payments, intrusive applications, lethargic court systems, inadequate staffing patterns, etc.). As such, it will be mandatory that national policies with adequate funding be adopted as part of any new legislation (NABSW, 1994, p.4).

REFERENCES

Adoption and Safe Families Act of 1997, P. L. No. 105–89, 111 Stat. 2115.

AFC Press Room: Children in Foster Care 1983–1998 (August 24, 2000). Retrieved April 15, 2001, from http://www.acf.dhhs.gov/news/stats/fc.htm.

Baldwin, J. (1981). Notes on an Africentric theory of black personality. *The Western Journal of Black Studies, 5*, 172–179.

Burgess, E. W. (1926). The family as a unity of interacting personalities. *The Family, 7*, 3–9.

Cooley, C. H. (1956). *Human nature and social order.* Glencoe, IL: Free Press. (Original work published in 1902).

Evan B. Donaldson Adoption Institute (2000). Adoption in the United States. Retrieved April 17, 2001, from http://www.adoptioninstitute.org/research/ressta. html.

Goddard, L. L. (1996). Transracial adoption: Unanswered theoretical and conceptual issues. *Journal of Black Psychology, 22*, 273–281.

Gutman, H. G. (1976). *The black family in slavery and freedom.* New York, NY: Random House.

Hill, R. D. (1977). *Informal adoption among black families.* Washington, DC: National Urban League.

Hollingsworth, L. D. (1997). Effect of transracial/transethnic adoption on children's racial and ethnic identity and self-esteem: A meta-analytic review. *Marriage & Family Review, 25*, 99–130.

Hollingsworth, L. D. (2000). Africentric theory as a predictor of adoption among African Americans: An exploratory study. *Journal of Ethnic and Cultural Diversity, 9*, 119–133.

Hollingsworth, L. D. (Unpublished manuscript). A content analysis of media-reported interviews with transracially adopted persons.

James, C. L. R. (1992). The Atlantic slave trade and slavery: Some interpretations of their significance in the development of the United States and the Western world. In F. W. Hayes. II (Ed.), *A turbulent voyage: readings in African American studies* (pp. 213–236). San Diego, CA: Collegiate Press.

Mbiti, J. S. (1969). *African religions and philosophy.* New York: Praeger.

McRoy, R. G. (1989). An organizational dilemma: The case of transracial adoptions. *The Journal of Applied Behavior Science, 25*, 145–160.

McRoy, R. G. (1994). Attachment and racial identity issues: Implications for child placement decision-making. *Journal of Multicultural Social Work, 3*, 59–74.

Multi-ethnic Placement Act of 1994, Pub. L. No. 103–382, S553, 108 Stat 4057 (1995).

National Association of Black Social Workers (1994). Preserving African American families: Position statement. Detroit, MI.

Patton, S. (1999). *Birthmarks: Transracial adoption in contemporary America*. New York: New York University Press.

Robbins, S. P., Chatterjee, P., & Canda, E. R. (1998). *Contemporary human behavior theory: A critical perspective for social work*. Boston, MA: Allyn and Bacon.

Silverman, A. R. (1993). Outcomes of transracial adoption. *The Future of Children, 3,* 104–118.

Simon, R. J., & Alstein, H. (1977). *Transracial adoption*. New York: John Wiley & Sons.

Simon, R. J., & Alstein, H. (1992). *Adoption, race and identity: From infancy through adolescence*. New York: Praeger Publishers.

Simon, R. J., Alstein, H., & Melli, M. S. (1994). *The case for transracial adoption*. Washington, DC: The American University Press.

Small Business Job Protection Act of 1996, P. L. 104–188, 110 Stat. §1807.

Stolley, K. S. (1993). Statistics on adoption in the United States. *Future of Children, 3,* 26–33.

United Nations High Commissioner for Human Rights: Convention on the Rights of the Child. (Adopted November 20, 1989, Entry into force September 2, 1990). Retrieved May 1, 2001, from http://www.umhchr.ch/html/menu3/b/k2crc.htm.

United Nations Convention on the Prevention and Punishment of the Crime of Genocide. (1948). Retrieved May 1, 2001, from http://www.hawaii-nation-org/genocide.html.

Waller, W. (1938). *The Family: A dynamic interpretation*. New York, NY: Dryden.

■ ■ ■ ■ ■ ▬▬▬▬▬▬▬▬▬▬▬▬▬▬▬▬▬▬▬▬▬▬ ▬

SHOULD GAYS AND LESBIANS BE ALLOWED TO ADOPT?

Editor's Note:
The question of gay and lesbian adoptions is another hot button in social policy. Gay organizations adamantly support the right of gays and lesbians to adopt, while fundamentalist Christian groups oppose it with equal determination. As editors, it was difficult for us to find someone to argue the opposing side. Specifically, much of the opposition to gay and lesbian adoptions comes from the religious right, whose rhetoric is hate-based and grounded in intolerance. We would not permit the inclusion of such hate-based and discriminatory material in this book.

Stephen Erich, Ph.D., L.M.S.W.-ACP, is the program director at the University of Houston Clear Lake Bachelor of Social Work program. He received his Ph.D. and M.S.W. from the University of Houston Graduate School of Social Work. Dr. Erich's research interests primarily center on the practice of adoption and specifically the support of families and children with special needs.

Howard Jacob Karger, Ph.D., is professor of social work at the Graduate School of Social Work, University of Houston.

YES

Stephen Erich

Yes, gays and lesbians should have the same opportunities to adopt children that heterosexuals do. All adults who want to be adoptive parents, regardless of their sexual orientation, should be judged on their ability to meet the needs of children eligible for adoption. Equality of opportunity for all potential adoptive parents is a matter of social justice that benefits all of us.

There are two groups of people who are directly affected by this issue. One group comprises gay men, lesbian women, and anyone else who doesn't have a strictly heterosexual lifestyle. The other group consists of children currently eligible for adoption and those children who may at some point become eligible for adoption. The first group is a minority in our society.

Their lifestyle is often narrowly characterized by their sexual orientation rather than by all that their lives encompass. The second group is also a minority, given the lack of power they have over their young lives.

We do harm to society and to both of these groups by continuing to discriminate against gays and lesbians. Our collective homophobia, along with a strong sense of heterosexism, provides the foundation for the pervasive discrimination that is levied against gays and lesbians. This discrimination, among other things, manifests itself as laws against gay and lesbian marriage and adoption, policies against same-sex partner health-insurance coverage, and violence and murder. This form of discrimination is based on irrational fear and heterosexual privilege that are carried on from generation to generation.

These irrational fears and our heterosexism lead us to make erroneous assumptions about what constitutes a successful family. In spite of all the different types of successful families we see in our society, we still only fully sanction families that have two parents: one woman and one man who are married and have a couple of children together. This myopic view implies that family form is more important than family function. Family form simply characterizes the composition and appearance of the family, while family function defines the tasks families have to achieve in order to ensure their own survival. In this context, family function is specifically characterized as the tasks parents must carry out to meet the needs of their children. In the United States and around the world, our children's needs are met by families with a variety of forms that are quite able to carry out their necessary functions. In fact, according to the U.S. Bureau of the Census (1996), the traditional and favored nuclear family makes up only about 25 percent of all American households. This represents a decline of 15 percent since 1970, a trend that is expected to continue (Ryan, 2000). Conversely, biracial, single-parent, blended, and multigenerational families are increasingly more common (Dubios & Miley, 1999). In addition, the total number of children living with gay or lesbian parents reportedly ranges from 6 to 14 million (Dubios & Miley, 1999). Gays and lesbians become parents in a variety of ways. Some have children in heterosexual marriages and relationships. Others plan families using donor insemination, foster care, or adoption (Patterson, 1992). Notably, there is no evidence suggesting that these family forms cannot carry out their necessary parenting functions.

Agency-based adoption practices, like the American family, have also changed over the past fifty years. Some of those changes include doing away with maximum-age requirements and minimum-income requirements for potential adoptive parents (personal communication). Furthermore, single women and men are now recognized as equally viable adoptive-parent alternatives (Groze, 1991). Just five decades ago, older, single adults with lower incomes had few if any options for adopting children. More recently, attention has focused on gay and lesbian adults and couples who are adopting children through available venues. Such individuals may adopt infants or children with special needs. They may adopt transracially or internationally, and they may adopt privately, through nonprofit adoption agencies or through Children's Protective Services. Though adoption professionals and investigators now recognize that a successful adoptive family may take many forms, this recognition has not been fully extended to gay or lesbian adults or couples.

This is disturbing because a sizable body of research, using a wide variety of psychological tests and psychiatric interviews, have found few differences between gays and lesbians and heterosexuals in terms of psychological adjustment and level of psychopathology (Bell & Weinberg, 1978; Gonsiorek, 1991). Moreover, several studies have examined the mental health of lesbian mothers and found no significant differences between them and heterosexual mothers (Green, Mandel, Hotvedt, Gray, & Smith, 1986; Rand, Graham, & Rawlings, 1982).

The results from studies on lesbian couple relationships are consistently favorable. In studies from the United States and Europe, lesbian mothers expressed satisfaction with their couple relationships. These same studies also report that lesbian couples were able to negotiate the division of labor equitably, including work outside the home and childcare responsibilities. In addition, lesbian nonbiological mothers were consistently described as more positively involved than their heterosexual fathers (Mitchell, 1996; Patterson, 1992, Polikoff, 1990; Riley, 1988; Tasker & Golombok, 1991; Weston, 1991).

Many studies have also considered whether gays and lesbians possess the appropriate parental attitudes to raise children. In fact, several studies of this issue have not found any significant differences between divorced lesbian and straight mothers in terms of appropriate parental attitudes (Golombok, Spencer, & Rutter, 1983; Mucklow & Phelan, 1979). Neither have studies found any significant differences in overall parenting attitudes between gay and heterosexual men. Specifically, Scallen (1981) compared parenting attitudes in gay and straight fathers and found no significant differences between the groups in terms of problem-solving ability or ability to provide recreation for children or encourage their autonomy. In another study, researchers asked four-to-eight-year-olds who were conceived through donor insemination by lesbian mothers about their perceptions of their relationship with their parents. All the children reported positive feelings about their parents (Brewaeys, Ponjaert, Van Hall, & Golombok, 1997). Furthermore, there were no differences when this group was compared with children conceived by heterosexual parents (Brewaeys, Ponjaert, Van Hall, & Golombok, 1997). The results of these studies strongly suggest that sexual orientation has little to do with effective family functioning and parenting attitudes and skills. Once again, the form of the family is less important than the family's ability to carry out its basic functions in raising children.

However, if we are to adequately assess the ability of gay and lesbian parenting, we must also examine outcomes of children parented by gay and lesbians. Ample evidence suggests that children raised by gays and lesbians are not any more likely to become gay or lesbian than children raised by straight parents (Patterson, 1992). Studies asking children of gay fathers to express their sexual preference found the majority of children to be hetero-sexual and the proportion of gay and lesbian children to be similar to that of any random sample (Patterson, 1992). Furthermore, the assessment of more than three hundred children of gay or lesbian parents in twelve different samples did not show any evidence of significant disturbances of any kind in the development of sexual identity (Patterson, 1992). Investigators have also compared the gender identity of children raised by lesbian parents to that of children raised by heterosexual parents using interviews and psychological testing. Each has concluded that the children of these parents appear to be as comfortable as other children with their biological sex and also exhibit con-ventional gender behavior (Golombok, Spencer, & Rutter, 1983; Green & Bozett, 1991; Hoeffer, 1981; Kirkpatrick, Smith, & Roy, 1981; Patterson, 1994).

Researchers have also studied the competencies, adaptive behavior, intelligence, and behavioral adjustment of children raised by gay and lesbian parents. McCandlish (1987) interviewed lesbian couples raising young chil-dren born to them through donor insemination. Results indicate that all the children displayed normal development and no significant behavior prob-lems. In a study comparing planned lesbian families with heterosexual fam-ilies in terms of the intelligence, behavior, and adaptive functioning of children, there were no significant differences between the two groups. Both groups also compared favorably to the standardization samples for each of the instruments used in the study (Flaks, 1995).

In 1994, Patterson studied four-to-nine year olds using a variety of stan-dardized measures. On the Achenbach and Edelbrock Child Behavior Check-list, scores for children of lesbian mothers on social competence and ability to internalize and externalize behavior problems did not differ from the scores for a large representative sample of children used to norm the test (Achen-bach & Edelbrock, 1983). The research to date on outcomes of children raised by gay and lesbian parents indicates that they are no different than those chil-dren raised by heterosexual parents. Patterson (1992) has reported that after the accumulation of a substantial body of knowledge, not a single study has found children of gay and lesbian parents to be adversely affected in any sig-nificant way relative to children of straight parents.

Successful families, regardless of their form, must achieve an adaptive fit with their environments. They must be able to exchange information, energy, and resources with their environments so that they can achieve optimal levels of family functioning while also supporting the continued healthy develop-ment of the environment (Germain & Gitterman, 1995). Achievement of this adaptive balance is within reach for most individuals and families but is very difficult, if not impossible, for those segments of our society who are the tar-gets of discrimination. The result is an unfavorable niche from where it is dif-ficult to achieve optimal individual and family functioning (Germain & Gitterman, 1995). Gays and lesbians are one of many disenfranchised groups who have to work harder to achieve this level of adaptive balance because of their niche in society. Unlike favored groups in our society, disenfranchised groups are likely to have weaker social-support networks, which are sources of information, energy, and resources. The absence of a strong social-support network makes it more difficult for these groups to achieve an optimal fit with their environment, which in turn supports higher levels of adaptive personal and family functioning (Germain & Gitterman, 1995).

Although the research on personal- and familial-support networks is somewhat limited, studies suggest that despite being the targets of institutionalized discrimination, gays and lesbians have social-support networks comparable to those of heterosexual parents. For example, two studies have found that divorced lesbian and heterosexual mothers are equally likely to seek support from their families of origin, ex-husbands, and partners (Lewin, 1981; Lewin & Lyons, 1982). Studies of gay and lesbian couples without children have also reported evidence of satisfactory social-support networks, although some studies have concluded that gay and lesbian couples view their friends as more prominent providers of emotional support than they view their families (Aura, 1985; Kurdek & Schmitt, 1987).

The research on gay and lesbian adoptive families strongly supports the contention that their children are as well cared for as their counterparts in heterosexual families. The research specific to gay and lesbian adoptive families is limited at this time. However, Erich, Leung, Kindle, and Carter (2001) conducted a yet-to-be-published study of exclusively gay and lesbian adoptive families. The results of this study indicate that all families scored in the "typical/average" range or the "family-strength" range on a standardized scale of family functioning. Less than 5 percent of the adopted children in this study scored in the clinically significant range of the total-problem scale of the Child Behavior Checklist (Achenbach & Edelbrock, 1983). The gay and lesbian parents in this study were also able to find adequate levels of help from a variety of social supports. In addition, the majority of parents in this study reported that they received significant help from members of the heterosexual community.

In conclusion, there is not a shred of credible evidence that gay and lesbian adults or couples are any less capable of being good parents than their heterosexual counterparts are. Parents must be judged on their ability to master the necessary functions of parenting rather than on their form alone. In spite of being the targets of institutional discrimination, gay and lesbian families continue to thrive. Their most significant problem remains society's reluctance to embrace change and social justice. By opening all avenues for gays and lesbians to adopt, we also help hundreds of thousands of children in our country and around the world to be adopted into loving and permanent families.

NO

Howard Jacob Karger

Those in their late forties or fifties might recall a 1940s "two brothers" movie, in which one brother was a priest and the other a gangster (played by Edmund O'Brien and James Cagney). The good-versus-bad-brother tale has been an enduring motif around Hollywood for decades. Although often overdone, the message is clear: Why in the same family does one brother turn out to be good and the other to be a criminal? Fifty years after these movies, and hundreds of research studies later, we still cannot answer this question. All we can know for sure is how little we really know about what makes people tick. This essay will not argue against gay and lesbian adoptions per se, but instead urge caution in enacting radical social experiments that are not grounded in sound social-science research. The policy of allowing gay and lesbian adoptions is an example of this kind of radical experiment.

In addition, I will not argue that gay and lesbians do not make fit parents. In fact, some make excellent parents while others make lousy parents. The proportion of good to bad homosexual parents is likely the same as in the heterosexual community. What I will argue is that we do not have the research evidence to know with certainty what long-term effects, if any, are experienced by children who are adopted into these relationships. The guiding principle in this essay is not whether gays and lesbians should have the right to adopt, but whether this kind of adoption is in the best interests of the child. In short, I am approaching this debate from a children's-rights perspective rather than a gay-rights perspective.

THE SHIFTING KNOWLEDGE BASE
OF SOCIAL-SCIENCE RESEARCH

In the middle 1970s, popular and academic wisdom held that ending a bad marriage worked to the long-term benefit of all concerned. Liberal social scientists argued that children in a conflict-ridden marriage suffered more than children whose parents divorced. It was assumed that the deleterious effects of divorce on children were short-lived and could be compensated by a loving parent who was living in a less stressful situation. Of course, some studies supported this contention. In contrast, Judith Wallerstein studied 131 children in 1970 whose parents were divorcing. Wallerstein reported that eighteen months after the breakup, "we didn't see a single child who was well adjusted. And we didn't see a single child to whom divorce was not the central event of their lives" (quoted in Van Biema, 1994, p. 12). Using six nationally representative data sets containing more than 25,000 children, Sara McLanahan and Gary Sandefur (1997) found that children raised with only one biological parent are disadvantaged in a multitude of ways. Compared to children who grow up in two-parent families, they are (1) twice as likely to drop out of school, (2) 2.5 times more likely to become teen mothers, and (3) 1.4 times more likely to be idle out of work and out of school. They also have (4) lower grade-point averages, lower college aspirations, and poorer attendance records, and (5) higher rates of divorce in adulthood. These patterns persist even after adjusting for differences in race, the education of parents, the number of siblings, and the child's geographic and residential location.

Conversely, new research suggests that divorce does not necessarily lead to children's problem behavior. Rather, mothers' delinquency before marriage accounts for many of the behavior problems found among children after divorce. The study also found that children of divorce were better off than those living in highly dysfunctional marriages. The authors point out two important limitations to their research: (1) the absence of data on the fathers of the children, and (2) the fact that the national sample is heavily weighted toward young parents and their children. At the least, the research on the effects of divorce on children is contradictory and points out how little we really know about this phenomenon. Conventional wisdom exists within a particular time period, and is therefore not necessarily an enduring form of wisdom.

Research on gay and lesbian adoptions is also in an infancy stage. An Internet search of "gay and lesbian adoptions" yielded about eight thousand hits, most of them from pro-gay and -lesbian organizations. In 1992, Charlotte Patterson (1992) analyzed the findings of twelve studies that had assessed more than three hundred children of gay or lesbian parents, often comparing them with the children of divorced heterosexual women. She found that adult children of gay people were no more likely to be gay than were the children of heterosexual parents. These children did not differ from "normal" children in terms of gender identity (how good they felt about being male or female) or gender role behavior (lesbians' children played just as often with "feminine" toys such as dolls, and as adults they were just as likely as others to choose jobs that fit into conventional sex roles). The studies found no differences in terms of intelligence, self-concept, emotional problems, and development of moral judgment. One study reported that lesbians' children saw themselves as more lovable and were rated by others as more affectionate and more protective toward younger children.

The conventional wisdom among liberal social scientists is reflected in a 2000 study done by Scott V. DiBartolo, a Yale University psychiatrist. According to DiBartolo, children thrive in same-sex families. DiBartolo argues that same-sex adoption does not generally have any significant detrimental effects on a child's development and can, in fact, add to a child's emotional and financial security. He concludes that permitting same-sex adoptions is in the best interests of the child.

Other emerging research paints a slightly different picture. Psychologists sympathetic to gay rights have long asserted that children raised by same-sex parents are no different from other children. But a new study done by Judith Stacey and Timothy Biblarz (2001) suggests that there are differences. Done by two University of Southern California sociologists, this study examined twenty-one studies dating back to 1980 on the subject of children raised in gay and lesbian households. The authors found that children with lesbian or gay parents are more likely to depart from traditional gender roles than children of heterosexual couples. These children also show more empathy for social diversity, are less confined by gender stereotypes, and are more likely to explore homosexual activity themselves. The authors found that teenage boys with homosexual parents were more sexually restrained than their counterparts who were raised by heterosexual couples. Boys raised by lesbian couples exhibited less aggressive and more nurturing social behavior than boys raised in heterosexual families. The teenage girls showed an opposite trend, with those raised by lesbians gravitating toward less stereotypical feminine dress, play, and occupations. Teenage girls raised by lesbians also appeared to be more sexually adventurous and less chaste than girls raised by heterosexuals. Stacey and Biblarz maintain that children raised in gay and lesbian families grow up to be more open to homoerotic relations. While these findings do not imply negative traits or harm, they do point out that contrary to conventional social-science wisdom, there may be differences between children raised in gay and lesbian families compared to those raised in traditional heterosexual homes.

Many studies of gay and lesbian adoptions have been focused through an ideological lens. Often conducted by individuals or organizations with a vested interest in the outcome, the results of research studies are contradictory. For example, studies linked to conservative political and religious groups show negative effects on children of gay and lesbian parents. On the other hand, studies that support homosexual parenting are said to reflect the bias of those who are themselves gay or who support gay rights. Clearly, we need definitive studies that will follow large numbers of children over a long period of time. The research on gay and lesbian adoptions is complicated by yet another factor. Namely, the number of homosexuals who have adopted children is unknown, and because of the controversial nature of the issue, their children are often reluctant to speak out. In short, despite a plethora of research studies, many of which are spurious, we know very little about (nor can we predict) the effects on children of growing up in a gay or lesbian family.

On the one hand, liberal social thought minimizes the differences between groups of people. We are told that we are all the same and should be treated that way. On the other hand, liberal social science celebrates multi-culturalism and diversity. Are we or are we not the same? We can't have it both ways.

If gay and lesbian culture has distinct attributes and values that separate it from heterosexual society (as diversity proponents maintain), then it would stand to reason that the experience of children growing up in those families would be different (but not necessarily worse) than children raised in heterosexual families. If this is true, we would expect children growing up in gay and lesbian families to have different values and attributes, which is congruent with the findings of Stacey and Biblarz. Because anti-gay scholars seek evidence of harm, sympathetic researchers defensively stress its absence and therefore tread lightly around the differences. It is obvious that children brought up in different social contexts will be different. Intellectual honesty dictates that we acknowledge the differences, despite our fear that this will inflame homophobia.

IS LOVE ENOUGH?: POTENTIAL STRUGGLES FACED BY CHILDREN GROWING UP IN GAY AND LESBIAN FAMILIES

Our current understanding of child development is based on the belief that loving a child is the key factor in his or her development. But is love enough? Even abusive parents love their children, albeit not in a healthy way. We don't doubt that gay and lesbians can make excellent parents. However, social-work theory informs us that children also live in a social environment in which much of their social cues and self-concept come from their peers as well as their parents. Anyone who has lived through parenting a teenager knows all too well the influence that peer acceptance plays in the lives of their children.

Nowhere are the consequences of anti-gay feelings more apparent than in the high number of suicides among gay youth. Studies have found that gay youth are three to seven times more likely to attempt suicide than heterosexual children (Horizons Foundation, 2001). Studies have found that gay youth—and youth who are perceived to be gay—are more likely to get beat up (40 percent report threats of attack, 17 percent have been physically assaulted, and 80 percent report verbal abuse), feel isolated, and have trouble in school (Horizons Foundation, 2001; National Adoption Information Clearinghouse, 2000). A study done for the former governor of Massachusetts found that 97 percent of public high school students reported hearing homophobic remarks regularly from their peers, and 53 percent reported hearing them from school staff. Gay teens are four times more likely than heterosexuals to be threatened with a weapon at school (Horizons Foundation, 2001). Given the fear and violence created by homophobia, it is not surprising that the Department of Justice concluded that gays are probably the most frequent victims of hate crimes (Horizons Foundation, 2001). Moreover, children of gays and lesbians suffer from the stigmatization of their parents as unfit and immoral. Schools, communities, and homes often become hostile places for children of gay and lesbian parents, and otherwise happy and healthy children can face mental-health problems because of anti-gay bigotry.

These deplorable conditions exist despite the fact that the American Psychological Association concluded in 1995 that "not a single study has found children of gay and lesbian parents to be disadvantaged in any significant respect relative to the children of heterosexual parents. Indeed, the evidence suggests that home environments provided by gay and lesbian parents are as likely as those provided by heterosexual parents to support and enable children's psychological growth" (quoted in National Adoption Information Clearinghouse, 2000).

CONCLUSION

The issue of gay and lesbian adoptions has taken on profound political importance. As such, gay and lesbian adoptions have become an important gay-rights issue. However, what has been lost is the fact that adoption is primarily a child-welfare issue. The fundamental goal of adoption is not to promote a more just society but to protect the best interests of an individual child. Unfortunately, these goals have been submerged in a battle (by both conservatives and progressives) that has more to do with gay rights than with the welfare of children. As such, the welfare of vulnerable children is being held hostage in a heated political battle for equal rights. Adoption decisions must be unlinked from the political struggle for equal rights, and the best interests of children must occupy the forefront of adoption policies. It is no minor hypocrisy that many states will allow gay and lesbian individuals and couples to adopt special-needs children while reserving "healthy" children for heterosexual couples. If adoption by gay and lesbians is deemed socially appropriate, then it should be appropriate across the board.

I am not arguing for a ban on gay and lesbian adoptions, nor are we disputing the fact that gay and lesbians can make excellent parents. They can, and many do. Nevertheless, the societal sanctioning of gay and lesbian adoptions represents a radical social experiment based on inconclusive, and highly subjective studies. In effect, we are attempting to make radical social-policy decisions based on spurious, ideologically driven studies. This will not be the first time decisions are made in this manner, nor will it be the last. Policy is often made in this kind of haphazard fashion. Unfortunately, the supposed beneficiaries of this policy (vulnerable children) have no say, nor are there many advocates who will speak on their behalf.

Knotty questions remain about the effects of gay and lesbian adoption. How will children in these families feel about themselves and their families? Will they be embarrassed because they have two mothers or two fathers, or because their single mother dates women or their unmarried father has a boyfriend? Children of gay men and lesbians are vulnerable to teasing and harassment, particularly as they approach adolescence, when any sign of difference is grounds for exclusion. How much of a problem is this stigma? Is it likely to cause lasting psychological damage? Will such children be more likely to be homosexual than children raised by heterosexual parents? And most important, how will having been raised by gay or lesbian parents affect children as they grow into adulthood? Despite the range of studies done, we still don't have definitive answers to these questions. Until we have more complete data, I urge caution in vigorously pursuing the radical social experiment of gay and lesbian adoptions.

REFERENCES

Achenback, T. M., & Edelbrock, C. (1983). *Manual for the Child Behavior Checklist and Revised Child Behavior Profile*. Burlington, VT: University of Vermont, Department of Psychiatry.

Aura, J. (1985). Women's social support: A comparison of lesbians and heterosexuals (unpublished doctoral dissertation, University of California, Los Angeles).

Bell, A. P., & Weinberg, M. S. (1978). *Homosexualities: a study of diversity among men and women.* New York, NY: Simon & Schuster.

Brewaeys, A., Ponjaert, I., Van Hall, E. V., & Golombok, S. (1997, April). Donor insemination: Child development and family functioning in lesbian mother families with 4 to 8 year old children. Paper presented at the 1997 Biennial Meeting of the Society for Research in Child Development, Washington, DC.

Dubios, B., & Miley, K. (1999). *Social work: An empowering profession* (3rd Ed.). Needham Heights, MA: Allyn & Bacon.

Emery, R. E., Waldron, M. C., Aaron, J., & Kitzmann, K. (1999). Delinquent behavior, future divorce or nonmarital childbearing and externalizing behavior among offspring: A 14-year prospective study. *Journal of Family Psychology, 13*(4), 56–67.

Erich, S., Leung, P., Kindle, P., & Carter, S. (2001). Analysis of gay and lesbian adoptive families. Unpublished raw data.

Flaks, D. (1995). Research issues: Issues in gay and lesbian adoption. *Proceedings of the Fourth Annual Peirce-Warwick Adoption Symposium.* Washington, DC: Child Welfare League of America.

Germain, C., & Gitterman, A. (1995). Ecological perspective In R. Edwards (Ed.), *Encyclopedia of social work* (19th Ed., Vol. 1) (pp. 816–822). Washington, DC: NASW.

Golombok, S., Spencer, A., & Rutter, M. (1983). Children in lesbian and single-parent households: Psychosexual and psychiatric appraisal. *Journal of Child Psychology and Psychiatry, 24,* 551–572.

Gonsiorek, J. C. (1991). The empirical basis for the demise of the illness model of homosexuality. In J. D. Weinrich & J. C. Gonsiorek (Eds.), *Homosexuality: Research implications for public policy* (pp. 197–214). Newbury Park, CA: Sage.

Green, G. D., & Bozett, F. W. (1991). Lesbian mothers and gay fathers. In J. D. Weinrich & J. C. Gonsiorek (Eds.), *Homosexuality: Research implications for public policy* (pp. 197–214). Newbury Park, CA: Sage.

Green, R., Mandel, J. B., Hotvedt, M. E., Gray, J., & Smith, L. (1986). Lesbian mothers and their children: A comparison with solo parent heterosexual mothers and their children. *Archives of Sexual Behavior, 15,* 167–184.

Groze, V. (1991). Adoption and single parents: A review. *Child Welfare, 70,* 321–331.

Hoeffer, B. (1981). Children's acquisition of sex-role behavior in lesbian-mother families. *American Journal of Orthopsychiatry, 51,* 536–544.

Horizons Foundation (2001). Open letter to Dr. Laura. Retrieved August 16, 2001, from http://www.horizonsfoundation.org/drlaura. htm.

Kirkpatrick, M., Smith, C., & Roy, R. (1981). Lesbian mothers and their children: A comparative survey. *American Journal of Orthopsychiatry, 51,* 541–551.

Kurdek, L. A., & Schmitt, J. P. (1987). Perceived emotional support from family and friends in gay, lesbian and heterosexual cohabiting couples. *Journal of Sex Research, 23,* 212–232.

Lewin, E. (1981). Lesbianism and motherhood: Implications for child custody. *Human Organisms, 40,* 6–14.

Lewin, E., & Lyons, T. A. (1982). Everything in its place: The coexistence of lesbianism and motherhood. In W. Paul, J. D. Weinrich, J. C. Gonsiorek, & M. E. Hotvedt (Eds.), *Homosexuality: Social, psychological, and biological issues* (pp. 249–274). Beverly Hills, CA: Sage.

McCandlish, B. (1987). Against all odds: Lesbian mother family dynamics. In F. Bozett (Ed.), *Gay and lesbian parents* (pp. 23–38). New York, NY: Praeger.

McLanahan, S., & Sandefur, G. (1997). *Growing up with a single parent*. Cambridge, MA: Harvard University Press.

Mitchell, V. (1996). Two moms: Contribution of the planned lesbian family to the deconstruction of gendered parenting. In J. Laird & R. J. Green (Eds.), *Lesbians and gays in couples and families: A handbook for therapists* (pp. 343–357). San Francisco, CA: Jossey-Bass.

Mucklow, B. M., & Phelan, G. K. (1979). Lesbian and traditional mother's responses to adult response to child behavior and self-concept. *Psychological Reports, 44,* 880–882.

National Adoption Information Clearinghouse. (2000, *April*). *Gay and lesbian adoptive parents: Resources for professionals and parents.* Retrieved August 16, 2001, from http://www.calib.com/naic/pubs/f_gay.htm.

Patterson, C. J. (1992). Children of lesbian and gay parents. *Child Development, 63,* 1025–1042.

Patterson, C. J. (1994). Children of the lesbian baby boom: Behavioral adjustment, self-concepts, and sex role identity. In B. Greene & G. M. Herek (Eds.), *Lesbian and gay psychology: Theory, research and clinical applications* (pp. 156–175). Newbury Park, CA: Sage Publications.

Polikoff, N. (1990). This child does have two mothers. Redefining parenthood to meet the needs of children in lesbian mother and other nontraditional families. *Georgetown Law Review, 78,* 459–575.

Rand, C., Graham, D. L. R., & Rawlings, E. I. (1982). Psychological health and factors the courts seek to control in lesbian mother custody trials. *Journal of Homosexuality, 8,* 27–39.

Riley, C. (1988). American kinship: A lesbian account. *Feminist Issues, 8,* 75–94.

Ryan, S. D. (2000). Examining social workers' placement recommendations of children with gay and lesbian adoptive parents. *Families in Society: The Journal of Contemporary Human Services, 15,* 517–527.

Scallen, R. (1981). An investigation of paternal attitudes and behavior in homosexual and heterosexual couples. *Dissertation Abstracts International, 42,* 3809B.

Stacey, J., & Biblarz, T. J. (2001). (How) does the sexual orientation of parents matter? *American Sociological Review, 66*(2), 159–169.

Tasker, F. L., & Golombok, S. (1991). Children raised by lesbian mothers: The empirical evidence. *Family Law, 21,* 184–187.

United States Bureau of the Census (1996, May). National households and families projections. *United States Bureau of the Census* Retrieved March 2, 2001, from http://www. census.gov/population/www/projections/nathh.html.

Van Biema, D. (1994, February 27). The price of a broken home. *Time,* 12–13.

Weston, K. (1991). *Families we choose: Lesbians, gays, kinship.* New York, NY: Columbia University Press.

SOCIAL-WORK EDUCATION AND PROFESSIONAL POLICY

SHOULD ABORTION RIGHTS BE AN ACCEPTED SOCIAL-WORK VALUE?

Editor's Note:

Abortion is one of the most controversial issues of our time, with strong opinions being expressed on both sides. Although some abortion opponents have tried to prohibit abortion in the United State through judicial and legislative action, the constitutional right to have an abortion remains in force. However, abortion opponents have succeeded in curtailing abortion programs and guidelines on several fronts. Supporters of these measures argue that abortion is an evil that the state should not condone. As an avowedly liberal profession, the field of social work has assumed almost *a priori* that the vast majority of social workers unequivocally support the right of a woman to choose abortion. However, there are dissenting elements within the profession.

John T. Pardeck is professor of social work in the School of Social Work at Southwest Missouri State University. Professor Pardeck is an advocate for persons with disabilities and for interpreting the Americans with Disabilities Act for both private- and public-sector organizations. He is author of *Social Work after the Americans with Disabilities Act: New Challenges and Opportunities for Social Services Professionals*. A prolific author, Dr. Pardeck has published articles on disabilities and related topics. His books include *Social Work: Seeking Relevancy in the Twenty-First Century, Using Books in Clinical Social Work Practice, Reason and Rationality in Health and Human Services Delivery* and *Post-modernism, Religion, and the Future of Social Work* (all by The Haworth Press, Inc.). Professor Pardeck is editor of the *Journal of Social Work Education in Disability and Rehabilitation* and is a research fellow at Southwest Missouri State University.

Roland Meinert has taught in and administered social-work education programs at all levels at Michigan State University, St. Louis University, and the University of Missouri-Columbia. He was one of the founders of the Inter

University Consortium for International Social Development, and for six years was coeditor of the journal *Social Development Issues*. His most recent books and articles deal with the influence of postmodernism on social work.

YES

John T. Pardeck

Social work is a value-based profession. These values guide the behavior of practitioners at both the policy and practice levels. Given the importance of values to the profession, it is imperative that practitioners conduct critical analysis of important social issues from a values perspective. This paper examines one important social issue, abortion, from such a perspective. Specifically, I look at the issue of abortion from numerous perspectives, including religious, historic, and legal. Obviously, each of these perspectives offers a different view on the topic of abortion. I conclude that the *Roe v. Wade* ruling in 1973 concerning a woman's right to an abortion makes perfect sense in terms of the religious, historic, and legal traditions surrounding this important issue. Given this conclusion, social workers should support a woman's legal right to an abortion.

RELIGIOUS PERSPECTIVE ON ABORTION

Christian ethics and teachings have varied on the topic of abortion. However, if one uses Christian ethics and teachings as a justification for banning a woman's right to an abortion, one is probably using a romanticized and distorted view of Christianity. The historical Christian position on abortion, not the romanticized view, suggests that the human fetus was not particularly viewed as having intrinsic worth, nor were children and women in general. A critical interpretation of historical Christianity suggests that the religion was more concerned with the control of sexuality, the social order, and the preservation of male prerogatives, not with morality issues related to abortion (Harrison, 1983). Thus to use Christian teachings as a focal point for claiming that abortion is immoral is less than candid concerning the evolution of Christian teachings on this issue.

Palley (1991) notes that the Western European welfare states view the right to abortion as a legitimate public concern. Abortion as a right in the European welfare states is as important as the right to a family allowance, day care, education, and healthcare. What is notable about the evolution of abortion rights in Western Europe and the United States is that both cultures have grounding in Christian ethics and teachings. Given this tradition, one can only speculate on why Western Europe gave women the right to an abortion much earlier than the United States did. Palley (1991) also argues that other patriarchal religions such as Judaism, Islam, and Confucianism have anti-abortion traditions. However, these religions have had variable influence on government policy in various parts of the world. For example, in an Islamic theocracy, abortion is obviously not viewed as a legitimate alternative for women, even though women continue to have abortions under this kind of rule. However, mainland China, which is influenced by Confucianism and other eastern religious traditions, uses abortion as a vital mechanism to control population growth (Childbirth By Choice Trust, 1995).

If one conducts an in-depth analysis of Christian teachings, the opposition to abortion is a relatively recent development. Saint Augustine, like Aristotle, believed that a fetus did not become a live soul until forty days after conception for boys and eighty days for girls. The medieval church was not necessarily opposed to abortion. A tolerant approach to abortion in the Roman Catholic church ended relatively recently, approximately in the mid nineteenth century. Presently, within the United States, the Roman Catholic church, as well as a number of Protestant churches, has actively attempted to influence social-welfare policy dealing with abortion (Childbirth By Choice Trust, 1995).

Other major religions in the United States have various positions on abortion. For example, the Anglican church allows abortion when a woman's physical or mental health is endangered by the pregnancy. Lutherans are divided on abortion and typically view the procedure as an option in rare circumstances. Presbyterians generally oppose abortion. The Baptist church sees abortion as an option when a woman's life is in danger. Even though historic Christianity often tolerated abortion, many modern-day Christian groups, including Roman Catholics and Protestants, view abortion as unacceptable or as an option only in certain circumstances (Childbirth By Choice Trust, 1995).

The paradox, however, is that women in virtually every society—regardless of the religious practices found in these societies—use abortion to end unwanted pregnancies. In primitive societies, even before recorded history, women induced abortion with herbs, sharp sticks or simply by exerting heavy pressure on the abdomen (Childbirth By Choice Trust, 1995). Regardless of whether a society outlaws abortion, women have always—and will continue—to abort unwanted pregnancies. What this means is that a right to an abortion must be made available to women to help ensure the safety of this procedure.

HISTORICAL PERSPECTIVE ON ABORTION

From the twelfth century to the nineteenth century, abortion before quickening (movement of the fetus) was not punished under English common law. Because most abortions took place prior to quickening, abortion was not particularly seen as a moral issue. When abortion was performed after quickening, it was usually treated as a misdemeanor (Childbirth By Choice Trust, 1995).

In the early nineteenth Century, abortions performed after quickening became a serious offense under English common law; lesser penalties accrued with abortions performed prior to quickening. Legislation in the United States regulating abortion also began to emerge in that same era. Much of this legislation was more concerned with protecting the health of the mother and not necessarily with ensuring any rights of the fetus. Supposedly, physicians in the nineteenth-century United States became heavily involved in abortion legislation not so much to protect the mother or fetus, but rather to consolidate their professional status and power (Childbirth By Choice Trust, 1995). The criminalization of abortion in the United States is largely a twentieth-century phenomenon. Abortion was highly restrictive through the 1960s. In that decade, a tremendous amount of cultural change occurred in the United States and Western Europe, including the belief that women have a right to control their fertility. During the twentieth century, virtually every European country legalized abortion. For example, the Netherlands legalized the procedure in 1981, even though it was freely available before that date. Norway did likewise in 1979. Sweden enacted its initial abortion legislation in 1938. The only countries in Western Europe that have not legalized abortion in some form are the Irish Republic, Northern Ireland, and Malta. In Ireland, even with its strict anti-abortion laws in place, an estimated four thousand Irish women every year go to Britain to have a legal abortion (Childbirth By Choice Trust, 1995).

LEGAL PERSPECTIVE ON ABORTION

Abortion in the United States was not seen as a moral issue in the nineteenth century. The moral issues surrounding abortion reflected in the law largely arose during the twentieth century. Through most of the first half of the twentieth century in the United States, abortion was highly restricted. During this time, illegal abortions became a serious health problem; many women suffered injury or infection, or died, because of illegal, unsafe abortions.

The most important legal ruling from the United States Supreme Court was *Roe v. Wade* in 1973. Under this ruling, states cannot ban abortion during the first trimester of pregnancy. One of the important considerations by the Court was that women who obtained abortions illegally under dubious medical conditions risked death or injury. Thus the Court in part viewed the legalization of abortion as a medical issue aimed at protecting women's health. The Court also recognized that it is impossible to prevent women from using abortion to end pregnancy, even when the procedure is illegal. Yet even with the *Roe v. Wade* ruling favoring a woman's right to an abortion, many Americans continue to oppose the procedure.

Since *Roe v. Wade*, a number of government regulations and court rulings have restricted access to abortion. In 1988, the United States Department of Health and Human Services forbade health-care providers under Title X of the Public Health Service Act to give clients information on abortion. In 1991, the Supreme Court upheld this so-called Gag Rule. As a result of this ruling, many low-income women have less access to information about abortion. In *Webster v. Reproduction Health Services* (1989), the United States Supreme Court upheld a Missouri law that prohibited abortion from being performed in any publicly financed facility, even if the client is willing to pay for the procedure. This is a clear example of how social class determines access to abortion services.

Many states tried to pass other restrictive abortion laws in the 1980s and 1990s. Restrictive abortion legislation has been enacted in Pennsylvania, Utah, and Guam. The appointment of Clarence Thomas to the United States Supreme Court was an example of how President George H. W. Bush attempted to change the Court's position on abortion.

Another threat to a woman's right to an abortion has emerged with the bombing of abortion clinics and the harassing and killing of clinic patients and staff. One might argue that the political process has even fueled these attacks on abortion clinics. For example, in 1991 President George Bush proclaimed that the federal judge in Wichita, Kansas, overstepped his authority when he issued a restraining order to keep anti-abortionists from harassing abortion-clinic patients and staff. Given the fact that President George W. Bush, like his father, clearly opposes abortion, there is a strong chance that he will attempt to appoint a justice to the Supreme Court who will favor overturning *Roe v. Wade*. The history of abortion in the twentieth-century United States was one of legal turmoil. There is nothing to suggest that the next century will be any different.

WHY ABORTION SHOULD BE LEGAL

Even though the final chapter of *Roe v. Wade* is far from written, there is little doubt in this author's mind that the right to abortion must continue to be protected. This position is based on religious, historic, and legal traditions surrounding the issue of abortion.

The notion that Christian teachings have historically opposed abortion and that this is why the procedure should be illegal today is unwarranted. As mentioned earlier in this paper, there is limited evidence that early Christians perceived abortion as a major moral issue. The romanticized Christian teaching suggesting that abortion is morally wrong is largely a modern invention.

The history of Western Europe and the United States suggests that abortion was not a major moral issue until relatively recently. If anything, abortion historically has been viewed as a common method of birth control.

Laws enacted in the nineteenth-century United States were often aimed at protecting the health of women, not necessarily protecting the fetus. As mentioned earlier, women in many parts of Western Europe now see abortion as a basic right similar to day care, family allowance, and other related welfare benefits.

Abortion did not become a constitutional right in the United States until 1973. Many women in Western Europe enjoyed the right to an abortion even in the 1930s. The United States' legal system evolved much more slowly on this front. As suggested earlier, a woman's right to an abortion in the United States may come under fire during the administration of President George W. Bush. Given the attacks on a woman's right to an abortion by a number of political and religious groups in the United States, *Roe v. Wade* may someday be overturned. However, regardless of this possibility, it is this author's opinion that women must have a constitutional right to an abortion for the following reasons:

1. Many women now believe that they have a right to determine whether to bear children or not. If this right is taken away, they will turn to acts of civil disobedience; that is, they will seek out illegal abortions.
2. The political institution is not well suited to resolve deep social, moral, and religious conflict. Thus the state does not have a right to regulate a woman's right to an abortion. Only women get pregnant, yet men have largely interpreted the morality surrounding abortion. And men have mandated laws restricting abortion. The political institution's role in this extremely moral issue should be to allow the right to abortion and to ensure that abortion procedures are safe.
3. Safe, legal abortions have protected women's health. If abortion is made illegal, women will continue to use the procedure to regulate family size. Illegal abortions are often unsafe and pose a threat to a woman's health.
4. If abortion is made illegal, the well to do will continue to have access to the procedure. For example, women who want an abortion and who can afford one will simply go to another country where the procedure is legal. Poor women will have to use illegal, unsafe abortion procedures.

CONCLUSIONS

The author wishes to make it very clear to the reader that abortion is a less-than-desirable option for terminating a pregnancy. However, as history suggests, women will continue to limit family size through the use of abortion, regardless of whether the procedure is legal.

Abortion might be viewed through a perspective found in the child-welfare literature, the "Least Detrimental Available Alternative" Standard.

This Standard means that an alternative is used on behalf of a child that does the least amount of harm to the child. For example, the choice between providing a sexually active adolescent with birth control versus the prospect of the child becoming pregnant appears to have a clear resolution under this Standard: Provide access to birth control.

The fact that women will continue to have abortions regardless of whether they are legal means that a choice must be made between the least harmful alternative—a safe, legal abortion—or one that is illegal and unsafe. In a certain sense, *Roe v. Wade* follows this line of reasoning. Legal abortion, even though a far from desirable option, helps to ensure that the procedure is safe.

Finally, abortion politics has far more to do with the regulation or outlawing of abortion. Opposing abortion is often a conservative ideology strategy used to gain political mileage on other causes. Anti-abortionists often oppose welfare entitlements, endorse the death penalty, and take stands on an array of other conservative issues. Abortion politics has prevented the passage of laws helping children, women, and the elderly. For example, during the 2000 Missouri legislative session, a law was introduced to prevent the abuse of the elderly in nursing homes in Missouri. Amendments concerning abortion were added to the bill that took the proposed legislation away from its intended purpose—protecting the elderly—to the arena of abortion politics. As an unfortunate outcome of this political ploy, the legislation was not enacted. Thus abortion politics continues, and the elderly continue to suffer abuse in residential settings.

Abortion politics continues to occur in state legislatures throughout the United States. This kind of politics must end.

NO

Roland Meinert

It is widely believed, though undocumented, that the majority of professional social workers support the position that women of any age have an unequivocal right to abortion on demand. Despite the absence of definitive data, there are several reasons to support this belief. First, the social-work journal literature about abortion and reproductive rights is decidedly skewed toward pro-choice positions. One searches unsuccessfully through main-line social-work journals in an attempt to identify articles that espouse a pro-life position. In fact, there is every reason to believe that social-work editorial boards are heavily biased toward a pro-choice orientation.

Second, the curricula in schools of social work have a blatant and one-sided pro-choice orientation and fairly present pro-life material in only a few programs. Pro-life perspectives are not only routinely ignored in the instructional process, but they are frequently denigrated. The avoidance of pro-life content in the curriculum is one measure of the lack of intellectual, philosophical, and ideological diversity in social-work education.

Last, the official policy of the National Association of Social Workers (NASW), representing about 155,000 social workers, supports abortion at any stage of pregnancy for any reason the woman selects (NASW, 2000). Thus the evidence shows that social work is firmly entrenched in the pro-choice camp and endorses abortion on demand. However, when the issue is examined in detail, there are compelling, logical, persuasive, and science-based arguments that the central value should be pro-life. Thus, in this writer's view, the answer to whether abortion should be an accepted social-work value is no.

IDEOLOGICAL FOUNDATIONS OF PRO-CHOICE RHETORIC

Social work has always occupied a marginal status within the helping professions and readily accommodated itself to influences and pressures from the environment. Lacking a firm theoretical framework to guide practice, it has borrowed from other disciplines. These frameworks varied, and the mission of social work changed, depending on which theory was prominent at the time. For example, during the decades when social work was a prisoner of psychoanalysis, that theory defined both the purpose of the profession and the behavior of practitioners. During the time of the sexual revolution, it is not surprising that the profession adopted a pro-choice orientation bolstered by support from academic, mass-media, entertainment, political, and professional elites—most of whom were pro-life unfriendly. When the abortion debate began in social work, the voices of those in the pro-life corner were drowned out by a cacophony of postmodern, radical feminist, existential, and moral relativistic voices. In most instances, the proponents of the pro-life position were treated judgmentally as extremist Christians, far-right conservatives, and ignorant zealots whose intelligence was questionable. Given this stereotype, the arguments of pro-life advocates were viewed as not befitting reasonable consideration. Thus, their central arguments were not to be examined.

By the 1960s and 1970s, most abortion advocates were inextricably entwined in the emerging philosophy about reproductive freedom and the separation of sex for pleasure from parenthood and family life. The proposition was accepted that if men could be sexually promiscuous and irresponsible, then the same right should be available for women. This sexual revolution became prominent as the larger culture, including social work, came under the dominance of postmodernism, radical feminism, social constructivism, and moral relativism. The postmodern influence in social work resulted in the diminution of value systems such as the Judeo-Christian, which had been the main philosophical orientation on which social work had been founded. Religion was replaced by the belief that individual subjective choice should be the supreme guide for human decision making. In the age of postmodernism, individuals were free to behave in whatever way they selected, because overarching religious, cultural, and institutional standards were deemed irrelevant. Postmodernists called these earlier standards for behavior meta narratives, and argued that their elimination would enable persons to maximize their human potential.

The social and cultural implications of postmodern and moral relativistic positions should not be ignored. For centuries, humans had made decisions based on reference to values that were transpersonal and lodged in culture, religious traditions, and institutional norms. These values existed outside the individual and served as guideposts and standards that informed the decision-making process and the behavior that emanated from it. Now, for the first time, it was argued that these systems of values should not only be ignored but should be demolished in favor of rampant individualism and subjectivism. This logic provided support for the pro-choice advocates who maintained that women had an absolute right to freedom and need not be influenced by context, cultural values, established systems of morality, or institutional guidelines.

The profession of social work swallowed the absolute-freedom principle that was being espoused and promoted. The NASW's official policy on family planning and reproductive choice had a profound influence on social-work education. The principle of the right to choose became a pro-choice mantra and was thought to be consistent with the concept of client self-determination, which has always been a central value in the profession. However, the major founders of social work who developed its intellectual foundation did not view the right of self-determination as an unqualified absolute. Self-determination was to be exercised in a responsible fashion that did not violate the rights of others and the traditionally accepted beliefs of right and wrong. The NASW policy on abortion does not address this qualification. It maintains that client self-determination is an absolute in terms of the decision to abort or not, and opposes any limits or restrictions on that decision, even with adolescents. Parenthetically, it describes those who support limits on absolute freedom of choice as members of a radical right wing who are assaulting women's rights for religious reasons.

The social-work education establishment and its curriculum policy reflect a postmodern and relativistic influence. This is best understood when the curriculum policy at the graduate (M.S.W.) level is examined. Graduate programs are expected to offer concentrations (specializations) around a specific range of practitioner roles or functions. Each program has the right and freedom to design concentrations and their constituent courses. The only requirement is that concentrations must be relevant to the mission of social work. But there is wide disparity within the profession about the nature of this mission. The result of this policy concerning curriculum is an inter-program range of course offerings without conceptual boundaries. Programs create concentrations based on roles, target populations, problem categories, regional social needs, fields of practice, and even individualized student preferences. This limitless and expansive curricular scope characterizes the entire profession of social work, which historically has struggled to find a definitive conceptual and practice niche. The relevance of this lack of boundaries to the abortion question is that social-work students are taught that absolute freedom, absolute client self-determination, and absolute pro-choice are unqualified values. Thus, abortion is to be endorsed at any time, under any conditions, and without consideration of any factors that exist outside the subjective decision-making sphere of the individual. This social construction of reality denies the existence of objective truth and knowledge and becomes relative to person, time, and place. It also removes social work from the family of professions based on truth seeking according to accepted canons of science. The entire structure of this line of thinking has been supported by radical feminist ideology, which has had an inordinate influence over both social-work practice and education.

THE NEGATIVE CONSEQUENCES OF ABORTION

In addition to the absolute right to choose, pro-choice proponents believe that abortions are justified because they result in positive outcomes for the women who have them. Frequently cited are a better quality of life, economic advancement, educational advancement, development of work skills, broadening of life experiences, a better life for future children, enhancement of emotional well-being, more satisfaction in interpersonal relationships, and others. It is further argued that these outcomes are particularly important and beneficial for minority women and those of lower socioeconomic status. Feminists and pro-choice advocates found it necessary to publicize these alleged positive outcomes in order to destigmatize abortion and make it readily available. Most of these outcomes are related to the feminist conviction that women will experience true happiness and fulfillment only in careers and work outside the home. Along with the promotion of this belief, it also became necessary to derogate women who sought their fulfillment as wives and mothers within the context of the family. It is the author's contention that the wide array of positive outcomes listed by abortion-rights advocates has not been convincingly documented and confirmed. In fact, there are sound reasons to conclude that the negative consequences of abortion far outweigh the alleged positive ones.

Mounting evidence from sound research studies reveals that women who have abortions, particularly adolescents, experience major problems that until recently have been unknown or purposefully denied. A list of some, but not all, of these problems include: an increased risk of breast, cervical, and uterine cancers; significantly higher suicide rates during the postabortion year; emotional problems including severe depression, grief, shame, anxiety, remorse, uncontrollable crying, and resentment; eating disorders;

unrealistic expectations for replacement children; substance abuse; and damaged interpersonal relationships. The professional social-work literature rarely reports on these post-abortion negative consequences. This constitutes a conspiracy of silence, because to openly examine these consequences weakens the entire pro-abortion movement and the possibility that freedom of choice should not be an absolute right. Space limitations preclude discussion of all these highly negative sequella from induced abortion, but two of them are major public health problems: an increased risk for breast cancer and suicide.

Several reports, especially a meta analysis by Brind (1996), of thirty-three studies worldwide have shown a markedly increased risk of breast cancer for women who have had induced abortions. The risk varies from 30 percent to 50 percent based on age at time of the abortion and other factors. The finding calls attention to the pernicious effect of the intrusion and assault on the normal biological functioning of pregnant women. Following pregnancy, there is an enormous increase in the level of estrogen and other hormones during the first trimester. This natural development stimulates the growth of the breasts in preparation for the production of milk. Toward the end of the pregnancy, other hormones are activated that kill off the cells not needed to produce milk. These transitional cells increase susceptibility to develop carcinogens. In induced abortion, the maturing effects of the later hormones are absent, and the changing and transitional cells have a much greater chance of becoming cancerous.

A study of more than nine thousand women in Finland over a period of seven years (Gissler, et. al, 1997) disclosed that the risk of dying within a year after an abortion was several times higher than the risk of dying after miscarriage or childbirth. Conclusions from the same data set reported the astonishing finding that the risk of death from suicide within the year of an abortion was seven times higher than the risk of suicide within a year of childbirth (Gissler, et al., 1996). Also, the risk of suicide following induced abortion was about twice that in the general population of women.

One of the persistent myths is that a professional dialogue takes place between a pregnant woman and her physician —a dialogue that leads to an informed decision about whether to abort. Evidence is hard to find that this kind of conversation actually occurs. To the contrary, most women who receive an abortion have had no prior contact with the physician who performs it, and the negative consequences of the procedure are never discussed. It is also likely that the pregnant woman has ended up in an abortion clinic that is more of a for-profit business than a medical facility. As abortions decline, the number of clinics also decreases and the competition for patients stiffens. In many cities, abortion clinics advertise for business, and price undercutting between them is becoming common. Legitimate questions can be raised about the ethics and the competence of physicians who work in such nonprofessional and blatantly commercial settings. The principle of informed consent should lead the medical abortionist to share the information about breast cancer, suicide, and other risks. However, it is unlikely that they do share it, since doing so would mean a loss of income.

It is not known how many abortions in the United States are performed merely because one of the parents did not like the sex of the unborn child. Nor is it known if any abortionist has ever refused to perform the procedure because the unborn child was of the wrong sex. In India, figures from the last census make it very clear that females are being regularly aborted at a far greater rate than males (Dugger, 2001). This practice became a trend beginning in the 1980s, when ultrasound technology became widely available. For example, in the prosperous farming state of Punjab, the birth ratio of girls to boys has plummeted to 793 girls per 1,000 boys. The pronounced gender imbalance has long been a feature of life in India, and its acceleration will cause long-term social consequences and injustices. Feminists show no concern about this trend and ignore the possibility of similar consequences in the United States. Furthermore, feminists who express a desire for equity and justice for women strangely do not abhor the fact that at least half of those aborted are female and will never experience an equal opportunity for life.

As repeat abortions become more frequent (and it is estimated that about 45 percent are second ones), it is difficult to rationalize the supposed benefits of the procedure. It is not likely that women who have had more than one abortion are lifting themselves out of poverty and the myriad other difficulties facing them. In fact, the higher likelihood is that there are many more negative social, health, and psychological consequences resulting from induced abortion than there are positive benefits.

REFRAMING THE DEBATE

Communication between the majority pro-choice and minority pro-life social-work advocates has been contentious. It occurs within contexts in which the former group has the most organizational and programmatic power and controls the reward structure. Discussions have been narrow in scope, because pro-choicers begin and end the encounters with the presupposition that absolute freedom of choice closes off any other considerations. The imbalance in favor of the pro-choice position increases due to enhanced support from political, medical, and media elites, thus placing pro-life proponents at a disadvantage. Social-work educators who endorse pro-life positions are very vulnerable, because their career advancement is in jeopardy within programs where strident pro-choice positions dominate. Pro-lifers seek engagement in a broader scope of issues such as when life begins, the nature of human life, abortion surgical procedures, the proliferation of new knowledge about the development of the child during pregnancy, and the negative social and health consequences for women who abort. If it is true that knowledge becomes obsolete at an increasingly rapid pace, then the social-work profession has an ethical obligation to reopen and reframe the abortion debate.

This should begin with an examination of the development of the child in the womb from the time of conception. Revolutionary advances in medical technology have confirmed that the heart begins to beat at day 18 in the womb, and that brainwaves are recorded, the skeletal structure is complete, and reflexes are present at day 42. Ultrasound and other technologies provide clear images of a child present in the womb. Pro-choice advocates need to confront the reality that these images confirm the existence of a living, growing human being rather than "biological material," "disposable tissue," "property," "gangrenous growths," "noxious waste products," or "parasites" in the woman's body. These words dehumanize the unborn child and rationalize the absolute right to choose (Brennan, 1999). After all, it is semantically logical and emotionally reassuring to abort a parasite rather than a child.

As abortion facilities become more commercialized, medical staff will be under pressure not to share findings about the negative consequences of the procedure. To do so might result in a loss of income for abortion providers driven by market conditions and profit motives. This may account for the fierce resistance against informed-consent procedures. In this regard, profit seems to win out over medical ethics. If the predictions about the higher incidence of breast cancer, suicide, and other social and health effects of abortion in later life for women bear out, legal actions can be expected in the future. Women will feel justified in filing lawsuits against abortion providers for reckless endangerment to their health and will rightly seek monetary damages. Just as tobacco companies failed to warn the public about the injurious effects of smoking, women who have abortions and later develop breast cancer will sue because they were not warned about the increased risks.

Perhaps the most difficult issue that needs to surface in the abortion question is philosophical and cultural in nature. The excessive premium placed on individual subjective choice within a climate of moral relativism completely ignores the necessity for society to seek the common good. A central tenet and value in social work is the functioning and interaction of the individual with society and the larger environment. In formulating policies and implementing practices, both the individual and the common good must be considered. In the pro-choice movement, the subjective interests of the individual are elevated and the common good is diminished. It is no longer a profession of "social" work but of "individual" work. To ask the question whether abortion should be an accepted social-work "value" is a perversion of the very concept. By definition, values are conceptions of the desirable that transcend the person and are lodged in larger cultural institutions. Values then serve to inform individual behavior and decision making. Support by the social-work profession for abortion is an occupational preference, but it is not a value. If social work is to retain any degree of legitimacy in regard to the abortion issue, it should support an open dialogue about the topic, reexamine the pro-choice bias of curricula in educational programs, become open to new scientific knowledge about the beginning of life, admit the moral and ethical issues pertaining to abortion, and encourage research about the negative social and health consequences for women who abort. Also, pro-life practitioners and educators must be allowed to present their views without fear of sullied reputations, retaliation, or threats to their professional careers.

REFERENCES

Brennan, W. (1999). Anti-fetal rhetoric: America's best-loved hate speech. *New Oxford Review, 65*(5), 18–21.

Brind, J. (1996). Induced abortion as an independent risk factor for breast cancer: A comprehensive review and meta-analysis. *Journal of Epidemiology and Community Health, 50*, 481–496.

Childbirth by Choice Trust (1995). *Abortion in law, history, and religion.* Toronto, Canada: Author.

Dugger, C. (2001, April 22). Abortion in India is tipping scales sharply against girls. *New York Times*, International Section, 10–11.

Gissler, M., Hemminki, E., & Lonnqvist, J. (1996). Suicides after pregnancy in Finland: 1987–1994 register linkage study. *British Medical Journal, 313*, 1431–1440.

Gissler, M., et al. (1997). Pregnancy associated deaths in Finland: Definition problems and benefits of record linkage. *Acta Obsetricia et Gynecologica Scandinavica, 76*, 651–657.

Harrison, B. W. (1983). *Our right to choose: Toward a new ethic of abortion.* Boston, MA: Beacon Press.

National Association of Social Workers (2000). Social work speaks: Family planning and reproductive choice. *National Association of Social Workers Press* (5th Ed.). Washington, DC, 109–116.

Palley, M. L. (1991). Women's rights as human rights: An international perspective. *Annals of the American Academy of Political and Social Sciences, 515*, 163–179.

■ ■ ■ ■ ■

SHOULD FAITH-BASED SOCIAL-WORK PROGRAMS BE REQUIRED TO COMPLY WITH NONDISCRIMINATION STANDARDS IF THEY VIOLATE THE BELIEFS OF THOSE INSTITUTIONS?

Editor's Note:

In recent years, the number of bachelor's and master's programs in social work has grown almost exponentially. This stems in part from the policy of the Council on Social Work Education to more easily accredit social-work programs, and to accredit a greater number of competing programs (social-work programs in close geographic proximity). As a result, the power of smaller B.S.W. and M.S.W. programs has grown within social-work education. Though this is not necessarily a negative trend, many of these smaller programs are in religiously based institutions that *can* be more conservative in their social orientation. The issues raised by some of these religious-based institutions cut to the core of the value base of social work and social-work education.

Karen E. Gerdes, Ph.D., is an associate professor in the school of social work at Arizona State University in Tempe. Her areas of research include women, children, diversity, and social justice. Dr. Gerdes has served as the B.S.W. coordinator, the M.S.W. coordinator, and associate director of the School of Social Work at ASU. She is coauthor of an introductory social-work textbook and is working on a social-work statistics text. *Elizabeth A. Segal, Ph.D.,* is a professor in the school of social work at Arizona State University in Tempe. Her areas of research include social-welfare policy, social justice, inequality, and poverty. Dr. Segal is the co-editor of the *Journal of Poverty.* She is the author of a social-welfare-policy text and several edited books on issues related to diversity and social justice.

Lawrence E. Ressler, Ph.D., joined the faculty of Roberts Wesleyan College in 1995. He holds the positions of associate chair of the division of social work and social sciences and director of the M.S.W. program. He has held teaching and administrative positions at Carver School of Church Social Work, the Southern Baptist Theological Seminary, Louisville, KY; Messiah College, Grantham, PA; and Malone College, Canton, OH. His areas of interest are family-conflict mediation, social research, social policy, community development, and the integration of social work and religion.

YES

Karen E. Gerdes and Elizabeth A. Segal

Some private, religious colleges and universities have social-work programs with policies that prohibit same-sex relationships. These programs ban the hiring of faculty and staff, as well as the admission of students, who engage in lesbian, gay, bisexual, and transgender relationships (LGBT). During the mid-1990s, these policies of exclusion were seen as contradicting the Counsel on Social Work Education (CSWE) accreditation standard of nondiscrimination (CSWE Evaluative Standard 3—Nondiscrimination and Human Diversity, 1994). Some religious institutions counterargued that the CSWE mandate for nondiscrimination based on sexual orientation violated their religious freedom.

The religious institutions further maintained that the CSWE could not legally mandate what is not in public law (that is, sexual orientation is not a protected status through public civil-rights law, as are race, sex, ethnicity, age, and physical ability). However, the religious institutions conceded that in terms of the *curriculum content* and *learning environment*, the CSWE could extend its mandates to prohibit discrimination based on sexual orientation.

In the wake of legal arguments made by religious institutions, the CSWE consulted many civil-rights and affirmative-action lawyers. The attorneys all seemed to agree: The CSWE could not mandate the inclusion of sexual orientation in nondiscrimination policies because sexual orientation is not a federally protected category. To do so, they claimed, would be suicide. The lawyers advised the CSWE that the courts would rule against them. In the worst-case scenario, the CSWE would not only lose, it would be deemed a monopoly with unfair practices, and dissolved.

In response to the legal argument of the religious institutions and the advice of counsel, the CSWE's new Educational Policy and Accreditation Standards (CSWE, 2001) eliminated the requirement that social-work programs must have a nondiscrimination statement that includes sexual orientation. However, the EPAS do emphasize the requirement that "students learn to understand and respect diversity and to practice nondiscrimination in their professional activities" (Beless, 2001, p. 22).

CSWE Nondiscrimination Policy

Though the EPAS document does not stipulate that schools must have a nondis-crimination policy, it does have clear guidelines about social-worker prepara-tion that promote nondiscrimination. For example, social-work programs must achieve a learning environment of nondiscrimination through such means as:

- Preparing social workers to practice without discrimination, with respect, and with knowledge and skills related to clients' age, class, color, culture, disability, ethnicity, family structure, gender, marital sta-tus, national origin, race, religion, sex, and sexual orientation.
- Preparing social workers to alleviate poverty, oppression, and other forms of social injustice (CSWE, 2001, p. 6).

The new EPAS also state that part of the foundation-year objectives must include the ability of graduates to understand the forms and mecha-nisms of oppression and discrimination and apply strategies of advocacy and social change that advance social and economic justice (CSWE, 2001, p. 8).

In addition, the diversity content of the foundation curriculum must demonstrate that social work programs integrate content that promotes understanding, affirmation, and respect for people from diverse back-grounds. The content emphasizes the interlocking and complex nature of culture and personal identity (CSWE, 2001, p. 9). And, the populations-at-risk and social- and economic-justice foundation content must demonstrate that the program integrates social and economic justice content grounded in an understanding of distributive justice, human and civil rights, and the global interconnection of oppression (CSWE, 2001, p. 9).

Finally, the EPAS stipulate that the program make specific and contin-uous efforts to provide a learning context in which respect for all persons and understanding of diversity is practiced, provide a learning context that is nondiscriminatory and reflects the profession's fundamental tenets, and describe how its learning context and educational program and curriculum model understanding and respect for diversity (CSWE, 2001, p. 16).

In summary, if we focus on the area of sexual orientation in all the above criteria, the Educational Policy and Accreditation Standards require that all programs, in order to be accredited, provide evidence that the program:

- Is preparing students with the necessary knowledge and skills to prac-tice without discrimination on the basis of sexual orientation;
- Is training students to practice social work without discrimination and with respect for people of all sexual orientations;
- Is providing a learning context in which respect and understanding of sexual orientation is practiced; and understanding and respect for diversity are modeled.

THE CONTROVERSY

The question we were asked to address is: "Should the CSWE mandate nondiscrimination policies that violate religious beliefs?" However, we do not think that is the relevant question. The fundamental questions from our perspective are: "Can a program that openly refuses to hire or admit LGBT people and refuses to create policies to protect LGBT people from discrimination *for whatever reasons* truly prepare students to practice social work without discrimination on the basis of sexual orientation? Can graduates from social-work programs that have exclusionary policies regarding LGBT people, respect people of all sexual orientations?" and moreover, "Can social-work programs with exclusionary policies create a learning context in which respect and understanding of sexual orientation is practiced, and in which understanding and respect for diversity are modeled?" We believe the answer to these questions is no.

THE IMPACT OF EXCLUSION

Discrimination, by definition, is *distinction* made on group status, *not* on merit or ability. From a social-work perspective, discrimination is "the prejudgment and negative treatment of people based on an identifiable characteristic" (Barker, 1999, p. 132). The policy of exclusion based on sexual orientation fits these definitions of discrimination because applicants for jobs and admissions are excluded based on their sexual orientation, not their ability or merit. Consider the following true case:

> Thomas Madsen (a pseudonym) received a master's in social work at a private religious university. As a teenager, Thomas had considered entering the ministry. However, he opted instead for a social-work degree, thinking that it would satisfy both his spiritual and professional ideals. After earning a doctoral degree from a different university, Thomas was recruited to teach at the religious school where he had finished his M.S.W.
>
> Thomas excelled as an assistant professor. He published his research in major journals, served on several committees, and sponsored clubs for undergraduate and graduate students. His students awarded him the Outstanding Teacher award after each of his three years in the classroom. Thomas's personal life was less successful. He dated occasionally but could not sustain a relationship with a woman. During his fourth year at the university, he began to consciously acknowledge a suppressed but lifelong suspicion that he was gay.
>
> At around this time, Thomas agreed to participate in a study on sexual abuse. As part of the study, he worked with a student named Brian. During the course of the research, Brian told Thomas that he had tried to kill himself because he was gay—and that he intended to "do it right" if he could not "make himself straight" by praying. Shaken by Brian's despair, Thomas confided that

he himself thought he might be gay, and that homosexuality was no reason for suicide. Later, Brian told his roommate about the conversation. The roommate, in turn, told his parents, who called the director of the social-work department.

The next day, Thomas was summoned and questioned by university authorities. Thomas was asked directly if he told a student it was "okay" to be gay. They also asked him if he was gay, a question he declined to answer. He was told to that if he did not leave the school he would have a very serious problem. Allowing Thomas to keep his job, the authorities explained, would send the message to students like Brian that homosexuality was acceptable—an idea that would violate university standards.

Thomas was embarrassed and shamed by the incident, but he eventually recovered. Yet although he has excelled in a new faculty position, he still has emotional scars. Imagine how Brian must have felt. As a student, he had even less power than Thomas and nowhere to turn for help. Students in religious institutions who are gay or think they might be gay live with the constant fear of being exposed. If they turn to the institutional authorities for assistance, they are likely to be referred to some type of reparative therapy or face expulsion.

Whether exclusion and discrimination of LGBT people are legal or not does not deny the harm done by these practices. The above case illustrates this. In addition, the American Academy of Pediatrics warned recently that the societal stigmatization, need for secrecy, and lack of opportunities for open socialization for LGBT youth place them at extreme risk for depression, failure in school, substance abuse, and suicide (Carmen, 2001). Furthermore, the American Medical Association publicly declared that exclusion based on sexual orientation such as those practices by the Boy Scouts of America cause psychological distress for adolescents (*Arizona Republic*, 2001). In the recent past, the American Psychological Association and the American Psychiatric Association have shared similar concerns.

EXCLUSION OF LGBT PEOPLE DIRECTLY CONTRADICTS CSWE POLICIES AND STANDARDS

How do we create an environment that is respectful and understanding of sexual orientation when we exclude people solely on their sexual orientation? If I am not safe to be who I am and if I am told clearly that my sexuality is forbidden, then I am not in a learning context that practices respect and understanding. Respect and understanding are inclusive practices, and dis-crimination is not. How does mandating nondiscrimination violate the beliefs of a school of social work? If nondiscrimination violates their beliefs, then it conversely follows that discrimination supports their beliefs. To knowingly and willingly allow schools of social work to discriminate on the basis of sexual orientation conflicts directly with all the values we hold as social workers and with the new EPAS.

Religious institutions often raise the counterargument that "we are not discriminating; we simply have strong religious beliefs that homosexuality is wrong." Religious beliefs are part of the personal-belief system. However, when we step into a profession by choice, we agree to the principles of the profession. Those principles include respect for all forms of sexual orientation. Respect is a *verb* that must be put into action through training, modeling, and advocacy. Anti-gay hiring and admissions policies do not allow for or respect diversity in sexual orientation.

In order to teach respect and nondiscrimination based on sexual orientation, it is important to understand the lives of LGBT persons. People who are LGBT are discriminated against all the time—in employment and housing, for example—and often fear for their personal safety. Hate crimes against LGBT people, such as the murder of Matthew Shepard in 1998, provide the most glaring example of why many LGBT people fear for their lives. In everyday life, LGBT people lack civil rights and human rights. In light of this, how can any religious institution advocate for the right to discriminate and oppress? Furthermore, nondiscrimination and respect for sexual orientation are not the same as promoting homosexuality, an erroneous claim often made to defend exclusion.

How can open exclusion based solely on sexual orientation lead to an environment in which nondiscrimination is taught, where LGBT people are protected from discrimination, and where understanding and respect for LGBT people are modeled? For a moment, replace sexual orientation with divorce. Some people have strong religious beliefs against divorce. Does that mean that those people are free to discriminate against people who are divorced, or against children of divorced parents? Do we prohibit divorcees from becoming social workers? What about a man and a woman who are living together without being legally married? Can a school of social work support discrimination toward this couple? If we are opposed to the use of birth control based on our religious values, should we then exclude from our social-work programs all men and women who use birth control?

It is dangerous for social work as a whole to allow groups to opt out of principles that are important to the profession. Where do we draw the line? Are legal nondiscrimination categories the only forms of nondiscrimination that we recognize? Does that mean that before the 1964 Civil Rights Act that there was no moral imperative *not* to discriminate against people of color? People with disabilities had to wait until 1990 to receive federal protection from discrimination. Does that mean that before 1990, social workers were ethically entitled to discriminate against people with disabilities? The profession has adopted and made clear its principles of nondiscrimination, which include sexual orientation.

Suppose the legal experts are right and that, as a monopoly, the CSWE cannot force religious institutions to have nondiscrimination policies that include sexual orientation. What the CSWE *can* uphold is a standard that "requires that nondiscrimination be taught and modeled in all social programs, but would not affect faculty hiring or admissions based on sexual orientation" (*NASW News*, 2001). At a minimum, every program must teach and model nondiscrimination of LGBT people. How can any institution actively model and teach this principle, if it is practicing discrimination? Even in schools with the best of intentions, this feat is impossible.

NO

Lawrence E. Ressler

The question being addressed in this essay is more than a theoretical issue. From 1982 to 1997, the CSWE had a policy that came to light in a 1996 memorandum to deans and directors of social-work programs (Norlin, 1996). The memo stated, "The social work community understood when these [1982 nondiscrimination] standards were promulgated that to require institutions to include political and sexual orientation violated their religious beliefs."

The purpose of this essay is to explore the ethical soundness of universally applied standards that knowingly violate religious beliefs. I will argue that the mindset undergirding the 1982 nondiscrimination standard, particularly as it was attempted to be rigidly implemented in 1995, is ethically and legally flawed in numerous ways. Beyond being a blatant violation of the free-exercise portion of the First Amendment and a potential transgression of antitrust laws, the violation of religious beliefs also violates basic ethical standards related to religious diversity. Furthermore, I will suggest that the issue is not, as is popularly argued, a simple matter of social justice. Rather, it's a complex ethical matter that involves different rankings of the profession's values, principles, and standards by equally committed social workers who are in their own way attempting to fulfill the mission of the profession. Finally, I will suggest that the 1995 attempt to impose one interpretation of the Code of Ethics on all institutions runs counter to two of the most important types of diversity inherent in the Code; namely diversity of context and diversity of thought.

While I was writing this essay, a colleague told me a story of a Christian student who confronted his gay professor and informed him that his behavior was an abomination to God and that his soul would rot in hell for it. The story made me cringe, and I hesitated to continue writing an apology that calls for flexibility when applying nondiscrimination standards. The argument in this essay is not against social justice or appropriate nondiscrimination, and it does not condone demeaning language and hateful actions against persons because of their sexual orientation. Such action would be viewed as unacceptable to the vast majority of social workers even in the faith-based institutions potentially excluded from the 1995 rigid application of the 1982 nondiscrimination statement. Social workers in these settings share the profession's commitment to social justice and work to teach students to interact constructively with all kinds of persons. Where there are conflicts of interest, including value conflicts, the programs help students learn to respond appropriately.

In the spirit of fairness, I will point out that it is not uncommon for Christian students to endure hateful and demeaning comments because of their beliefs. In a national study of religious discrimination (Ressler & Hodge, 2000), 50 percent of the respondents (n = 111 of 222) provided examples of what they felt was religious discrimination. The incidents included being told that they did not belong in social work, being ridiculed publicly for their beliefs, having grades lowered or being failed in class, being denied travel funds, being denied admission to programs, and not being hired, to name a few. These stories also make me cringe. Though I recognize that some religious people have prejudicial attitudes and commit inappropriate discriminatory actions, I will proceed with arguing against universally applied nondiscrimination standards that knowingly violate religious beliefs.

Some personal disclosures may be useful first. I am a Christian who comes from a family with a long Christian tradition. I have also been an NASW member for twenty-five years. I've served in numerous leadership positions, including a term on the state board, a term as regional president, and a term as an NASW Assembly delegate. Furthermore, I have taught social work for twenty years in five different faith-based social-work programs, having helped two undergraduate and one graduate program get initial accreditation. I have been involved in the North American Association of Christians in Social Work (NACSW) for a decade, including being president for seven years; and I have been an active participant in the Society for Spirituality and Social Work for most of its existence. I have found that social workers on both sides of the question at hand have far more in common than they might acknowledge. The challenge is to affirm that which is held in common, to learn to discuss the differences with civility, and to find ways to resolve conflicts constructively. In keeping with the spirit of the NASW Code of Ethics, it is imperative that the profession increase its commitment to respect diversity and give greater attention to resolving tensions.

A HISTORY OF THE NONDISCRIMINATION STANDARD CONFLICT

The question posed in this essay is rooted in an accreditation evaluative standard developed in 1982. That standard extended mandatory nondiscrimination to political and sexual orientation. The approved standard read, "The program must be conducted without discrimination on the basis of race, color, gender, age, creed, ethnic or national origin, disability, political orientation, or sexual orientation." According to the 1996 COA memorandum, the nondiscrimination statement was both "a source of pride and a source of concern." The standard was a source of pride for advocates of universal mandatory nondiscrimination. At the same time, it was a source of concern for supporters of faith-based institutions who felt that the policy wrongfully disregarded religious-diversity principles and ignored the educational model and context in which they operated.

Few, if any, of the schools who had concerns about the 1982 standard discriminated on the basis of political and sexual orientation. Their concern centered on the right of institutions to have community lifestyle standards that were consistent with the theological beliefs of the affiliated denomination. The most controversial of these standards is a commonly held "sexual intimacy in marriage only" policy. However, the nondiscrimination-standard conflict goes well beyond the literal words of the nondiscrimination policy. The nondiscrimination standard and the phrase "sexual orientation" have taken on symbolic crusade characteristics that connect to profound differences in broader society. Hunter (1991) refers to the conflict as a culture war between persons with a progressive and orthodox worldview. This issue is discussed in the latter part of this essay.

The conflict lay dormant from 1982 to 1995 because the standard was not enforced. Unbeknownst to most social-work educators and social-work programs, faith-based programs were quietly and routinely granted an exemption by the COA from the nondiscrimination standard when aspects of the standard conflicted with the religious beliefs of the institution. Religious institutions did not challenge the policy because they were being exempted. Moreover, other social-work educators did not challenge the exempting process because they were not aware that exemptions were being given. The conflict erupted in 1995 when, for reasons that are not entirely clear, the unofficial exemption policy changed. That year, a number of religiously affiliated schools were told they would not be accredited because they were not in compliance with the nondiscrimination statement. The public uproar that emerged did not arise from faith-based institutions' effort to change the 1982 nondiscrimination standard. Rather, it stemmed from COA's attempt to threaten faith-based institutions if they did not change their policy statements.

According to a document distributed by the Council on Social Work Education (1996), a group of religiously affiliated schools threatened to file a class-action lawsuit. After reviewing the matter, the CSWE concluded that there was a "substantial likelihood that the position of the COA would not prevail" and that the CSWE would be subjected to the following consequences: the CSWE would have been responsible for paying the other side's legal expenses; it would have lost credibility and possibly have been subjected to additional lawsuits; and a permanent injunction could have given a judge the authority to review and modify standards of the COA. As a consequence, "after long deliberations and examination of all the evidence presented to it and upon the strong recommendation of the Council's accreditation attorneys, the Commission voted to revise its standards so as to create the possibility of an exemption for programs located in religious institutions."

The COA then abandoned the exemption approach and replaced the nondiscrimination statement with the following standard: "Programs must make specific, continuous efforts to provide a learning context in which understanding and respect for diversity (including age, color, disability, ethnicity, gender, national origin, race, religion, and sexual orientation) are practiced." In addition, the interpretive guidelines added the statement that programs "must provide a context that is nondiscriminatory." Though the proposed standard that emphasized learning context was highly controversial, it was approved by the CSWE board of directors in 1996, albeit by the narrowest of margins.

This solution temporarily eased the conflict until January 2001, when a proposed revision of the standards reinserted mandatory nondiscrimination language. The second draft of the Educational Policy and Accreditation Standards (EPAS) proposed the following:

> The program does not discriminate against any person or group on the basis of age, culture, class, disability, ethnicity, family structure, gender, national origin, race, religion, and sexual orientation. The program makes specific, continuous efforts to provide a learning context in which understanding and respect for diversity are practiced. The program demonstrates and documents a nondiscriminatory context for learning in faculty, staff, and student composition, agency selection and client composition, constituent group composition, resource allocation, special programs, and research and community service and other initiatives (www.cswe.org/epas.htm).

Numerous social workers and faith-based institutions viewed the proposed standard as a renewed threat to their accreditation status and as discrimination that violated the profession's commitment to religious diversity. Numerous non-social-work education groups also saw the standard as a threat to educational diversity. These included the American Association of Presidents of Independent Colleges and Universities (AAPICU), several Washington Higher Education Secretariat organizations, the National Association of Independent Colleges and Universities (NAICU), and the Council on Christian Colleges and Universities (CCCU). Legal reviews, like those in 1996, concluded that nondiscrimination standards that violated the religious beliefs of religiously affiliated institutions would likely be found unconstitutional and that CSWE would face problems if it approved the proposed standard. As a result, the wording was withdrawn and further changes were proposed:

> The program makes specific and continuous efforts to provide a learning context in which respect for all persons and understanding of diversity (including age, class, color, disability, ethnicity, family structure, gender, marital status, national origin, race, religion, sex, and sexual orientation) are practiced. Social work education builds upon professional purposes and values; therefore, the program provides a learning context that is nondiscriminatory and reflects the

profession's fundamental tenets. The program describes how its learning context and educational program and curriculum (including faculty, staff, and student composition; selection of agencies and their clientele as field education settings; composition of program advisory or field committees; resource allocation; program leadership; speakers series, seminars, and special programs; research and other initiatives) model understanding of and respect for diversity (Council on Social Work Education, 2001, 81).

Though much of the proposed standard has the approval of both sides, it is likely to remain controversial. For universal nondiscrimination advocates, the emphasis on learning context may give unwanted flexibility to programs. For faith-based institutions, the requirement that "the program provides a learning context that is nondiscriminatory" may suggest a denial of the right of faith-based institutions to hire faculty who embrace the religious beliefs of the affiliated denomination and to have lifestyle standards that flow from those religious beliefs. Efforts continue to find wording that satisfies the concerns of all social-work educators and programs.

THE LEGAL ISSUES: RELIGIOUS FREEDOM

In large part, the tension around the 1982 nondiscrimination statement centers on the legality of requiring religiously affiliated institutions to hold to standards that violate beliefs central to their mission and identity. Note that the NASW Code of Ethics acknowledges the need to consider the law—along with ethical theory and principles, social-work theory and research, policies, and other codes of ethics—when making ethical decisions. Religiously affiliated social-work programs that oppose the 1982 nondiscrimination standard viewed the standard as a straightforward violation of the free-exercise portion of the First Amendment that states, "Congress shall make no law respecting an establishment of religion, or prohibiting the free exercise thereof." Free exercise of religion has been given great latitude historically in both church organizations and in religiously affiliated educational institutions. Even the Civil Rights Act of 1964 provided an exemption to religious institutions. More recently, the Religious Freedom Restoration Act of 1993, with support from a broad coalition of groups including the America Civil Liberties Union, reaffirmed religious freedom by requiring a "compelling reason" to any limitation to religious expression.

ANTITRUST

An additional legal concern stems from the CSWE's status as the only accrediting body for social-work education. Policies such as the 1982 nondiscrimination standard potentially violate antitrust laws by eliminating an entire class of educational institutions from accreditation. This would produce an unfair trade dynamic for students from religiously affiliated institutions, because many state-certification or licensing standards and federal job requirements require graduation from CSWE-accredited schools.

Seldom does the rhetoric around the issue demonstrate a valuing of religious belief, religious diversity, and the benefit of educational pluralism. From a legal perspective, I would suggest that advocates of a universally applied nondiscrimination standard are undervaluing the importance of religious freedom in U.S. culture. Continued efforts to establish one rigidly applied policy to all makes the CSWE vulnerable to lawsuits. These efforts also jeopardize the CSWE's autonomy and ability to serve as the only accrediting body for social-work education.

THE ETHICAL ISSUES: THE NASW CODE OF ETHICS

There are four standards in the 1997 NASW Code of Ethics (www.naswdc .org) that mention religion as a specially named diversity category. Standard 1.05(c) states that "social workers obtain education about and seek to understand the nature of diversity and oppression related to . . . religion." Standard 2.01(b) suggests that "social workers should avoid unwarranted negative criticism of colleagues in communications with clients or with other professionals." This standard goes on to state that "unwarranted negative criticism may include demeaning comments that refer to colleagues' level of competence or to individuals' attributes such as . . . religion." The fourth standard, which focuses directly on discrimination, has this admonition: "Social workers should not practice, condone, facilitate, or collaborate with any form of discrimination on the basis of . . . religion" (4.02). Finally, the section of the Code related to social workers' responsibility to broader society states, "Social workers should act to prevent and eliminate domination of, exploitation of, and discrimination against any person, group, or class on the basis of . . . religion" [6.04(d)]. Furthermore, the preamble to the NASW Code of Ethics makes this statement: "Social workers also should be aware of the impact on ethical decision-making of their clients' and their own personal values and cultural and religious beliefs and practices."

RELIGION DIVERSITY, DISCRIMINATION, UNWARRANTED CRITICISM, AND OPPRESSION

A policy that knowingly violates religious beliefs calls into serious question adherence to the profession's commitment to religious diversity. Unfortunately, in spite of the profession's roots in religion, the 1982 policy reveals a neglect of religion in social work (Cnaan, 1999) and the broader trivializing of religion described by Carter (1993).

My deeply rooted faith orientation and affinity for the First Amendment protection of religious freedom is shared by many clients, social-work professionals, and faith-based institutions. From this perspective, attempts to impose CSWE standards that knowingly violate religious beliefs suggest a desire to oppress religious beliefs by yet another well-meaning group. Though the pain inflicted on others by Christians who have used theology to justify their behavior is evident in history, so is the pain inflicted against Christians by others who have used their own justification to oppress. Like social justice, oppression and the general welfare of society are complex issues that defy simple solutions. In our discussion, we must also have a high respect for religious beliefs, which have all too frequently been ignored in the professional discourse.

Underneath the 1982 nondiscrimination standard and the 1995 decision to require strict conformity lie ethical concerns related to all of the NASW standards regarding religion. The 1982 policy appears to be based on a lack of understanding and respect for religious education—something that violates standard 1.05(c). Evidence suggests that education in these situations is typically excellent, with students able to demonstrate respect for all forms of diversity, including sexual orientation. Opponents of faith-based institutions frequently lace their arguments with stereotypic and prejudicial language. Some even refuse to engage in civil discourse about the issues involved. The CSWE Commissions are grossly underrepresented by persons who understand and can fairly represent social-work programs and faculty at faith-based institutions.

The 1995 threat to eliminate religious institutions from accreditation appears to directly violate the profession's commitment not to discriminate based on religious diversity (4.02). It also ignores the call to prevent oppression based on religion. Remember: There was no outcry over the 1982 nondiscrimination standard for thirteen years because the COA was not actively discriminating against religiously affiliated programs. During the three initial accreditation and two reaffirmation processes I have been involved in at faith-based institutions, the issue of nondiscrimination was never taken lightly. Furthermore, programs were required to explain how they met the standard. Extensive writing and conversation took place on each occasion about how the programs were addressing nondiscrimination concerns. The controversy arose in 1995 when programs were threatened with elimination of accreditation, an action that I suggest is inappropriately discriminatory.

The attempts to eliminate faith-based programs from accreditation may be the tip of a much larger problem of religious oppression in the profession as a whole. Emerging research (Ressler & Hodges, 2000; 2001) indicates that clients and social workers, as well as organizations, are experiencing what they believe to be religious discrimination. The problem appears to be most serious for social workers or clients who embrace a theology that is at the more conservative end of the spectrum. Indeed 56 percent of such persons in the 2000 report indicated they had personally experienced religious discrimination.

There is no indication in the Code of Ethics that respect for religious diversity applies only to those religious beliefs that are moderate, liberal, or radical.

Finally, the dialogue that has taken place in the past few years has at times involved vitriolic charges against religious social workers and social-work programs. These charges sometimes borders on violating the professional standards against unwarranted negative criticism. This became most evident at the 1996 CSWE Annual Program Meeting open discussion on the proposed exemption standard. Faculty at faith-based programs were stunned by the vociferousness of those who opposed the provision of an exemption. Opponents used language that would swiftly be ruled unacceptable if applied to any other group. The research referred to above (Ressler & Hodge, 2000) indicated that they commonly experience unwarranted criticism by social workers who embrace a very conservative theology against which the NASW Code of Ethics does not protect.

DIVERSITY OF THOUGHT

Those favoring a universally applied nondiscrimination standard frequently frame the nondiscrimination-standard conflict as a matter of social justice. For example, according to the 1996 CSWE memorandum, the standard was put in place because:

> The social work community wanted to position itself against nondiscrimination for all people. Thus, it felt it had a philosophical and moral responsibility to at least require social work programs to state their intention not to discriminate, even though they were housed in institutions that for religious reasons could not, or would not, include sexual orientation in their nondiscrimination policy statement.

Yet social-work programs in religiously affiliated institutions share a commitment to social justice and to working for the general welfare of society. The Ressler and Hodges (2001) study found that all of the conservative subjects (n = 12) fully support the values behind social justice, viewing social justice as a fundamental theological tenet. There is no disagreement between those for and against universal nondiscrimination standards about the importance of social justice.

However, there is a second way to frame the conflict: different rankings of social-work values, principles, and standards that reflect worldview diversity and diversity of contexts in the profession. The worldview-diversity analysis has received some, but not much, attention in the literature (Parr & Jones, 1996; Van Soest, 1996; Ressler & Hodges, 2000). All three of these articles point to the work of famed sociologist Hunter (1991) in explaining the tensions. According to Hunter, there is a clash between those with a progressive worldview and those with an orthodox worldview. In the words of Van Soest (1996), the tension is between cultural conservatives and cultural progressives "whose ideologies are grounded in divergent moral vision" (p. 54).

A worldview-diversity analysis views the tension not as a struggle between the just and unjust but as a difference in resolving ethical dilemmas among social-work values, principles, and standards. Five areas play a large role in catalyzing the tension between those with orthodox and progressive worldviews: diversity, social justice, client well-being, general well-being, and advocacy. Chief among the dilemmas are choices that we must make between respect for diversity and respect for social justice. Religious diversity *and* sexual orientation are included in the list of characteristics deserving special respect and understanding in both the NASW Code of Ethics and the CSWE's accreditation standards. When the theology of the religious group in question is progressive, the mandate to respect religious diversity and the mandate to respect sexual orientation converge. The dilemma emerges when the religious group in question holds that sexual intimacy is best reserved for heterosexuals who are married, as is the belief held by some religiously affiliated institutions. The 1982 nondiscrimination standard resolved the dilemma by giving religious diversity a lower priority than social-justice goals related to sexual orientation. Religiously affiliated institutions that have chosen not to include sexual orientation in the nondiscrimination statement resolve the same dilemma by giving religious diversity the higher priority and asking faculty and students to follow a limiting lifestyle while employed by or attending the institutions.

Social workers must also reconcile dual commitments to clients as well as to the general welfare of society. The sixth and final standard of the NASW Code of Ethics focuses on social workers' responsibility to broader society. For example, standard 6.10 states, "Social workers should promote the general welfare of society, from local to global levels, and the development of people, their communities, and their environments. . . ." At the same time, the Code acknowledges the importance of individual rights. For example, standard 1.01 begins by stating, "Social workers' primary responsibility is to promote the well-being of clients. In general, clients' interests are primary." It concludes with this complication: "However, social workers' responsibility to the larger society or specific legal obligations may, on limited occasions, supersede the loyalty owed clients, and clients should be so advised." In other words, sometimes the well-being of individuals is paramount, and at other times the well-being of society is paramount.

There is no dilemma as long as individual choices are equated with the well-being of society. However, as the NASW Code suggests, on occasion it is appropriate to limit individual behavior for the good of the group or society. Based on the commitment to the general welfare of society, many individual freedoms are curtailed. For example, laws prohibit use of certain drugs, prostitution, and other harmful activities. Society has the right to tax, and to forcibly hospitalize a person who is considering suicide. Each of these situations involves deciding whether the individual choice is more critical than social well-being.

Such tension also exists relative to sexual orientation. Those favoring placement of sexual orientation in the nondiscrimination statement see individual choice around sexual behavior as consistent with the well-being of society. Religious institutions that see sexual intimacy as appropriate only for married heterosexual persons base their views on a concern for the well-being of society. The refusal to include sexual orientation in the nondiscrimination statement and the willingness of such institutions to limit student and faculty behavior in this area reflect an orthodox worldview of what the general welfare of society entails.

This tension is exacerbated by the expectation that social workers engage in social and political action to bring about the well-being of society (6.02, 6.4). The diversity of worldviews, combined with the mandate to engage in advocacy, guarantees that social workers will not only have different opinions about general welfare but will also advocate for different policies to bring about the implementation of these diverse worldviews. We might argue that efforts to obstruct those who advocate for a different policy are violating the spirit of the Code of Ethics. The free expression of ideas and inclusive advocacy, especially in the face of diversity, is critical for a healthy society and profession.

Finally, matters grow even more complicated with the different definitions of clients. The preamble to the NASW Code of Ethics defines clients as including "individuals, families, groups, organizations, and communities." The CSWE CPS acknowledges a similar range of systems. Proposed solutions to the sexual-orientation/religious-diversity dilemma change considerably depending on the system one is emphasizing. Those favoring the nondiscrimination standard place an emphasis on individual diversity while minimizing the importance of institutional diversity. On the other hand, religious institutions opposing the nondiscrimination standard place a premium on institutional diversity while minimizing the importance of individual diversity. The Code does not prioritize individual over institutional diversity.

DIVERSITY OF CONTEXT

The NASW Code of Ethics specifically recognizes the importance of context in applying the standards. The purpose section of the Code states: "Specific applications of the *Code* must take into account the context in which it is being considered and the possibility of conflicts among the *Code's* values, principles, and standards." When conflicts arise, the Code suggests that social workers consider other sources of information, including "ethical theory and principles generally, social work theory and research, *laws, regulations, agency policies*, and other relevant codes of ethics" (italics added). In particular, the discussion around ethical decision-making cautions, "Social workers also should be aware of the impact on ethical decision-making of their clients' and their own personal values and cultural and religious beliefs and practices."

The 1995 rigid application of the 1982 nondiscrimination policy seems to disregard the impact of the nondiscrimination policy on religious beliefs and practices in some faith-based institutions. The link between education and religion is not a recent phenomenon. The earliest institutions were all religiously affiliated, including such prestigious institutions as Harvard, Yale, and Princeton. Many faith-based institutions threatened with elimination from accreditation are part of a religious educational system that has a long history and is rich in diversity. Indeed, it is the publicly funded institution that is the more recent development in education. The diversity extends not only to the type of religious affiliation but to the core missions of the institutions themselves. Sandin (1990) identifies a fourfold taxonomy of the role of religion in faith-based institutions: pervasively religious, religiously supportive, nominally church related, and independent with historical religious ties.

The ethical tensions are greatest for institutions that have a pervasively religious mission. In these institutions, faith is a central part of the educational model. At the undergraduate level, students in many institutions are required to participate in activities that have religious functions, including attending chapel and taking religious courses. This is not to suggest that the educational exposure is narrow and the explanations simplistic. Such institutions typically have an equally strong commitment to providing a liberal-arts education. Moreover, these schools make an effort to expose students to different ways of thinking and living, and even to different religious perspectives.

The pervasively religious model has another outcome that many institutions embrace. The theology is often pietistic in nature. This theology suggests that religious beliefs should shape one's way of living and the social context. Consequently, students are asked to conduct themselves in a manner that respects various worldviews, even if they, individually, do not embrace them. In this respect, social-work students and faculty are asked to be culturally respectful and sensitive. The list of lifestyle expectations that emerge from some religious beliefs include the nonuse of alcoholic beverages and tobacco and the misuse of drugs; it also includes abstaining from certain behaviors related to sexuality, including sexual harassment, the use of pornography, and sexual intimacy between homosexuals. Furthermore, to achieve the goal of integrating a Christian worldview, faculty are frequently required to share a Christian religious commitment. Within this context, the social-work programs are fully committed to a learning context that teaches respect for and understanding of diversity. The model embraced by such programs is equivalent to that which is required of individual social workers who have personal values but extend self-determination as much as possible to clients.

It is appropriate for faculty who work for private, faith-based institutions and for students who attend such institutions to be asked to conduct themselves in ways that respect the cultural standards and theological beliefs of the religious group at such times as their lives intersect with the community. Such expectations also apply to public institutions that must apply much broader standards because of the broader constituency they serve. It is wrongheaded for CSWE policies to ignore the context of religious institutions and deny them accreditation because they interpret and rank the profession's values, principles, and standards differently.

THE ALTERNATIVE: MAKING ROOM FOR DIVERSITY OF THOUGHT AND DIVERSITY OF CONTEXT

Differences of worldview are anticipated in the NASW Code of Ethics, with significant attention given to resolving conflict that emerges. The Code's preface makes explicit room for what can be called diversity of thought and diversity of contexts for social workers. The preface acknowledges that differences of opinions exist among social workers and does not specify which values, principles, or standards are most important in a conflict. It recognizes the importance of the context in which ethical conflict emerges and decries the attempt to resolve ethical dilemmas simply and with prescriptive rules. Ethical decisions, it suggests, must draw on the informed judgment of social workers, or educational institutions in this case, based on a variety of factors. These factors include ethical theory and principles, social-work theory and research, the law, regulations, and agency policies. The impact of ethical decision-making on religious beliefs and practices counts among the specific outcomes to be considered.

The nondiscrimination language found in the 1982 standard and in the proposed second draft of EPAS violates many of these principles. They attempt to apply a simple solution to a complex ethical issue. They give no leeway for diversity among educational institutions. They do not take into adequate account the context of pervasively religious schools and the model in which they approach education. The standards insist on one particular ranking of the Code's values, principles, and standards, and it denies persons who hold other worldviews the right to their ranking. As acknowledged on January 22, 1996, the 1982 nondiscrimination standard was built on a disregard for the policy's potential impact on the beliefs and practices of religiously affiliated institutions.

The tension around religion and sexual orientation points to the presence of diverse worldviews within the profession that must be embraced, not repressed. The NASW Code of Ethics rightfully acknowledges the presence of diversity of thought and makes room for differences that emerge from that diversity. In contrast to the CSWE COA, which attempted in 1995 to insist that all come to the same conclusions about the complexity of the ethical issues related to sexual orientation, the Code acknowledges the complexity of such situations and calls for thoughtful, ethical decision making. The tension in CSWE related to the nondiscrimination standard is not so much a disagreement about the goal of nondiscrimination but the lack of flexibility allowed institutions in how they resolve dilemmas. The most permanent solution to the nondiscrimination-standard conflict may *not* be to determine whether to have a nondiscrimination standard nor to decide which groups to include. Rather, the solution may be to add language that overtly acknowledges different worldviews among institutions and that permits all programs to explain how they resolve dilemmas.

REJECTING THE TOTALITARIAN SOLUTION TO DIFFERENCES

As the only accrediting body for social work in the United States, the CSWE serves a quasi-governmental function with monopoly power. It does not have the freedom to establish policies as the majority of members will them, particularly when the position violates the laws of the land—as the nondiscrimination standards do with respect to the First Amendment and Title VII of the Civil Rights Act of 1964. In a democracy, there are arenas for discourse and decision making that include checks and balances designed to keep any one group from imposing a single viewpoint on all. The "slippery slope" that some fear will arise when respect for diversity is extended to worldview and context is not nearly as troublesome as the attempt to make the profession ideologically pure and contextually similar through use of universally applied, mandatory nondiscrimination standards. History reminds us that many of the most horrific social movements arose from attempts to achieve purity of context or thought. These movements include the Holocaust, the killing fields of Pol Pot in Kampuchea, the ethnic cleansing advocated by Slobodan Milosevic in Yugoslavia, the slaughter of the Tutsis by the Hutus in Rwanda, the brutality used to achieve a classless society by Josef Stalin in the Soviet Union, and the Red Scare tactics of Joseph McCarthy in the United States. It is possible to have strong nondiscrimination standards *and* honor diversity of context and diversity of thought. More important, it is ethically imperative to do so. However, this means avoiding "one-size-fits-all" policies. Rather, we should use accountability processes that enable social workers and institutions to explain the ethical issues they face and the way they resolve them. They should be asked to demonstrate the outcomes of their programs, with equal emphasis given to all of the groups identified. I would submit that religious ignorance and even outright hatred in social-work programs is one of the more neglected topics of discussion.

Possibly the most profound challenge posed by the tension between sexual orientation and religion is the need to discover how to deal with differences constructively. As the profession rightly acknowledges, diversity is a basic reality of life, and that includes diversity of thought. But so is the tension that emerges from diversity. Tensions over differences arise within families, between groups, and in and between organizations and countries. Tensions related to religion and sexuality are among the most powerful in our day. I wish that individuals and institutions could point to the social-work profession when facing their own conflicts and say, "I hear that social workers have learned to deal with these tensions constructively. Let us learn from them." Sadly, we have little to offer in this regard. The 1982 nondiscrimination policy models institutional intolerance and oppression. The language of some colleagues is demeaning and offensive, and reveals little attempt to achieve understanding. Maybe the most powerful lesson we can learn from the nondiscrimination-standard struggle is that we can learn much from to the diversity that we have within our own profession.

REFERENCES

Arizona Republic. (2001, June 20). Doctors urge halt to gays' exclusion, p. A8.

Barker, R. L. (1999). *The social work dictionary.* Washington, DC: National Association of Social Workers.

Beless, D. W. (2001). Grappling with nondiscrimination and diversity. *CSWE Social Work Education Reporter, 49*(2), 2, 22.

Bracht, T. (1837). *Martyrs' mirror.* Lancaster, PA: D. Miller.

Carman, D. (2001, March 22). Gay teens need our support. *Denver Post,* p. A7.

Carter, S. (1993). *The culture of disbelief.* New York: Basic Books.

Cnaan, R. A. (1999). *The newer deal: Social work and religion in partnership.* New York, NY: Columbia University Press.

Council on Social Work Education. (1996, February 13). Commission on Accreditation Information Sheet Regarding Accreditation and Non-Discrimination. Alexandria, VA.

Council on Social Work Education (2001). *Educational Policy and Accreditation Standards.* Alexandria, VA: Author.

CSWE standard reviewed. (2001). *NASW News, 46*(5), 8.

EPAS second draft. Retrieved May 1, 2001, from www.cswe.org/epas.

Gaustad, E. (1993). *Neither king nor prelate: Religion and the new nation.* Grand Rapids, MI: Eerdmans.

Hunter, J. D. (1991). *Culture wars.* New York: Basic Books.

Norlin, J. (1996, January 22). Proposed changes in accreditation standards. Memo addressed to deans and directors by Commission on Accreditation Chair Julia Norlin. Alexandria, VA.

Parr, R., & Jones, L. (1996, Fall). Should CSWE allow social work programs in religious institutions an exemption from the accreditation nondiscrimination standard related to sexual orientation? *Journal on Social Work Education, 32*(3), 297–313.

Ressler, L. E., & Hodge, D. R. (Spring, 2000). Religious discrimination in social work: An international survey of Christian social workers. *Social Work and Christianity, 27*(1), 49–70.

Ressler, L. E., & Hodge, D. R. (2001, March 8–11). Silenced voices: The oppression of conservative narratives. Council on Social Work Education. Dallas, TX.

Sandin, R. T. (1990). *Autonomy and faith: Religious preference in employment decisions in religiously affiliated higher education.* Atlanta, GA: Center for Constitutional Studies, Mercer University and Omega.

Van Soest, D. (1996). The influence of competing ideologies about homosexuality on nondiscrimination policy: Implications for social work education. *Journal of Social Work Education, 32*(1), 53–64.

www.naswdc.org. NASW Code of Ethics. NASW Web site.